Table of Contents

Canadian Rockies

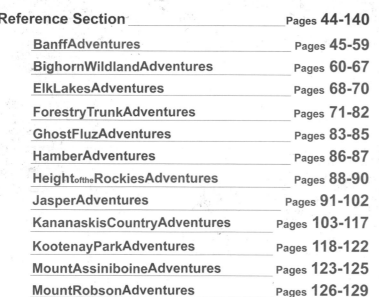

Image © allcanadaphotos.com (Mount Assiniboine Provincial Park)

Backroad Mapbooks

Alberta
Land Area... 661 848 km²
Population...3 290 350
Capital...Edmonton
Largest City...Calgary
Highest Point...Mount Columbia
3 747 metres (12 294 feet)
Tourism info...1.800.ALBERTA
www.travelalberta.com

Official Partners: ALBERTA PARKS · Alberta Fish & Game Association

Acknowledgements

Published by

Backroad Mapbooks

Mussio Ventures Ltd.
#106- 1500 Hartley Ave,
Coquitlam, BC. V3K 7A1
Toll Free: 1-877-520-5670
E-mail: info@backroadmapbooks.com
www.backroadmapbooks.com

Backroad Mapbooks

DIRECTORS
Russell Mussio
Wesley Mussio
Penny Stainton-Mussio

ASSOCIATE DIRECTOR
Jason Marleau

VICE PRESIDENT
Chris Taylor

COVER DESIGN & LAYOUT
Farnaz Faghihi

COVER PHOTO
Allcanadaphotos.com
(Mount Assiniboine Provincial Park)

CREATIVE CONTENT
Russell Mussio
Wesley Mussio

PROJECT MANAGER
Andrew Allen

PRODUCTION
Shaun Filipenko,
Justin Quesnel,
Dale Tober, Jonathan Wang

SALES / MARKETING
Joshua Desnoyers
Chris Taylor

WRITER
Trent Ernst

Library and Archives Canada Cataloguing in Publication

Ernst, Trent
Canadian Rockies backroad mapbook [cartographic material] : outdoor recreation guide / [Trent Ernst]. -- 2nd ed.

(Backroad mapbooks)
Includes index.
ISBN 978-1-897225-53-0

1. Recreation areas--Rocky Mountains, Canadian (B.C. and Alta.)--Maps. 2. Outdoor recreation--Rocky Mountains, Canadian (B.C. and Alta.)--Guidebooks. 3. Rocky Mountains, Canadian (B.C. and Alta.)--Maps. 4. Rocky Mountains, Canadian (B.C. and Alta.)--Guidebooks. I. Title. II. Series: Backroad mapbooks

G1167 R6E63 E76 2009 796.509711 C2009-906184-8
Copyright © 2010 Mussio Ventures Ltd.

Acknowledgement

Thanks to all the people who have helped make this updated Canadian Rockies book even better than the previous edition. These folks include: Kevin Witranen, Roger Meyer and Wayne Crocker at Alberta Sustainable Resource Development, while Scott Sunderwald at Tourism, Parks and Recreation gave us feedback on the Willmore/Forestry Trunk area.

Duane Fizor and his team gave us a whole bunch of edits for Kananaskis Country, Greg Horne provided feedback on Jasper National Park, Ross MacDonald who does communications for Yoho and Kootenay National Parks gave us feedback on those two parks and Backcountry Supervisor Chris Worobets provided feedback on our Banff Section, Glenn Kubian who is the backcountry operations coordinator helped us with Yoho National Park. Scott Sunderwald provided feedbad on Alberta region & Wesley Eror on Sundre region.

Jeff Volp and Hugh Ackroyd gave us feedback on Elk Lakes and Height of the Rockies Provincial Parks in BC. Tay Hanson and Alex Green knows about all there is to know about Mount Assiniboine, while Wayne Van Velzen made sure our sections on Mount Robson and Hamber Provincial Parks were perfect.

This book is also the result of the dedicated and talented people at Mussio Ventures Ltd. A hats off to Trent Ernst for his diligent work on the research and writing. The mapping team of Andrew Allen, Justin Quesnel, Dale Tober and Jonathan Wang did some amazing improvements on the maps. When combined with the work of Chris Taylor and Farnaz Faghihi on the book layout and graphic work we are able to produce a visually stimulating and the most informative book on this truly spectacular region of Canada.

We would like to express our gratitude to the helpful map providers GeoBase©, Department of Natural Resources Canada, and BC's Ministry of Water, Land and Air Protection.

Finally we would like to thank Allison, Devon, Jasper, Madison, Nancy and Penny Mussio for their continued support of the Backroad Mapbook Series. As our family grows, it is becoming more and more challenging to break away from it all to explore our beautiful country.

Sincerely,

Russell and Wesley Mussio

Disclaimer

Mussio Ventures Ltd. does not warrant that the backroads, paddling routes and trails indicated in this Mapbook are passable nor does it claim that the Mapbook is completely accurate. Therefore, please be careful when using this or any source to plan and carry out your outdoor recreation activity.

Please note that traveling on logging roads, river routes and trails is inherently dangerous, and without limiting the generality of the foregoing, you may encounter poor road conditions, unexpected traffic, poor visibility, and low or no road/trail maintenance. Please use extreme caution when traveling logging roads and trails.

Please refer to the Fishing and Hunting Regulations for closures and restrictions. It is your responsibility to know when and where closures and restrictions apply.

Help Us Help You

A comprehensive resource such as Backroad Mapbooks for Canadian Rockies could not be put together without a great deal of help and support. Despite our best efforts to ensure that everything is accurate, errors do occur. If you see any errors or omissions, please continue to let us know.

All updates will be posted on our web site: www.backroadmapbooks.com

Please contact us at:
Mussio Ventures Ltd.
#106 - 1500 Hartley Ave,
Coquitlam, BC, V3K 7A1

Email: updates@backroadmapbooks.com
P: 604-521-6277 F: 604-521-6260
Toll Free 1-877-520-5670
www.backroadmapbooks.com

Welcome

Canadian Rockies

Image © Travel Alberta

Welcome to the second special edition of the Backroad Mapbook for **Canadian Rockies.** This book focuses on the Canadian Rocky Mountain Parks system, an interconnected system of provincial and national parks covering more that 30,000 square kilometres–about the size of Belgium.

From the world famous Banff National Park to the much quieter and smaller Elk Lakes Provincial Park there is a lifetime of recreation to enjoy in this spectacular area. If you are a follower of the series, you will notice a different twist to the book. Rather than split up the book by various activities (fishing, paddling, trails, etc.), this book focuses on the individual parks in the area as well as Kananaskis Country and the Forestry Trunk Areas of Alberta that are found in the Rocky Mountain Foothills to the east. By focusing on each park we are able to provide more details than ever before. Of course we include our ever-popular maps as well as a few helpful inset maps to help guide the people to the places we write about.

The park system in the area has a long colourful history. Back in 1885, the government of the then Dominion of Canada drew a box around the Basin Hot Springs and Sulphur Mountain Cave in order to protect the springs from commercial development. Two years later, the borders were redrawn, taking in 673 square kilometres. It was named the Rocky Mountains National Park and it was Canada's first national park. By the late 1880s people flocked to see this new and magical landscape, making the long trip by train.

Today people still flock to the Canadian Rockies by the millions. Over four million people a year visit Banff alone. And while new roads and railways have opened up new areas for these people to explore, it still remains true that only a small percentage of people take the time to explore these parks very far off the road. While short, popular trails can often resemble a line-up to see the latest Hollywood Blockbuster, once you get more than a couple kilometres away from the main roads, the crowds thin out. While it is unlikely that you will have any but the longest and most difficult trail to yourself in a place like Banff, the number of people you encounter will drop to a few groups a day.

This book is dedicated to those who want their Rocky Mountains a little more rugged. Who pass on the five-star luxury accommodations of the Fairmont in Lake Louise and spend the night in a tent or a trailer. Who chose to see the Bow River from water level in a canoe or raft, rather than from the confines of a car passing by along the Trans-Canada Highway. Who want to see the high mountain peaks by standing on top of them, not just by driving past them. Who are willing to live out of a pack on their back for days on end for the sheer joy of exploring this amazing area.

Unlike many of our books, the word backroad is almost misleading in this area of epic treks. There are few actual backroads to explore, but enough trails to keep you busy for several lifetimes. In addition to 3,000 km (1,800 miles) of hiking trails, you will find river after sparkling river to paddle, endless mountains to climb and a lifetime's worth of lakes to fish. We hope this edition of the Backroad Mapbook Series helps guide you through this truly spectacular part of the country.

History

The Backroad Mapbook idea came into existence when Wesley and Russell Mussio were out exploring. They had several books and a few maps to try to find their way through the maze of logging roads around southern BC. The brothers were getting very frustrated trying to find their way and eventually gave up. Not to be outdone, the two ambitious brothers started brainstorming. Eventually the Backroad Mapbook idea was born.

They published their first book in January 1994 and it quickly sold out. Rather than simply reprinting it, they listened to the feedback of customers and made several alterations that helped improve the book. This formula of continuing to make the product better continues today and has helped establish the Backroad Mapbook series as the top selling outdoor recreation guidebook series in the country. From the tiny beginnings in that Vancouver apartment with maps strewn all over the walls, to one of the most sought after outdoor products in the country, the Backroad Mapbook series has truly come a long way.

Russell & Wesley Mussio -
Founders of Backroad Mapbooks

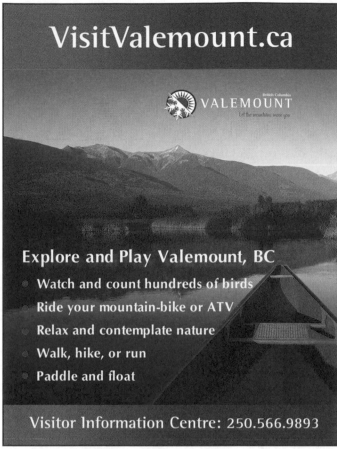

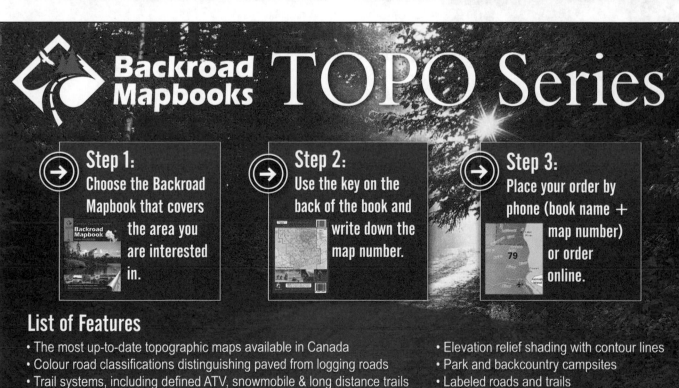

Legend

C A N A D A

Scale Bar

Scale 1:200 000 1 Centimetre = 2.0 Kilometres

2km 0km   4km   8km   12km

Map Information

Map Projection:
Universal Transverse Mercator Zone 11

Map Datum:
North American Datum 1983 (NAD 83)

Elevation Bar:

over 2000m
1750m-2000m
1500-1750m
1250-1500m
1000-1250m
750-1000m
500-750m
250-500m
0-250m

Area Indicators:

Provincial / National Park	City
Conservation / Natural Area	First Nations
Swamps	Glaciers
Water	Forest Land Use Zone (FLUZ) or Restricted Area

Contour Lines:

20m Intervals	100m Intervals
100m Intervals	500m Intervals

Contour Intervals
approximately 20m
or approximately 100m
(see map for details)

Population Indicators:

◎ Village / Railstop
● Town
⊕ Capital City

Line and Area Classifications:

═══════	Freeways	═✿═	Trans Canada Trail
━━━━━━	Highways	━━━━━━	Long Distance Trail
▬▬▬▬▬	Secondary Highways	━━━━━━	Duo Sport Trails
▬▬▬▬▬	Arterial Paved Roads	━━━━━━	Snowmobile Trails
───────	Rural Paved Roads	━━━━━━	ATV Trails
───────	Local Paved Roads	─ ─ ─ ─	Developed Trail
───────	Forest Service / Main Industry Roads	· · · · · ·	Routes (Undeveloped Trails)
───────	Active Industry Roads (2wd)	─ ─ ─ ─	Ferry Routes
───────	Other Industry Roads (2wd / 4wd)	─·─·─·─·	Lake / River Paddling Routes
───────	Unclassified / 4wd Roads	─·─·─·─·	Powerlines
─────────	Deactivated Roads	─ ─ ─	Pipelines
┼──┼──┼─	Railways	──────	Saltwater Fishing Area
──────	Alberta Township Grid	▬▬▬▬	Wildlife Management Zones

Recreational Activities:

⚓	Anchorage	🪂	Hang-gliding
🚤	Boat Launch	🚶	Hiking
🏖	Beach	🐎	Horseback Riding
⛺	Campsite / Limited Facilities	🏍	Motorbiking / ATV
🏕	Campsite / Trailer Park	🛶	Paddling (canoe-kayak)
⛺	Campsite (trail / water access only)	☰	Picnic Site
⚐	Canoe Access Put-in / Take-out	Ⓟ	Portage
🎿	Cross Country Skiing	Ⓡ	Resort
🚴	Cycling	🧗	Rock Climbing
🤿	Diving	🛷	Snowmobiling
⛷	Downhill Skiing	🎿	Snowshoeing
🐟	Fishing	🔭	Wildlife Viewing
⛳	Golf Course	🏄	Windsurfing

Miscellaneous:

✈ ✈	Airport / Airstrip	─¥─	Marsh
──	Arrow / Location Pointer	⚒	Microwave Tower
✳	Beacon	✕	Mine Site (abandoned)
⚑	Cabin / Hut	Ⓟ	Parking
✂	Customs	✛	Pictograph
🛬	Float Plane Landing	★	Point of Interest
═	Gate	P 50	Portage Distance
◢	Gas Plant	⚓	Ranger Station
🏁	Highway: Trans Canada	ⓘ	Travel Information
🏁	Highway: Yellowhead	🚚	Truck Weigh Scale
▢	Highway: Primary	🏃	Viewpoint / Forestry Lookout (abandoned)
◻	Highway: Secondary	↘	Waterfalls
◇	Interchange	⌁	Wilderness, Wildlife Area or Reserve
🍁	Long Distance Trail	🍇	Winery

Map Features

Recreational Features

You will find the maps mark points of interest, paddling routes, parks and conservation areas, trail systems and even wildlife viewing opportunities. **ATV, snowmobile trails** and **long distance trails** are highlighted with a background colour to aid users in tracking these systems. Hunters and anglers will also be happy to see that we have included the **Management Units** on the maps. The big green number notes the zones while the boundaries are marked with a faint green border. For a complete list of symbols and what they mean please refer to our Map Legend.

Road Features & Map Legend

By combining city and rural roads with current forestry and logging road maps our maps are designed for people wishing to get outdoors. However, they are very detailed and the myriad of current logging and industrial roads in addition to the various trail systems can be confusing. We provide a **map legend** at the start of each section of the maps to illustrate the region we cover as well as how to decipher the various grades of roads and symbols used on the maps.

Below are some more common features of our maps:

Roads & Trails

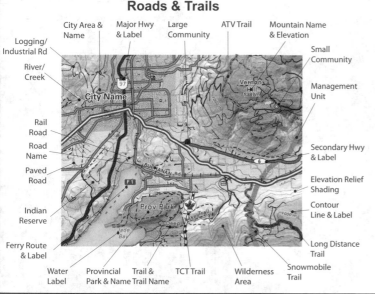

Recreational & Misc

UTM Grid & Longitude and Latitude

A useful navigational feature on our maps is the small numbers provided around our map borders. These blue numbers represent UTM Grids and the black numbers represent Longitude and Latitude reference points. Although most GPS units are set to longitude and latitude, switching the unit to UTM (NAD 83) is both easier and more accurate for land-based travel. Since our maps provide UTM grid lines that are 10,000 metres apart (both east & north), users can accurately pinpoint the location of features by dividing the grid into 10 equal parts (both east & north). Counting the number of tics from the nearest coordinate value and multiplying by 1,000 will give you the UTM coordinate. Do this for both the Easting (the numbers along the top and bottom of the map border) and the Northing (the numbers along the side) and you will have an accurate GPS waypoint.

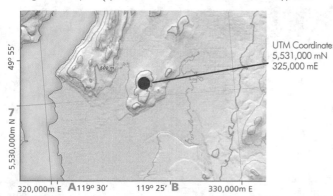

How to use the Scale Bar

To use the scale bar provided for each map, you can do one of the following things:

1) Use a piece of paper & mark the distance intervals from the scale bar. Then put that piece of paper on the map and measure the distance between two points. In example below the distance between "Adventure" & "Discovery" is 2 units or 3 kilometres.

2) Measure your distance with a piece of string, then place the string on the scale bar to find out the kilometres.

3) You can draw the approximate unit lines on the map itself (the green bars below) and then estimate the distance.

Note that all measurements are approximate.

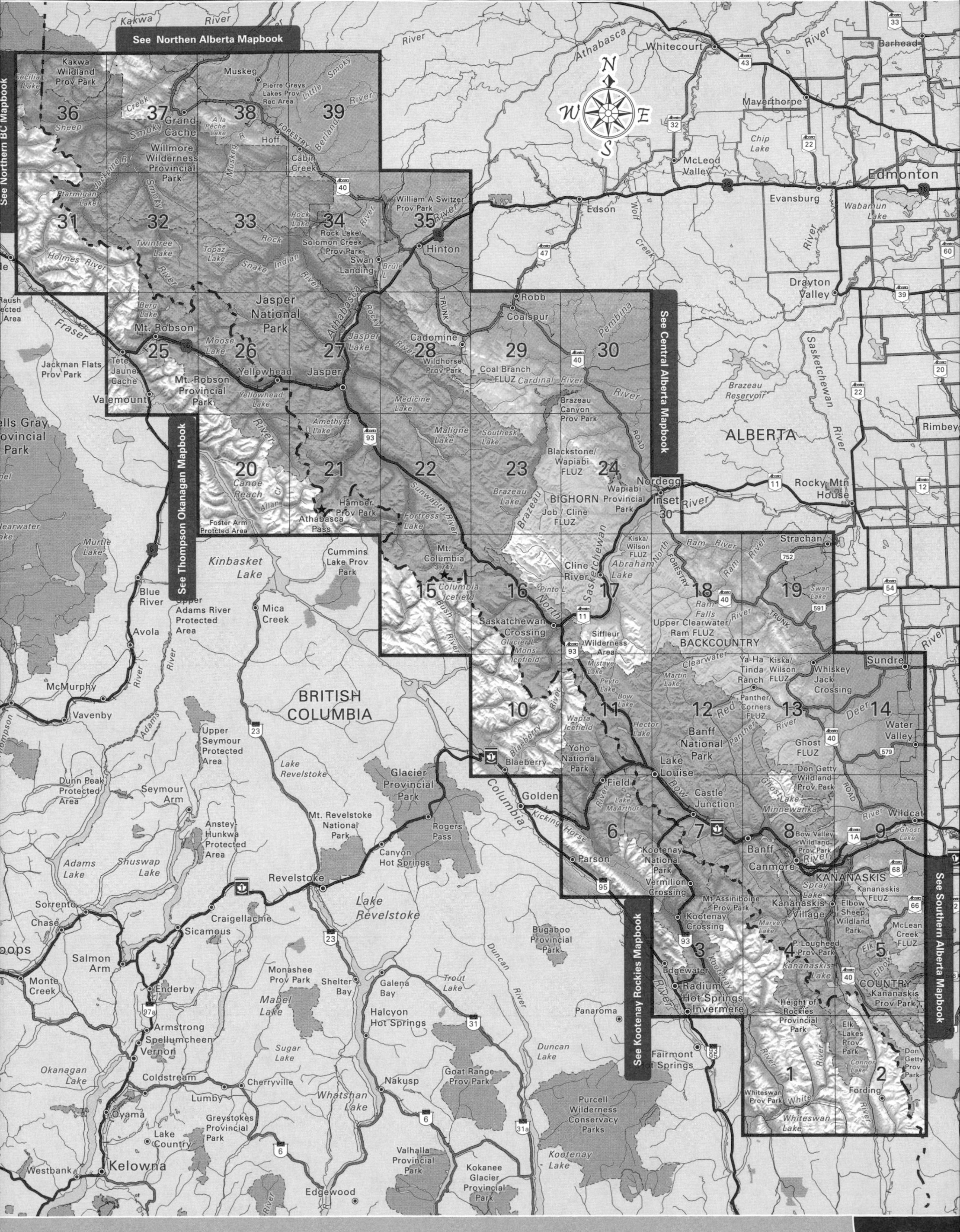

See Northen Alberta Mapbook

See Northern BC Mapbook

See Thompson Okanagan Mapbook

See Central Alberta Mapbook

See Kootenay Rockies Mapbook

See Southern Alberta Mapbook

N E S W (compass)

ALBERTA

BRITISH COLUMBIA

Kakwa Wildland Prov Park — 36
Sheep — 36
37 Grand Cache
38 Hoff
39
Muskeg
Pierre Greys Lakes Prov Rec Area
Little Smoky River
A la Pèche Lake
Cabin Creek
Willmore Wilderness Provincial Park — 32
Smoky River
31 Ptarmigan Lake
Holmes River
Twintree Lake — 32
33
Topaz Lake
Rock Lake — 34
Rock Lake/Solomon Creek Prov Park
Swan Landing
35 Hinton
William A Switzer Prov Park
Edson
Robb
Coalspur
Cadomine
Wildhorse Prov Park
Coal Branch FLUZ
Cardinal River
29
30
Pembina River
Brazeau Reservoir
Rocky Mtn House
Nordegg
Wapiabi Provincial Park — 24
Blackstone/Wapiabi FLUZ
Job/Cline FLUZ
BIGHORN
Cline River
Kiska/Wilson FLUZ
Abraham Lake
Strachan
Ram River
Ram Falls
Upper Clearwater/Ram FLUZ
BACKCOUNTRY
18
19
Swan Lake
Sundre
Saskatchewan Crossing
Glacier L.
Mons Icefield
Siffleur Wilderness Area
Mistaya Lake
Peyto Lake
Bow Lake
Hector Lake
Clearwater
Ya-Ha-Tinda Ranch
Kiska/Wilson FLUZ
Whiskey Jack Crossing
Martin Lake
Panther Corners FLUZ
12
Banff National Park
13
Ghost FLUZ
14
Water Valley
Don Getty Wildland Prov Park
Lake Louise
Castle Junction
7
8
Banff
Canmore
Bow Valley Wildland Prov Park
9
Ghost Lake
Wildcat
KANANASKIS
Spray Lake
Kananaskis FLUZ
Kananaskis Village
Elbow Sheep Wildland Park
McLean Creek FLUZ
COUNTRY
Kananaskis Prov Park
5
Height of Rockies Provincial Park
Elk Lakes Prov Park
Connor Lakes
Don Getty Prov Park
1
2
Fording
Whiteswan Prov Park
Whiteswan Lake
White River

Mt. Robson — 25
Tête Jaune Cache
Valemount
Mt. Robson Provincial Park
Yellowhead — 26
Moose Lake
Yellowhead Lake
Jackman Flats Prov Park
Fraser River
Raush Protected Area
20
Canoe Reach
Foster Arm Protected Area
21
Hamber Prov Park
Athabasca Pass
22
Sunwapta River
Fortress Lake
23
Brazeau Lake
Southesk Lake
Amethyst L'ake
Medicine Lake
Maligne Lake
Jasper National Park
27
Jasper
Jasper Lake
Athabasca River
Rocky River

Kinbasket Lake
Upper Adams River Protected Area
Mica Creek
Blue River
Avola
Cummins Lake Prov Park
15
Columbia Icefield
Mt. Columbia 3,747
16
Saskatchewan Crossing
17
North Saskatchewan River
McMurphy
Vavenby
Murtle Lake
Wells Gray Provincial Park
Clearwater Lake
10
Wapta Icefield
Blaeberry
Yoho National Park
11
Field
Lake O'Hara
Golden
Kicking Horse River
Parson
Rogers Pass
Glacier Provincial Park
Mt. Revelstoke National Park
Canyon Hot Springs
Revelstoke
Lake Revelstoke
Craigellachie
Sicamous
Dunn Peak Protected Area
Seymour Arm
Upper Seymour Protected Area
Anstey-Hunkwa Protected Area
Adams Lake
Shuswap Lake
Monashee Prov Park
Shelter Bay
Galena Bay
Halcyon Hot Springs
Trout Lake
Duncan River
Bugaboo Provincial Park
Mt Assiniboine Prov Park
Kootenay National Park
Vermilion Crossing
6
7
Kootenay Crossing
3
Edgewater
Radium Hot Springs
Invermere
4
Marvel Lake
Salmon Arm
Monte Creek
Sorrento
Chase
Enderby
Armstrong
Spellumcheen
Vernon
Coldstream
Lumby
Cherryville
Mabel Lake
Sugar Lake
Whatshan Lake
Nakusp
Goat Range Prov Park
Panaroma
Duncan Lake
Fairmont Hot Springs
Purcell Wilderness Conservancy Parks
Okanagan Lake
Oyama
Lake Country
Westbank
Kelowna
Greystokes Provincial Park
Valhalla Provincial Park
Kokanee Glacier Provincial Park
Kootenay Lake
Edgewood

Athabasca River
Whitecourt
Mayerthorpe
McLeod Valley
Chip Lake
Edmonton
Evansburg
Wabamun Lake
Drayton Valley
Saskatchewan River
Rimbey
Barhead

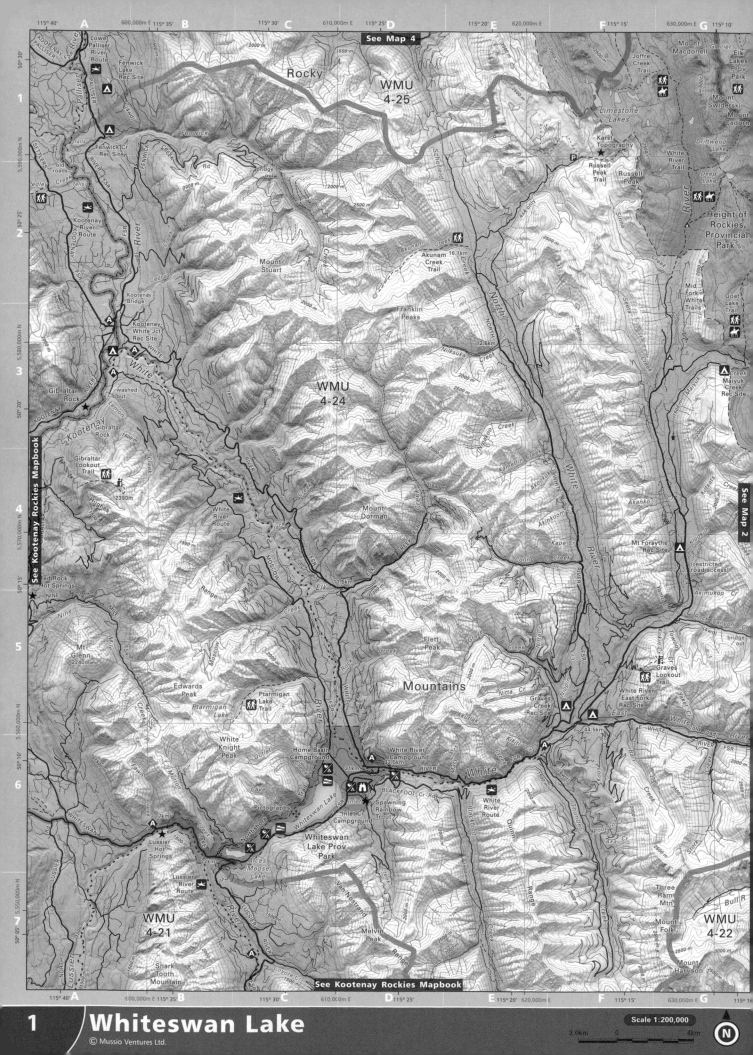

Whiteswan Lake

1

Scale 1:200,000

2.0km   0   4km

© Mussio Ventures Ltd.

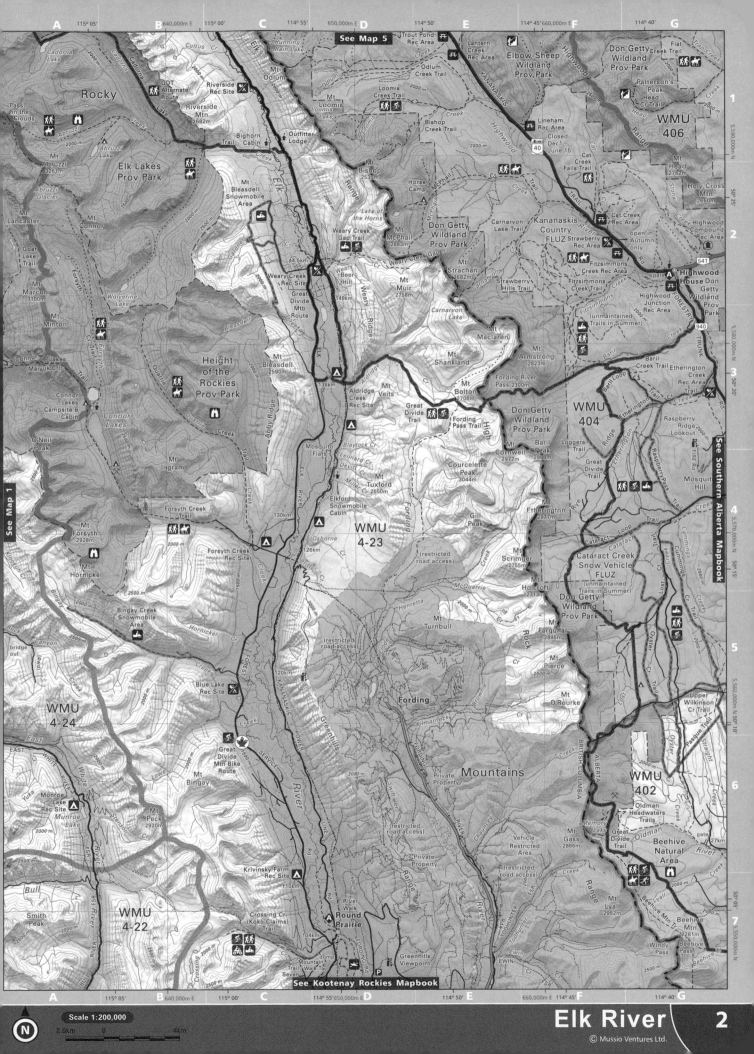

Rocky

Cadorna Lake

Pass in the Clouds

Mt Lancaster

Mt Abruzzi 3261m

Abruzzi Glacier

Elk Lakes Prov Park

Mt Connor

Goat Lake Trail

Mt Marconi 3100m

Mt Minton

Wolverine Lake

Connor Lakes (Maiyuk Cr)

O'Neil Peak

Connor Lakes Campsite & Cabin

Connor Lakes

Height of the Rockies Prov Park

Mt Ingram

Mt Forsyth 2928m

Forsyth Creek Trail

Mt Hornickel

Forsyth Creek Rec Site

bridge out

WMU 4-24

Bingay Creek Snowmobile Area

Monroe Lake Rec Site

Munroe Lake

Mt Bingay

Mt Peck 2920m

Blue Lake Rec Site

Smith Peak

WMU 4-22

Krivinsky Farm Rec Site

Crossing Cr (Koko Claims) Trail

GDT Alternate Route

Riverside Rec Site

Riverside Mtn 2682m

Mt Odlum

Bighorn Trail

Outfitter Lodge

Bighorn Cabin

Mt Bleasdell Snowmobile Area

Weary Creek Gap Trail

Weary Creek Rec Site

Weary Beer Hill

Great Divide Mtb Route

44.5km

149km

Mt Bleasdell 2590m

Aldridge Creek Rec Site

138km

Abby Ridge

Mosquito Flats

Blaylock Cr

Leonard Cr

Devitt Cr

Miller Cr

Elkford Snowmobile Cabin

130km

Osborne Cr

126km

Blue Lake Rec Site

Great Divide Mtn Bike Route

120km

Fording

110km

River Walk

Round Prairie

104km

Greenhills Viewpoint

Mt Loomis Lake

Mt Bishop 2530m

Lake of the Horns

Mt McPhail 2883m

Horse Camp

Mt Muir 2758m

Mt Strachan 2682m

Mt Veits

Aldridge Creek Trail

Great Divide Trail

Fording Pass Trail

Fording River Pass 2300m

Mt Bolton 2706m

Mt Shankland

Mt Maclaren

Mt Tuxford 2550m

Courcelette Peak 3044m

Gill Peak

Mt Cornwell 2972m

Baril Peak 2998m

Mt Etherington 2877m

Mt Scrimger 2755m

Mt Holcroft 2713m

Mt Turnbull

Mt Farquhar 2895m

Mt Pierce

Mt O'Rourke

Mountains

Private Property

(restricted road access)

(restricted road access)

(restricted road access)

Private Property

Vehicle Restricted Area

Mt Gass 2866m

Mt Lyall 2952m

Windy Pass

Beehive Mtn 2281m

Beehive Pass

Beehive Natural Area

WMU 402

Oldman Headwaters Trails

Upper Wilkinson Cr Trail

Pasque Trail

Memory Lake

27km

gate

See Map 5

Trout Pond Rec Area

Lantern Creek Rec Area

Elbow-Sheep Wildland Prov Park

Don Getty Wildland Prov Park

Flat Creek Trail

Patterson's Peak Head Cr Trail

WMU 406

Odlum Creek Trail

Loomis Creek Trail

Bishop Creek Trail

Lineham Rec Area

Closed Dec 1 – June 15

Mt Head 2782m

Holy Cross Mtn 2650m

Highwood Compound Rec Area

open in Autumn only

Cat Creek Falls Trail

Kananaskis Country FLUZ

Carnarvon Lake Trail

Strawberry Rec Area

Fitzsimmons Creek Rec Area

Fitzsimmons Creek Trail

Carnarvon Lake

Strawberry Hills Trail

40

541

Highwood House

Highwood Junction Rec Area

(unmaintained Trails in Summer)

Don Getty Wildland Prov Park

940

WMU 404

Baril Creek Trail

Etherington Creek Rec Area Trail

Raspberry Ridge Lookout

Mosquito Hill

Great Divide Trail

Loggers Trail

Baril Loop

Raspberry Trail

Great Divide Trail

Cataract Creek Snow Vehicle FLUZ

(unmaintained Trails in Summer)

Don Getty Wildland Prov Park

Great Divide Trail

See Map 1

See Southern Alberta Mapbook

ALBERTA

BRITISH COLUMBIA

Scale 1:200,000

2.0km 0 4km

Elk River

2

© Mussio Ventures Ltd.

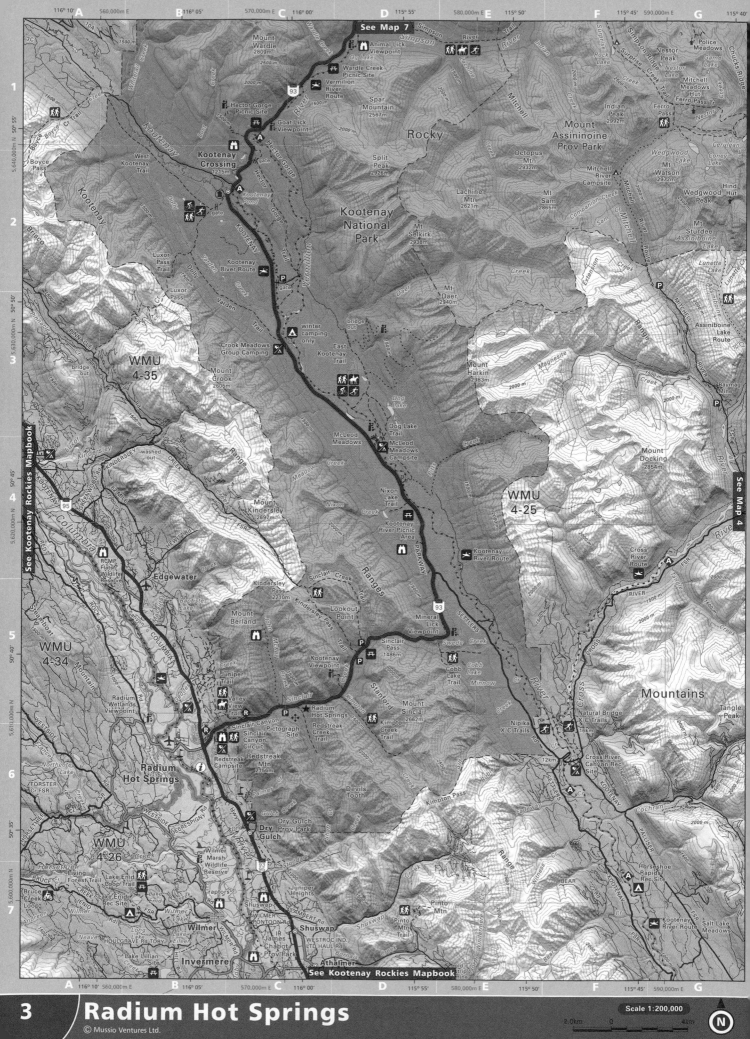

See Kootenay Rockies Mapbook

See Map 4

See Kootenay Rockies Mapbook

3   Radium Hot Springs

© Mussio Ventures Ltd.

Scale 1:200,000

2.0km   0   4km

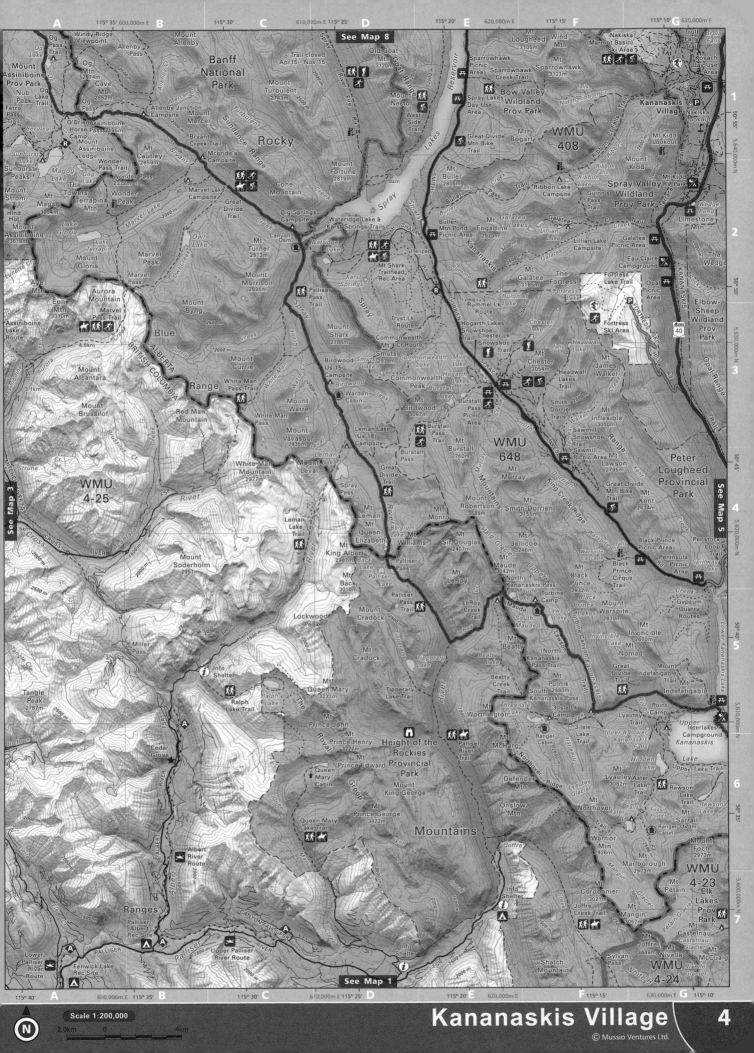

Kananaskis Village

4

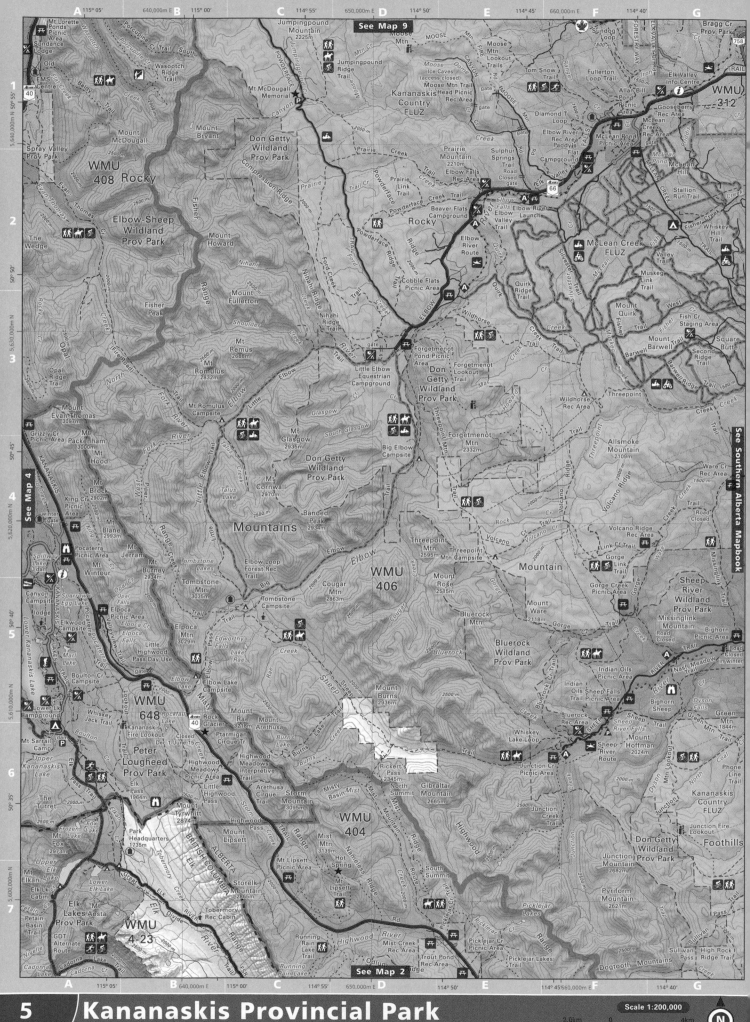

5 Kananaskis Provincial Park

Scale 1:200,000

2.0km   0   4km

© Mussio Ventures Ltd.

Scale 1:200,000

2.0km   0   4km

Field

6

© Mussio Ventures Ltd.

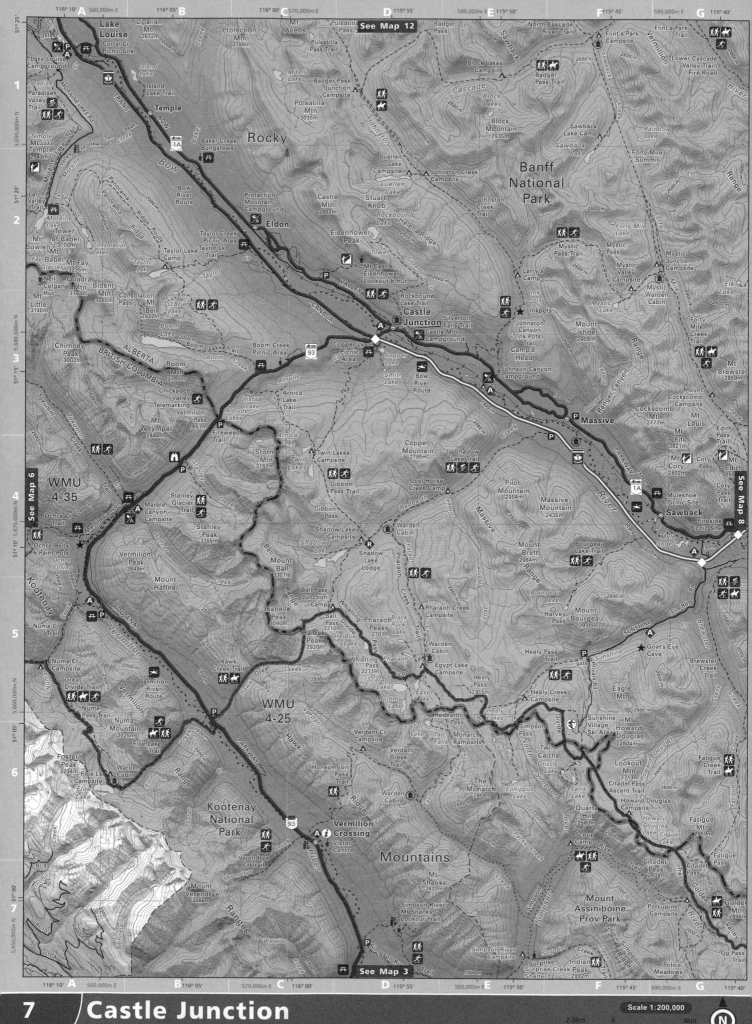

Scale 1:200,000

© Mussio Ventures Ltd.

2.0km   0   4km

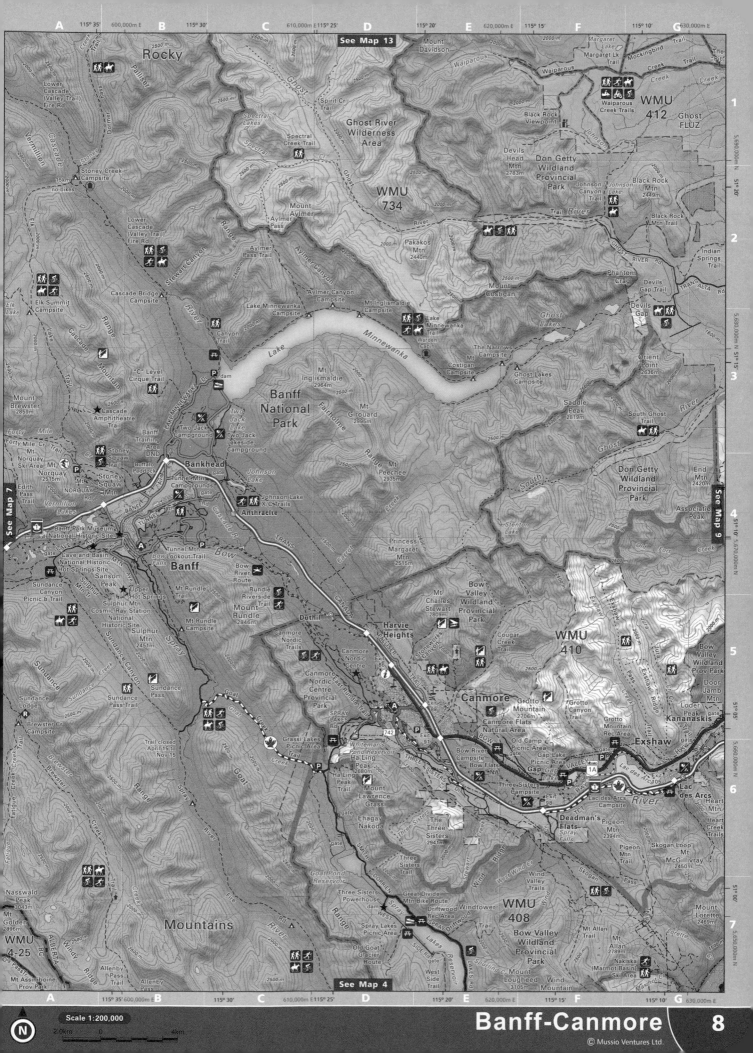

Rocky

Ghost River Wilderness Area

WMU 734

WMU 412

Ghost FLUZ

Don Getty Wildland Provincial Park

Banff National Park

Lake Minnewanka

Spectral Lakes

Mount Aylmer

Mount Costigan

Ghost Lakes

Mount Brewster 2859m

Mt Norquay 2515m

Banff

Sulphur Mtn 2451m

Mount Rundle 2846m

Canmore Nordic Centre Provincial Park

Canmore

WMU 410

Bow Valley Wildland Provincial Park

Exshaw

Kananaskis

Lac des Arcs

Don Getty Wildland Provincial Park

Ha Ling Peak 2680m

Mount Lawrence Grassi

Ehagay Nakoda

The Three Sisters 2941m

WMU 408

Bow Valley Wildland Provincial Park

Mount Lorette 2469m

WMU 4-25

Mountains

See Map 13
See Map 7
See Map 9
See Map 4

Scale 1:200,000
2.0km · 0 · 4km

Banff-Canmore

8

© Mussio Ventures Ltd.

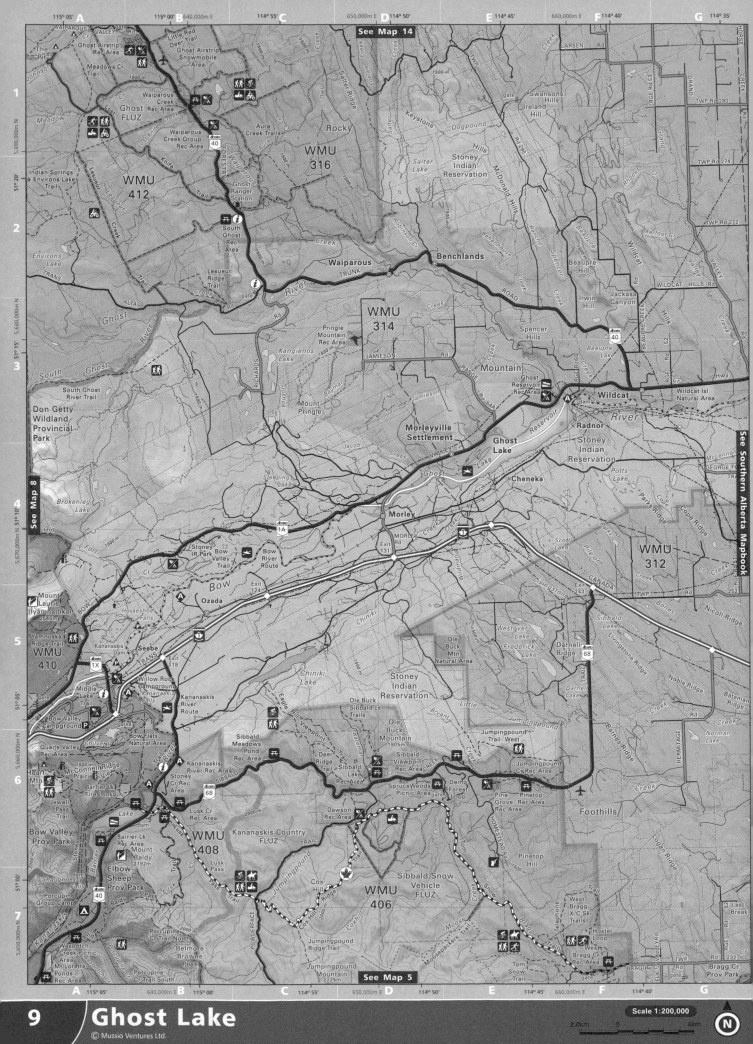

9 Ghost Lake

See Map 5

Scale 1:200,000

© Mussio Ventures Ltd.

See Southern Alberta Mapbook

See Map 8

Banff National Park

WMU 4-36

See Kootenay Rockies Mapbook

WMU 4-34

See Kootenay Rockies Mapbook

Yoho National Park

See Map 11

Scale 1:200,000

2.0km   0   4km

N

Blaeberry   **10**

© Mussio Ventures Ltd.

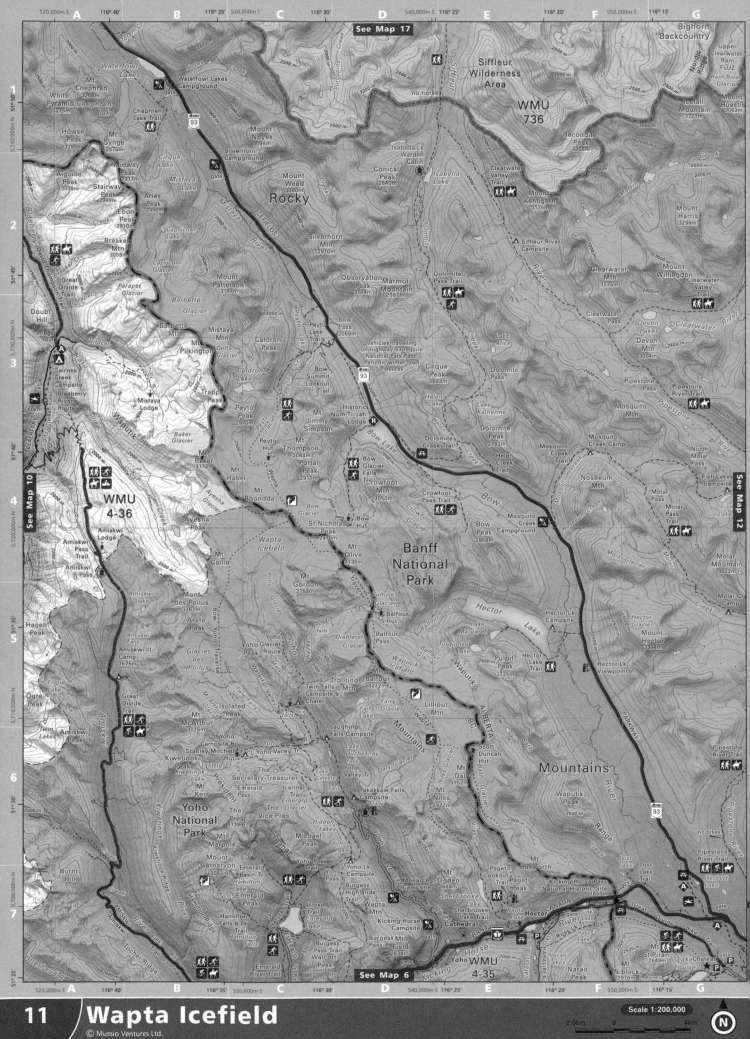

11 Wapta Icefield

© Mussio Ventures Ltd.

Scale 1:200,000

2.0km   0   4km

Lake Louise

12

Scale 1:200,000

© Mussio Ventures Ltd.

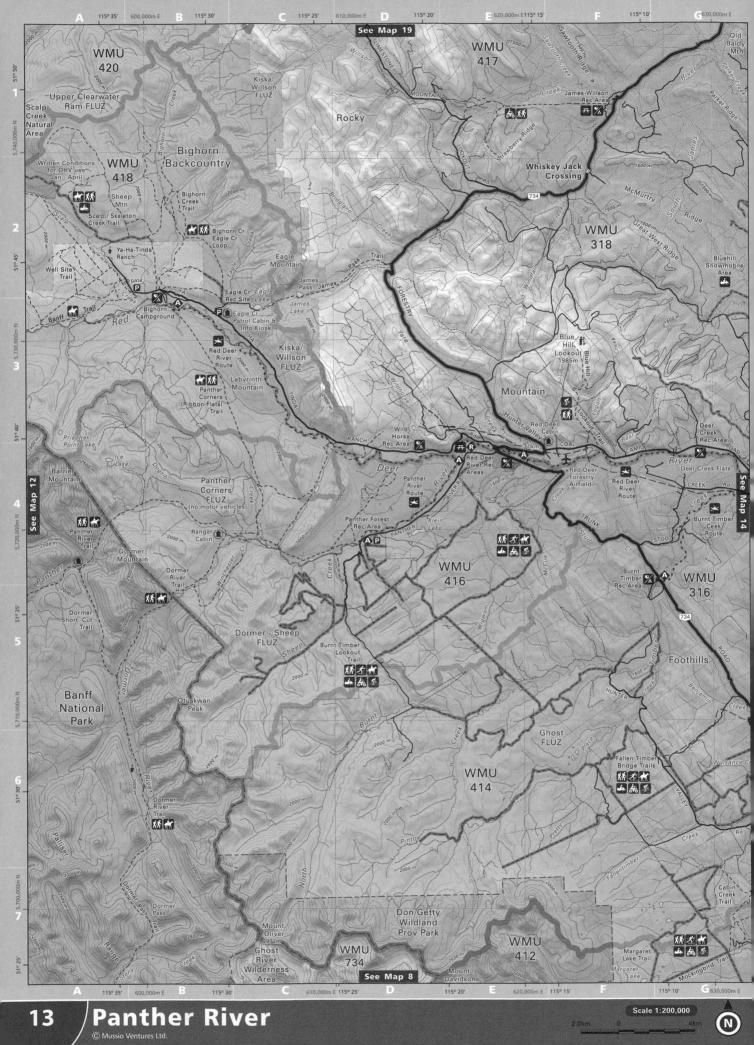

WMU 420

Upper Clearwater Ram FLUZ

Scalp Creek Natural Area

WMU 418

Written Conditions for OHV use Jan - April

Sheep Mtn

Scalp/ Skeleton Creek Trail

Ya-Ha-Tinda Ranch

Well Site Trail

Bighorn Campground

Bighorn Trail

Banff Trail

Red Deer River Route

Panther Corners (Ribbon Flats) Trail

Labyrinth Mountain

Bighorn Backcountry

Kiska/ Willson FLUZ

Bighorn Creek Trail

Bighorn Cr / Eagle Cr Loop

Eagle Cr Rec Site

Eagle Mountain

Eagle Lake

Eagle Cr Patrol Cabin & Info Kiosk

Kiska/ Willson FLUZ

James Pass Trail

James Pass

James Lake

Rocky

WMU 417

James-Willson Rec Area

Whiskey Jack Crossing

WMU 318

Sawtooth Ridge

Strawberry Ridge

McMurtry Ridge

Great West Ridge

Old Baldy Mtn

Parker Ridge

Bluehill Snowmobile Area

Blue Hill Lookout 1985m

Mountain

Hunter Valley

Red Deer Cabin

Deer Creek Rec Area

Prisoner Point Lake

Barrier Mountain

Ice Lake

Panther Corners FLUZ (no motor vehicles)

Ranger Cabin

Dormer Mountain

Panther River Trail

Dormer River Trail

Dormer Short Cut Trail

Banff National Park

Otuskwan Peak

Dormer River Trail

Mount Oliver 2972m

Ghost River Wilderness Area

Dormer Pass

Dormer Pass Trail

Mount Davidson

Dormer - Sheep FLUZ

Burnt Timber Lookout Trail

Wild Horse Rec Area

Panther River Route

Panther Forest Rec Area

Red Deer River Rec Areas

Red Deer Forestry Airfield

Red Deer River Route

Deer Creek Flats

Burnt Timber Creek Route

Burnt Timber Rec Area

WMU 316

Foothills

WMU 416

Klein Lake

WMU 414

Ghost FLUZ

Fallen Timber Bridge Trails

WMU 412

Margaret Lake Trail

Margaret Lake

Mockingbird Trail

Don Getty Wildland Prov Park

WMU 734

See Map 12

See Map 14

734

50km

Scale 1:200,000

2.0km   0   4km

N

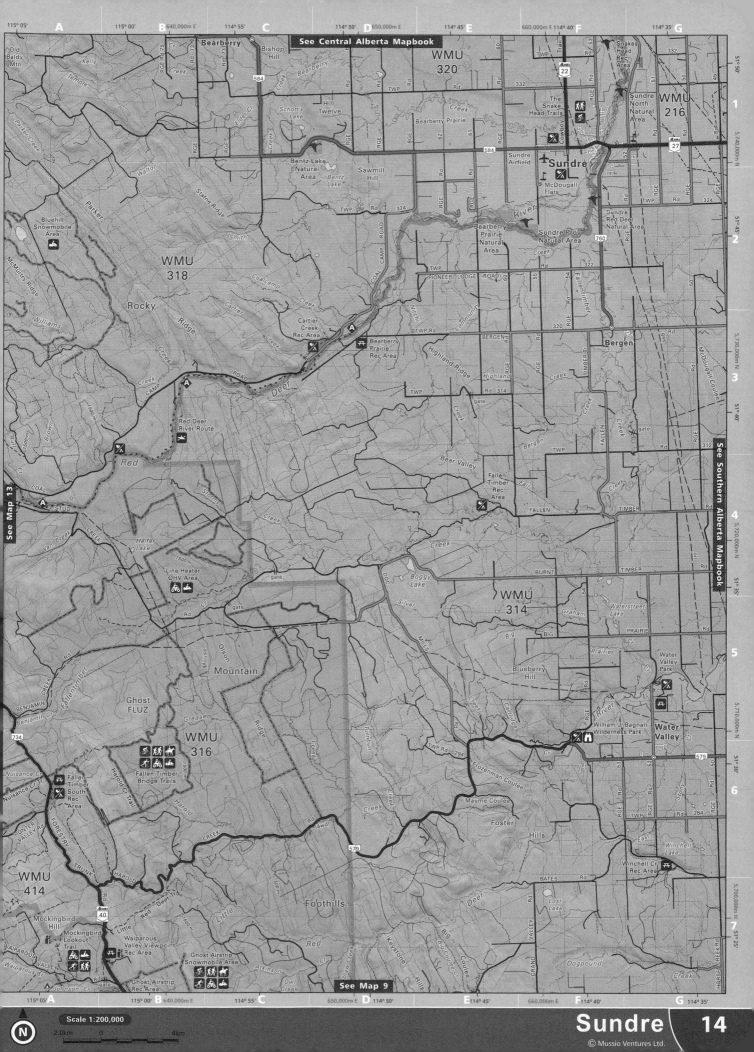

See Map 13

See Southern Alberta Mapbook

See Map 9

Scale 1:200,000

2.0km   0   4km

Sundre   14

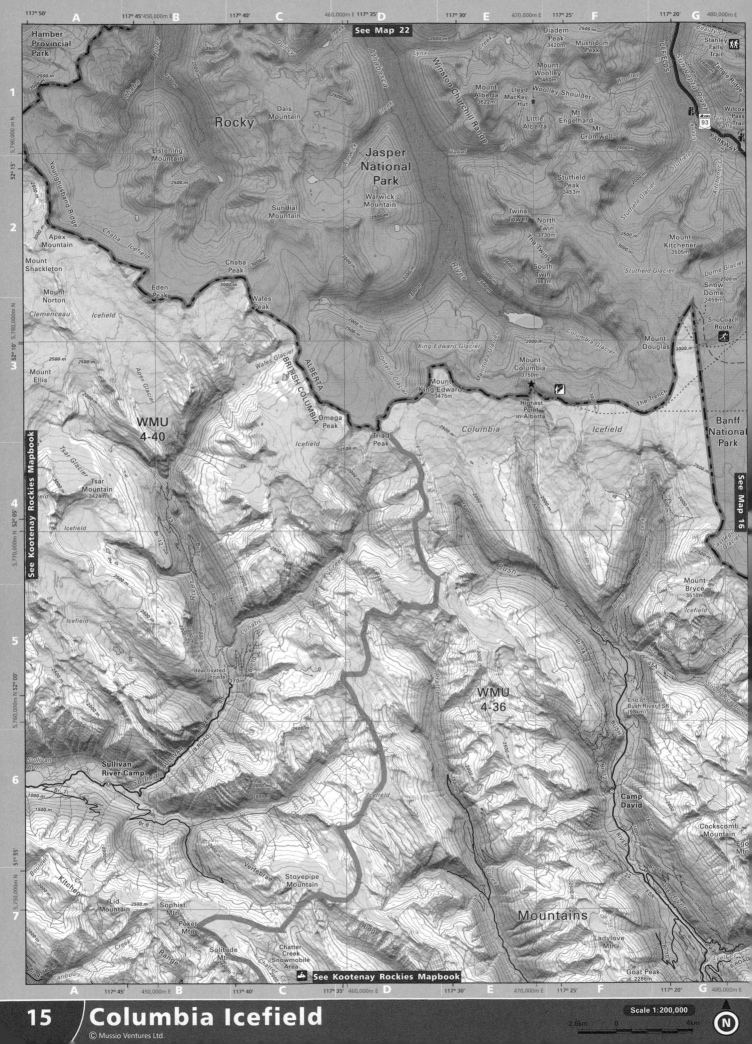

See Map 22

Hamber Provincial Park

Rocky

Dais Mountain

Listening Mountain

Jasper National Park

Warwick Mountain

Sundial Mountain

Diadem Peak 3420m

Mushroom Peak

Mount Woolley 3460m

Mount Alberta 3622m

Lloyd MacKay Hut

Woolley Shoulder

Little Alberta

Mt Engelhard

Mt Cromwell

Stutfield Peak 3453m

Stutfield Glacier

Twins Tower

North Twin 3730m

The Twins

South Twin 3561m

Mount Kitchener 3505m

Stutfield Glacier

Dome Glacier

Snow Dome 3459m

SnoCoach Route

Stanley Falls Trail

Wilcox Pass

Tangle Falls

PARKWAY

93

Apex Mountain

Mount Shackleton

Mount Norton

Clemenceau Icefield

Chaba Icefield

Eden Peak

Chaba Peak

Wales Peak

Columbia Glacier

Mount Douglas

Youghusband Ridge

Mount Ellis

Wales Glacier

BRITISH COLUMBIA

ALBERTA

Omega Peak

Icefield

Triad Peak

Ontario Glacier

Manitoba Glacier

King Edward Glacier

Mount King Edward 3475m

Mount Columbia 3750m

Highest Point in Alberta

Columbia Icefield

The Trench

Banff National Park

See Map 16

See Kootenay Rockies Mapbook

WMU 4-40

Tsar Glacier

Tsar Mountain 3424m

Apex Glacier

Icefield

Icefield

Lunatic

Creek

Bush

Mount Bryce 3510m

Icefield

deactivated roads

170m

SULLIVAN RIVER (19 ROAD)

WMU 4-36

Prattle

Bush

End of Bush River FSR (98km)

Sullivan Arm

Sullivan River Camp

Sullivan

Icefield

Camp David

Cockscomb Mountain

Ego Mtn

Boulde

Kitchen

Lid Mountain

Sophist Mtn

Poker Mtn

Vertebrae

Stovepipe Mountain

Solitude Mtn

Chatter Creek Snowmobile Area

Ridge

Mountains

Ladylove Mtn

Goat Peak 2286m

Lyell

BROOK

Caribou

Range

Chatter Cr

See Kootenay Rockies Mapbook

15 Columbia Icefield

© Mussio Ventures Ltd.

Scale 1:200,000

2.0km   0   4km

N

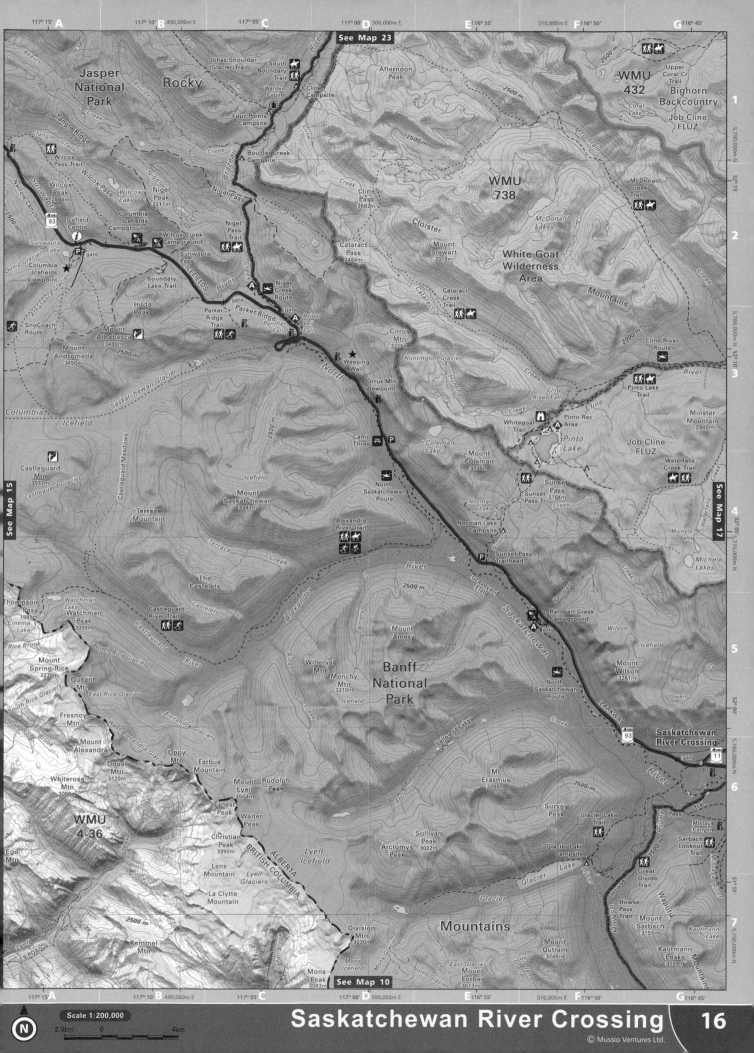

Jasper National Park

Rocky

Johas Shoulder (Glacier) Trail
South Boundary Trail
Cline Campsite
Warden Cabin
Four Points Campsite
Boulder Creek Campsite

Afternoon Peak

Beauty Cr

WMU 432

Bighorn Backcountry

Job Cline FLUZ

Upper Coral Cr Trail

2500 m

Tangle Ridge

Tangle Creek

Wilcox Pass Trail
Wilcox Peak 2884m

Nigel Creek

Boulder Creek

Brazeau River

Cline Creek

McDonald Creek

Cline Pass 2682m

WMU 738

McDonald Lakes

McDonald Creek Trail

Narrow Canyon

Sunwapta

93

Icefield Centre

Wilcox Lake

Nigel Peak 3211m

Columbia Icefields Campground

Nigel Pass

Nigel Pass Trail

Cataract Pass 2484m

Cline Pass

Cloister

Mount Stewart 3315m

White Goat Wilderness Area

Mountains

2000 m

P

gate

Wilcox Creek Campground

Sunwapta Pass

ICEFIELDS

Creek

Cataract Creek Trail

Cataract

2500 m

Columbia Icefields Viewpoint

Dome Glacier

Sunwapta Lake

Hilda Peak

Boundary Lake Trail

River

Nigel Creek Route

gate

A

Parker Ridge Trail

Parker Ridge

gate

Panther Falls

Bridal Veil Falls

Cirrus Mtn 3215m

Huntington Glacier

Huntington

Cline River Route

Cline River Falls

Pinto Lake Trail

Minster Mountain 2940m

Athabasca Glacier

SnoCoach Route

Mount Athabasca 3490m

North

Weeping Wall

Cirrus Mtn Viewpoint

Cline

Whitegoat Trail

Pinto Rec Area

Pinto Lake

Job Cline FLUZ

Mount Andromeda 3450m

2500 m

Saskatchewan Glacier

Camp Three

P

Coleman Lake

Mount Coleman 3135m

A

Sunset Pass 2164m

Waterfalls Creek Trail

Columbia Icefield

See Map 15

Castleguard Mtn 3077m

Castleguard Glacier

Castleguard Meadows

Terrace Mountain

Icefield

Mount Saskatchewan 3342m

North Saskatchewan Route

Alexandra River Trail

Norman Lake

Norman Lake Campsite

Sunset Pass Tr

A

Norman Creek

P

Sunset Pass Trailhead

Michele Falls

See Map 17

Michele Lakes

Terrace Creek

The Castelets

Castleguard River Trail

Castleguard River

Castelets Cr

Alexandra

River

River

2500 m

Graveyard Flats

Rampart

Saskatchewan

Rampart Creek Campground

A

gate

Wilson

Icefield

Owen Cr

Thompson Pass 1985m

Watchman Lake

Watchman Peak 3009m

North Rice Glacier

Rice Brook

Mount Spring Rice 3275m

Quéant Mtn 3261m

East Rice Glacier

Alexandra Glaciers

West Alexandra Glacier

Willerval Mtn

Monchy Mtn 3210m

Icefield

Mount Amery

Amery Cr

River

Banff National Park

2500 m

North Saskatchewan Route

Mount Wilson 3261m

Icefield

PARKWAY

52° 00'

Cinema Lake

Fresnoy Mtn

Mount Alexandra

Douai Mtn 3120m

Whiterose Mtn 3066m

WMU 4-36

South Rice Glaciers

South Rice Brook

Oppy Mtn

Farbus Mountain

Mount Lyell 3504m

Rudolph Peak

Ridges

Castleguard

Creek

Valley of Lakes

Mt Erasmus 3265m

Arctomys Cr

93

Saskatchewan River Crossing

11

gate

Mistaya Canyon

Sarbach Lookout Trail

Ego Mtn

Lyell Cr

Ernest Peak

Walter Peak

Christian Peak 3390m

ALBERTA

BRITISH COLUMBIA

Lens Mountain

Lyell Icefield

Lyell Glaciers

La Clytte Mountain

Sullivan Peak 3022m

Arctomys Peak

Survey Peak

Glacier Lake Trail

Glacier Lake Campsite

Howse

River

Great Divide Trail

Mount Sarbach 3155m

Mistaya River

2500 m

Lyell 6 ROAD

Kemmel Mtn

Icefall Brook

Division Mtn 3030m

Mons Icefield

Mons Glacier

Mons Peak 3083m

North Glacier

East Glacier

Mount Forbes 3612m

Mountains

Glacier

Glacier Lake

Mount Outram 3240m

Howse Pass Trail

Waputik

Mountains

Kaufmann Lake

Kaufmann Peaks 3109m

See Map 10

117° 15' 117° 10' 490,000m E 117° 05' 117° 00' 500,000m E 116° 55' 510,000m E 116° 50' 116° 45'

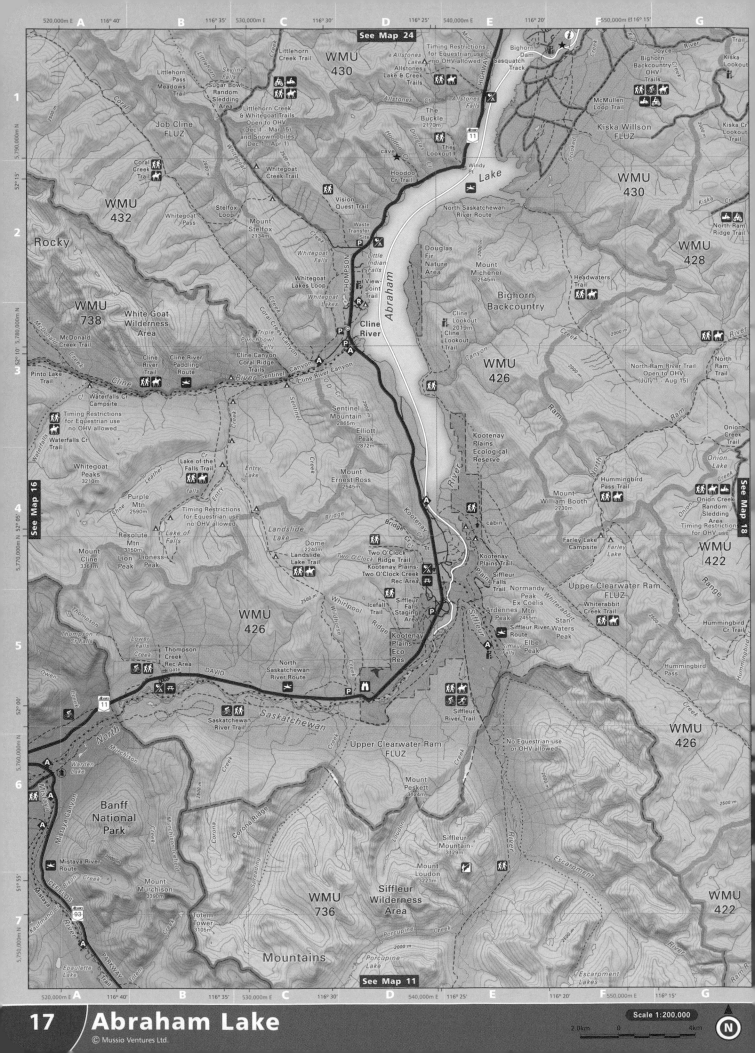

See Map 17

See Map 19

See Map 12

Joyce R

Joyce River Trail

Bighorn Dam Trail

Kiska Creek Lookout Trail

Kiska/ Willson FLUZ

North Ram Ridge Trail

North Ram River Trail

WMU 428

Jock Lake

Rocky

North Ram River Trail

North Ram River Trail Open to OHV (July 1 - Aug15)

North Cripple Creek Trail

Gap Lake Trail

North Ram- Nice Creek Natural Area

Esker Trail

WMU 429

Mountain

South Ram River Route

WMU 326

Table Rock Falls

Tapestry Falls

Onion Creek Trail

(Timing Restrictions for OHV use)

Hummingbird Creek Trail

Hummingbird Creek Route

Canary Creek Trail

(Timing Restrictions for OHV use)

Bighorn Backcountry

Falls Lookout 2460m

Ram Ridge Trail

Ram Falls Rec Area

Upper South Ram Canyon River Route

Hummingbird Rec Area

(Timing Restrictions for OHV use)

Ranger Creek Trail

Ram Falls

Kiska/ Willson FLUZ

Peppers Lake Trail

Peppers Lake Rec Area

Peppers Lake

Elk Creek Rec Area

South Ram River (Allenby) Trail

WMU 422

Upper Clearwater/ Ram FLUZ

Foothills

Cutoff Cr Rec Area

WMU 426

Whiterabbit Creek Trail

South Ram Patrol Cabin

Tin Roos - Headwaters Historical Patrol Cabin (not used)

Ranger Creek Random Sledding Area (Timing Restrictions for OHV use)

WMU 420

(Timing Restrictions for OHV use)

Clearwater River Trail

Lost Guide Canyon Trail

Wampum Peak

Headwaters Trail

Lost Guide Lake

Banff National Park

Indian Lookout Mtn

Clearwater River Trail

Forty Mile Flats

Forty Mile Patrol Cabin

Skeleton Creek Trail

Harrison Flats

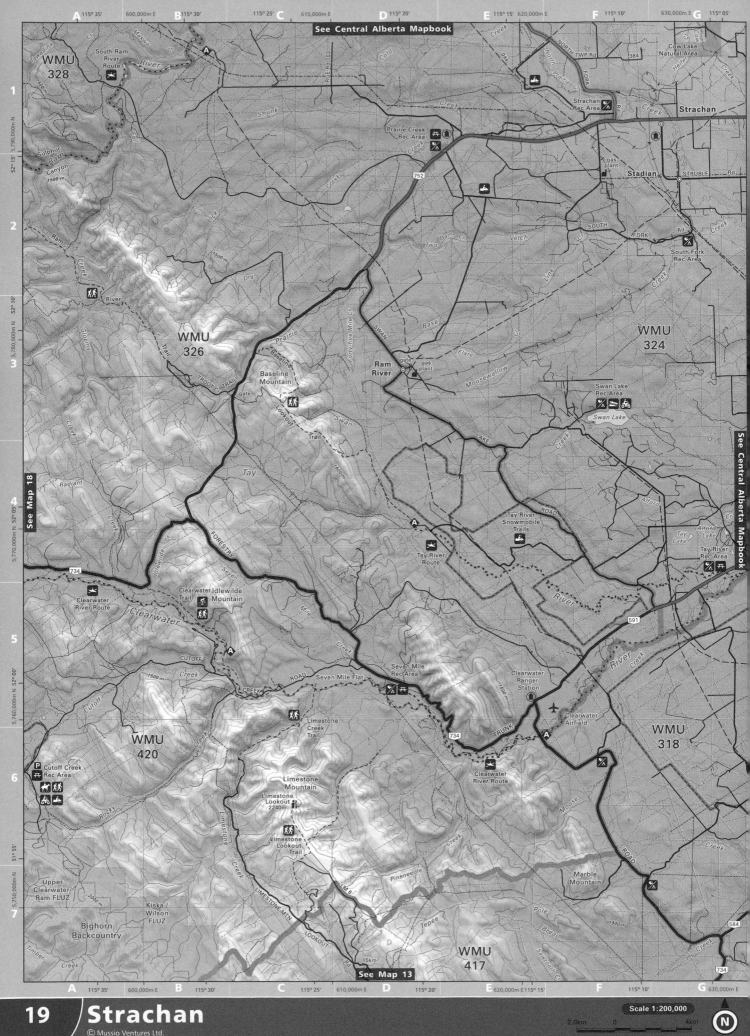

A 115° 35′ 600,000m E B 115° 30′ 115° 25′ C 610,000m E D 115° 20′ E 115° 15′ 620,000m E F 115° 10′ 630,000m G 115° 05′

WMU
328

South Ram
River
Route

WMU
326

Baseline
Mountain

Baseline

Lookout

Trail

Swan

Tay

Radiant

FORESTRY

TROUT C. TRAIL

Idlewilde Cr

Clearwater

Clearwater
River Route

Clearwater
Idlewilde
Mountain

CUTOFF

Creek

CREEK

ROAD

Seven Mile Flat

Limestone
Creek
Trail

WMU
420

Cutoff Creek
Rec Area

Cutoff

Rocky

Limestone
Mountain

Limestone
Lookout
2240m

Limestone
Lookout
Trail

Upper
Clearwater/
Ram FLUZ

Kiska /
Wilson
FLUZ

Bighorn
Backcountry

Timber

LIMESTONE MTN

LOOKOUT

15km

Ram

Maskwa

River

Shunk

Creek

Lick

Dry

Prairie

Prairie Creek
Rec Area

Cold

Creek

Ram River

gate

gas
plant

Ram
River

Forty-five Mile Cr

SWAN

Base

Flare

Moosewallow

LAKE

Creek

ROAD

Seven Mile
Rec Area

Clearwater
Ranger
Station

Tay River
Route

Tay River
Snowmobile
Trails

734

734

TRUNK

Clearwater
River Route

Clearwater
Airfield

Pineneedle

LM 6

Tepee

Moose

Pole

Sawtooth Cr

Bread

WMU
417

See Map 13

North Prairie Cr

NORTH TWP Rd

FORK

Creek

Strachan
Rec Area

Strachan

gas
plant

Stadian STRUBLE Rd

SOUTH

FORK

Rd

South Fork
Rec Area

WMU
324

Swan Lake
Rec Area

Swan Lake

Alford

Tay
Lake

Alford
Lake

Tay River
Rec Area

River

591

WMU
318

Marble
Mountain

ROAD

584

734

Cow Lake
Natural
Area

384

Heifer Cr

Cow
Lake

RGE Rd 103

752

52° 15′ N
5,790,000m N
52° 10′
5,780,000m N
52° 05′
5,770,000m N
52° 00′ N
5,760,000m N
51° 55′
5,750,000m N

See Map 18

19 Strachan

© Mussio Ventures Ltd.

Scale 1:200,000

2.0km 0 4km

N

Selwyn

Rocky

WMU
7-1

Mount
Robson
Provincial
Park

Tonquin Ridge

Barbican
Peak

ALBERTA
BRITISH COLUMBIA

Fraser River

Geikie Creek

Portcullis
Peak
Gateway
Peak
Jade
Lake

Minotaur
Peak

Range

Rocky

CANOE

WMU
7-2

PTARMIGAN

private road

Ptarmigan
Bay

Ptarmigan

Creek

Brûlé
Hill

Morning Glory
Basin Trail

Clemina
Creek
Snowmobile
Trails

CLEMINA Cr
FSR

Saddle
Lakes

Canoe

Mountain

FSR

Creek

See Map 21

EAST

Lake)

(Kinbasket

Blackman

Creek

Mountains

WMU
3-43

Columbia

Dominion
Cr

Deer

Creek

Grouse

WEST

Mount
Blackman

Goatlick

CANOE RIVER TRAIL

FSR

1600 m

CANOE

Hugh Hugh

Hugh Allan Ridge

LITTLE
FROG
FSR

Dominion
Mountain
3048m

2000 m

Windfall
Bay

EAST EXT
Hugh Allan
Bay

Reach

Howard
Bay

HOWARD CREEK

Creek

Monashee

Torii
Mountain

Windfall

FSR

Howard

Creek

BUSTER/HOWARD FSR

ALLAN

Allan

SILVERTIP

SOUTH FORK

FSR

Bryan
Peak

Oventop
Ridge

Oventop
Peak

2000 m

Mountains

Oventop Glacier

Pancake Cr
Pancake Glacier

Mountains

Foster Arm
Protected
Area

Trench

Anderson
Mtn

Edward
Peak

Amie
Peak

Baker

Creek

WMU
4-40

Scale 1:200,000

2.0km   0   4km

Meadow Glacier

Caniche Peak

Rocky

Tonquin Hill 2396m

Tonquin Pass 1950m

Moat Lake

Trident

Circus Valley

Majestic Mtn 3085m

Vertex Peak

Portal Campsite

Peveril Peak

Lectern Peak 2774m

Astoria River Route

Wabasso Campsite

Wabasso Campground Trail

Otto's Cache Picnic Area

Athabasca River Route

Mount Geikie 3308m

Turret Mountain

Maccarib Campsite

Maccarib Pass Tonquin Valley Trail

Maccarib Pass 2180m

Chak Peak 2798m

Aquila Mtn 2880m

Astoria River

Mt Edith

Cavell Warden Station

Meeting of the Waters Picnic Area

93

Barbican Peak

Bastion Peak 2969m

The Ramparts

Tonquin Valley

Amethyst Lakes

Mt Clitheroe 2794m

Amethyst Campsite

Clitheroe Maccarib Campsite

Tonquin Valley Trail

Cairn

Chrome Lake

Cldhorn Mountain

Astoria River Trail

Astoria Campsite

Angel Glacier

Mt Edith Cavell 3383m

Cavell Lake

Path of the Glacier Trail

Cavell Meadows Trail

Mt Edith Cavell Hostel

16 1/2 Mile Lake

Edwards Lake

Horseshoe Lake

Horseshoe Lk Trail

Drawbridge Peak

Redoubt Peak 3077m

Postern Mtn 2969m

Geikie Icefall

Portcullis Peak

Casemate Mtn 3089m

Dungeon Peak

Paragon Peak

Parapet Peak

Simon Peak

Surprise Point Campsite

Switchback Campsite

Eremite Valley Trail

Outpost Peak

Thunderbolt Peak 2681m

Arrowhead Lake

Chrome Lake

Campus

Throne Mtn 3120m

Buttress Lake

Blackhorn Peak 3000m

Beryl Lake

Chevron Mountain 2879m

Verdant Pass 2105m

Ranges

Verdant Creek

Whirlpool River Route

Athabasca Pass Trail

Geraldine Lookout

Fryatt Trail

Athabasca Falls

Warden Station

Jade Lake

Gateway Glacier

Goodair Peak

Rufus Peak

Scarp Glacier

Simon Glacier

Bennington Glacier

McDonell Peak

Mt Fraser 3000m

Gibson Hut

Bennington Peak

Eremite Glacier

Mt Erebus 3118m

Eremite Mtn

Alcove Mtn 2890m

Angle Peak 2909m

Park

Simon Creek Campsite

Tie Campsite

closed to bikes here

Athabasca Pass Trail

First Geraldine Lake

Second Geraldine Campsite

Second Geraldine Lake

Geraldine Lakes

Fryatt Valley Trail

Brussels Campsite

Mount Robson Park

Scarp Mountain 2999m

Mastodon Mtn 2939m

Mastodon Glacier

Elephas Mtn

Reunion Peak

Jasper National Park

Simon Creek

Simon

Whirlpool River

Divergence Creek

Mt Fryatt 3360m

Fryatt Valley Trail

See Map 22

WMU 7-1

Fraser River

Blackrock Mtn 2909m

Whitecrow Mtn 2830m

Beacon Lake

Needle Peak 2969m

Whirlpool River

Middle Forks Campsite

warden cabin

See Map 20

The Cube Ridge

Beacon Peak 2985m

Chalk Lake

Beaverdam Ridge

Divergence Peak 2826m

Alnus Peak 2975m

Fraser Pass 2010m

Whirlpool Pass 1810m

Middle

Ross Creek

Scott Creek

Mt Lapensée 3105m

Mt Belanger 3107m

Headwall Campsite

Fryatt Lake

Fryatt (Sidney Vallance) Hut

WMU 7-2

Mallard Peak 2843m

Scott Campsite

Athabasca Pass Trail

Whirlpool River

Mt Scott 3267m

Mt Ross Cox 2999m

North Alnus Glacier

Mt Oates 3119m

Alnus Glaciers

Alnus Creek

Lick Creek

Lick Peak 2879m

Kane Meadows Campsite

Canoe Pass 2050m

Mt Evans 3209m

Mount Kane 3089m

Scott Glacier

Mount Scott

Mt Oates

South Alnus Glacier

Serenity Mountain 3220m

Hamber Provincial Park

High Allan Creek

McGillivray Ridge

Kane Glacier

Hooker

ALBERTA

BRITISH COLUMBIA

Mount Ermatinger 3059m

Serenity Glacier

Iroquois Creek

East Creek

Athabasca Pass 1748m

Athabasca Pass Historic Site

Mt Hooker 3306m

Hooker Glacier

Mt Hooker

Icefield

Serenity Creek

Fortress Lake

Mount Brown

Mount Brown Icefield

Mountains

WMU 4-40

Wood

Falls

Ghost Glacier

Ghost Mountain 3204m

Chisel Peak

Dawson Creek

Jeffrey Creek

Pacific Creek

Bras Croche

Clemenceau River

Ghost Creek

Maligne Lake

Scale 1:200,000

2.0km 0 4km

© Mussio Ventures Ltd.

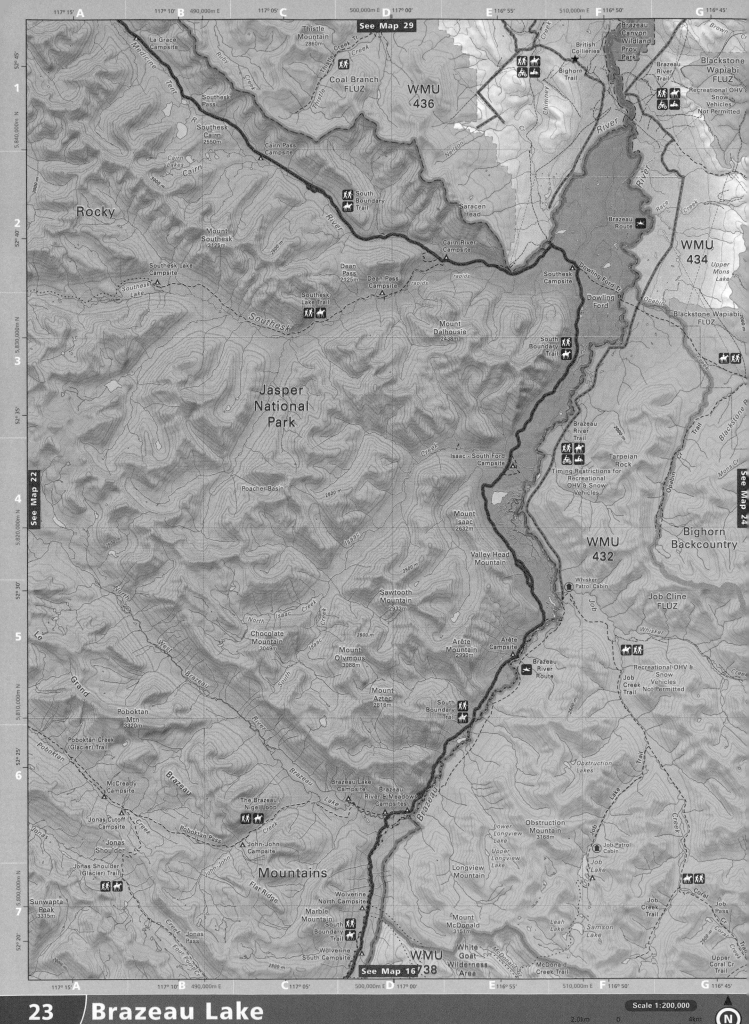

Scale 1:200,000

2.0km   0   4km

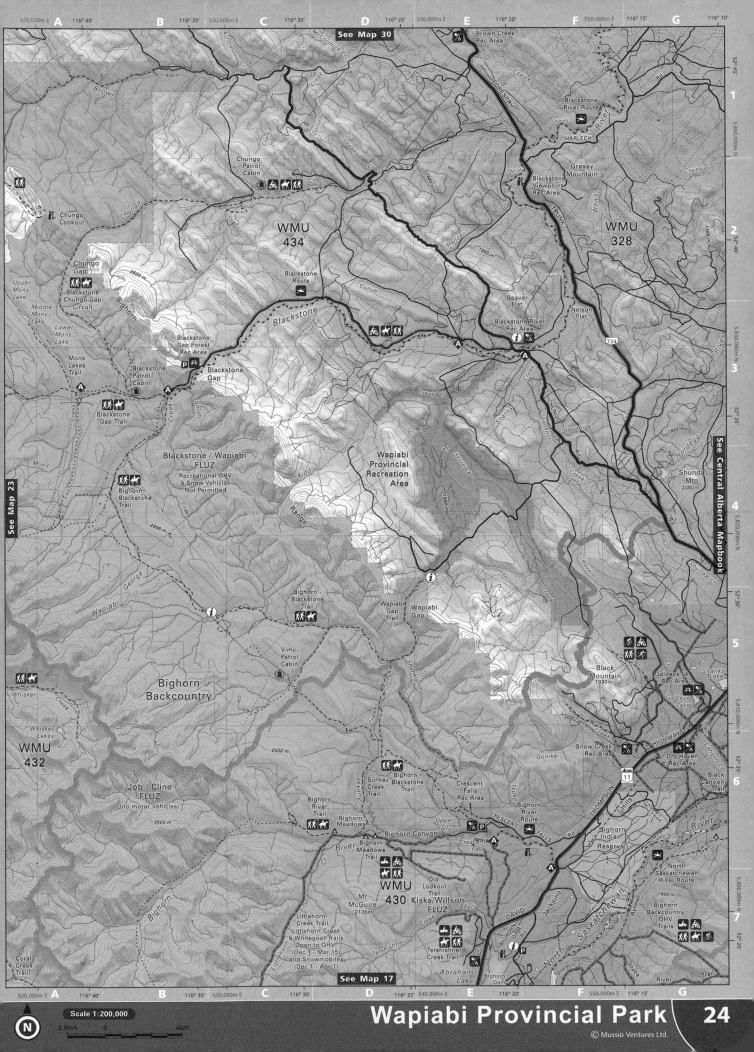

WMU 434

WMU 328

WMU 432

WMU 430

Brown Creek Rec Area

Blackstone River Route

HARLECH

Blackstone River Rec Area

Grassy Mountain

Blackstone Viewpoint Rec Area

Chungo Patrol Cabin

Chungo Lookout

Chungo Gap

Blackstone Chungo Gap Circuit

Upper Mons Lake
Middle Mons Lake
Lower Mons Lake

Mons Lakes Trail

Blackstone Patrol Cabin

Blackstone Gap Forest Rec Area

Blackstone Gap

Blackstone Gap Trail

Blackstone Route

Beaver Flat

Blackstone River Rec Area

Nelson Flat

734

Shunda Mtn 2080m

Blackstone / Wapiabi FLUZ
Recreational OHV & Snow Vehicles Not Permitted

Bighorn Blackstone Trail

Wapiabi Provincial Recreation Area

Bighorn - Blackstone Trail

Vimy Patrol Cabin

Wapiabi Gap Trail

Wapiabi Gap

Black Mountain 1930m

Goldeye Lk Rec Area

Goldeye Lake

Shanks Lake

Bighorn Backcountry

Whisker Creek

Whisker Lakes

Snow Creek Rec Area

Dry Haven Rec Area

Black Canyon Trail

Job / Cline FLUZ
(no motor vehicles)

Sunkay Creek Trail

Bighorn Blackstone Trail

Crescent Falls Rec Area

Bighorn River Route

HIGHWAY
11

Thompson Hills

Bighorn River Trail

Bighorn Meadows

Bighorn Canyon

Bighorn Meadows Trail

Upper Falls

Crescent Falls

CRESCENT FALLS

Bighorn Indian Reserve

North Saskatchewan River Route

Bighorn Backcountry OHV Trails

Mt McGuire 2135m

Old Lookout Trail

Kiska/Willson FLUZ

Littlehorn Creek Trail
Littlehorn Creek & Whitegoat Trails
Open to OHV (Dec 1 - Mar 15) and Snowmobiles (Dec 1 - Apr 1)

Tershishner Creek Trail

BIGHORN DAM Rd

Bighorn Dam

Abraham Lake

DAVID THOMPSON

North Saskatchewan River

Coral Creek Trail

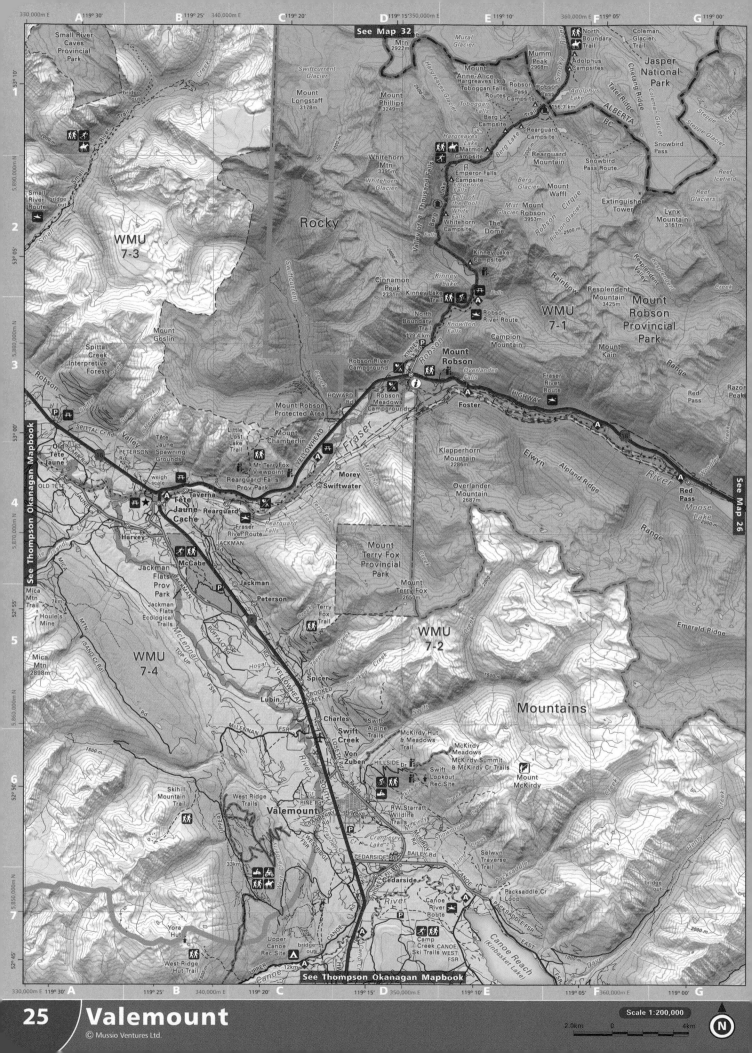

Rocky

Small River
Caves Provincial
Park

Small River
Route

WMU
7-3

WMU
7-1

WMU
7-2

WMU
7-4

Mount Robson
Provincial
Park

Jasper National
Park

ALBERTA
BC

Spittal Creek
Interpretive
Forest

Mount
Goslin

Mount
Longstaff
3178m

Mount
Phillips
3249m

Whitehorn
Mtn
3395m

Mount
Anne-Alice

Mumm
Peak
2968m

Adolphus
Campsites

North
Boundary
Trail

Coleman
Glacier
Trail

Mural
Glacier

156.7 km

Rearguard
Campsite

Rearguard
Mountain

Snowbird
Pass Route

Snowbird
Pass

Lynx
Mountain
3161m

Mount
Waffl

Mount
Robson
3953m

Berg
Glacier

Mount
Kain

Resplendent
Mountain
3425m

Resplendent
Valley

Mount
Robson
Range

Red
Pass

Razor
Peak

Kinney Lake
Campsite

Campion
Mountain

Fraser
River
Route

Overlander
Falls

Robson
River Route

Cinnamon
Peak
2731m

Kinney Lake
Trail

Mount
Robson

Robson River
Campground

Robson
Meadows
Campground

HOWARD Rd

North
Boundary
Trail
179.4 km

Knowlton
Falls

Foster

Old Tête
Jaune

Tête
Jaune
Spawning
Grounds

Little
Lost Lake
Trail

Mount
Chamberlin

Mt Terry Fox
Viewpoint

Rearguard
Falls
Prov Park

Morey
Swiftwater

Klapperhorn
Mountain
2286m

Overlander
Mountain
2687m

Elwyn

Alpland Ridge

Red
Pass

Moose
Lake

Emerald Ridge

Tête
Jaune
Cache

Taverna

Rearguard

Fraser
River Route

Rearguard
Falls

Harvey

Jackman
Flats
Prov
Park

McCabe

Jackman

Peterson

Jackman
Flats
Ecological
Trails

Mount
Terry Fox
Provincial
Park

Mount
Terry Fox
2650m

Terry
Fox
Trail

Mountains

Mica
Mtn
Trail
7km

Houle's
Mine

Mica
Mtn
2898m

Spicer

Lubin

Charles

Swift
Creek

Von
Zuben

Swift
Alpine
Trails

McKirdy Hut
& Meadows

McKirdy
Meadows
McKirdy Summit
& McKirdy Cr Trails

Mount
McKirdy

HILLSIDE Dr

Swift
Lookout
Rec Site

Skihill
Mountain
Trail

West Ridge
Trails

Valemount

Cranberry
Lake

R.W. Starratt
Wildlife
Trails

CEDARSIDE

Cedarside

Selwyn
Traverse
Trail

Packsaddle Cr
Loop

Yora
Hut

West Ridge
Hut Trail

Upper
Canoe
Rec Site

bridge
out
12km

Canoe
River
Route

Camp
Creek CANOE
Ski Trails WEST
FSR

Canoe Reach
(Kinbasket Lake)

25 Valemount

© Mussio Ventures Ltd.

Scale 1:200,000

2.0km   0   4km

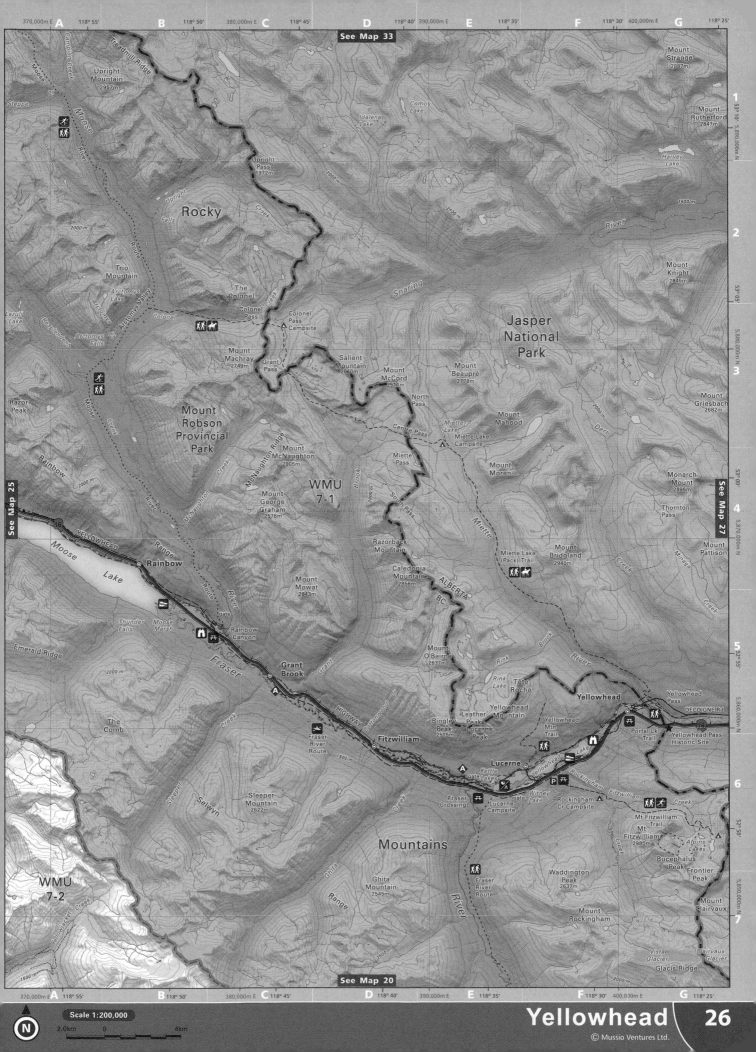

Mount Strange 2887m

Mount Rutherford 2847m

Harvey Lake

Moose Cr

Steppe

Campton Creek

Treadmill Ridge

Upright Mountain 2957m

Rocky

Upright Pass 1972m

Upright Falls

Trio Mountain

Arctomys Lake

Arctomys Valley

Arctomys Falls

Lazuli Lake

Razor Peak

The Colonel

Colonel Pass

Colonel Pass Campsite

Idalene Lake

Comoy Lake

River

Jasper National Park

Mount Knight 2845m

Mount Griesbach 2682m

Mount Machray 2749m

Grant Pass

Salient Mountain 2640m

Mount McCord 2511m

Mount Beaupré 2778m

Snaring

Mount Mahood

Monarch Mount 2896m

Mount Robson Provincial Park

McNaughton Ridge

Mount McNaughton 2905m

Mount George Graham 2576m

North Pass

Centre Pass

Miette Lake

Miette Lake Campsite

Mount Moren

Thornton Pass

WMU 7-1

Brook

Miette Pass

South Pass

Razorback Mountain

Derr

Mount Pattison

Rainbow

Range

River

Moose

Mount Mowat 2843m

Caledonia Mountain 2856m

Mount Bridgland 2940m

Miette Lake (Pack) Trail

Moose Lake

YELLOWHEAD

Rainbow

Thunder Falls

Moose Marsh

Rainbow Canyon

Grant Brook

Grant

Cottonwood Cr

Mount O'Beirne 2637m

ALBERTA BC

River

Rink

Rink Lake

Tête Roche

Leather Peak

Yellowhead Mountain

Bingley Peak 2615m

Lucerne Peak

Yellowhead Mtn Trail

Yellowhead

Yellowhead Pass

DECOIGNE Rd

Portal Lk Trail

Yellowhead Pass Historic Site

Emerald Ridge

Fraser

HIGHWAY

Fitzwilliam

Fraser River Route

Lucerne

Lucerne Lake

Witney Lake

Rockingham Cr Campsite

Kettle Lakes

Rockingham

Fitzwilliam

The Comb

Sleeper Mountain 2622m

Selwyn

Sleeper

Creek

Ghita Range

Fraser Crossing

Lucerne Campsite

Fraser River Route

Ghita Mountain 2545m

River

Mount Fitzwilliam Trail

Mt Fitzwilliam 2980m

Alpine Lakes

Bucephalus Peak

Frontier Peak

Waddington Peak 2637m

Mount Rockingham

Mount Clairvaux

WMU 7-2

Mountains

Vista Glacier

Cinnvaux Glacier

Glacis Ridge

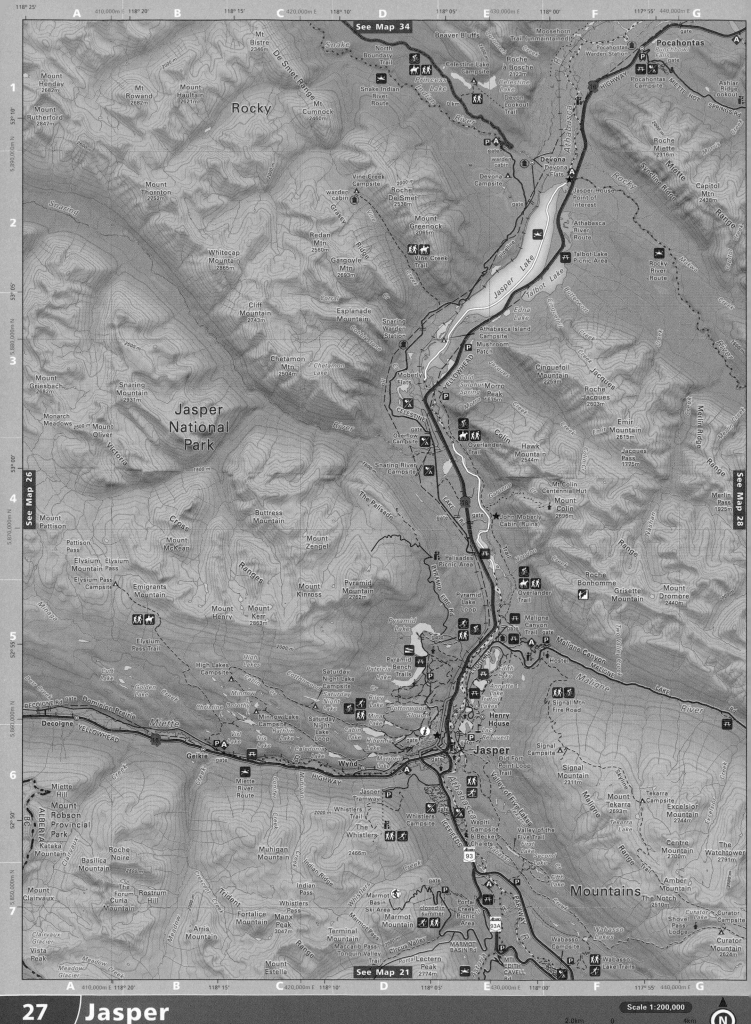

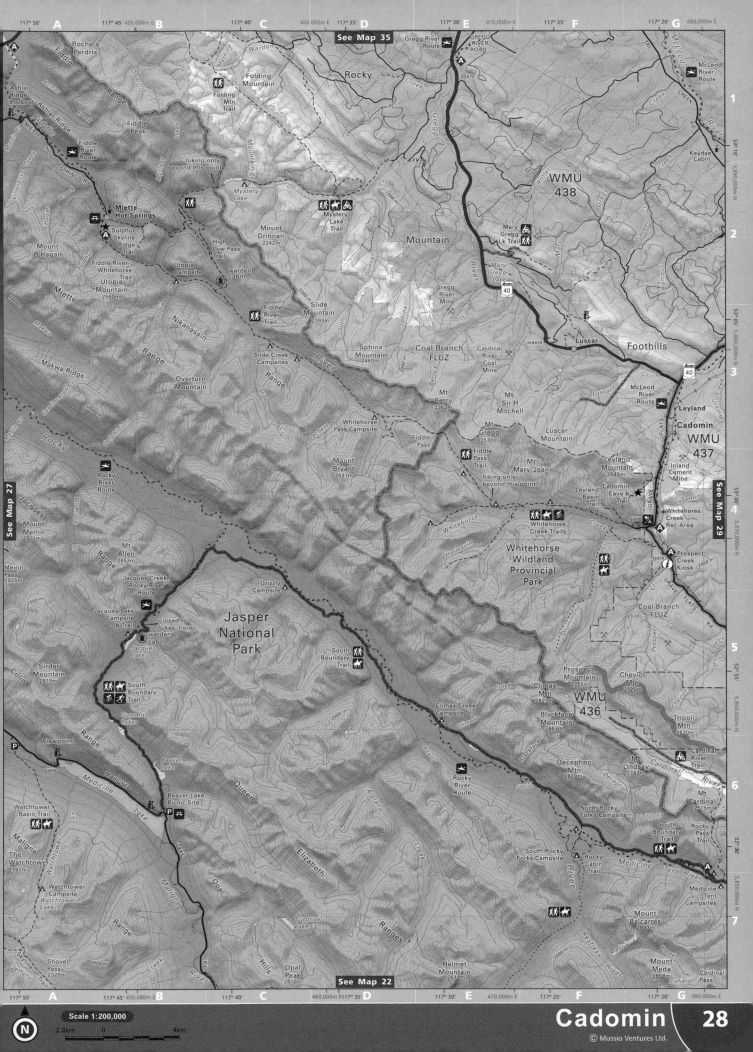

See Map 35

Gregg River Route

GREGG RIVER ROAD

Roche à Perdrix

Fiddle

Ashlar Ridge Lookout

Ashlar Ridge

Fiddle Peak

Fiddle River Route

Folding Mountain

Folding Mtn Trail

Rocky

Mountain

McLeod River Route

Kaydee Cabin

WMU 438

MIETTE

SPRINGS Rd

Miette Hot Springs

Sulphur Skyline Ridge Trail

hiking only beyond this point

Mystery Lake

Mystery Lake Trail

Mountain

Mary Gregg Lk Trail

Mary Gregg Lake

Mount O'Hagan

Fiddle River / Whitehorse Trail

Utopia Mountain 2560m

High Low Pass Trail

Utopia Campsite

warden cabin

Mount Drinnan 2242m

Gregg River Mine

40

Luscar

Foothills

Miette

Makwa Ridge

Nikanassin

Fiddle River Trail

Slide Mountain 2393m

Sphinx Mountain 2460m

Coal Branch FLUZ

Cardinal River Coal Mine

waste

40

McLeod River Route

Leyland

Range

Overturn Mountain

Slide Creek Campsites

Range

Sphinx

Mt Berry 2362m

Mt Sir H Mitchell

Luscar

Cadomin

WMU 437

Rocky

Range

Whitehorse Pass Campsite

Fiddle Pass

Mt Gregg 2530m

Luscar Mountain

Leyland Mountain 2545m

Inland Cement Mine

See Map 29

Rocky River Route

Mount Bryant 2621m

Fiddle Pass Trail

Mt Mary-Jean

Leyland Basin Trail

Cadomin Cave & Trail

GRAVE

Jacques

Mount Merlin 2711m

Mt Allen 2653m

hiking only beyond this point

Whitehorse

Whitehorse Creek Trails

gate

Whitehorse Creek Rec Area

Merlin Pass 1925m

Range

Jacques Creek / Rocky River Route

Grizzly Campsite

Harlequin

Whitehorse Wildland Provincial Park

gate

Prospect Creek Kiosk

Jacques Lake Campsite & Trail

closed to bikes here

warden cabin

Jasper National Park

Coal Branch FLUZ

Sirdar Mountain 2819m

Jacques Lake

South Boundary Trail

South Boundary Trail

Climax Creek Campsite

Prospect Mountain 2755m

Cheviot Mtn 2720m

WMU 436

Colin

Osborne

Summit Lakes

Climax Mtn 2823m

Blackface Mountain 2867m

Tripoli Mtn 2620m

Viewpoint

gate

Beaver Lake

Queen

Climax

rapids

Deception Mtn 2819m

Mt Lindsay 2743m

Cardinal River Trail

Medicine

Beaver Lake Picnic Site

Range

MALIGNE

Alpland

Rocky River Route

North Rocky Forks Campsite

Mt Cardinal 2515m

Watchtower Basin Trail

Elizabeth

Beatty

Creek

Cardinal

South Boundary Trail

Maligne The Watchtower 2791m

LAKE

Opal

South Rocky Forks Campsite

Rocky Cabin Trail

Medicine

Rocky Pass Trail

Watchtower Campsite

Watchtower Lake

Maligne

Surprise Lake

Opal

Hills

Ranges

River

Restless River

Mount Balcarres 2897m

Medicine Tent Campsites

Shovel Pass 2320m

Skyline Trail

Jeffery

River

Opal Peak 2810m

See Map 22

Helmet Mountain 2612m

Mount Meda 2858m

Mount Cardinal Icefield

Cardinal Pass

Scale 1:200,000

2.0km   0   4km

N

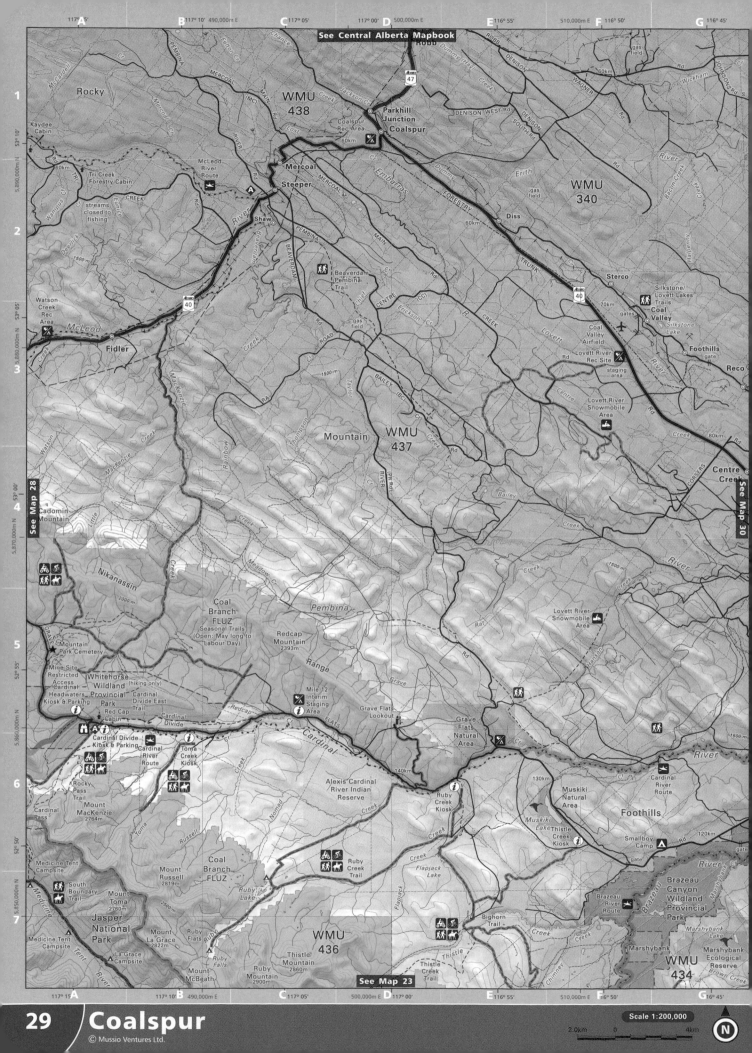

WMU 438

WMU 340

WMU 437

WMU 436

WMU 434

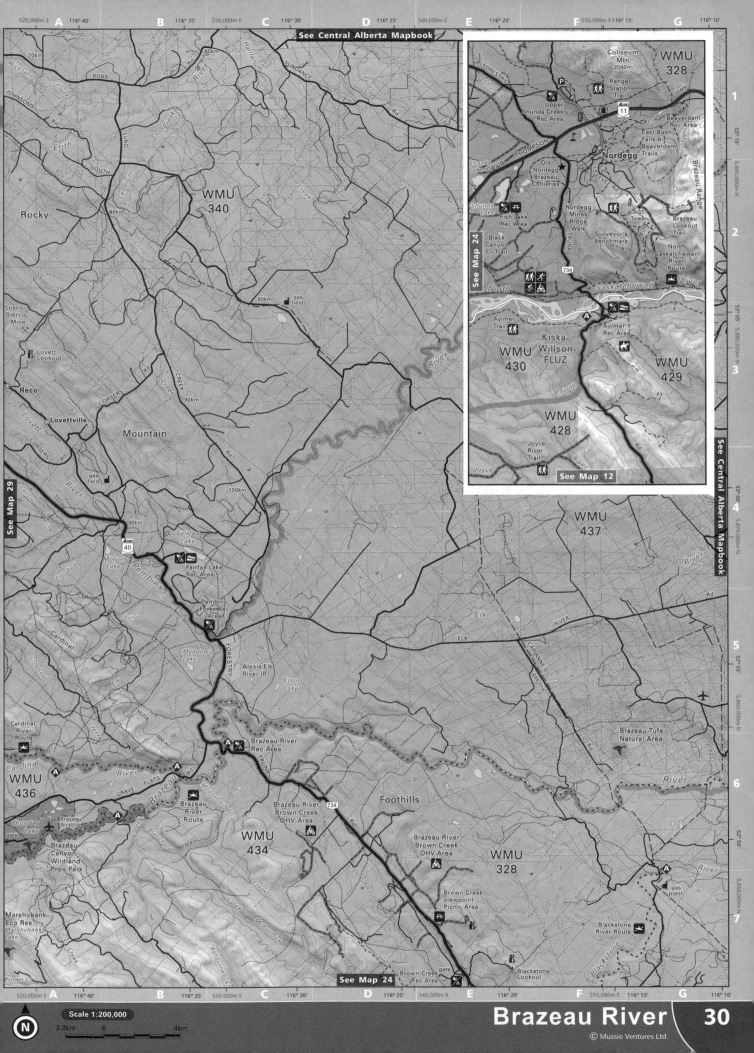

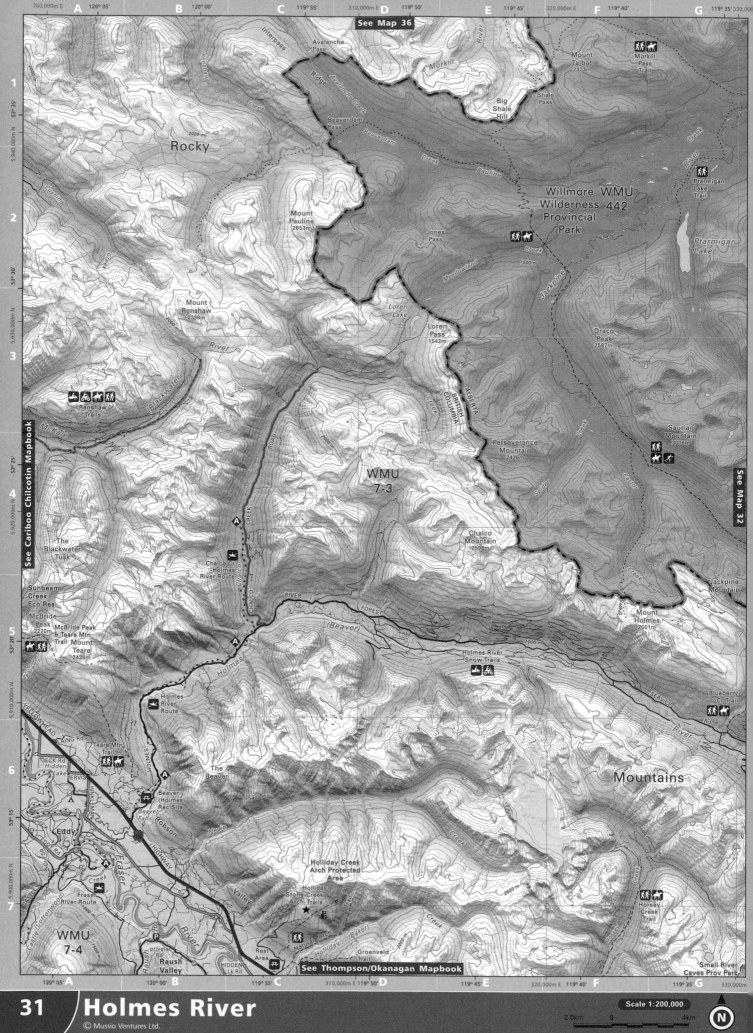

See Cariboo Chilcotin Mapbook

See Map 32

Interpass

Avalanche
Pass

Ridge

Avalanche Creek

Beaverdam
Pass

Beaverdam
Creek

Renshaw
Creek

Rocky

2000 m

Mount
Pauline
2653m

Mount
Renshaw
2398m

River

Blackwater

McKale
Creek

2000 m

Renshaw
Trails

The
Blackwater
Tusk

Sunbeam
Creek
Eco Res

McBride
Peak
2270m

McBride Peak
& Teare Mtn
Trail Mount
Teare
2438m

Teare Cr

YELLOWHEAD

LAING Rd

Teare Mtn
Trail

JERVIS

DECK Rd
Hidden
Lake

HINKLEMAN

Eddy

Epp Rd

Rd

Fraser

Creek

Fraser
River Route

1000 m

WMU
7-4

Raush

River

ROAD

CHALCO

CREEK

CHALCO

Chalco Cr
-Holmes
River Route

Chalco

Holmes

RIVER

River
(Beaver)

FOREST

1000 m

Morkill

River

Mount
Talbot
2373m

Shale
Pass

Big
Shale
Hill

Morkill
Pass
Trail

Ptarmigan
Lake Trail

Ptarmigan
Lake

Willmore WMU
Wilderness 442
Provincial
Park

Pauline
Creek

Jones Pass

Meadowland

1500 m

Loren
Lake

Loren
Pass
1542m

Jackpine

Creek

BRITISH
COLUMBIA

ALBERTA

Draco
Peak
2587m

WMU
7-3

Perseverance
Mountain
2426m

Spider

Creek

Castor

Creek

Saurian
Mountain
3016m

Chalco
Mountain
2598m

Jackpine
Mountain

Mount
Holmes
2501m

1000 m

Holmes River
Snow Trails

SERVICE

River

Rd

Blueberry
Cr Trail

Mountains

Holmes

HOLMES

Robson

Beaver
Falls

Beaver
(Holmes)
Rec Site

The
Beaver

1500 m

Nexio

Holliday Creek
Arch Protected
Area

Holliday
Stone Creek
Arch. Trails

★

Natural Arch

Holliday

(Baker)

Creek

Groenveld
Trail

2000 m

2500 m

Horsey
Creek
Trail

Small River
Caves Prov Park

HIGHWAY

HIDDEN
Lk Rd

P

private
Rd

Raush
Valley

Rest
Area

Valley

31 Holmes River

© Mussio Ventures Ltd.

Scale 1:200,000

2.0km   0   4km

N

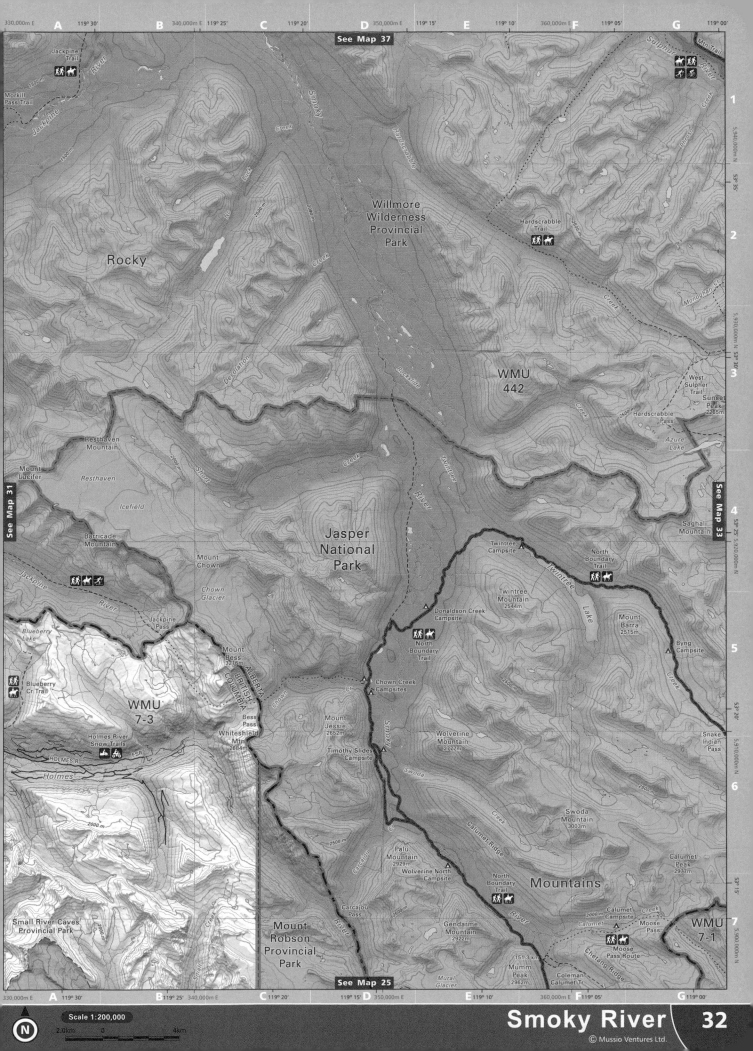

330,000m E A 119° 30' B 340,000m E 119° 25' C 119° 20' D 350,000m E 119° 15' E 119° 10' F 360,000m E 119° 05' G 119° 00'

Jackpine Trail
Morkill Pass Trail
Jackpine

Rocky

Willmore Wilderness Provincial Park

Hardscrabble Trail

Sulphur River

Mtn Trail

WMU 442

West Sulphur Trail
Sunset Peak 2265m
Hardscrabble Pass
Azure Lake

Resthaven Mountain
Mount Lucifer
Resthaven
Icefield
Barricade Mountain

Jackpine River

Mount Chown

Jasper National Park

Short Creek

Twintree River

Chown Glacier

Jackpine Pass
Blueberry Lake
Blueberry Cr Trail
WMU 7-3

Mount Bess 3216m

ALBERTA
BRITISH COLUMBIA

Bess Pass
Whiteshield Mtn 2684m

Holmes River Snow Trails
HOLMES R FSR
Holmes

Small River Caves Provincial Park

Mount Robson Provincial Park

Small Creek

Carcajou

Mount Jessie 2652m

Timothy Slides Campsite

Chown Creek Campsites

North Boundary Trail

Donaldson Creek Campsite

Twintree Campsite

Twintree Mountain 2544m

Twintree Lake

North Boundary Trail

Mount Barra 2515m

Saghali Mountain

Byng Campsite

Snake Indian Pass

Smoky River

Swoda

Wolverine Mountain 2777m

Swoda Mountain 3003m

Calumet Ridge

Calumet Peak 2977m

Palu Mountain 2929m
Wolverine North Campsite

North Boundary Trail

Mountains

Calumet Creek
Calumet Campsite
Moose Pass

Carcajou Pass

Gendarme Mountain 2922m

Calumet River

Chetang Ridge

Coleman Calumet Tr

Moose Pass Route

WMU 7-1

151h.3 km
Mumm Peak 2962m

Mural Glacier

© Mussio Ventures Ltd.

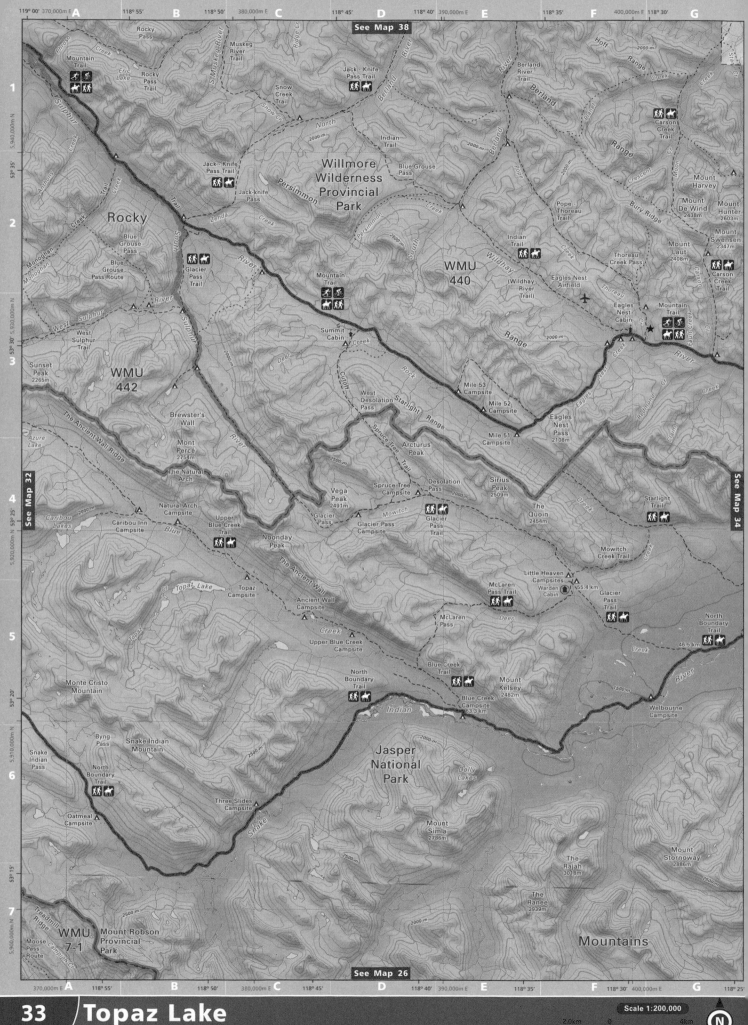

See Map 32

See Map 34

33 Topaz Lake

© Mussio Ventures Ltd.

Scale 1:200,000

2.0km 0 4km

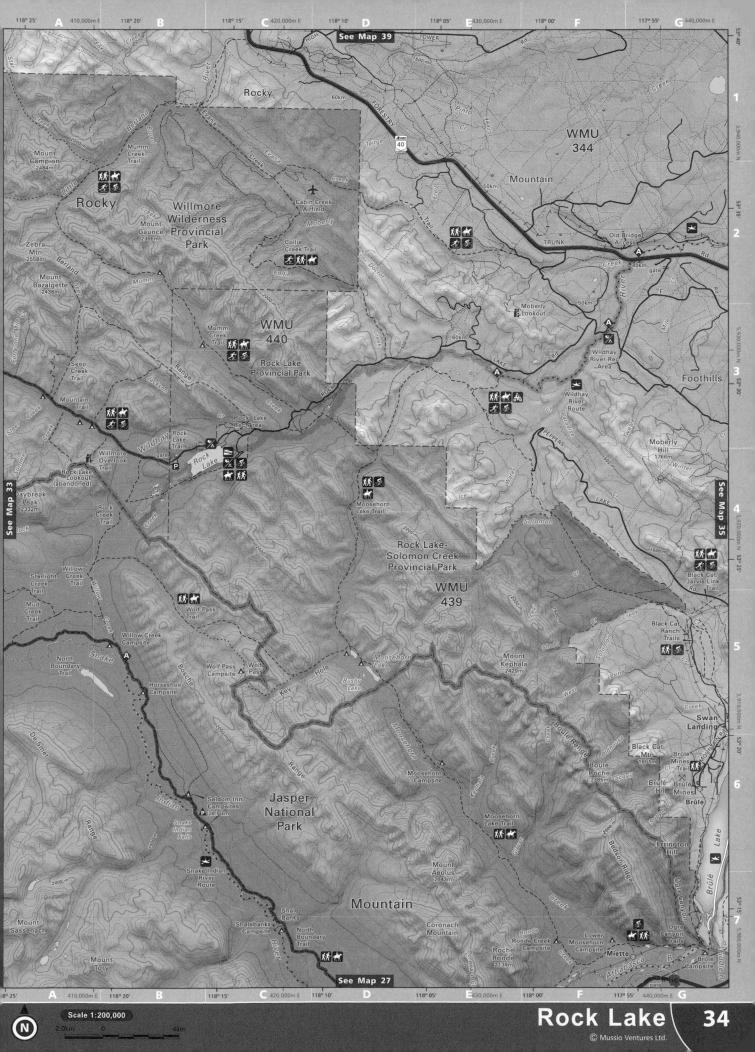

WMU 344

Rocky

Willmore Wilderness Provincial Park

Mount Campion 2484m

Rocky

Zebra Mtn 2558m

Mount Bazalgette 2438m

Mount Gaunce 2386m

Mumm Creek Trail

Collie Creek Trail

WMU 440

Rock Lake Provincial Park

Mumm Creek Trail

Cabin Creek Airfield

Moberly

Moberly Lookout

TRUNK

Wildhay River Rec Area

Wildhay River Route

Old Bridge Access

Foothills

Moberly Hill 1766m

Seep Creek Trail

Mountain Trail

Willmore Overlook Trail

Rock Lake Lookout (abandoned)

Rock Lake Trails

Rock Lake Rec Area

Rock Lake

Moosehorn Lake Trail

Rock Lake-Solomon Creek Provincial Park

WMU 439

Daybreak Peak 2332m

Rock Creek Trail

Starlight Creek Trail

Mud Creek Trail

Willow Creek Trail

Willow Creek Campsite

Wolf Pass Trail

Wolf Pass Campsite

Wolf Pass

Key Hole

Busby Lake

Moosehorn Lake

Mount Kephala 2429m

Black Cat Ranch Trails

Swan Landing

North Boundary Trail

Snake

Horseshoe Campsite

Bosche Range

De Smet

Indian

Snake Indian Falls

Seldom Inn Campsites 26.5 km

Jasper National Park

Snake Indian River Route

Moosehorn Range

Moosehorn Campsite

Boule Range

Boule Roche 2385m

Black Cat Mtn 1801m

Brûlé Mines Trail

Brûlé Hill

Brûlé Mines

Brûlé

Errington Hill

Mount Sassenach

Mount Tory

Shalebanks Campsite

Shale Banks

North Boundary Trail

Moosehorn Lake Trail

Mount Aeolus 2643m

Mountain

Coronach Mountain

Roche Ronde 2138m

Ronde Creek Campsite

Lower Moosehorn Campsite

Miette

Ogre Canyon Trails

Ogre Canyon

Brûlé Lake

Brûlé Campsite

Athabasca R.

Middle R.

Scale 1:200,000

2.0km 0 4km

Rock Lake 34

© Mussio Ventures Ltd.

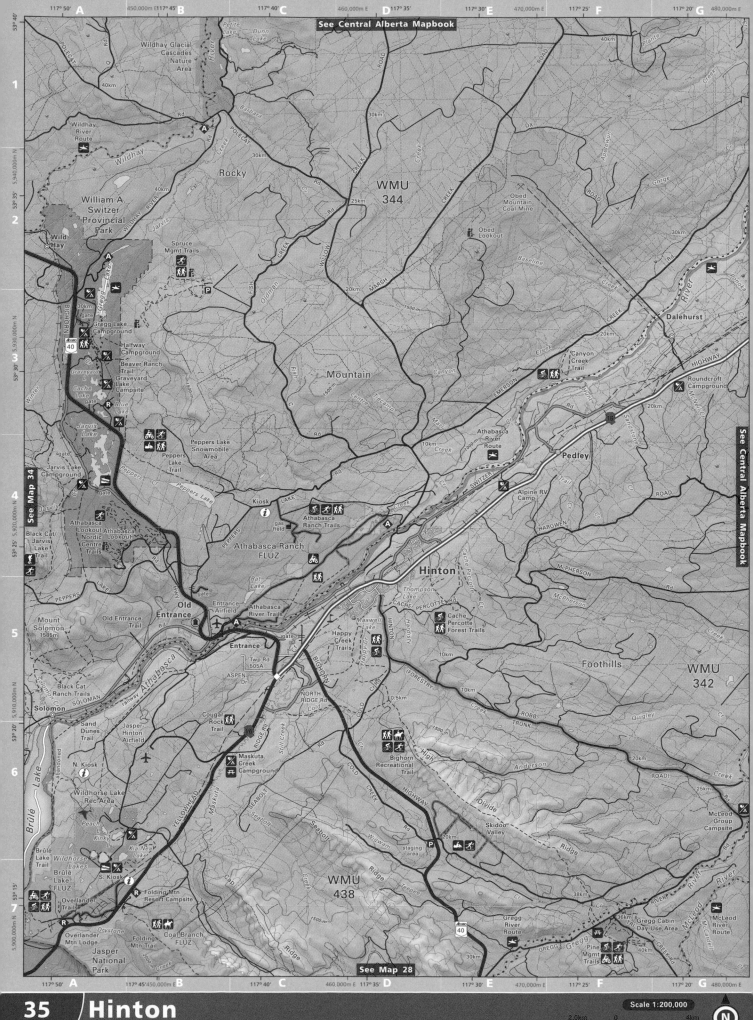

WMU
344

Obed
Mountain
Coal Mine

Obed
Lookout

Wildhay Glacial
Cascades
Nature Area

Rocky

Dalehurst

Mountain

Canyon
Creek
Trail

William A.
Switzer
Provincial
Park

Wild
Hay

Roundcroft
Campground

Spruce
Mgmt Trails

Athabasca
River Route

Pedley

Gregg Lake
Campground

Halfway
Campground

Alpine RV
Camp.

Beaver Ranch
Trail
Graveyard
Lake Campsite

Blue
Lake

Peppers Lake
Snowmobile
Area

Athabasca
Ranch Trails

Hinton

Jarvis
Lake

Cache
Percotte
Forest Trails

Peppers
Lake
Trail

Kiosk

Jarvis Lake
Campground

Athabasca
Lookout

Thompson
Lake

Foothills

WMU
342

Athabasca
Lookout Athabasca
Nordic
Centre
Trails

Athabasca Ranch
FLUZ

Black Cat/
Jarvis Lake
Trail

Rat
Lake

Old
Entrance

Entrance
Airfield

Athabasca
River Trails

Maxwell
Lake

Happy
Creek
Trails

Mount
Solomon
1585m

Old Entrance
Trail

Entrance

Twp Rd
505A

Black Cat
Ranch Trails

Aspen
Dr

Solomon

Sand
Dunes
Trail

Cougar
Rock
Trail

Jasper-
Hinton
Airfield

NORTH
RIDGE Rd

Bighorn
Recreational
Trail

Skidoo
Valley

McLeod
Group
Campsite

N. Kiosk

Wildhorse Lake
Rec Area

Maskuta
Creek
Campground

WMU
438

Peach

staging
area

Brûlé
Lake

Kia Neg
Lake

Brûlé
Lake
Trail

S. Kiosk

Brûlé
Lake
FLUZ

Folding Mtn
Resort Campsite

Gregg Cabin
Day Use Area

Gregg
River
Route

Overlander
Trails

McLeod
River
Route

Overlander
Mtn Lodge

Folding
Mtn Trail

Coal Branch
FLUZ

Gregg
Mgmt
Trails

Jasper
National
Park

Scale 1:200,000

2.0km 0 4km

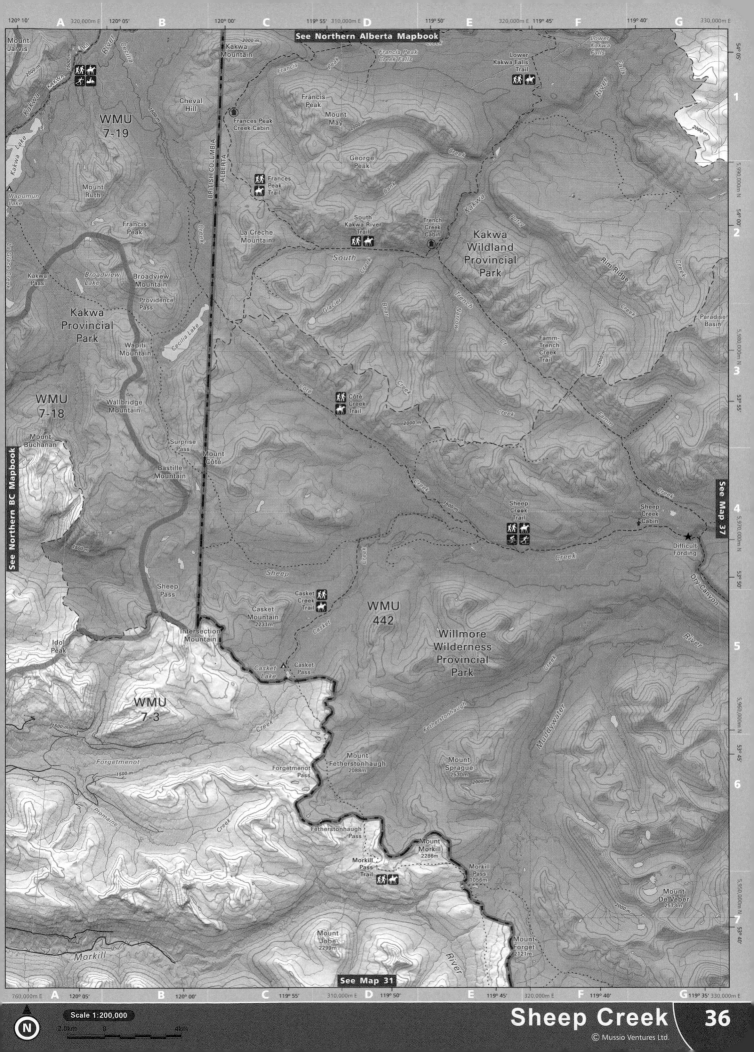

A 320,000m E 120° 05' B 120° 00' C 119° 55' 310,000m E D 119° 50' E 320,000m E 119° 45' F 119° 40' G 330,000m E

54° 05'

Mount Jarvis

WMU 7-19

Cheval Hill

Kakwa Mountain

2000 m

Francis Peak

Francis Peak Creek Falls

Lower Kakwa Falls

Lower Kakwa Falls Trail

1

Mount Ruth

Wapumun Lake

Frances Peak Creek Cabin

Francis Peak

Mount May

George Peak

Francis Peak Trail

La Crèche Mountain

South Kakwa River Trail

South

Kakwa Creek

Trench Creek Cabin

Kakwa Wildland Provincial Park

Rim Ridge

54° 00'

5,990,000m N

2

Kakwa Lake

Kakwa Pass

Broadview Lake

Broadview Mountain

Providence Pass

Kakwa Provincial Park

Wapiti Mountain

Glacier Creek

Bear Creek

Trench Creek

Narrows

Famm-Trench Creek Trail

Famm

Paradise Basin

5,980,000m N

53° 55'

3

WMU 7-18

Wallbridge Mountain

Côté Creek

Côté Creek Trail

2000 m

Creek

2000 m

Mount Buchanan

Surprise Pass

Mount Côté

Bastille Mountain

Sheep Creek Trail

Sheep Creek Cabin

Difficult Fording

See Map 37

53° 50'

5,970,000m N

4

Sheep Pass

Sheep

Creek

1500 m

Creek

Creek

Dry Canyon

River

5

Idol Peak

Intersection Mountain

Casket Mountain 2231m

Casket Creek Trail

WMU 442

Willmore Wilderness Provincial Park

5,960,000m N

53° 45'

Casket Lake

Casket Pass

Casket

Creek

WMU 7-3

Forgetmenot

1500 m

Forgetmenot Pass

Mount Fetherstonhaugh 2088m

Fetherstonhaugh

Mount Sprague 2530m

2000 m

Muddywater

6

Promaine

Morkill

Fetherstonhaugh Pass

Morkill Pass Trail

Mount Morkill 2286m

Morkill Pass 1056m

2000 m

Mount De Veber 2573m

5,950,000m N

53° 40'

7

Mount Jobe 2299m

River

Mount Forget 2121m

See Map 31

A 760,000m E 120° 05' B 120° 00' C 119° 55' 310,000m E D 119° 50' E 119° 45' 320,000m E F 119° 40' G 119° 35' 330,000m E

BRITISH COLUMBIA / ALBERTA

N

Scale 1:200,000

2.0km 0 4km

Sheep Creek 36

© Mussio Ventures Ltd.

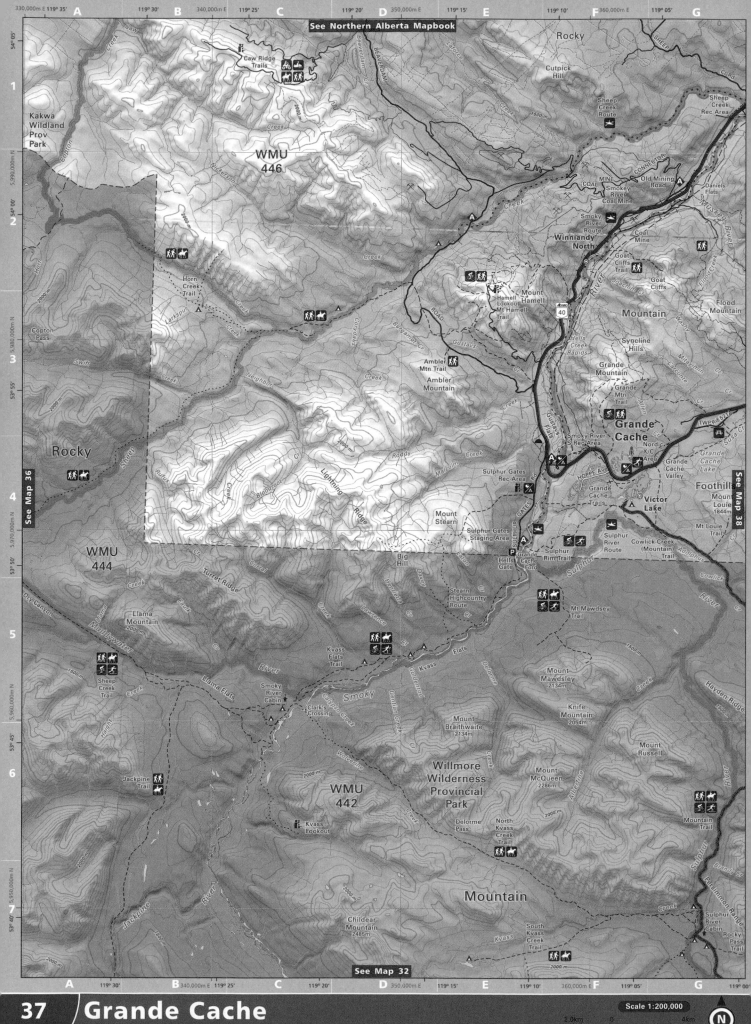

Rocky

Cutpick Hill

Kakwa Wildland Prov Park

WMU 446

Caw Ridge Trails

Horn Creek Trail

Copton Pass

Sheep Creek Route

Sheep Creek Rec Area

Daniels Flats

MINE
COAL
Smokey River Coal Mine
Old Mining Road
CONNECTOR

Smoky River Route

Winniandy North

Coal Mine

Goat Cliffs Trail

Goat Cliffs

Flood Mountain

Mountain

Syncline Hills

Grande Mountain

Grande Mtn Trail

Hamell Lookout
Mt Hamell
Mt Hamell Trail
Mount Hamell

Hells Creek Rapids

Grande Cache

Ambler Mtn Trail

Ambler Mountain

Nordic X/C Area

Grande Cache Lake

Grande Cache Valley

Rocky

See Map 36

Smoky River S Rec Area

Grande Cache Trails

Foothills

Mount Louie 1844m

Victor Lake

Mt Louie Trail

See Map 38

WMU 444

Big Hill

Sulphur Gates Rec Area

Sulphur Gates Staging Area

Hells Gate

Grande Cache Ford

Sulphur Rim Trail

Sulphur River Route

Cowlick Creek (Mountain) Trail

Turret Ridge

Llama Mountain

Mount Stearn

Stearn Highcountry Route

Mt Mawdsey Trail

Dry Canyon

Muddywater

Sheep Creek Trail

Llama Flats

Kvass Flats Trail

Kvass

Kvass Flats

Mount Mawdsley 2134m

Knife Mountain 2054m

Mount Russell

Smoky River Cabin

Clark's Crossing

Smoky

Mount Braithwaite 2134m

Mount McQueen 2286m

Jackpine Trail

WMU 442

Willmore Wilderness Provincial Park

Delorme Pass

North Kvass Creek Trail

Mountain Trail

Kvass Lookout

Childear Mountain 2485m

Mountain

South Kvass Creek Trail

Sulphur River Cabin

Rocky Pass Rte

37 Grande Cache

© Mussio Ventures Ltd.

Scale 1:200,000

2.0km 0 4km

N

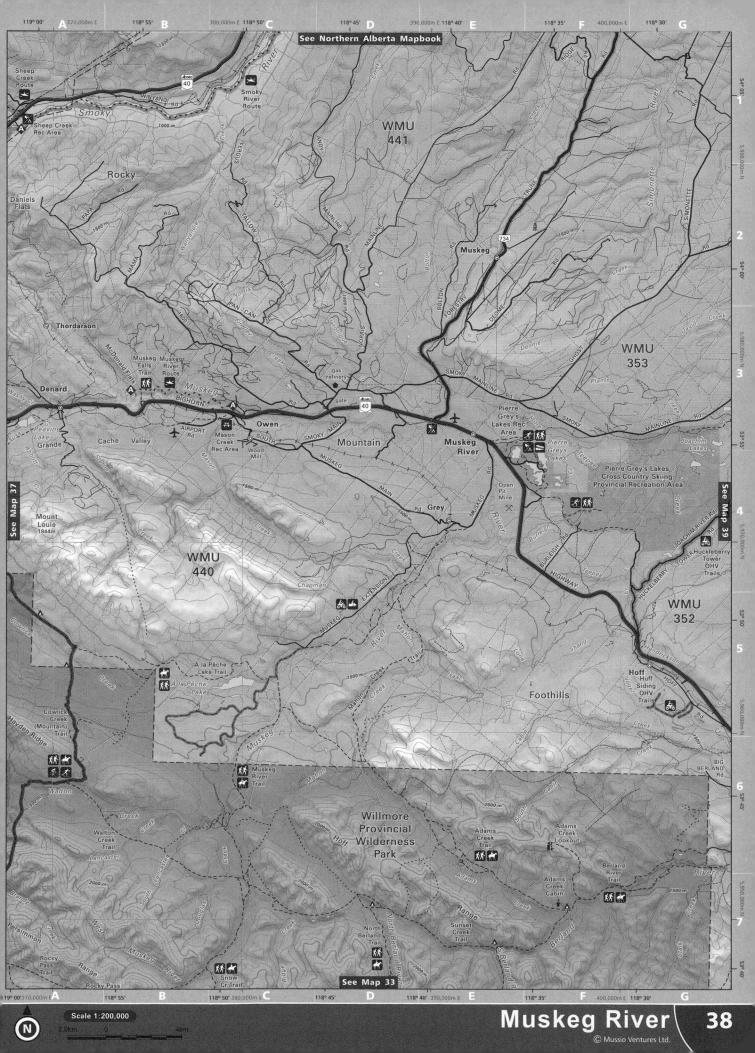

WMU 441

WMU 353

WMU 440

WMU 352

Muskeg

Muskeg River

Pierre Grey's Lakes Rec Area

Pierre Greys Lakes

Pierre Grey's Lakes Cross Country Skiing Provincial Recreation Area

Huckleberry Tower OHV Trails

Hoff
Huff Siding OHV Trails

Foothills

Open Pit Mine

Mountain

Owen

Grey

Denard

Thordarson

Rocky

Daniels Flats

Sheep Creek Route

Sheep Creek Rec Area

Smoky

Smoky River Route

Muskeg Falls Trail

Muskeg River Route

AIRPORT Rd

Mason Creek Rec Area

Wood Mill

Cache Valley

Mount Louie 1844m

gas refinery

gate

A la Pêche Lake Trail

A la Pêche Lake

Muskeg River Trail

Cowlick Creek (Mountain) Trail

Hayden Ridge

Walton Creek Trail

Lancaster

Rocky Pass Trail

Rocky Pass Range

Rocky Pass

Snow Cr Trail

North Berland Trail

Willmore Provincial Wilderness Park

Adams Creek Trail

Adams Creek Lookout

Adams Creek Cabin

Berland River Trail

Sunset Creek Trail

Range

Peavine Grande

BIG BERLAND Rd

See Map 37

See Map 39

See Map 33

Scale 1:200,000

2.0km   0   4km

Muskeg River   38

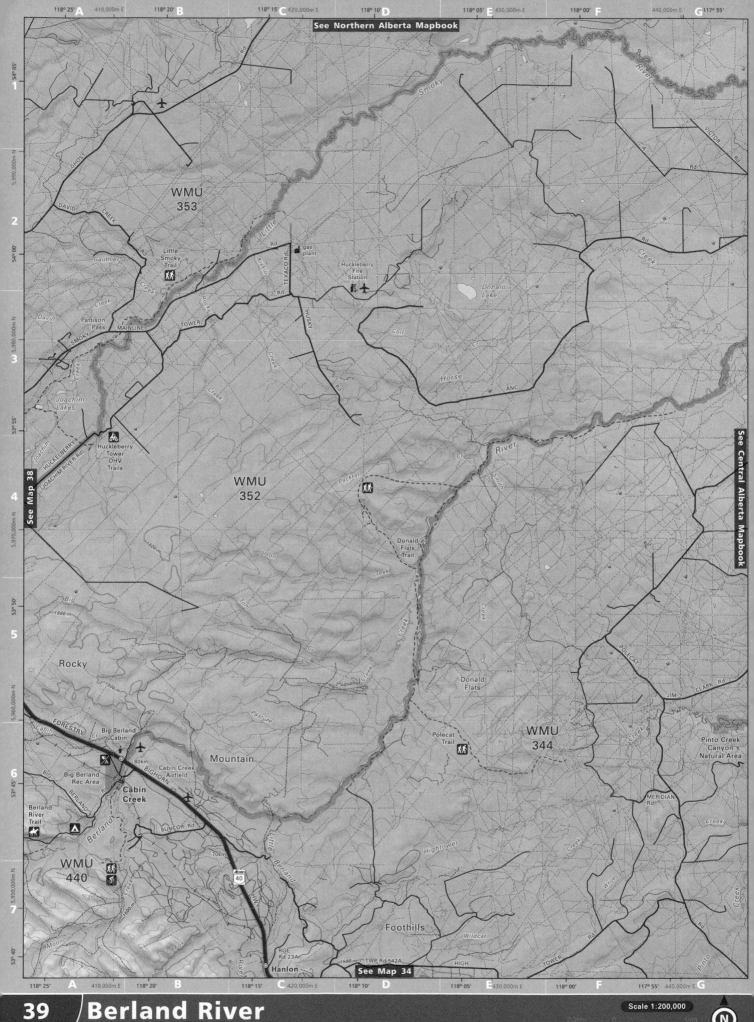

WMU
353

WMU
352

WMU
344

WMU
440

Little Smoky Trail

Huckleberry
Fire Station

Donald
Lake

gas plant

Huckleberry
Tower
OHV
Trails

Packrat

Donald Flats
Trail

Donald Flats

Polecat
Trail

Pinto Creek
Canyon
Natural Area

Rocky

Big Berland
Cabin

Big Berland
Rec Area

Cabin
Creek

Cabin Creek
Airfield

Mountain

Berland
River
Trail

Hanlon

Foothills

Pattison
Pass

Joachim
Lakes

See Map 38

See Central Alberta Mapbook

39 Berland River

© Mussio Ventures Ltd.

Scale 1:200,000

Lake Minnewanka

dam

Cascade Mountain

"C" Level Cirque Trail

Banff National Park

Cascade Pond

Two Jack Campground

Two Jack Lake

2900 m
2800 m
2700 m
2600 m
2500 m
2400 m
2300 m
2200 m
2100 m
2000 m
1900 m
1800 m
1700 m
1600 m
1500 m

Banff Training Area DND

Cascade Amphitheatre Trail

Elk Lake Trail

Mile Cr.

Stoney Squaw Trail

Mt Norquay Mystic Ridge Ski Area

Stoney Squaw Mountain 1884m
Stoney Squaw Lookout

Narquay Road

Mt Norquay Drive

Buffalo Paddock

gate

Compound Ave.

Caribou St.

Gopher St.

Tunnel Mtn.

hostel

Bankhead

Johnson Lake

gate

Johnson Lake X/C Trails

Cascade Highway

Fenland Loop

Banff

Whiskey Cr.

Whiskey Jack Cres
Cougar
Spruce

Hawk
Eagle Cres

Pika Ct. St.

Marmot St
Antelope St Ln.
Antelope St

Moose Mountain

Banff Int'l Hostel

coyote

Road

Hoodoos Viewpoints

Banff Springs Golf Course

Anthracite

To Canmore

Bow River Route

Vermilion Lakes

1st Lake
2nd Lake

Echo Creek

Bow River

Wolf St
Grizzly St.
Elk St.
Lynx St.
Bear St.
Banff Ave.
Buffalo St.
Squirrel St.
Muskrat St.
Beaver St.
Otter St.
Deer St.
Moose St.
Martin St.

Rabbit St.
Wolverine
Caribou St.

Banff Park Museum National Historic Site

Central Park

Birch

Cascade Gardens

Tunnel Mountain 690m

Road Closed to vehicles in Winter & Summer after dark
Tunnel Mtn Lookout Trail

Tunnel Mtn Trailhead

Road Closed to vehicles in Winter & Summer after dark

Bow River Route

Rundle

Riverside Tr.

Bow River

Marsh Loop

Jasper Way
Middle Springs Dr.
Nahanni Dr.
Kluane Dr.
Rundle Ave.
Rosedale Ave.

Cave Ave.

Discovery Trail

Cave and Basin National Historic Hot Springs Site

gate Fairholme
Park Ave.
Glen Ave.
Rainbow Pl

Bow Falls Hoodoos Trailhead

Bow Falls

Glen Ave.

Fairmont Banff Springs Hotel

1600 m
1700 m
1800 m
1900 m
2000 m
2100 m
2200 m
2300 m
2400 m
2500 m

Middle Springs Wildlife Corridor

Sanson Peak 2270m

Spray Mountain Tr.

Spray River

Observatory Trail

Upper Hot Springs

Spray River Loop

Banff Gondola

Mt. Rundle

Mount Rundle 2846m

Fire Road

TCT Road

Spray River

Sundance Canyon Trail

Sundance Canyon

Sulphur Mtn

2800 m
2700 m

2600 m
2700 m

Scale 1:50,000 or 1cm = 0.5km
0.5km   0km   1.0km

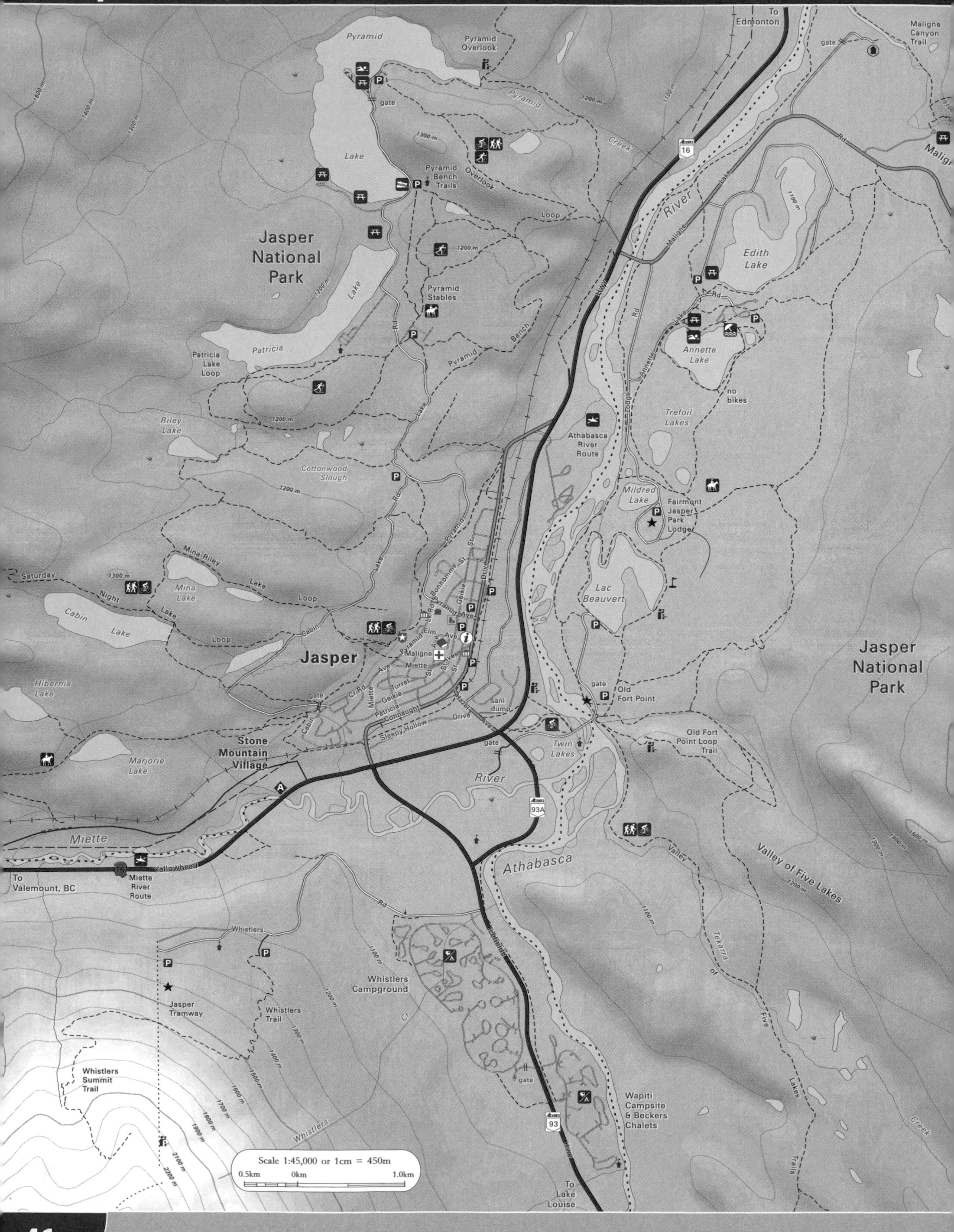

To Edmonton
Maligne Canyon Trail
gate
Pyramid
Pyramid Overlook
gate
Pyramid
Creek
Lake
Pyramid Bench Trails
Overlook
Loop
16
River
Maligne
Lake
Rd
Jasper National Park
Lake
Pyramid Stables
Edith Lake
Rd
Hwy
Patricia
Patricia Lake Loop
Rd
Pyramid
Bench
Lake
Annette
Annette Lake
no bikes
Lodge
Riley Lake
Lake
Trefoil Lakes
Athabasca River Route
Cottonwood Slough
Rd
Mildred Lake
Fairmont Jasper Park Lodge
Pyramid
Saturday
Night
Mina-Riley
Mina Lake
Lake
Loop
Cabin
Lake
Lake
Loop
Cabin
Lac Beauvert
Bonhomme St.
Pyramid Ave
Elm Ave
Maligne
Miette
Geikie
Turret
Patricia
Connaught
Jasper
Jasper National Park
Hibernia Lake
gate
Cabin
Cr Rd
Miette
Sleepy Hollow
Drive
Ave
sani dump
gate
Old Fort Point
Old Fort Point Loop Trail
Stone Mountain Village
Marjorie Lake
Twin Lakes
gate
River
A
93A
Miette
Yellowhead
Athabasca
To Valemount, BC
Miette River Route
Valley
Valley of Five Lakes
Rd
Whistlers
Icefields
Tekarra
P
Jasper Tramway
Whistlers Trail
Whistlers Campground
Cr
of
Five
Whistlers Summit Trail
gate
Wapiti Campsite & Beckers Chalets
93
Lakes
Creek
Whistlers
Hwy
Trails
Scale 1:45,000 or 1cm = 450m
0.5km 0km 1.0km
To Lake Louise

Peter
Lougheed
Provincial
Park-
anaskis Lakes

Peter
Lougheed
Provincial
Park-
Kananaskis Lakes

To Canmore

To Kananaskis Village

To Kananaskis Village

Penstock Loop Snowshoe Trail

Pocaterra Day Use

Rolly Rd Tr

Spillway Lake

Sounding Lake

Pocaterra Camp

Peninsula Day Use

Interpretive Trail

Canyon Camp

Visitor Centre

Rockwall Lake

Canyon Day Use

sani dump

Meadow

Come Along Trail

Canyon Trail

Lower Lake Trail

Lodgepole Trail

Wolley Trail

Sparrow's Egg Lake

Opal

Pocaterra

Falls Creek

Elpoca Viewpoint

Braille Trail

Lynx Tr

Spotted

Elpoca Creek

Marsh Loop Snowshoe Trail

Elkwood Camp & Amphitheatre

Kananaskis

Kananaskis

Marl Lake Interpretive Trail

Access 40

Mt Indefatigable 2670m

Lake

Marl Lake

Wheeler

Amos

Lakeview Day Use

Indefatigable Trail

Mt Indefatigable

1700 m

Trail

Wolf

Trail

To Longview

Windy Elekes Viewpoint

Lake

Three Isle Lake Trail

Lake Trail

Circuit

Panorama dam

North Interlakes Day Use

Lower Lake Camp

Lower Lake Day Use

Lower Lake Camp

Packers

Boulton Creek Camp

Whiskey

Jack

LAKES

Upper

Interlakes Camp

Boulton Cr Tr

Lakeside Tr

Boulton Bridge

Boulton Day Use

Boulton Creek Trail Loop

Point Camp

Upper Kananaskis

Lake

Canadian Mt Everest Interpretive Trail Loop

Mt Sarrail Camp

Moraine Trail

Peter Lougheed Provincial Park- Kananaskis Lakes

Hidden Lake

Elk Pass Day Use

gate

Elk

Fox Creek Trail

fire lookout 2125m

Upper

Lake

Falls

Circuit

Upper Lake Day Use

Boulton

Creek

Aster Lake Route

Rawson Lake Trail

Sarrail Cr

Fox Pass Tr

Hydroline Trail

Lookout

:50,000 or 1cm = 0.5km

0km   1.0km

Canadian Rockies

Image © allcanadaphotos.com (Mount Assiniboine Provincial Park)

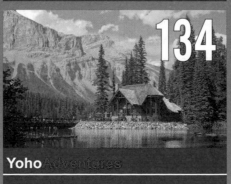

BanffAdventures

Image © Gord McKenna

THINGS TO KNOW

Area: 664,100 hectares

Highest Point: Mount Forbes 3,612 metres (11,850 feet)

Total Vehicle Accessible Campsites: 2,468

THINGS TO SEE

❶ Lake Louise

❷ Cave and Basin National Historic Site

❸ Johnston Canyon

CONTACT INFORMATION

Campground Reservations:
1.877.737.3783   www.pccamping.ca

Parks Canada: (430) 762.1550,
banff.vrc@pc.gc.ca, www.pc.gc.ca/banff,
www.friendsofbanff.com

Banff Visitor Centre: (403) 762.8421

Lake Louise Visitor Centre:
(403) 522.3833

Upper Hot Springs Pool: (403) 762.1515

Warden Office: (403) 762.1470,
1.888.927.9967

Avalanche Information: 1-800-667-1105,
www.avalanche.ca

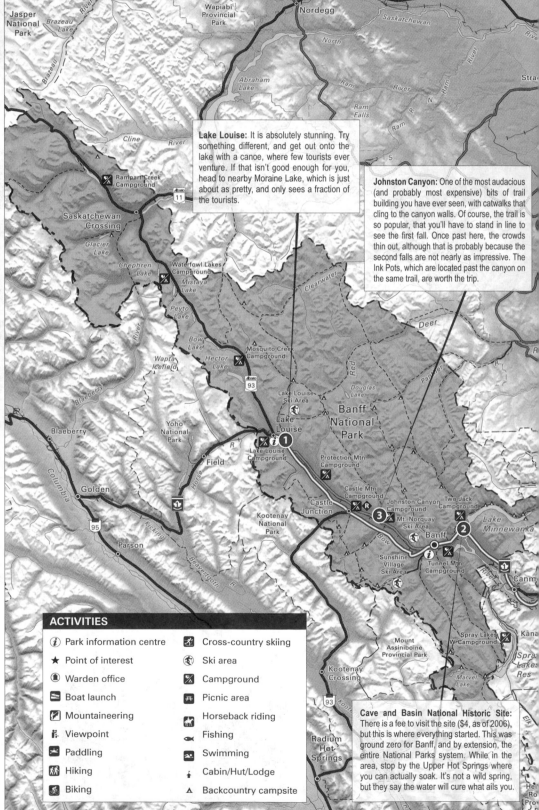

Lake Louise: It is absolutely stunning. Try something different, and get out onto the lake with a canoe, where few tourists ever venture. If that isn't good enough for you, head to nearby Moraine Lake, which is just about as pretty, and only sees a fraction of the tourists.

Johnston Canyon: One of the most audacious (and probably most expensive) bits of trail building you have ever seen, with catwalks that cling to the canyon walls. Of course, the trail is so popular, that you'll have to stand in line to see the first fall. Once past here, the crowds thin out, although that is probably because the second falls are not nearly as impressive. The Ink Pots, which are located past the canyon on the same trail, are worth the trip.

ACTIVITIES

ⓘ	Park information centre	🎿	Cross-country skiing
★	Point of interest	⛷	Ski area
⌂	Warden office	📷	Campground
🛥	Boat launch	⛱	Picnic area
🧗	Mountaineering	🐴	Horseback riding
🧍	Viewpoint	🎣	Fishing
🛶	Paddling	🏊	Swimming
🥾	Hiking	🛖	Cabin/Hut/Lodge
🚴	Biking	⛺	Backcountry campsite

Cave and Basin National Historic Site: There is a fee to visit the site ($4, as of 2006), but this is where everything started. This was ground zero for Banff, and by extension, the entire National Parks system. While in the area, stop by the Upper Hot Springs where you can actually soak. It's not a wild spring, but they say the water will cure what ails you.

BanffAdventures

Banff is a world famous destination that is the crown jewel in the National Parks system. Known for its spectacular vistas and friendly and abundant wildlife, Banff offers easy access to all extremes of outdoor adventure. Whether you are looking for an enjoyable car camping experience or looking to explore some remote and rugged trails, Banff National Park has many wilderness camping options to choose from.

However, with more than 4 million people visiting the park every year, the campgrounds and trails are often packed, especially in the heart of summer. For this reason, the park is governed by a strict set of rules to balance the extremely heavy pressure put on it by humans with the need to conserve and protect the environment. All groups entering the park are required to pay a fee (on top of any accommodation or camping fees) and are given a parks guide outlining the basic rules.

Historically, Banff had been visited by a number of First Nations groups, although none ever really settled. In 1754, Anthony Henday, a representative of the Hudson's Bay Company became the first non-native person to see the Rocky Mountains, but the first real explorer to this area was David Thompson, who, along with Duncan MacGillivry explored the Bow River Valley a half century later. It was Thompson who discovered Athabasca Pass, which for years was the main route for trade into the area that is now British Columbia.

In 1871, BC joined confederation and the government of the newly formed Dominion of Canada begins working on a Trans-continental railway to bind the large, disparate country together. The original plan was to build through the Yellowhead Pass, but in 1882, a bill is passed, authorizing the use of the most direct route through Kicking Horse Pass. The route is indeed more direct, but much more difficult, along a route surveyed by civil engineer Major A.B. Rogers.

In 1883, three railway workers, William and Thomas McCardell and Frank McCabe found a series of hot springs (known today as the Cave and Basin), at the foot of Sulphur Mountain. While it's generally accepted they weren't the first non-natives here, they were the most ambitious, dreaming of starting a private resort. But that wasn't to be and two years later, the 26 sq. km (10 sq mile) Banff Hot Springs Reserve was established in order to protect the springs from commercial development.

Soon after a group of parliamentarians made the trip from Ottawa to Banff to see the hot springs. They saw the springs and the surrounding mountains first-hand and quickly moved to protect a much larger chunk of land. In 1887, the park was renamed the Rocky Mountain Park and the boundaries were expanded to cover 673 sq km (260 sq miles). It is considered Canada's first National Park, even though the National Park Act wasn't passed until 1930.

In 1888, the Canadian Pacific Railway opened the first of a series of grand hotels in the Rockies, the Banff Springs Hotel to attract rich Europeans to the park. The building of the town soon followed. By 1902, the boundaries of the park were expanded again, to encompass Lake Louise and the area around Canmore, but the park's boundaries were reduced to 6,641 sq km (2,564 sq miles) in 1930, which is when the park was renamed Banff National Park.

HOT SPRINGS

The entire national parks system is founded on the Cave and Basin Hot Springs, which were discovered during the construction of the railway through this area. Although these are now closed to the public, nearby Upper Hot Springs are the most popular hot springs in the country.

Cave and Basin Hot Springs (Map 8/A4)
Before the European settlers arrived, many native groups used this spring for centuries, but it was the European settlers who first had the idea of charging money to soak here. The hot springs were commercially developed and used for over a hundred years, but in 1993, the pools were closed to bathing. Nowadays, the springs have been set aside as habitat for a unique snail that resides here. There are four springs here, including the famous Cave Springs. These springs are located in a 12 metre (40 foot) circular cave; early visitors had to lower themselves through a small hole in the roof until a tunnel was

blasted to provide access. The cave used to have a number of stalactites, but souvenir hunters long ago broke these off. The other main spring here is the Basin Spring, which was the original bathing pool here. It was closed in 1971. Two smaller springs can also be found along the Discovery Trail.

Upper Hot Springs (Map 8/B5)
With the closure of the Cave and Basin Springs, these are now the only commercial hot springs in Banff. They are also the most popular hot springs in the country. They are commercially developed and are known for being strongly influenced by the weather; the temperature can vary from 47.3°C (117°F) to 29°C (84°F). In spring, when the temperature is the coolest, the water is sometimes heated. In winter, when the flow is the lowest, water is sometimes added to the mix. In fact, from 1998–2001 the springs stopped flowing altogether for a period of a few weeks to a few months each winter. The outdoor pool is located on the slopes of Sulphur Mountain, with great views over Mount Rundle and the Bow Valley.

Other Hot Springs (Map 8/B5)
Also in the area are a couple other hot springs that have been closed to the public to help protect one of the last remaining habitats of the Banff Springs Snail. The Kidney Spring is a very small spring that was closed to bathing in 2002. It is found just below the Upper Hot Springs. The Middle Springs are located between the Upper Springs and Cave and Basin Springs on Sulphur Mountain.

CAMPING

The vehicle accessible campsites are extremely busy throughout the season. If you don't have a reservation, finding a spot can be difficult late in the day. To improve your chances, drop by a campsite before checkout time (11 am) and watch for people packing up. In addition to the park permit, there is a daily fee for vehicle camping. For those looking for a campfire, there is a small fire permit charge.

Campground reservations have recently been introduced in the park and sites can be reserved at Tunnel Mountain and Lake Louise. To make a reservation, visit www.pccamping.ca or call 1-877-RESERVE (1-877-737-3783). International callers can call 1-905-426-4648.

Castle Mountain Campground (Map 7/D3)
Located 34 km (21.1 miles) from Banff on the Bow Valley Parkway, this campsite is open from mid-June to the first week of September. There are 43 sites situated in a beautifully wooded area. Some of the facilities that are close by are a small store, gas bar and restaurant.

Johnston's Canyon Campground (Map 7/F3)
Found across from Johnston's Canyon, 25 km (15.5 miles) from Banff, this picturesque 132 unit campground is located next to the creek and is a short walk from the Johnston Canyon Falls. It is open from June to mid-September. It is the most popular campground on the scenic Bow Valley Parkway and offers showers and a sani-dump. Group camping is available by reservation.

Lake Louise Campground (Map 7/A1)
This is one of the most popular campgrounds in Banff because of its proximity to Lake Louise and wide range of amenities and activities. Campers who aren't in a soundproofed RV might want to think twice about staying here. While the site is close to Lake Louise, the highway is closer and the railway closer still. The RV site is open year round and has 189 sites with electric hook-up, while the 210 tenting sites are only available from mid-May to October. This is also one of only two sites with an interpretive program.

Mosquito Creek Campground (Map 11/F4)
Many of the sites here offer a superb view of Mount Hector. Found 24 km (14.9 miles) north of Lake Louise, this rustic campground has 32 sites with pit toilets. The campground is open year round.

Protection Mountain Campground (Map 7/C2)
This campground found is 48 km (29.8 miles) from Banff and is opened from July to September. The area, with lots of wildlife, is great for hiking. This campground has 89 sites and flush toilets.

Rampart Creek Campground (Map 16/F5)
Found on the Icefields Parkway 88 km (54.7 miles) north of Lake Louise, this is the most remote of the vehicle accessible campgrounds in Banff. It is also the cheapest to stay at. The small, 50 site campground offers pit toilets and is open from late June to September.

Tunnel Mountain Campgrounds (Map 8/B4)

The three sites that make up the Tunnel Mountain Campgrounds contain almost half of the campsites in the park. No wonder, as the campgrounds are within easy walking distance of downtown Banff. The area offers a spectacular view of the valley, hoodoos and the Banff Springs Golf Course. Services, such as food, laundry and a waterslide are close by. There are 321 full service sites in the Trailer Court, 188 electric only sites in Village II, plus 618 non-serviced sites in Village I. Showers are available at all three areas. Tunnel Mountain Village II is open year round with only group camping available in the summer (reservations are required). The other sites are open from early May until October. The ever popular interpretive programs are offered at all 3 campgrounds.

Two Jack Campgrounds (Map 8/B3)

Two Jack Main is 12 km (7.5 miles) from Banff and opened from late May to early September. This campground is situated on the Minnewanka Lake Drive in a wild and beautiful wooded area. There are 380 secluded campsites with flush toilets, picnic shelters and a sani-dump. Group camping is available by reservation. Located across the road is the Two Jack Lakeside Campground. This is a small (well, for Banff, with only 74 sites) campground with shower facilities that is open from mid-May to mid-September. The ruins of the coal-miners town of Bankhead are nearby. There is a lot of wildlife in the area, so proper food storage is a must.

Waterfowl Lakes Campground (Map 11/B1)

Located 57 km (35.4 miles) north of Lake Louise on the Icefields Parkway, this pretty campground is found where the bubbling Mistaya River enters Waterfowl Lake. Trails also lead to Cirque and Chephren Lakes. Open from mid-June to the first week of September, the campground has 116 sites with flush toilets and sani-dump.

BACKCOUNTRY CAMPSITES

There are more than 54 different backcountry campsites in Banff. An informative Backcountry Visitors' Guide lists all of the backcountry campsites available or you can visit us on-line for a chart that lists all of the sites and their access trail. Currently, there is a small fee, plus a reservation fee for the busier backcountry campsites. There is also a grazing fee and a horse permit required for horseback riders. Facilities often include pit toilets, picnic tables and bear-proof storage. Some of the more popular sites include:

Baker Lake Backcountry Campsite (Map 12/C6)

There are ten sites found at this popular site, which can be accessed by a number of trails, including the Baker Creek Trail (20.5 km/12.7 miles) and the Skoki Trail (12 km/7.5 miles). Open fires are not permitted at this campsite, but camp stoves are allowed.

Hidden Lake Backcountry Campsite (Map 12/B7)

This site is found near Boulder Pass at the Hidden Lake Trail junction. Ten sites are available with pit toilets, picnic tables and bear-proof storage. Pack a camp stove because open fires are not permitted.

Merlin Meadows Backcountry Campsite (Map 12/B6)

There are ten sites at Merlin Meadows, a lovely site with excellent views of Mount Richardson.

Red Deer Lakes Backcountry Campsite (Map 12/B6)

This ten unit campsite is found near Red Deer Lakes through a number of trail options.

BACKCOUNTRY HUTS

If your interest lies in exploring some remote regions, the Alpine Club of Canada maintains several backcountry huts in the Canadian Rockies. These sites range from rustic shelters to cozy log cabins. They serve as a base for hikers, climbers and backcountry skiers to explore remote mountainous areas. Call (403) 678-3200 or visit www.alpineclubofcanada.ca for more information on location and cost.

Abbot Pass Hut (Map 6/F1)

This stone structure can hold up to 24 mountaineers exploring Victoria Glacier and Mount Lefroy.

Balfour Hut (Map 11/D5)

Located to help travellers explore the famous Wapta Traverse (Wapta Icefield), up to 16 people can use the hut. Access is difficult and only folks who are well experienced in glacier travel should attempt to use the hut, which is set below Mount Balfour.

Bow Hut (Map 11/D4)

The largest hut on the Wapta Icefield, there is space for 30. It is used as a base for mountaineering, glacier travel and backcountry skiing. It is found above Bow Lake.

Castle Mountain Hut (Map 7/D2)

Accessed by rock climbers on Castle Mountain, this rustic cabin holds six people.

Neil Colgan Hut (Map 7/A2)

The highest habitable structure in North America (higher than the Abbott Pass Hut by a mere 33 metres/100 feet), this hut is found in the Valley of the Ten Peaks south of Lake Louise. It holds up to 16 climbers and requires glacier travel to reach it.

Peter & Catharine Whyte [Peyto] Hut (Map 11/C4)

This is the northern most huts on the Wapta Icefield and is found above Peyto Lake. It holds up to 16 people who are well experienced in glacier travel. Allow up to 8 hours to reach it from the highway.

Scott Duncan Hut (Map 11/E6)

Holding 12 people who are well experienced in glacier travel, this hut is found at the base of Mount Daly. It is the southernmost hut on the Wapta Icefield.

BACKCOUNTRY LODGES

Banff National Park is also home to several backcountry lodges for those looking to pamper themselves while exploring the wild. These include the Sundance Lodge, which is located at the base of the Sundance Range next to Brewster Creek. The lodge holds up to 20 people and makes a fine ski-in destination about 10 km from Healy Creek. The Shadow Lake Lodge is a popular destination for visitors to the Redearth Creek area. It is found 14 km from the trailhead and provides access to several other trails in the area. The Num-Ti-Jah Lodge is situated on the shores of majestic Bow Lake and can be accessed by vehicle. Explorers working their way up to Bow Summit and the Bow Hut often use it. Perhaps the most famous of them all is the Skoki Lodge, which is located in the beautiful high alpine region northeast of Lake Louise. It is an ideal destination for hikers and skiers looking for a rustic backcountry experience.

FISHING

Due to its sheer size, there are a lot of lakes and streams to sample within Banff National Park. Although, the easily accessed water bodies see a lot of pressure there are many remote lakes that see few anglers and contain good numbers of fish. Add in the natural beauty of the Rocky Mountains and you can see why Banff is an excellent fishing destination.

Anglers will find that the lakes and streams are no longer stocked, which may result in slower fishing for generally larger fish. There is a zero catch and possession limit on both cutthroat and bull trout. There is no bait fishing allowed in the park and lead sinkers are banned. Also unique to National Parks is the fact they are governed under their own regulations and you will need a special license to fish. Check with Parks Canada for more information. Regulations can be downloaded from www.parkscanada.gc.ca.

Alexandra River (Map 16/D5)

Located by trail north of the Saskatchewan River Crossing, this short river flows into the North Saskatchewan River. The river contains some bull trout, lake trout and rocky mountain whitefish best caught by fly-fishing or spincasting. The river is hard to reach, as you have to ford the North Saskatchewan River. Like most rivers in the area it is heavily silted, which means poor fishing, especially during summer.

Altrude Lakes (Map 7/B3)

These two small lakes are found next to Highway 93. The lakes have small cutthroat with the lower lake producing the most fish. Spincasting or fly-fishing from shore or a belly boat work.

Altrude Creek (Map 7/C3)
The Trans-Canada Highway (Highway 1) crosses the creek at its junction with Highway 93. The creek has small cutthroat near the estuary with the Bow River.

Arnica Lake (Map 7/C3)
Arnica Lake is reached by trail (Arnica Trail) from Highway 93. The lake holds some good-sized cutthroat but is usually not ice-free until July.

Baker Creek (Map 7/C1–12/C7)
Baker Creek is a Bow River tributary that drains Baker Lake. The creek has brook, bull and cutthroat trout with the best fishing found near the Bow Valley Parkway (Highway 1A).

Baker Lake (Map 12/B6)
This lake is reached by a 12 km (7.4 mile) hike up the Skoki Valley. The lake holds good-sized brook and cutthroat trout. If you are not having any luck here, try nearby Little Baker Lake, which holds slightly smaller versions of cutthroat. Tilted Lake is right next to Little Baker Lake, but holds few, if any, fish.

Black Rock Lake (Map 7/D5)
Black Lake is reached by the Shadow Lake Trail up Redearth Creek and then a trail along Pharaoh Creek. An alternative route is to park near the end of Sunshine Road and hike up the Healy Pass Trail. The lake holds cutthroat to 30 cm (12 inches).

Block Lakes (Map 7/E1)
Accessed by a long, difficult hike/climb up the Cascade River Valley from Lake Minnewanka, getting to this lake is recommended only for experienced climbers. Those who make it will find cutthroat trout to 40 cm (16 inches). The lake was once stocked with Quebec Red Trout, but there have been no reports of these trout for years.

Boom Lake (Map 7/B3)
Getting to Boom Lake involves a 5 km (one-way) hike from Highway 93. The lake has rainbow as well as cutthroat.

Bow Lake (Map 11/D4)
Located next to the Icefields Parkway (Highway 93) north of Lake Louise, Bow Lake is not quite the headwaters of the Bow River (that would be the Bow Glacier), but for most people, it is close enough. The lake has bull trout, lake trout and rocky mountain whitefish. Despite its proximity to Highway 93, the lake still produces well throughout the ice-free season by spincasting or fly-fishing. Try the outflow to the river at the south end of the lake for best success.

Bow River (Map 7, 8, 11, 12)
The Bow is one of Alberta's, if not Canada's, most famous trout rivers. The upper reaches of the river flow through the park and are easily accessed from the Icefields Highway, the Trans-Canada Highway and even the Bow Valley Parkway. There are many enticing pools to cast a fly, with favourite patterns being various Adams, caddis fly and nymph imitations.

Bourgeau Lake (Map 7/F5)
It is 7 km (4.3 miles) from the Trans-Canada Highway (Highway 1) to the lake itself. The lake holds brook trout to 30 cm (12 inches).

Brewster Creek (Map 7/G4–8/B7)
Hiking/horse trails follow Brewster Creek almost all the way to its headwaters, providing good access to the creek. The creek is home to small bull and cutthroat.

Bryant Creek (Map 4/C2–B1)
Bryant Creek, which flows into the south end of the Spray Lakes Reservoir, holds cutthroat and whitefish to 30 cm (12 inches) and bull trout to 60 cm (24 inches). The latter two species are found only in the lowest sections of the creek. This creek is accessed by trail only.

Carrot Creek (Map 8/D4)
Carrot Creek is a Bow River tributary that crosses the Trans-Canada Highway (Highway 1) just inside the Banff boundary. Your best chance for success is near the confluence, as most of the fish in Carrot Creek swim up from the Bow.

Cascade River (Map 7/E1–8/B3)
The Cascade River flows into and out of the west end of Lake Minnewanka and is home to brook, bull, cutthroat and rainbow trout as well as rocky mountain whitefish. The best fishing is for the cutthroat in the upper reaches of the river. There is good hiking/biking access along most of the river via the Cascade Fire Road.

Chephren Lake (Map 11/A1)
This lake is reached by trail from the north end of Waterfowl Lakes on the Icefields Parkway (Highway 93). The lake has small cutthroat and rainbow trout caught by spincasting or fly-fishing. Camping is provided at the south end of Waterfowl Lake.

Cirque Lake (Map 11/B1)
This lake is reached by the same trail used to access Chephren Lake. The silty lake has small cutthroat and rainbow trout caught by spincasting or fly-fishing.

Citadel Lake (Map 7/G7)
This small lake is found just south of the Citadel Pass off the Citadel Pass Trail. The trail doesn't actually pass the lake, or even get within eyeshot, so very few people visit the lake. Those who do will find rainbow trout in the 30-35 cm (12-14 inch) range.

Consolation Lakes (Map 7/A2)
These gorgeous lakes are located 3 km (1.8 miles) from the Moraine Lake parking lot. During times of high grizzly activity, you will have to travel in groups of at least four people for safety. The lakes hold brook trout to 30 cm (12 inches), while the lower lake has a few cutthroat, too.

Copper Lake (Map 7/D3)
Located just a short ways from the Trans-Canada Highway (Highway 1), Copper Lake offers good (but not great) fishing for rainbow to 40 cm (16 inches).

Corral Creek (Map 7/A1–12/A7)
Corral Creek flows into the Bow River south of Lake Louise. The creek, which is best fished upstream from the estuary, has bull, cutthroat and rainbow trout.

Cuthead Creek (Map 7/G1–12/G7)
Cuthead Creek is a tributary of the Cascade River and holds bull and cutthroat trout. The creek is reached by the Cascade Fire Road.

Cuthead Lake (Map 12/F7)
Cuthead Lake is reached by the Cascade Fire Road then by bushwhacking up Cuthead Creek. The lake has bull and cutthroat trout, which are easily caught by spincasting and fly-fishing from shore or a float tube.

Deer [Pipestone] Lake (Map 12/A4)
This lake is found about 2 km (1.2 miles) south of Fish Lakes. There is no trail to the lake, but you should be able to pick out the route in. The lake has lots of cutthroat to 40 cm (16 inches), which take readily to a fly.

Egypt Lake (Map 7/D5)
Egypt Lake is reached by the Shadow Lake Trail up Redearth Creek and then a trail along Pharaoh Creek. An alternative route is to park near the end of Sunshine Road and hike up the Healy Pass Trail. The lake contains brook and cutthroat trout.

Elk Lake (Map 8/A3)
Elk Lake is reached by hiking up the Cascade Fire Road to the Stoney Creek Campsite and then heading south. An alternative route is to walk the Elk Pass Trail from the Forty Mile Trail. The lake contains cutthroat trout to 45 cm (18 inches).

Forty Mile Creek (Map 8/A4)
Forty Mile Creek flows into the Bow River within the townsite of Banff. The creek has bull trout, brook trout and cutthroat but is closed to fishing near the town. It is best to hike up the Forty Mile Trail from the end of Mount Norquay Road to sample some of the larger pools.

Forty Mile Lake (Map 7/F2)
After a 20 km (12 mile) return hike up the Forty Mile Trail from the top of Mount Norquay Road, anglers wishing to get to this lake must bushwhack their way up a small creek that drains the lake. Those who make it will find brook trout to 30 cm (12 inches).

Ghost Lakes (Map 8/F3)
The Ghost Lakes are located at the east end of Lake Minnewanka and are reached by boat or trail. The lakes have a few bull trout, lake trout and rocky mountain whitefish but do not offer great fishing. The best place to try is in the narrows between the lakes.

Glacier Lake (Map 16/F7)
Glacier Lake gets murky during hot weather because of the glacier run-off. As a result, fishing for the rocky mountain whitefish and lake trout is best during the spring and late fall. The lake is accessed by hiking from the Saskatchewan River Crossing off Icefields Parkway (Highway 93) for about 15 km (9 miles) one-way.

Haiduk Lake (Map 7/D5)
Haiduk Lake is accessed by following the Hawk Creek Trail from Highway 93 or the Shadow Lake Trail from the Trans-Canada Highway (Highway 1). The lake holds some fairly large cutthroat trout, to 1.5 kg (3 lbs).

Hector Lake (Map 11/E5)
Located in Banff National Park, this large lake is reached by a short trail off Highway 93. However, the hike involves crossing the Bow River. The lake, which has a rustic campsite on the eastern shores, offers fishing for brook, bull and rainbow trout as well as rocky mountain whitefish. If fishing is slow, you may wish to venture to Lake Margaret, which offers good numbers of small cutthroat taken by spincasting or fly-fishing.

Herbert Lake (Map 11/G7)
Herbert Lake is a small lake sandwiched between the Icefields Parkway (Highway 93) and the Bow River just north of Lake Louise. The lake contains a few small brook trout and cutthroat best caught by spincasting a small lure. Less than a kilometre to the south is Little Herbert Lake, which holds a few rainbow.

Howard Douglas Lake (Map 7/G7)
This small lake is found 6 km (3.6 miles) from Sunshine Village on the Citadel Pass Trail. The lake holds plenty of small brook trout, but the odd fish grows to 30 cm (12 inches) or larger.

Howse River (Map 10/G1–16/G6)
The Howse River is a major tributary of the upper North Saskatchewan River. A hike/horse trail follows the silty river to its source. Due to the water clarity, you will find slow fishing for bull trout, whitefish and, oddly enough, lake trout.

Isabella Lake (Map 11/D2)
Isabella Lake is the only lake or stream on the Siffleur River system that is open to fishing. Access to the lake is along the Dolomite Creek Trail and you will need at least a day to hike the 24 km (14.9 miles) to the lake. Once you get there, expect good fishing for rainbow that average 30 cm (12 inches) but often get much bigger.

Johnston Creek (Map 7/D1–E3)
Johnston Creek flows into the Bow River east of Castle Mountain and is accessed along its entire length by the Johnston Creek Trail. There is decent fishing for bull and cutthroat trout in the pools above the Inkpots (Map 20/D7) since the crowds begin to thin out after the first falls. You will want to get above Johnston Canyon, anyway, before trying to fish the creek.

Johnson Lake (Map 8/C4)
Johnson Lake is open to fishing, but most anglers take a pass on this poor fishing lake. There are a few rainbow and brook trout.

Lake Annette (Map 6/G1)
This small lake is set beneath Mount Temple in the Paradise Valley. It contains a few cutthroat and rainbow to 30 cm (12 inches). It is not worth making the trip just to fish the lake, but if you are making the trip, it is worth fishing. Shore fishing is difficult, but not impossible.

Lake Gloria (Map 4/A2)
The lovely Lake Gloria (Glorious Gloria?) is accessed by following the Bryant Creek Trail from the south end of Spray Reservoir and then heading southwest on the Wonder Pass Trail. Gloria contains fair numbers of cutthroat to 1.5 kg (3 lbs), but shore fishing can be tricky.

Lake Helen (Map 11/D3)
It is a 6 km (3.6 mile) hike to get to this alpine lake set high above the Icefields Parkway (Highway 93). The lake holds brook trout to 30 cm that take well to flies.

Lake Katherine (Map 11/E3)
The 8.1 km (5 mile) trail to Lake Katherine climbs up to Helen Lake, over a ridge (at 2500 m/8125 ft) and down to Lake Katherine, at 2373 m (7712 ft), climbing 575 m (1869 ft) to the ridge. Basically, you will need to put in a bit of work to get to this pretty alpine lake. You may have to do a bit of work to catch one of the cutthroat trout that inhabit this lake, but it is worth it, as they can get to 50 cm (18 inches). Fly fishing works well.

Lake Louise (Map 6/G1)
Arguably one of the best-known lakes in the province, let alone the country, Lake Louise is known for its turquoise waters and dramatic mountain scenery. It is not, however, known for its fishing. It does contain whitefish to 30 cm (12 inches) and bull trout to about twice that size, but only the most persistent angler will have any success.

Lake Merlin (Map 12/B6)
A small, high elevation lake, Merlin Lake is accessible by foot along a rough trail from the Skoki Valley. The last section involves scrambling up a scree slope to access the hanging valley the lake is set in. Because of its high elevation, the lake is not free of ice until July. It contains brook trout to 30 cm (12 inches).

Lake Minnewanka (Map 8/C3–E3)
Lake Minnewanka is a large murky lake located east of the Banff townsite. It is considered to be one of the top ten lakes in the province for trophy lake trout, which can get to 20 kg (45 lbs). You will also find bull trout (to 4 kg/8 lbs), rainbow (to 1.5 kg/3 lbs) and rocky mountain whitefish (to 1 kg/2 lbs). The fishing can be very slow in summer but if you can get deep, you do have a chance to catch those big lakers. Fishing starts to heat up in the fall, but just as it gets good, the lake closes (September 3). Unlike other lakes in the park, motorized boats are allowed on the lake so it is best to bring a boat and try trolling or spincasting near one of the tributaries.

Leman Lake (Map 4/D4)
Leman Lake is located by hiking the trail leading south along the Spray River from the reservoir. It does hold small trout.

Louise Creek (Map 12/A7)
Louise Creek drains Lake Louise into the Bow River and is easily accessed by the main road to the town of Lake Louise. Bull and cutthroat trout can be found in the deeper pools.

Luellen Lake (Map 7/D2)
Luellen Lake is accessed by following the Johnston Creek Trail from the Bow Valley Parkway (Highway 1A). A rustic campground is located at the lake, which is populated with a lot of good-sized cutthroat that reach 50 cm/20 inches on occasion. Note that the outflow area and logjam are closed to fishing.

Marvel Lake (Map 4/B2)
Marvel Lake is accessed by following the Bryant Creek Trail from the south end of Spray Reservoir and then heading southwest on the Wonder Pass Trail. It is 15 km (9.3 miles) from the trailhead to the lake, which means that packing a belly boat is a bit of a proposition (heaven forbid you try carrying a canoe). But because the lake is so big (4 km/2.4 miles long and 75 m/230 ft deep), fishing from the shore often does not produce. If you do try from shore, try around the inflow/outflow streams. Part of the lake is closed to angling year round. Nearby Lake Terrapin does hold cutthroat to 40 cm (16 inches), but the silty water and shallow, weedy area around the shoreline make fishing here almost more hassle than it is worth.

Mistaya Lake (Map 11/B2)
The Mistaya River flows into and then out of Mistaya Lake, which is hidden from the Icefields Parkway (Highway 93) by a screen of trees. Accessed by trail from Waterfowl Lakes, few people make the trip, preferring to sample the good fishing at Waterfowl Lakes. Mistaya Lake can produce well for cutthroat to 30 cm (12 inches).

Mistaya River (Map 11/C3–17/A6)
The Mistaya River (Mistaya translates as Grizzly) runs from Peyto Lake north through Mistaya Lake, Waterfowl Lakes and into the North Saskatchewan River. The river is never more than a few hundred metres from the Icefields Parkway (Highway 93) for its entire length. However, it is the glacier run-off that affects the fishery, especially in the summer.

Moraine Creek (Map 7/A2)
Moraine Creek drains Moraine Lake. It contains brook and cutthroat trout.

Moraine Lake (Map 7/A2)
If you are looking for sheer scenic beauty, it is hard to beat Moraine Lake. Even better, the lake is accessible by road. Anglers, however, will have to take consolation in the scenery, because their chances of pulling one of the few cutthroat or bull trout from the lake are poor, although certainly not non-existent. Fly-fishing or spincasting from shore can work, as can fishing from a canoe, which are available for rent at the lake.

Mud Lake (Map 12/A7)
Located near Lake Louise, this small lake is reached by a short trail leading up the Pipestone River from Trans-Canada Highway (Highway 1) near the Tourist Bureau. The lake can be fished from shore or belly boat for small brook and cutthroat trout. Spincasting seems to produce the best.

Mummy Lake (Map 7/D5)
Mummy Lake is reached by the Shadow Lake Trail up Redearth Creek and then a trail along Pharoah Creek. An alternative route is to park near the end of Sunshine Road and hike up the Healy Pass Trail. The lake is home to a small population of cutthroat that reach a nice 35 cm (14 inches) in size.

Mystic Lake (Map 7/F3)
Mystic Lake is accessed by either following the Forty Mile Trail from the Mount Norquay Road or the Johnston Creek Trail from the Bow Valley Parkway (Highway 1A) and then walking the Mystic Pass Trail. The lake, which holds

bull and cutthroat trout, is surprisingly popular despite the 19 km (11.7 mile) trek in.

Norman Lake (Map 16/E4)
Norman Lake is reached by hiking along the Sunset Pass Trail for about 6 km (3.6 miles) one-way from the Icefields Parkway (Highway 93). The lake has small brook trout best caught by casting a small lure or fly.

North Saskatchewan River (Map 16/C3–17/D4)
The glacier fed North Saskatchewan River is one of the largest rivers in Alberta. The section found in Banff National Park is not known as a great fishery as the water is silty. Bull trout, cutthroat and whitefish are the main sportfish in the park.

O'Brien Lake (Map 7/D3)
O'Brien Lake is not a big lake, but it holds plenty of good-sized cutthroat, some of which can get up to 50 cm (20 inches).

Owl Lake (Map 4/B2)
Owl Lake is accessed by following the Bryant Creek Trail from the south end of Spray Reservoir and then heading southwest on the Owl Lake Trail. There are brook trout to 1.5 kg (3 lbs) in the lake as well as smaller cutthroat.

Panther River (Map 12, 13)
The headwaters of the Panther River are in Banff National Park. If you wish to fish this section (accessed by a couple long trails through the Cascade Valley or from Bighorn Wildland Recreation Area), you will need a National Park Fishing Permit. Bull trout, cutthroat and whitefish all roam the river.

Peyto Lake (Map 11/C3)
Peyto Lake is accessed by a steep 2 km (1.2 mile) one-way trail leading down from the viewpoint on the Icefields Parkway (Highway 93). The lake holds fair numbers of cutthroat best caught by fly-fishing or spincasting from a float tube. If you are fishing from shore, the outlet and inlet streams are the best place to try. Fishing is best just after the ice is off the lake and again in fall.

Pharaoh Creek (Map 7/D5)
All of Egypt drains into Pharaoh Creek, or at least, all of the Egyptian-themed lakes found south of Sunshine Village. The creek holds small cutthroat and brook trout.

Pharaoh Lake (Map 7/D5)
Pharaoh Lake is reached by the Shadow Lake Trail up Redearth Creek and then a trail along Pharaoh Creek. An alternative route is to park near the end of Sunshine Road and hike up the Healy Pass Trail. The lake holds some cutthroat trout to 30 cm (12 inches).

Pipestone River (Map 11/G3–12/A7)
Pipestone River flows in a southern direction into the Bow River near Lake Louise. The Pipestone River Trail leads from the Trans-Canada Highway (Highway 1) near the Tourist Bureau to the headwaters offering a chance to test your luck for the cutthroat trout to 30 cm (12 inches) and bull trout to 50 cm (20 inches). The best place to fish is in the large pools downstream from the canyon.

Ptarmigan Lake (Map 12/B6)
Ptarmigan Lake is reached by the Skoki Valley Trail from the Lake Louise Ski Area and has a few small brook and cutthroat trout. The lake is prone to high winds, making fishing, especially fly-fishing, difficult. The lake is usually not ice-free until July.

Rainbow Lake (Map 7/F1)
A small lake set in a bowl just north of the Forty Mile Summit, Rainbow Lake contains lots of rainbow trout, some of which will get to 1.5 kg (3 lbs). Access to the lake is via a difficult 30 km (19 mile) hike up the Forty Mile Trail from the top of Mount Norquay Road or by a 40 km (25 mile) hike up the Cascade Fire Road from Lake Minnewanka.

Red Deer Lakes (Map 12/B6)
The two lakes that make up the Red Deer Lakes are accessed by long trail up the Red Deer River or by trails to the south and west. The eastern most lake has brook trout whereas the western most lake has brook and cutthroat trout. Both lakes are fairly shallow and subject to winterkill.

Redearth Creek (Map 7/E4)
Redearth Creek drains into the Bow River. The creek contains brook, bull, cutthroat and rainbow trout with the best fishing being in the canyon near the estuary.

Redoubt Lake (Map 12/B7)
Redoubt Lake is reached by trails leading up Baker Creek and Redoubt Creek from the Bow Valley Parkway (Highway 1A). The lake has small cutthroat trout

and mostly small brook trout, although occasionally you will come across a monster (to 60 cm/24 inches). The lake is usually covered by ice until July.

Rockbound Lake (Map 7/D2)
Rockbound Lake is reached by trail up Silverton Creek from the junction of the Trans-Canada Highway (Highway 1) and the Bow Valley Parkway (Highway 1A). The trail climbs steeply up to the lake, which holds some good-sized brook trout and cutthroat.

Sawback Lake (Map 7/F1)
Sawback Lake is reached by a difficult 30 km (19 mile) hike up the Forty Mile Trail from the top of Mount Norquay Road or by a 40 km (25 mile) hike up the Cascade Fire Road from Lake Minnewanka. A rustic campground is found near the lake. For those willing to put in the effort, the lake has cutthroat to 2 kg (4 lbs).

Scarab Lake (Map 7/D5)
Scarab is reached by the Shadow Lake Trail up Redearth Creek and then a trail along Pharaoh Creek. An alternative route is to park near the end of Sunshine Road and hike up the Healy Pass Trail. You will find a few cutthroat trout to 1.5 kg (3 lbs).

Shadow Lake (Map 7/C4)
The shadow cast on Shadow Lake falls from Mount Ball, which towers above the lake. Some anglers might argue that the shadow is the result of the fact that this lake does not hold as many fish are others in the area. Access to the lake is via a 14 km (8.6 mile) hike along the Shadow Lake Trail. It contains good-sized cutthroat, brook and rainbow trout caught by spincasting or fly-fishing from shore or a belly boat.

Siffleur River (Map 11/F2–17/E5)
The headwaters of the Siffleur are reachable by trail. In fact, the entire river is accessible by trail, but only the portion within Banff is open to fishing (although none of its tributaries are). It is a pretty river, with a lot of small bull trout and whitefish. For many, the quality of fishing is not worth the long hike in along the Dolomite Pass Trail.

Skoki Lakes (Map 12/B6)
Of the two Skoki Lakes, only Myosotis Lake (the lower lake) has fish in it. But the fishing is slow and often fruitless as there are only a few rainbow left in the lake. While not above treeline, Myosotis Lake has an open shore, with lots of casting room.

Smith Lake (Map 7/D3)
Smith Lake is reached by a short trail (1 km one-way) leading south of the junction of Highway 1 and Highway 93. It contains cutthroat and brook trout. The lake was once known for large cutthroat, but they have mostly been fished out.

Spray River (Map 4/C3; 8/B4–D7)
Spray River flows north into and out of the Spray Lakes Reservoir, eventually draining into the Bow River at the town of Banff. The river contains brook, cutthroat and rainbow trout as well as rocky mountain whitefish. Anglers willing to hike above the reservoir will find cutthroat, while below the reservoir, you will start finding a few brown trout in addition to the other fish species. Most of the lower reaches of the river are accessible by the trail (hike/bike) linking Banff and the reservoir. Most of this trail is closed from April 15 to November 15, though.

Stoney Creek (Map 8/A1)
Stoney Creek is a tributary of the Cascade River. There is a backcountry campsite at the confluence, which is about a 15 km (9 mile) trip up the Cascade Fire Road on foot or by bike. The Dormer Pass Trail provides access to the upper reaches of the creek.

Sundance Creek (Map 8/A5)
This creek flows into the Bow River just west of the Banff townsite. The creek has a series of beaver dams that hold good numbers of brook trout. The creek is best accessed by the Sundance Canyon Trail from Banff.

Taylor Lake (Map 7/B2)
The cutthroat trout that populate the waters of Taylor Lake average 30 cm (12 inches) in size. It is a 6 km (3.6 mile) hike to the lake from the Trans-Canada Highway (Highway 1).

Tower Lake (Map 7/D2)
A small lake on the way to Rockbound Lake, Tower Lake holds a small population of small cutthroat.

Twin Lakes (Map 7/C4)
These two small lakes are best reached by trail from Highway 93. An alter-

nate route is to park next to the Altrude Creek Bridge near the junction of Highway 1 and 93 and hike the steep trail to the two lakes. Both lakes have small cutthroat with the lower lake producing the most fish. Spincasting or fly-fishing from shore or a belly boat works. A rustic campsite is found at the north end of the upper lake.

Two Jack Lake (Map 8/C3)
This small lake is located just south of Lake Minnewanka and has cutthroat, lake and rainbow trout as well as rocky mountain whitefish. Spincasting and fly-fishing in the spring and fall is your best bet. The lake is home to a campground and sees heavy fishing pressure.

Vermilon Lakes (Map 8/A4)
In the Bow Valley just west of Banff, there are a series of three small, shallow lakes that offer slow fishing for small rainbow and brook trout. The lakes are reached by Vermilon Lakes Drive.

Vista Lakes (Map 7/C3)
These small hike-in lakes are reached by the Arnica Lake Trail from Highway 93. The lakes have small cutthroat that can be caught by spincasting or fly-fishing from shore or a belly boat.

Waterfowl Lakes (Map 11/B1)
These two lakes—actually, they are widenings of the Mistaya River caused by glacial silt—see a lot of fishing pressure, due in no small part to the large campground here. The lakes hold cutthroat and brook trout to 30 cm (12 inches).

PADDLING

Spend a couple hours relaxing on one of the prettiest lakes in the world, spend a couple days paddling down the Bow River or spend as much time as you like challenging some of Banff's whitewater. While the park is not known for having a tremendous amount of paddling opportunities (as there are very few roads that allow you to reach the upper reaches of the rivers), there are enough to bring along your canoe or kayak.

For each river, we have included the put-in and take-out locations. The length of each run, the season and general comments are also provided. To grade the rivers, we have used a modified version of the International River Classification System. Please remember that river conditions are always subject to change and advanced scouting is essential. The information in this book is only intended to give you general information on the particular river you are interested in. You should always obtain more details from a local merchant or expert before heading out on your adventure.

Bow River (Map 7, 8)
The Bow River is a large volume river draining in an eastward direction from Banff National Park. Most of the river can be paddled by canoe without much unexpected danger. The dramatic scenery in the Bow River Valley makes paddling the river truly a lasting experience.

> **Put-in:** Lake Louise (Map 7/A1)

> **Take-out:** Castle Junction (Map 7/F3)

This section starts from the bridge over the Bow River about 3 km (1.8 miles) south of the Lake Louise interchange on the Trans-Canada Highway. This Grade II paddle takes you 40 km (24.9 miles) to the Redearth Creek Picnic Area. It is a fast flowing stretch of water with two short rapids, plenty of standing waves and an abundance of back eddies. At the put-in, there are some Class II rapids, which can be avoided by putting your canoe/kayak in about a kilometre downstream from the bridge. The river shifts frequently throughout its course and there is the occasional sweeper to be wary of. The water level remains high enough to paddle most of the year because the river is glacier fed. Mount Temple, which looms to the east, offers a spectacular backdrop.

> **Put-in:** Castle Junction (Map 7/F3)

> **Take-out:** Banff Townsite (Map 8/B4)

Below the Redearth Creek Picnic Site, the Bow River becomes more exciting as it passes through the Redearth Creek Rapids, which are rated Class II (Class III at low water) and should be scouted. Once through these rapids, the river slows down and begins to braid. You must take-out before you hit Bow Falls, which should not be attempted.

> **Put-in:** Below Bow Falls (Map 8/B4)

> **Take-out:** Canmore (Map 8/D6)

This section of the Bow is a gentle Grade II paddle. The Trans-Canada Highway parallels the river all the way.

Lake Louise (Map 6/G1)
Arguably one of the best-known lakes in the province, let alone the country, Lake Louise is known for its turquoise waters and dramatic mountain scenery. Chateau Lake Louise rents canoes and the lake can be circumnavigated in a few hours.

Mistaya River (Map 17)
The Mistaya River is a small river flowing in a northwestern direction into the North Saskatchewan River near Saskatchewan River Crossing in Banff National Park. The Icefields Parkway parallels the river, offering good access.

> **Put-in:** 8 km south of Mistaya River Canyon (Map 17/A7)

> **Take-out:** Mistaya River Canyon (Map 17/A6)

Watch for a short trail off the highway, 8 km (5 miles) south of the Mistaya River Canyon Parking Area. This will take you to the start of an 8.2 km (5.1 mile) Grade II/III paddle to the top of the canyon (don't try paddling the canyon itself!). This section of river has a lot of obstacles, which can make for a fun or annoying run, depending on whether you like obstacles.

> **Put-in:** Mistaya River Canyon (Map 17/A6)

> **Take-out:** Highway 93 Bridge (Map 17/A6)

Don't try and put-in at the top of the Mistaya Canyon; it just won't be any fun. Instead, walk downstream along the canyon wall to a spot where you can easily access the river. From here, paddle 3.5 km (2.2 miles/2–2.5 hours) to the Highway 93 Bridge. This section is a tight and technical Grade III route through the lower section of the canyon. There are lots of obstacles to avoid and plenty of rapids.

Moraine Lake (Map 7/A2)
If you are looking for sheer scenic beauty, it's hard to beat Moraine Lake. The lake is well sheltered by a stand of towering mountains, and doesn't get too rough, although storms can blow up quickly in the high mountains. There are canoe rentals at the lake, which is accessed by a paved road.

Nigel Creek (Map 16/C3)
This small, fast flowing creek offers a short, 2.5 km (1.6 mile/1–2 hour) paddle near its confluence with the North Saskatchewan River. The paddle begins from the Highway 93 Bridge and ends anywhere you can access the North Saskatchewan River along Highway 93. Along the way, there are a multitude of challenges including many drops, obstacles and boulder gardens. The first part of the paddle is tough, but as you near the river the creek flows out into a plain and slows.

North Saskatchewan River (Map 16, 17)
The North Saskatchewan River is one of the largest rivers in Alberta. Most of its length can be paddled with minimal difficulty as it lacks the canyon and treacherous sections of other foothill rivers. However, there are some faster sections in the mountains.

> **Put-in:** Nigel Creek (Map 16/C3)

> **Take-out:** Rampart Creek (Map 16/F5)

When running this section of the North Saskatchewan, make sure you portage around the 10 metre (33 feet) high falls (in the canyon). Also, watch out for sweepers around tight corners. The river is mostly a Grade II paddle through an open valley with lots of braiding, but there is a 3 km long (1.8 miles) canyon, with some nice rapids and standing waves. And the falls. Don't forget the falls. Below the canyon, the river again becomes braided and flows over a gravel bottom. There is a short stretch where the river channel narrows, offering some standing waves and rapids. To reduce the length of the paddle, you can put-in or take-out at a number of locations along Highway 93.

> **Put-in:** Rampart Creek (Map 16/F5)

> **Take-out:** Highway 93 Bridge (Map 17/A6)

The scenery is spectacular along all the upper North Saskatchewan, and, while the water is very chilly, this is a mostly easy 16 km (9.8 mile) paddle through an open valley. Mostly easy, but there is a 1.5 km long (1 mile) canyon with two Class IV/V drops and a number of Class III standing waves.

> **Put-in:** Highway 93 Bridge (Map 17/A6)

> **Take-out:** Highway 11 near the Cavalcade Campsite (Map 17/D4)

As the river flows out of the mountains, the difficult parts become fewer and fewer. This section is a steady, 27 km (16.8 mile/4–6 hour) Grade I/II paddle. The river at this location is braided and flows over a gravel bottom with few obstacles.

TRAILS

The spectacular alpine scenery, abundant wildlife and over 1,600 km (1,000 miles) of trails attract visitors year round. The usual hiking season ranges from mid-May to mid-October, with high elevation trails sporting snow later into the year. The trails in this park see a lot of activity, especially those around the towns of Banff and Lake Louise. Remember, there is a daily fee and a backcountry camping permit required when in the park. Please ensure you have (voluntarily) registered before heading out on the trails. Note also that trails can close at any time for a variety of reasons, including, but not limited to, wildlife in the area, physical hazards or trail maintenance. In particular, the trails in the Moraine Lake area are closed until July 17 each year due to grizzly bear activity.

Alexandra River Trail (Map 16/D4–B5)
Beginning at the Icefields Parkway, this old fire road runs along the North Saskatchewan River for a few kilometres, before heading west to parallel the Alexandra River. The 11.7 km (7.3 mile) trail takes you through spectacular terrain and scenic views. While the old fire road continues on to the junction of the Alexandra and Castleguard Rivers, there are numerous stream crossings. Most people stop at the difficult Terrace Creek crossing.

Allenby Pass Trail (Map 7/G4–8/B7)
This long trail will take hikers three or four days to complete. It can be accessed from Sunshine Road, along the Brewster Creek Trail. It is a moderate 27 km (16.8 mile) trail that climbs steeply to the Allenby Pass. Along the way you catch views of the Sundance Range. An option to continue to the Bryant Creek Trail is possible. From August 1 to September 30, hikers or horse groups must have a special permit to travel over Allenby Pass for safety reasons, as this is prime grizzly bear country. Permit conditions for hikers include a minimum group size of four adults (minimum age 16 and over) with larger groups recommended and for riders a minimum of 2 is required. Permits are available by personal appointment at the Banff Information Centre 403.762.1550.

Arnica & Twin Lakes Trail (Map 7/C3)
Found at the Vista Lake Viewpoint on Highway 93, 2 km (1.2 miles) east of the BC border, the Arnica Lake Trail is a popular 5 km (3 mile) hike. The trail actually drops down to Vista Lake before climbing 580 m (1,885 ft) through the woods to Arnica Lake. The lake provides good fishing for cutthroat trout. Most choose to explore the scenic routes up (800 m/2,600 ft) Storm Mountain or onto the Twin Lakes. The trail to Twin Lakes climbs 675 m (2,215 ft) over 16.8 km (10.4 miles) return. The trail does continue through Gibbon Pass to Redearth Creek and Shadow Lake. The best time of year for this hike is mid-June through September.

Aylmer Pass Trail (Map 8/C2)
A popular overnight trip, this trail begins at Lake Minnewanka before ascending towards Mount Aylmer. Along the way, many visitors take the side trail to the scenic lookout. The 27 km (16.8 mile) hike to the pass is difficult and should be left to those hikers who are fit. It is possible to link up with the Ghost River Trail outside of the park. Reservations are required for camping in the park. From July 15 to September 30, group access will be required along the Aylmer Pass Trail for the section from the Lake Minnewanka trail to the Park boundary, including the trail to Aylmer Lookout. This means that people must travel in a tight group of four or more for safety reasons. Anyone not complying with a minimum group size of four may be fined up to $5000.

Badger Pass Trail (Map 7/D1)
Accessed off the Johnston Creek Trail, this difficult, 21 km (13 mile) hike takes you through remote, high alpine terrain. In fact, it is one of the highest trail access passes in Banff Park. The trail connects with the Cascade River Trail and is best hiked from August through to September. Give yourself the better part of a day to complete this hike.

Baker Lake Trails (Map 12/B6)
The shortest route to this good fishing lake is from Boulder Pass off the Skoki Valley Trail (see below). The moderate side trail is only 4.5 km (2.8 miles) long but it is hilly and the route is often muddy as it follows the north shore of Ptarmigan Lake. The longer, more difficult route in follows the Baker Creek Trail and is quite rough in places.

Boom Lake Trail (Map 7/B3)
Anglers looking for a relatively easy hike-in lake may wish to pick this 5 km (3 mile) trail. However, the trail starts off with a tough climb before descending to the lake. It is possible to continue along more difficult routes leading to O'Brien, Taylor and Moraine Lakes. The trail climbs 170m (560 ft) to the lake and is used throughout the year.

Boundary Lake Trail (Map 16/B2)
The trailhead for this short, 1.5 km (0.9 mile) scramble is found on Icefields Parkway (Highway 93) at Sunwapta Pass. Most visitors also follow the side trail at the lake to view Boundary Glacier.

Bourgeau Lake Trail (Map 7/F4)
Accessed off the Trans-Canada Highway, this is an 8 km (5 mile) trail that is home to a lot of wildlife. It should take a couple of hours as you ascend through the Douglas-fir forest to a fairly high elevation. At the 7.5 km (4.7 mile) mark, there is a side trail to Harvey Pass. This is a 3 km (1.8 mile) trail that will take you around Bourgeau Lake and up to the pass.

Bow Glacier Falls & Hut Trail (Map 11/C4)
Num-ti-jah Lodge on the Icefields Parkway is the access point for this 4.5 km (2.8 mile) hike. You first skirt along the Bow Lake shoreline before climbing steeply to the edge of a canyon, where the trail leads to the base of some beautiful falls. It is a moderate hike in which you gain 170 m (553 ft). Mountaineers use this trail to gain access to the Bow Hut. The difficult route up climbs 440 m (1,430 ft). On the descent, it is possible to visit the source of Bow Glacier Falls.

Bow River Loop (Map 12/A7)
Found at the end of Sentinel Road in Lake Louise, this is an excellent trail for the hiker, biker or skier who is interested in nature. The 7.2 km (4.5 mile) trail follows both banks of the Bow River and would take about 1.5 hours to walk.

Bow Summit Lookout Trail (Map 11/C3)
Accessed from the Bow Summit parking area, this is an easy trail to an old fire lookout. The 3 km (1.8 mile) trail only climbs 32 m (105 ft) to the summit. From here, the Timberline Trail begins its loop through a sub-alpine meadow.

C Level Cirque Trail (Map 8/B3)
This 4 km (2.5 mile) one-way hike is one of the more attractive walks in the Banff townsite region. Look for it off of Lake Minnewanka Road at the Upper Bankhead Picnic Area. It takes you part way up the Cascade Mountain as it leads to a glacier-carved bowl. Within half an hour of your hike you will encounter two old buildings, which are the remains of an anthracite coal operation. As well, expect some uphill climbing through forest before it finally opens up to views of the Three Sisters and the Bow Valley.

Cascade Amphitheatre Trail (Map 8/A3)
A popular 15 km (9.3 mile) hike begins at the Mount Norquay Ski Area. The trail gains 610 m (1,983 ft) through scenic country to view the glacier-carved cove. A crossing of Forty Mile Creek and some steep switchbacks make the trip a bit strenuous. It should take about five hours to hike.

Cascade Fire Road (Map 8/B3–12/E3)
After the collapse of two bridges in the summer of 1984, the Cascade Fire Road was converted to a multi-use trail. This 75 km (46.6 mile) road runs from the Sawback Range to the Bare Mountains, passing the Palliser Range along the way. Wildlife such as bear, elk and sheep can be seen along the route. Creek and river crossings are necessary, including the Panther River. The trail can be broken down into two sections: the Lower Cascade Fire Road, which leads north from the Lake Minnewanka Road at the Upper Bankhead Picnic Area to Stoney Creek and the Upper Cascade Fire Road, which continues to the Red Deer River Valley. The Lower Cascade Fire Road is 15.2 km (9.4 miles) long, gaining 256 m (832 ft) of elevation and losing 70 m (228 ft). Because of its high Grizzly Bear population, this section has been designated as a biking path in order to minimize furry encounters of the unfriendly kind. The Upper Cascade Fire Road is 55.5 km (34.5 miles) long, gaining 830 m (2,698 ft) and losing 850 m (2,763 ft). It takes three days to hike this section one-way. The northern access is found at the Ya Ha Tinda Ranch (look for the spur road south of the locked gate before the ranch building).

Castle Mountain Lookout Trail (Map 7/C2)
This 4 km (2.5 mile) trek up the side of Castle Mountain leads to the old Mount Eisenhower Fire Lookout. You can find the trailhead 5 km (3 miles) west of Castle Junction on the Bow Valley Parkway (Highway 1A). Although short, the trail is quite steep, gaining 520 m (1,690 ft) in elevation. The trail leads from the forest to meadows full of wildflowers (in season) and an exposed cliff, which offers great views of the Bow Valley. Experienced rock climbers can continue from the scenic lookout and onto Goat Ledge.

Castleguard Meadows Trail (Map 16/B5)
The Castleguard Meadows Trail follows the Alexandra River Trail to the Castleguard River. From here, the trail becomes a route as it makes its way to the spectacular alpine meadows. The meadows are some of the most

impressive in Banff and because of the long, difficult access, few people visit them. It is a 35 km (21.7 mile) trip that should take two or three days. Experienced glacier travellers can continue onto the Saskatchewan Glacier. Check at the Lake Louise Visitor Centre for conditions.

Chephren Lake Trail (Map 11/B1) 🚶🏔️

This 7 km (4.3 mile) trail is accessed at the Waterfowl Lake Campground. It leads to a glacier-fed lake after climbing 90 m (293 ft). At the 2 km (1.2 mile) junction, it is possible to head left to arrive at Cirque Lake. The best hiking time is mid-June through October.

Citadel Pass Trail (Map 7/F6) 🏕️🚶🎿🚻

Accessed from the Sunshine Village Ski Area, this is a 9.5 km (5.9 mile) hike that gains 615 m (1,999 ft) in elevation. The trail climbs through alpine meadows and then descends to a lake and campground below. It is possible to continue to Lake Magog in Mount Assiniboine Park through the Golden Valley. Allow two days to hike that 28 km (17.4 mile) trail.

Clearwater Valley Trail (Map 11/E1–12/E1) 🏕️🚶🎿🐴🐟🚻

This long, difficult trek leads 58 km (three or four days) from the Siffleur River to the Clearwater River Valley. Hiking this trail takes you through some of the most remote regions in Banff National Park. You will pass Upper Devon Lake (good fishing) as well as a warden's cabin. One good location to camp is the east end of Trident Lake. Watch for the elk that often congregate here. There are several joining trails including the Divide Creek Trail and the Clearwater River Trail, which continues east into the Bighorn Wildland.

Consolation Lakes Trail (Map 7/A2) 🚶🐟🚻

This is a short, easy 5 km (3 mile) hike, which begins at Moraine Lake. The trail climbs past a rockslide to a beautiful open meadow with wildflowers in season. At Lower Consolation Lake enjoy the view of Bident Mountain and Mount Quadra before continuing on over a narrow ridge and discovering Upper Consolation Lake. When grizzly bears are active in the area, hikers need to hike in groups of six or more. There is a sign-up sheet at the trailhead.

Cotton Grass Pass Trail (Map 12/B6) 🚶🚻

The Cotton Grass Pass Trail is 5.8 km (3.6 mile) long and can be started from either direction. It takes you between Baker Lake and Red Deer Lakes. This trail is quite appealing as most of is above tree line, offering splendid views of the cliffs of Fossil Mountain and Pipestone Mountain.

Crowfoot Pass Trail (Map 11/E4) 🚶🎿🚻

If you are an adventurous hiker or skier, you are going to love this trail, or rather, route. Finding the unmarked trail is tough. From the Icefields Parkway, 1.3 km (0.8 miles) south of the Crowfoot Glacier Viewpoint, make your way down to Bow River, which you must cross. You then climb steeply for 7 km (4.3 miles) to the pass, with magnificent views. It is possible to continue on to the Mount Balfour viewpoint.

Divide Creek Trail (Map 12/C1–D3) 🚴🚶🐴🚻

This difficult multi-use trail begins off the Red Deer River Trail. It runs through meadows and forests and requires some creek crossing as you climb 625 m (2,031 ft) to the Divide Summit. From here, enjoy the great views of the surrounding mountains before descending to Peters Creek and Clearwater River. Wildlife may be encountered along the 26 km (16.2 mile) one-way route. Most hikers choose to follow the Clearwater River Trail back into Banff Park (the ford of the Clearwater River is best left until August at the earliest). From the Clearwater River/Peters Creek end, the trail gains 900 m (2,925 ft) in elevation.

Dolomite Pass & Creek Trail (Map 11/D4–E1) 🏕️🚶🎿🐴🐟🚻

The Dolomite Pass Trail is a 9 km (5.6 mile) one-way multi-use trail that is accessed at the Crowfoot Glacier Viewpoint. The climb to the pass is rather steep (650 m/2,112 ft gain), but if you travel it in the summer, you will be surrounded by colourful meadows with great views and access to Lake Helen (12 km/7.5 miles return). From the pass, the Dolomite Creek Trail continues to Isabella Lake passing some waterfalls along the way. It is a difficult, 10 hour hike that gains 550 m (1,788 ft). There is also a 7 km (4.3 mile) option from the pass heading down past Katherine Lake to Dolomite Peak, but this route is seldom used and you may have to bushwhack. These trails are best left to the fit hiker to do from mid-July through October.

Dormer Pass & River Trails (Map 8/A1–13/B4) 🏕️🚶🐴🚻

Accessed from the Cascade Fire Road at the 15 km (9.3 mile) mark, the trail up Dormer Pass is 13 km (8 mile) and requires a few stream crossings. From the pass it is a steep descent to the river, which also needs to be crossed. The trail has many scenic viewpoints and side trails to Stoney Pass, Dormer Mountain and Panther River.

Edith & Cory Pass Trails (Map 7/G4–8/A4) 🚶🚴🚻

Accessed from the Fireside Picnic Area, off the Bow Valley Parkway is a pair of strenuous 13 km (8 mile) hikes. The Edith Pass Trail gains 520 m (1,690 ft) in elevation and offers glimpses of Mount Norquay and Mount Edith along the way. The Cory Pass Trail will take about 6 hours to climb the 900 m (2,925 ft) up through a beautiful alpine forest. The rocky ascent is steep, but the scenic reward makes it worth it. It is possible to link the trails or continue north from Edith Pass to the Forty Mile Creek Trail. The later option is a 12.8 km (8 mile) one-way hike to Mount Norquay.

Eiffel Lake Trail (Map 6/G2–7/A2) 🚶🚻

While this trail is no longer maintained or promoted, Eiffel Lake is still a popular destination with those in the know. Alpine flowers bloom in profusion near the lake and Eiffel Lake is set in the heart of the stark Desolation Valley. The trip is 10 km (6.2 miles) return from the trailhead at Moraine Lake, although many people make their way past the lake (there is no trail here) to connect up with the Wenkchemna Pass Trail, 10 km (6.2 miles) one-way. You will gain 400 m (1,300 ft) to the lake, taking you through forests and meadows. Climbing to the pass takes you up another 350 m (1,138 ft) through fabulous rock formations and past the foot of the Ten Peaks. This trail can only be hiked after July 17 in groups of 4 or more people due to grizzly bears in the area.

Elk Lake & Pass Trail (Map 8/A2) 🏕️🚶🐴🎿🚻

Accessed from the Mount Norquay Ski Area, this multi-use trail begins. It is a 14 km (8.7 mile) one-way trip to the lake that gains 610 m (1,983 ft) in elevation. It is 12.8 km (8 miles) one-way to Elk Pass proper. There are many small lakes and scenic viewpoints along the way. Before reaching the lake, you will find a campsite a popular trail linking to the beautiful Cascade Valley. Allow five hours to hike to the lake.

Elkhorn Summit Trail (Map 12/F4) 🚶🚻

This 13 km (8 mile) hike leads to a series of meadows, found between the Red Deer and Panther Rivers.

Fatigue Creek Trail (Map 7/G6) 🚶🚻

Accessed from the Allenby Pass Trail, this is a 13 km (8 mile) trail that crosses the creek many times on your way to Fatigue Pass. You gain 780 m (2,535 ft) in elevation, making it a gruelling route. However, once you are above the treeline the views are great. The trail can be used as a link to Citadel Pass.

Flint's Park Trail (Map 12/F7) 🏕️🚴🚶🐴🚻

This 8 km (4.6 mile) connecting trail follows the Cascade River from the Cascade Fire Road to the Forty Mile Creek Trail. The campsite at Flint's Park is a popular equestrian destination and makes a good hub for exploring the area.

Forty Mile Creek Trail (Map 8/A3–7/F1) 🏕️🚶🐴🎿🐟🚻

This trail follows the Cascaded Amphitheatre Trail for less than a kilometre before splitting off to follow Forty Mile Creek. From the junction to Flint's Park—the end of the Forty Mile Creek Trail—is 27.8 km (17.2 miles) one-way. It should take backpackers at least three days to hike out and back. The trail can get muddy, so try to hold out for dry weather. Highlights include the excellent view of Sawback Lake once you reach Forty Mile Summit. Sawback Lake and Rainbow Lake are accessed off the trail, just north of the summit. It is very easy to create a multi-day loop trail with the many connecting trails. Popular options include following the Badger Pass Trail to the Johnston Creek Trail or the Flint's Park Trail to the Cascade Fire Road.

Gibbon Pass Trail (Map 7/C4) 🏕️🚶🚻

A 6 km (3.7 mile) hiking trail begins from the Shadow Lake Campsite. It gains 470 m (1,528 ft) in elevation on its way to the pass, before dropping down to the Twin Lakes.

Glacier Lake Trail (Map 16/F7) 🏕️🚶🐟🚻

Accessed from the Icefields Parkway, it will take the better part of a day to hike this 20 km (12.5 mile) trail. It is a climb 685 m (2,226 ft) up through open forest to Glacier Lake where there are great views of the surrounding mountains. To continue past Glacier Lake, you must bushwhack your way along Glacier River. A campsite by the lake provides a base for further explorations or anglers.

Goat Creek Trail (Map 8/B4–C6) 🚶🚴🐴

Follow the Spray River Fire Road south to the disused dirt road that follows Goat Creek east towards Spray Lakes Reservoir. The east end of the route is rougher and requires creek crossings. The moderate 9 km (5.6 mile) multi-use trail is accessed from the Banff Springs Hotel or at the Bow River Bridge in town. For the biker looking for a challenging loop, combine the Goat Creek

Trail with the Rundle Riverside Trail and the golf course road to complete a 48 km (29.8 mile) loop.

Great Divide [Ross Lake] Trail (Map 11/F7)

In reality the Great Divide Trail is an epic trip that runs along the BC Alberta boundary, stretching almost 500 km (300 miles) from tip to tail. However, that route follows many, many other trails and requires tremendous route finding skills and endurance to part take in. The stretch of trail found around Chateau Lake Louise is a lot easier since it follows the route of the old Highway 1A to the boundary. There is an exhibit here about the divide and you can continue into Yoho National Park and Ross Lake. From the parking lot to the divide is 7.5 km (4.7 miles), gaining 120 m (390 ft) in elevation. Along the route to Ross Lake is Minewakun Lake Trail, a 4.5 km (2.8 mile) trail that starts at the intersection of Minewakun Creek and the Ross Lake Trail. The beautiful colours of this lake will make this detour worthwhile. However one must be extremely careful when scaling steep rocky slopes, especially when wet.

Headwaters [Indianhead Creek] Trail (Map 12/B1–18/A6)

This 13 km (8 mile) one-way hike starts from the Clearwater Valley Trail (at the 27.4 km/17 mile mark) and leads to the Indianhead Creek headwaters. It begins by paralleling the Clearwater River before climbing steeply to a saddle. From here on, the open trail provides nearly continuous views of nearby summits as it makes its way to the old Headwaters Patrol Cabin (outside of Banff) via the Indianhead Creek Drainage.

Healy Pass Trail (Map 7/E6)

From the Bourgeau parking lot, two different routes provide access to the pass. The most scenic involves hiking up to Sunshine Village, while the more direct route follows the old road up Healy Creek. No matter what route you take, you will find beautiful meadows, ponds, wildflowers and streams. In the winter, frozen waterfalls provide you with some ice climbing opportunities. Egypt Lake can be accessed from the main trail, which is 20 km (12.5 mile) long and gains 215 m (699 ft). Another popular side trail is the easy 2.5 km (1.6 mile) Redearth Pass Trail. From the scenic pass, it is possible to continue toward East Verdant Creek, which will eventually take you down to Highway 93 in BC. June through September is the best hiking time.

Hector Lake Trail (Map 11/F5)

Accessed from the Icefields Parkway, this 2 km (1.2 mile) hike requires fording the Bow River, which is not safe until late in the season when water levels are low. The trail runs along the Bow River for a while and is often used by fishermen to access to some great fishing spots. There is camping by Hector Lake as well as a 5 km (3 mile) trail leading to Lake Margaret, where you will find an excellent view of Mount Hector.

Helen Creek Trail (Map 11/E4)

This 5 km (3 mile) trail begins off the Icefields Parkway, south of Crowfoot Glacier Viewpoint. The trail, which gains 490 m (1,593 ft) in elevation, is an alternate route to Helen Lake.

Howse Pass Trail (Map 10/F1–17/A6)

The trailhead for this 54 km (33.6 mile) multi-day trip is located by the Mistaya River Bridge at the Mistaya Canyon Pullout off the Icefields Parkway. The trail provides access to the Freshfield Range Glacier Area, a popular rock climbing area. This trail runs by Howse River and requires a bit of bushwhacking to avoid those icy stream crossings. Early June through September is the best time to hike the trail.

Johnson Lake Trails (Map 8/C4)

The 11.7 km (7.3 mile) network of trails in and around Johnson Lake is a series of ski trails that follow old roads around the lake. These trails can be hiked in the summer. In fact, they are some of the first trails in Banff to be relatively snow free in spring. The busiest of the trails is an easy 8 km (5 mile) circuit of the lake. Also in the area is a 700-year-old Douglas-fir, one of the oldest known fir trees in Alberta and the old Anthracite Mine site, found below some Hoodoos.

Johnston Canyon & Creek Trails (Map 7/E3–12/C7)

The Johnston Canyon Trail is a popular 3 km (1.8 mile) trail that leads to an impressive limestone canyon that is home to a series of waterfalls. The trailhead is accessed off the Bow Valley Parkway at the Hillsdale Meadows parking area. This was probably one of the most expensive trails to build in the park, as there are hundreds of feet of catwalks and a tunnel that bringing hikers through the heart of the canyon. Past the upper falls, the Johnstone Creek Trail continues to the Ink Pots and beyond. This two or three day 38.5 km (24 mile) hike weaves it's way through a valley bottom and is best undertaken from mid-July to September. It has several points of interest including

Pulsatilla Pass, Badger Pass and Mystic Pass. For those who plan to camp, there is a campsite at Luellen Lake (16.1 km/10 mile) and another on a small scenic knoll (20 km/12.5 miles).

Lake Agnes Circuit (Map 6/G1–11/G7)

Climbing the trail to Lake Agnes with the Big Beehive and Plain of Six Glaciers creates a truly sublime circuit. As an added bonus, you will pass both of the backcountry teahouses on this 14.5 km (9 mile) circuit. The trails to Lake Agnes and the Plain of the Six Glaciers are both extremely popular, but the trail linking the two together, over the Big Beehive, is not quite as popular, so you might have a few kilometres of solitude. Might. The trail to Lake Agnes will take about 4 hours as you climb 438 m (1,424 ft over 8 km (5 miles) return. Alternatively, try the Highland Trail, which starts at Mirror Lake off of the Lake Agnes Trail. This trail takes the hiker or horseback rider through trees to open slopes, revealing the whole length of Lake Louise. This demanding 14 km (8.7 mile) return trail does not see the crowds other trails do.

Lake Louise Shoreline Trails (Map 11/G7–6/G1)

A 3 km (1.8 mile) walk or ski around the lake provides great views of Mount Victoria towering above. At the far end of the lake is rock climbing opportunities (Wicked Gravity and Exquisite Corpse are two popular routes). The Fairview Lookout Trail is a short 2 km (1.2 mile) trail that provides you with an excellent view of Lake Louise. Accessed from the Boathouse in Lake Louise, the trail is rather steep. An alternate route back is the South Lakeshore Trail.

Lake Louise Ski Hill (Map 12/A7)

The lower slopes of the Lake Louise Ski Hill have been designated Grizzly habitat and are closed to hikers. However, the gondola remains in operation over the summer and fall, taking hikers to mid-mountain. From here, it is possible to hike across the valley as well as up the mountain along ski runs and trails. The views across the valley to Lake Louise, the lake, are phenomenal and get better as you climb. To get to the summit of the mountain from the gondola station, give yourself at least two hours up and make sure you fill up with water before heading out. Because this is active Grizzly Bear habitat, it is recommended that you hike in groups of six or more.

Lake Minnewanka Trail (Map 8/B3–F3)

This trail runs along the north shore of the large, beautiful Lake Minnewanka and past the three Ghost Lakes to the Devil's Gap, which marks the park boundary. The first Ghost Lake is dried up and the second is marshy, but the third is a beautiful blue. You will find signs directing you to other trails, including the Devil's Gap Trail. There is camping at the second Ghost Lake.

Lakes and Larches Hike (Map 7/E6–D5)

Ease of access and post card perfect scenery make this series of trails attractive to the hiker. This route strings together a series of trails to create a point-to-point hike, so you will need a shuttle. While it is possible to do this 40.3 km (25 mile) one-way route in two days, don't rush. Spend three or four days exploring this gorgeous area. From the Sunshine Road, this route follows the Healy Pass Trail to Egypt Lake. Here, branch trails take you to Pharaoh Lake and Black Rock Lake to the North and Scarab and Mummy Lake (3.5 km/2.2 miles) to the south. Through hikers should follow the Whistling Pass Trail to Shadow Lake (although you can take the Pharoah Creek Trail to the Shadow Lake Lodge, a great place to overnight if you have the funds). From here, a trail runs through Gibbon Pass to Twin Lakes and the Arnica Lake Trail. If you left your vehicle at the Vista Lake Trailhead, go left. If you left it at the Copper Lake Trailhead, go right.

Larch Valley Trail (Map 6/G2–7/A2)

This trail is spectacular in the fall when the larch trees turn a bright golden yellow. It is 9.5 km (5.9 miles) return to the valley, gaining 500 m (1,625 ft) along the way. Once at the valley, the hiker has the option to go north to Sentinel Pass, which requires another three hours to climb 720 m (2,340 ft). Once there, the views are magnificent. Going through Sentinel Pass, the fit hiker can descend 500 m (1,625 ft) to Paradise Valley to the west or go east to Lake Annette. Eventually, both options will lead back to Moraine Lake Road. Please note this trail requires people to travel in groups of four or more people after July 17 of each year due to traversing grizzly bear habitat.

Leman Lake Trail (Map 4/C4)

Bringing you into Banff National Park in Alberta, this trail is accessed at the end of the Albert River Road northwest of Invermere. It is a 5 km (3 mile) 2–3 hour moderate hike to an alpine lake that offers fishing lake. From the lake, a series of trails lead into the Spray River valley.

Lost Lake Trails (Map 11/G7)

Off the Trans-Canada Highway, 9 km (5.6 miles) west of the Lake Louise overpass there are a couple of routes that will get you to Lost Lake. The rougher Bath Creek Route is 2 km (1.2 mile) long, starting across the CPR tracks near the creek. The Hillside Route is 1 km (0.6 mile) long and is the steeper of the two routes. It begins at the trail sign. Both trails will take you to this green lake, surrounded by a heavy canopy of trees and mountains.

Louise Creek Trail (Map 12/A7) 🥾🐟
This trail is the quickest way from the village to Lake Louise Ski Hill. The trailhead for this 3 km (1.8 mile) trail starts at the campground on the southwest side of the Bow River Bridge and takes the hiker or fisherman through heavy forest as it follows along Louise Creek. The elevation gain is 200 m (650 ft).

Marvel Pass & Owl Lake Trails (Map 4/C2–B2) 🏕️🥾🚴🐟🅿️
Marvel Pass is 9.3 km (5.8 miles) from the Bryant Creek Trail Junction, which in turn is 11.7 km (7.3 miles) from the Mount Shark parking area. Head west on Bryant Creek Trail, until you come to the Owl Lake Trail junction (it is 4 km/2.5 miles to the pretty lake). Follow the trail past Owl Lake and on to Marvel Pass. This trip could easily be done in a day. However, many people connect this trail with Marvel Lake via a rough, ill-defined route south from Marvel Pass to connect with the Wonder Pass Trail, which passes by Marvel Lake. This 46.5 km (28.9 mile) loop is best left for experienced route finders carrying topographical maps. Be forewarned that the area at the south end of Marvel Lake is boggy and there may or may not be some log bridges over the creek. Expect to get your feet wet. From the BC side, a 20 km (12.2 mile) hike on a well-marked trail leads to the alpine meadows of Marvel Pass. The trailhead is located off the Cross River Road northwest of Invermere.

Molar Pass Trail (Map 10/A5–11/G4) 🏕️🥾🐎🅿️
The Molar Pass Trail is a 10 km (6.2 mile) hike. One can expect miles of rolling alpine meadows below looming glaciers. After the first 1.5 km (0.9 mile) the trail parallels Mosquito Creek until it splits at 6.5 km (4 miles) and begins to climb uphill to Molar Pass (2,377 m/7,725 ft). The rocky towers of Molar Mountain, which indeed looks like the titular tooth, can be seen to the south. You can also continue on to North Molar Pass but be prepared for a stiff climb (up to 760 m/2,470 ft) and the possibility of seeing grizzly bears. Snow can also be a problem until late July.

Moraine Lake Trail (Map 7/A1) 🥾🚴
This 8.5 km (5.9 mile) one-way trail begins on the banks of the Bow River in the village of Lake Louise. For those riding mountain bikes there is a longer version (30 km/18.6 miles), which loops around and follows Paradise Creek up the Giant Steps past Lake Annette. For most, the shorter version is a terrific journey that climbs up the side of Mount Temple and leads to the beautiful Moraine Lake. The trail essentially parallels Moraine Lake Road and in July and August the forest floor is a high mountain flower garden. A popular viewpoint at the north end of Moraine Lake is accessed by the Rockpile Trail. This short interpretive trail leads 1 km (0.6 miles) through a jumble of boulders to a viewpoint overlooking the lake and the Ten Peaks. At sunrise and sunset, the viewpoint is usually teeming with photographers.

Mosquito Creek Trail (Map 11/F4) 🏕️🥾🐎🐟🅿️
The trail up Mosquito Creek starts at a fairly high elevation and just gets higher. You climb quickly to the alpine around North Molar Pass before dropping down to the first of the Fish Lakes. There is camping and good cutthroat trout fishing at the lakes. Plan for an overnight trip since the 15 km (9.3 mile) one-way trail is difficult to hike in a day.

Mount Coleman Route (Map 16/E4) 🥾🚴🅿️
Getting to the summit of Mount Coleman is tough, but well worth the effort. Beginning at the 1 km (0.6 mile) mark of the Sunset Pass Trail off the Icefields Parkway, you ascend some 1,180 m (3,835 ft) over 4.8 km (3 miles) to reach the summit. This trail is not for the inexperienced as parts of this route qualify as scrambling and can be dangerous. Carry an ice axe. But once at the 3,135 m (10,189 ft) peak, the view offers a magnificent panorama of Banff National Park. Look northwest where Mount Columbia lies; the highest point in Alberta at 3,747 m (12,178 ft).

Mount Rundle Trail (Map 8/C5) 🥾🚴🅿️
While this trek offers great views of the Spray Valley and Banff townsite, the ascent is a steady, arduous 10.6 km (6.5 mile) return climb up the southwest slope of the mountain. The trailhead is near the first green at the Banff Springs Golf Course, along the Spray River Loop. At the 5.3 km (3.3 mile) mark the main trail ends, but for experienced rock climbers the peak lies a gruelling 1,120 m (3,640 ft) above. Be careful; many inexperienced climbers have lost their lives here.

Mystic Lake & Pass Trail (Map 7/F2) 🏕️🚻🥾🐎🐟🅿️
This 14.5 km (9 mile) one-way trail links lower Johnston Creek with Forty Mile Creek. The trail starts at the 15.2 km (9.5 miles) mark of the Forty Mile

Creek Trail (at the Mystic Junction Campground and warden cabin) and will take you the better part of the day to hike as it gains some 550 m (1,788 m) in elevation. It is quite a scenic trek with stark limestone walls and scatterings of larch, which are a striking gold colour in the fall. The difficult trail has numerous creek crossings and tiresome climbs, but the scenery, especially at Mystic Pass itself, is well worth the effort. Many choose to stop at Mystic Lake to try their luck fishing. This alternative is a 19.5 km (12.1 mile) trek from Mount Norquay.

Nigel Pass Trail (Map 16/C2) 🏕️🥾🐎🐟🅿️
A 16 km (10 mile) hike leads from the Icefields Parkway up to Nigel Pass. It gains 370 m (1,203 ft) in elevation as it runs through open meadows with great views of Mount Athabasca to the south. Late June through September is the best time to hike the trail, which should take about six hours to the pass. However, many who venture here also continue north into the Brazeau Lake area of Jasper. The return trip is about 32.5 km or if you are really ambitious, the Brazeau Loop is a daunting 78.5 week long trip through some of the best the Rockies has to offer. The terrain can become tricky at times, so take extra care and be prepared. Several campgrounds are located along the way. The scenic Jonas Pass Trail can be accessed at the 14 km (8.7 mile) point. This adjoining trail is 19 km (11.8 miles) long one-way, including a 13 km (8 mile) section above the treeline. It leads past towering peaks, through wildflower meadows and through prime mountain caribou habitat.

North Fork Pass Trail (Map 12/F6) 🥾🅿️
This 12 km (7.4 miles) trail starts at the 30 km (18.6 miles) mark of the Lower Cascade Fire Road, making it a 42 km (26 mile) one-way hike. It gains 540 m (1,770 ft) in 12 km (7.4 miles). The hike begins alongside the Panther River, before crossing over to reach a narrow valley. From here the climb starts to the pass. Excellent views of the surrounding mountain ranges are provided once up on top. The North Cascade River Route is a rough 9.6 km (6 mile) route that continues down to Flint's Park Campsite. You can hike out via Forty Mile Creek or the Flint's Park Trail back to the Cascade Fire Road. Be wary of Grizzly Bears in the area.

Panorama Ridge Route (Map 7/A2–C3) 🏕️🥾🐟🅿️
This difficult, 23 km (14.3 mile) route extends from the Boom Creek Picnic Site (off Highway 93) through to Moraine Lake south of Lake Louise. The first 2.3 km (1.4 miles) follows the trail to Boom Lake. But after the climb up to the first ridge the route becomes rough, indistinct and even boggy. You will need a lot of patience and a good topographic map as you search for the occasional 70-year-old blaze to assure you that you are on the right route. Overall, you gain 650 m (2,112 ft) in elevation. There is camping at Taylor Lake.

Panther River Trail (Map 12/G5–13/B4) 🏕️🚻🥾🐎🐟
A 15 km (9.3 mile) trail follows along the north side of Panther River. It connects the Cascade Fire Road with the Dormer Mountain Trail and continues on into the Bighorn Wildland Area. It should take most people about six hours to hike this trail.

Paradise Valley Trail (Map 6/G2–7/A2) 🏕️🥾🏃🅿️
From the Moraine Lake Road, this trail leads 18 km (11.2 miles) along the shores of Lake Annette, past the falls of the Giant Steps and to the foot of the Horseshoe Glacier. The route, enjoyed by hikers and backcountry skier, gains 390 m (1,268 ft) elevation gain. Like other trails in the area, access is restricted to groups of 4 or more people after July 17 of each year due to grizzly bear activity.

Parker Ridge Trail (Map 16/C3) 🥾🅿️
This is a 5 km (3 mile) hike that takes you to a fine viewpoint of the Saskatchewan Glacier. The ridge is over 2,000 m (6,500 ft) above sea level, so be prepared for some cold temperatures. The trailhead is found off the Icefields Parkway, 4.5 km (2.8 miles) north of the Nigel Pass parking area.

Peyto Lake Trails (Map 11/C3) 🥾🐟🅿️
Off the Icefields Parkway at the Mistaya Mountain Viewpoint, there are two trails that drop to Peyto Lake. The shortest is 1.5 km (0.9 miles), while the longer trail is 2.5 km (1.6 mile). A 5 km (3 mile) route continues southwest to Caldron Lake.

Pharaoh Creek Trail (Map 7/D5) 🏕️🚻🥾🐎🐟
This 9 km (5.6 mile) trail along the Pharaoh Creek is mainly used as an access trail to and from Egypt Lake. It gains 260 m (845 ft) in elevation. A side trail takes you to Pharaoh Lake. The trail is accessed from the Egypt Lake Campground via the Healy Pass Trail.

Pipestone River Trail (Map 11/G3–12/A7)
The Pipestone River Trail follows the Pipestone River for 36 km (22.4 miles) to the Pipestone Pass. The first 7 km (4.3 miles) are open to bikers, while the rest of the trail is open to hikers and equestrians. Most hikers avoid the trail, which is rough (from all the horse traffic) and uninspiring. A shorter, prettier route to the pass is via the Mosquito Creek Trail through North Molar Pass. The view from the pass is inspiring, allowing views of the Siffleur Valley all the way to the Kootenay Plains. Other branch trails include the Little Pipestove Creek Trail, a difficult trail providing access to Red Deer Lakes and Drummond Glacier, as well as a trail up Molar Creek.

Plain of Six Glaciers Trail (Map 6/G1)
This is one of the most scenic trails in an area famous for scenic trails. The route offers the visitor great views of towering mountains, majestic glaciers (yes, there really are six of them), mountain goats, and, just to be different, a teahouse at the end of the trail. Past the teahouse you can continue 1.5 km (0.9 miles) to view Abbot Pass and the Death Trap. It should take about three hours to hike this popular 10.8 km (6.7 mile) return trail, gaining 335 m (1,089 ft). In winter, the trip takes you through avalanche country and is recommended for experienced backcountry skiers only.

Red Deer River Trail (Map 12/C6–13/A3)
This long, but moderately graded trail begins at the Ya Ha Tinda Ranch. Allow at least two days to complete the trail one-way. It gains 345 m (1,121 ft). An alternate is to start from the south end and travel the 14.5 km (9 miles) from the Lake Louise Ski Area to Red Deer Lakes before camping.

Redoubt Lake Trail (Map 12/B7)
This trail is best accessed from the Baker Creek Trail. The 5.5 km (3.4 mile) hike has some steep sections on route to the meadows around the lake. Mountain goats, deer and elk frequent the area.

Rock Isle Lake Trail (Map 7/F6)
From the Sunshine Village Ski Area, a moderate 5 km (3 mile) hike leads south to Rock Isle Lake in British Columbia. Most of the 100 m (328 ft) elevation gain is found at the beginning, as you climb up from the Strawberry Chairlift to the top of Rock Isle Road. It is possible to extend the hike or ski to several destinations. Quartz Ridge is 10 km/6 miles return, Citadel Pass is 20 km/12.4 miles return and if you are really ambitious Mount Assiniboine Park and Highway 93 in Kootenay National Park are overnight options.

Rockbound Lake Trails (Map 7/D2)
This five hour, 15 km (9.3 mile) trail climbs 730 m (2,373 ft) past Tower Lake to the rich, deep blue waters of Rockbound Lake. Fishermen can try their luck for cutthroat and rainbow trout. Along the way, the trail passes rocky alpine meadows and sparkling mountain streams. There are a few other trails that are accessed from this one. Silverton Falls, a 90 m (293 ft) high waterfall found at the base of Castle Mountain, is found at the end of a short trail near the Castle Mountain Warden Cabin. Another route leads to Castle Mountain from the southeast shore of Rockbound Lake. This difficult four hour trail gains 870 m (2,828 ft) and loses 230 m (748 ft) as it climbs Castle Mountain and the north end of Helena Ridge.

Rundle Riverside Trail (Map 8/B4–C5)
This 8 km (5 mile) trail starts at the Banff Springs Golf Course road and follows the river to the park boundary. From here it is possible to continue along the well developed Banff Trail to the Canmore Nordic Trails. The Banff side of the trail is quite rooty and crosses rocky avalanche paths. Early summer to early fall is the best season for this trail.

Saddleback Trail (Map 6/G1)
A strenuous, 7 km (4.3 mile) hike takes you from the Giant Steps Trail to a fabulous viewpoint. The trail gains 580 m (1,885 ft) in elevation to the Saddleback summit. However, you can continue another 400 m (1,300 ft) up Fairview Mountain for better views. An alternate access begins 2.5 km (1.6 miles) up the Moraine Lake Road.

Sarbach Lookout Trail (Map 16/G6–17/A6)
This 10.5 km (6.5 mile) hike begins at the Mistaya Canyon Parking area. The trail starts by descending into Mistaya Canyon, a spectacular pot-marked gorge. Those that venture on will follow a windy trail up Mount Sarbach to the site of this former lookout, gaining 580 m (1,885 ft) in elevation. Many will be disappointed by the views from the lookout site, which are mostly blocked by the surrounding forest. But old trails, cut by the occupants of the lookout, will take you to better viewpoints of the valley below. To the north lies the junction of three rivers: Howse, Mistaya and North Saskatchewan.

Saskatchewan Glacier Trail (Map 16/C3)
From the Icefields Parkway to the toe of the Saskatchewan Glacier requires hiking a 12 km (7.4 mile) return trail. The trail, which gains 155 m (504 ft), is not marked, making it hard to follow. To actually reach the ice is treacherous and proper equipment is required.

Sawback Circuit (Map 7/E3–D1)
This is a multi-day trip, running 73 km (45.4 miles) through the Sawback Range. The route is filled with beautiful lakes, creeks, valleys and mountain passes. It is not one trail, but a combination of trails that starts along the Johnston Creek Trail. You loop through the mountain range by cutting over Badger Pass to the Forty Mile Creek Trail. Head south and cut back to Johnston Creek via Mystic Pass.

Sentinel Pass Trail (Map 6/G2–7/A2)
Sentinel Pass is the highest trail accessed pass in the Canadian Rockies. The 12 km (7.4 miles) hike offers unbelievable views of Moraine Lake and Ten Peaks along the way. In all you climb 790 m (2,568 ft) from the lake to the pass. To complete your journey, you may return the same way or continue to north Paradise Valley. This is another group hiking only area that can not be accessed until after July 17 of each year.

Shadow Lake Trail (Map 7/D4)
Accessed from the Trans-Canada Highway at the Redearth Creek Trailhead, this popular trail is enjoyed by hikers and bikers in summer and skiers in winter. The moderate trail takes you to the lake where you can continue (on foot or ski) to Ball Pass, Gibbon Pass, Ball Glacier Ice Cave, Haiduk Lake or Egypt Lake. It is 14.5 km (9 miles) to the Shadow Lake Lodge, climbing 325 m (1,050 ft) along the way. Haiduk Lake is an additional 14 km/8.7 miles return to the lodge, while Ball Pass is 12 km/7.5 miles return.

Skoki Valley Trail (Map 12/A7–B6)
The Skoki Valley area is one of the premier hiking and skiing destinations in Canada. Although day trips are possible it is simply too beautiful of an area not to spend more time in. If you are looking to explore in style, there is no better option that to use Skoki Lodge, which is found 11 km from the Lake Louise Ski Area, as a base camp. If you are roughing it, there are backcountry campsites at Hidden Lake, Red Deer Lake, Merlin Meadows and Baker Lake. From the Fish Creek parking lot, you gain 450 m (1,463 ft) in elevation to the pass. The lodge sites at 2,164 m (7,100 ft). Easy destinations from the Skoki Valley are Hidden Lake (less than a kilometre), Baker Lake, Merlin Lake and ridge (3 km to the lake) and Skoki Mountain (climbs an additional 220 m/720 ft).

Smith Lake Trail (Map 7/D3)
For fishermen and hikers, a 5 km (3 mile) trail heads uphill to Smith Lake. It is accessed off the Trans-Canada Highway at the Altrude Picnic Area. It begins along the same path taken for Twin Lakes, then heads left up a steep incline. Once at the lake, you can continue up a ridge overlooking the lake, 122 m (397 ft) higher.

Spray River Fire Road (Map 8/B4–4/D2)
From the Banff Springs Hotel, this old fire road runs to the Spray Lakes Reservoir, outside the park's eastern boundary. Most hikers will not want to bother with the valley bottom hike that covers 51.5 km (32 miles). Mountain bikers, however, will love it. It is easy and strong bikers can bike it in a day, return. There are ever a number of backcountry campsites, to turn this into a great overnight trip.

Spray River Loop (Map 8/B4)
This 12.5 km (7.8 mile) multi-use trail runs from the Banff Springs Hotel alongside the Spray River on the Spray River Fire Road (see above), before looping back to the golf course. Along the fire road, you are provided with great views. The Goat Creek Trail can also be accessed along this route.

Stoney Squaw Trail (Map 8/A4)
A biking/hiking trip for all ages begins at the Mount Norquay Ski Area. It is a 5 km (3 mile) round trip, with an elevation gain of 150 m (488 ft). The trail leads along the Stoney Squaw Ridge, to a lookout point. From here, panoramic views of the Bow River Valley, the Cascade Mountain Ridge, Lake Minnewanka and Mount Rundle are seen. June through September is the ideal time to explore this route.

Sulphur Mountain Trails (Map 8/B5)
This is one of Banff's most popular peaks, due in no small part to the fact that there are splendid views of Banff townsite and the Bow Valley and people can ride the gondola to the top. Some hikers and bikers will eschew this mechanized method of getting to the top. Instead, they can take a 12 km (7.4 miles) trail to the top and back from the Upper Hot Springs parking lot. It should take about five hours for hikers prepared to climb the 670 m (2,178 ft). A restaurant and

cafeteria are located at the top. Other options are to continue over the mountain to Sundance Canyon or follow the short boardwalk trail leading to Sanson Peak.

Sundance Canyon Trails (Map 8/A4)
Found close to the Banff townsite, this popular 2.5 km (1.6 mile) trail starts at the Sundance Picnic Area off of Cave Avenue. Be warned that this trail is quite busy and you will likely share the path with cyclists, rollerbladers, strollers, horseback riders or skiers and snowshoers in winter. The impressive rocky canyon and the view of Bow Valley are your rewards for climbing the many stairs along the route. The 3 km (1.8 mile) Marsh Loop can be accessed from the Sundance Trail. On this loop, you can enjoy the many species of birds as you travel past beaver dams and lodges along the Bow River. Also in the area is the Healy Creek Connector. The 4.8 km (3 mile) one-way trail follows the same route as Sundance Canyon but branches off, ultimately connecting with the Sunshine Road.

Sunset Pass Trails (Map 16/E4)
This 13.7 km (8.5 mile) trail climbs up to Sunset Pass through an extensive meadow system at the base of Mount Coleman. The first few kilometres climb steeply from the Icefields Parkway for about 3 km (1.8 miles), then levels out a bit as it passes into the Norman Meadows and Norman Lake. Sunset Pass is 4 km (2.4 miles) beyond. The Sunset Lookout Trail branches west for a 6 km (3.6 mile) return jaunt. The old fire lookout is set on the lip of an impressive limestone cliff and provides amazing views over the North Saskatchewan River. From the pass, the trail continues on to Pinto Lake, losing 415 m (1,349 ft) in 5 km (3 miles). At Pinto Lake, there are a number of trail options, including a 7 km (4.3 mile) trail around the lake and a 65 km (40.4 mile) multi-day backpack along the Pinto Lake Trail to the trailhead on Highway 11.

Taylor Lake Trail (Map 7/B2)
The trailhead to this 16 km (10 mile) trail is located at the Taylor Creek Picnic Area, off the Trans-Canada Highway. Taylor Lake is a glacier-fed lake surrounded by Mount Bell and the Panorama Ridge. There are many options to explore for this trail. From the lake, you can continue another 2 km (1.2 miles) to O'Brien Lake or 2 km (1.2 miles) to the Panorama Ridge. Optional accesses to Taylor Lake can be found at the Boom Creek Picnic Site and at Moraine Lake.

Tramline Trail (Map 12/A7)
This 4.5 km (2.8 mile) trail follows an old railway from the Station Restaurant on Sentinel Road in Lake Louise. The route climbs steadily to gain 200 m (650 ft). The Louise Creek Trails can be added on to make a 7 km (4.3 mile) loop.

Tunnel Mountain Lookout Trail (Map 8/B4)
To reach a viewpoint overlooking Bow Valley and the Banff townsite, follow this 5 km (3 mile) hiking trail. It begins in Banff, by the Banff Centre for the Performing Arts. The trail climbs steadily gaining over 250 m (813 ft).

Tunnel Mountain–Hoodoo Loop Trail (Map 8/B4)
Accessed from the Bow Falls Viewpoint, on Tunnel Mountain Road, this popular 12 km (7.4 mile) multi-use trail runs along the pretty river through forest and meadows. It eventually leads to the Hoodoos Viewpoint. The Hoodoos Interpretive Trail can be accessed at the 2.7 km (1.7 mile) T-junction.

Tyrrell Creek Trail (Map 12/F3)
The Tyrrell Creek Trail starts at the 6.4 km (4 mile) mark of the Upper Cascade Fire Road (heading southwest from Ya Ha Tinda Ranch). This difficult 11.3 km (7 mile) route travels from Red Deer River up Tyrrell Creek. It takes up to 3.5 hours one-way and gains 585 m (1,901 ft) in elevation.

Upper Hot Springs Trail (Map 8/B4)
For those looking to hike to the relaxing hot springs, a 2 km (1.2 mile) trail is available. It begins at the signed trailhead behind the Banff Springs Hotel.

Warden Lake Trail (Map 17/A6)
This hike begins at the Saskatchewan River Crossing Warden's Station and concludes at beautiful Warden Lake. The trail is 4 km (2.5 mile) return and gains 30 m (98 ft). Mid-summer to early fall is the best time to hike this trail.

Whistling Pass Loop (Map 7/D5)
This 27 km/16.8 mile wilderness circuit can be accessed by any one of three trails but the Shadow Lake Trail is the least strenuous. The loop, which climbs 820 m (2,665 ft) to a height of 2,280 m (7,410 ft), is dotted with alpine lakes and offers great views of the surrounding peaks, including the towering Pharaoh Peaks. There are four campsites along the loop, which can be used as base camps to explore the many side trails that exist (including a short trail to Scarab and Mummy Lakes).

White Man Pass Trail (Map 4/C4)
This scenic, well developed trail leads along the Upper Cross River northwest of Invermere into Banff National Park. The pass is 5.5 km (3.4 miles) from the

trailhead on the north side of the river. It is also possible to access the pass from the Palliser Pass Trail, which begins at the south end of Spray Lakes Reservoir.

Wonder Pass Trail (Map 4/B2)
This wonderful trail begins at Mcbride's Camp, 14 km (8.7 miles) along the Bryant Creek Trail. The 8.9 km (5.5 mile) trail runs past Marvel Lake and up to pass along the Great Divide. The pass is very scenic, with great views over both the southern corner of Banff and Mount Assiniboine Provincial Park, in BC. Most visitors continue down to Lake Magog.

WINTER RECREATION

Banff is a winter wonderland. Not only does the park sport three downhill ski areas (Norquay, Sunshine and Lake Louise), but also there are many, many kilometres of groomed and ungroomed cross-country trails. Add to that an almost endless opportunity for back-country ski touring and snowshoeing and you have a great place to go in the winter. The following is a list of trails that are groomed or not covered in the trails section.

Baker Creek Trail (Map 7/B1–12/C6)
This a track set trail that follows Baker Creek for 6 km (3.6 miles) and then a powerline for another 3.5 km (2.2 miles). It climbs 185 m (600 ft) and is a slightly more challenging trails for beginners.

Banff Golf Course (Map 8/B4)
Although not groomed, and often short of snow, this is an easy place for beginners to get the feel for a pair of cross-country skis.

Boom Lake Trail (Map 7/B3)
Another ungroomed trail that sees a fair bit of activity in winter, this trail is 5 km (3 mile) long. The trail climbs 170 m (560 ft) to the lake, before the cruise home.

Bow River Loop (Map 12/A7)
From the Station Restaurant or the Samson Mall in Lake Louise, this is an easy groomed and track set loop that covers 6.9 km (4.3 miles). There are a few ups and downs, but the trail is mostly level as it follows the edge of the river. It does connect with the Campground Loop.

Brewster Creek Trail (Map 7/G4–8/B7)
The Brewster Creek Fire Road branches from the Healy Creek Trail (see below), leading to the Sundance Lodge. Backcountry skiers/snowshoers can follow a network of trails beyond the lodge, but most people turn around (or stay) here. If you turn around at the lodge, you will cover 22 km (13.7 miles) by the time you get back to the parking lot. The trail is groomed and track set to this point.

Campground Loop (Map 12/A7)
A pair of short, easy loops known as the inner and outer loop cover a total distance of 4.5 km (2.8 miles). The trails connect with the Bow River Loop and are track set and groomed with a skating lane.

Cascade Trail (Map 8/B3–12/E3)
From the gate on the Lake Minnewanka Road, this long but easy backcountry trail follows the road and then turns up the Cascade valley on an old fire road. The trail is groomed and is usually in good condition. A return trip to the ranger station is 28 km (17.4 miles), with an elevation gain of 180 m (590 ft).

Castle Junction Trails (Map 7/D3)
Providing 8.7 km (5.4 miles) of track set trails in the forests surrounding the Castle Junction, these are easy trails, with little elevation gain. There are occasional views of the surrounding mountains to take in. For more backcountry options, jump over to the Forty Mile Creek area.

Fairview Loop (Map 7/A1)
From the Moraine Lake Road, this 2 km (1.2 mile) route follows the Tramline Trail to the Lake Louise parking lots, where it takes a left into the trees. The trail loops back and down to the road. There is one steep hill on this loop, which makes it a route for better skiers. Due to the hill, doing this loop in reverse is not recommended.

Forty Mile Creek (Map 8/A3–7/F1)
This trail system provides access to several great backcountry options. A good half-day trip is to follow the moderate ungroomed 5 km (3 mile) trail from the Mount Norquay parking lot to Edith Pass, losing 150 m (488 ft) along the way. If it is not quite long enough for you, you can continue another 15 km (9.3 miles) on to Mystic Lake by climbing 270 m (878 ft). This

winds up being a 40 km (24.8 mile) round trip and some skiers may have difficulty doing it on one of the short winter days, especially if they are breaking trail. Branching from the Forty Mile Creek Trail is a route up to Elk Lake. Following the Elk Pass Trail down to the Cascade River Valley can extend this route. Another option is to return via Johnson Creek. A second vehicle is recommended for these alternatives.

Great Divide Trail (Map 11/F7)
An easy groomed and track set trail follows the route of the old Highway 1A to the BC Alberta boundary. There is an exhibit here about the divide and you can continue into Yoho National Park along the Ross Lake Trail, which is an old road that is not groomed. From the parking lot to the divide is 7.5 km (4.7 miles).

Healy Creek & Pass Trail (Map 7/E5)
From the top of the Wa-Wa Chairlift at Sunshine Village Ski Area, head northeast towards a notch in the ridge, then head west across an open meadow to the top of a long descent through an open forest. Watch out for a cliff band as you head down! If you keep right, you will eventually hook up with the Healy Creek Trail, which is a steep, tricky descent. This 10 km (6.2 mile) trip is best left to advanced backcountry skiers. Alternatively, the **Healy Pass Trail** starts from the Sunshine Road climbs 640 m (2,080 ft) up to the pass and then drops 340 m (1,105 ft) down to Egypt Lake. The pass provides some good backcountry skiing (downhill) options for strong intermediate skiers.

Johnson Lake Trails (Map 8/C4)
A series of ungroomed trails follow old roads around the lake. There is one moderate section, but the majority of the 11.4 km (7 miles) of trails are easy. The longest trail is an easy 8.2 km (5 miles) circuit of the lake.

Johnston Creek Trail (Map 7/E3–12/C7)
From the Johnston Canyon parking lot, this long day trip covers 34 km (21.1 miles) to Luellen Lake, gaining 520 m (1,690 ft). A shorter option along the same trail is the Inkpots, which are only 10 km (6.2 miles) return. It is also possible to head over Mystic Pass and return via Forty Mile Creek.

Lake Louise (Map 6/G1–11/G7)
A popular area for people to get out and experience some of the charm that winter brings. From the resort, most people follow the moderate track-set ski trail along the lakeshore or snowshoe across the lake to Louise Falls to the southwest end of the lake. It is a 2.4 km (1.5 miles) one-way trip to the end of the lake. Travel beyond here is not recommended without appropriate avalanche safety equipment and knowledge.

Lake Louise Ski Area (Map 12/A7)
Located across the valley from the titular feature, the ski area at Lake Louise is the biggest in the Canadian Rockies. It is also one of the biggest resorts in North America with 4,200 skiable acres and 139 named runs. There are also plenty of off piste areas where hardcore skiers can enjoy some of the most challenging lift-accessible skiing anywhere. From top to bottom, skiers will cover 991 vertical metres (3,250 ft), with the longest run on the mountain being a quad burning 8 km (5 mile) long run. There are five chairlifts, a platter lift to the top of the West Bowl, a T-bar, a magic carpet and a gondola that takes skiers from the parking area at the base of the mountain to a ridge overlooking both the front and backsides of the mountain.

Moraine Lake Road (Map 7/A1)
Do not be fooled by the forested setting in the beginning, this is one of the prettier places to visit in winter. The route follows the unploughed road for an easy 16 km (9.6 mile) one-way trip. Although there is some elevation gained on the way to the lake, coming back is a lot easier.

Mount Norquay Ski Area (Map 8/A4)
One of Western Canada's oldest ski resorts, Mount Norquay has been a downhill destination for Banff skiers since 1926. The mountain has a reputation for offering some hardcore runs, especially off the North American Chair, one of four chairlifts and one surface lifts that service the area's 28 runs. There is 503 vertical metres (1,659 ft) and the longest run is just over a kilometre long (3,828 ft).

Paradise Valley Trail (Map 6/G2–7/A2)
Beginning from the Moraine Lake Road, this is an ungroomed (but often tracked) touring trail that climbs 410 m (1,333 ft) to the spectacular Paradise Valley Meadows. Give yourself the better part of a day to ski the popular 20 km (12.4 mile) return trip.

Pipestone Loops (Map 12/A7)
Five different loop trails are found in the Pipestone area of Lake Louise. The shortest trail is a difficult 1.5 km (1 mile) loop, while the longest is 12.6 km (7.8 miles). The rest of the trails are less than 3 km (1.8 miles) and are mostly

easy, but watch out for the occasional steep hill. Check at the Visitor Centre for information on grooming and snow conditions.

Plain of the Six Glaciers (Map 6/G1)
A spectacular backcountry trip that takes you past some of the best scenery that Banff has to offer. From the postcard-perfect Lake Louise, the 10 km (6.2 mile) return trail climbs 200 m (650 ft) into the gorgeous meadows that make up the Plain of the Six Glaciers. This trip takes you through avalanche country and is recommended for experienced backcountry skiers only.

Rock Isle Lake Trail (Map 7/F6)
Although the lake lies in British Columbia, the easiest access to it is from the Sunshine Ski Village. It is only 4 km (2.4 miles) return to the lake, gaining 110 m (358 ft). Almost all of it at the beginning of the run as you climb up from the Strawberry Chairlift to the top of Rock Isle Road. This is a perfect place for getting the feel for touring skis. From here, it is possible to continue on up Quartz Ridge (10 km/6 miles return), to Citadel Pass (20 km/12.4 miles return) or even on through Mount Assiniboine Park to Highway 93.

Rockbound Lake Trail (Map 7/D2)
This difficult 14 km (8.7 mile) trip climbs steeply up to a beautiful open valley and Rockbound Lake. You will gain 760 m (2,470 ft) on your way to the lake, but the real trick is coming down the fairly narrow, sometimes icy trail.

Shadow Lake Trail (Map 7/D4)
From the trailhead on the Trans-Canada Highway, 20 km (12.4 miles) west of Banff, this moderate track set trail takes you 14.5 km (9 miles) to the Shadow Lake Lodge, climbing 325 m (1,050 ft) along the way. From here it is possible to continue on to Haiduk Lake (14 km/8.7 miles return to the lodge) or Ball Pass (12 km/7.5 miles return).

Skoki Valley (Map 12/A7–B6)
Built in the 1930s, the Skoki Lodge makes a great winter destination since it is situated in a perfect valley for backcountry touring. From the lodge, possible routes include the Skoki Mountain Loop (an easy 9 km/5.6 mile return trip), the Natural Bridge (an easy 16 km/10 mile return trip), Fossil Mountain (a moderate 11 km/7 mile return trip), Oyster Lake (a moderate 12 km/7.5 miles return trip) and Merlin Valley (a difficult 6 km/3.6 miles return trip). There are also a number of great slopes to sample, including Packers Peak, Merlin Ridge and the Wolverine Slopes. Accessing the lodge requires a moderate 11 km (6.8 mile) trip from the Lake Louise Ski Area.

Spray River Loop (Map 8/B4)
From the Bow Falls parking lot, an easy 12.5 km (7.8 mile) loop tracks through the rolling forested terrain around the Banff townsite. The trail is groomed and track set, with an elevation gain of 200 m (660 ft).

Sundance Canyon Trail (Map 8/A4)
From the Cave and Basin Historic Site, it is an easy 3.7 km (2.3 mile) climb up to the Sundance Canyon. Well. It climbs, but only 30 m (100 ft). The route is track set, but lack of snow and sometime high winds can make the conditions sketchy. Hikers/snowshoers also use this route and not all of them stay off the groomed trail. Also in the area is the Healy Creek Connector. The 4.8 km (3 mile) one-way trail follows the same route as Sundance Canyon but branches off, ultimately connecting with the Sunshine Road.

Telemark Loop (Map 11/G7)
Divided into two sections above and below the Great Divide Trail, people will find the upper trail is much more difficult to ski. The Lower Telemark Loop is an 8.3 km (5.2 mile) track set trail that meanders through the forest near the Great Divide, while the upper section is a 9.3 km (5.8 miles) trip.

Tramline (Map 12/A7)
An easy 4.5 km (2.7 mile) trail that follows an old railbed from Lake Louise the town to Lake Louise the lake. The route begins at The Station Restaurant on Sentinel Road and climbs steadily, gaining 200 m (655 ft). The Louise Creek Trails can be added on to make a 7 km (4.3 mile) loop.

Wapta Icefield (Map 11/B3–D5)
One of the prime destinations for backcountry skiers and mountaineers in Canada, there are many advanced routes in this area that require good route finding skills and the ability to cross glaciers. If you are interested in exploring this area, contact the Alpine Club of Canada, who maintains a number of huts in the area.

WILDLIFE VIEWING

Where can you see wildlife in Banff? Where can't you see it? It is the rare trip down the Trans-Canada where you don't see a herd of elk or a group of bighorn sheep or a deer or a bear. The ease with which wildlife is spotted is one of the big draws to the park. Still, there are some places that are better than others. Here are a few of the best.

Banff Townsite (Map 8/B4)
Birders will find a number of areas around the Banff townsite great places to see songbirds, swallows and some raptors. The best places to find birds are at the foot of Tunnel Mountain and the Bow River (above the Bow River Bridge). Spring is a good time to see songbirds here, as the valley melts faster than elsewhere in the park. Dippers overwinter at Bow Falls, while elk are commonly seen along the road to the golf course.

Bow River & Summit (Map 11/D3–8/B4)
The Bow River is important habitat for waterfowl and shorebirds and there are a number of breeding areas along its shores. The valley is also home to large number of deer. The open sub-alpine forest of the Bow Summit (20 km/12 miles north on the Icefields Parkway) provides good habitat for mountain birds, like thrushes, Clarks Nutcrackers, ptarmigan, Water Pipts and Mountain Bluebird.

Cave and Basin Marsh (Map 8/B4)
Located 2 km (1.2 miles) west of the Banff townsite, these large wetlands is fed by the hot springs, which means that it usually remains partially ice-free over winter. It is a good place to see song and shore birds and waterfall, especially in spring and fall.

Johnston Canyon (Map 7/E3)
Johnston Canyon is one of only three known breeding sites in Alberta for the Black Swift. The nests can be hard to spot, high on the canyon walls, but you stand a good chance of spotting one around dawn and dusk. The area is also home to a large population of dippers and the surrounding forest is home to a number of songbirds.

Lake Minnewanka (Map 8/D3)
The rocky terrain around the lake is good bighorn sheep terrain and it is extremely common to come across groups of sheep wandering alongside the road.

Mount Norquay Road (Map 8/B4)
The road up to Mount Norquay is surrounded by rocky cliffs and is good bighorn sheep terrain. Sightings are very common.

Sulphur Mountain (Map 8/B5)
Bighorn sheep are commonly seen at the top of the Sulphur Mountain Skyride.

Vermilion Lakes (Map 8/B4)
The Vermilion Lakes are a large wetland area found west of the Banff townsite. It is the best place in the park to see wildlife, especially waterfowl. You will also find shorebirds and raptors like osprey and Bald Eagles. Large ungulates, especially elk, are also common in the area.

LIST OF BACKCOUNTRY CAMPSITES

Campsite	Map	Type	Accessed By
Allenby Junction	4/B1	hike	Bryant Creek Trail
Aylmer Canyon	8/D3	hike, bike, horse	Lake Minnewanka Trail
Badger Pass Junction	7/D1	hike, horse	Johnston Creek Trail
Baker Lake	12/C6	hike, horse	Skoki Valley Trail, Baker Creek Trail
Ball Pass Junction	7/C5	hike, horse	Whistling Pass Loop
Big Springs	4/C2	hike	Bryant Creek Trail
Birdwood	4/D3	hike, horse	Palliser Pass Trail
Block Lakes Junction	7/E1	hike, horse	Badger Pass Trail
Bow River-Canoe	7/E3	paddle	Bow River
Brewster Creek	8/A6	hike, bike, horse	Brewster Creek Trail
Cascade Bridge	8/B2	hike, bike, horse	Lower Cascade Fire Road

Campsite	Map	Type	Accessed By
Castlerguard	16/A4	hike, horse	Castleguard Meadows Route
Egypt Lake	7/D5	hike, horse	Pharaoh Creek Trail, Healy Pass Trail
Elk Lake Summit	8/A3	hike, horse	Elk Lake Trail
Fish Lakes	11/G4	hike	Fish Lakes Trail
Flint's Park	12/F7	hike, horse	Forty Mile Creek Trail, Flint's Park Trail
Ghost Lakes	8/E3	hike, horse	Devil's Gap Trail
Glacier Lake	16/F7	hike, horse	Glacier Lake Trail
Healy Creek	7/E5	hike, bike	Healy Pass Trail
Hector Lake	11/F5	hike, horse	Hector Lake Trail
Hidden Lake	12/B6	hike	Skoki Valley Trail
Howard Douglas	7/F6	hike, horse	Citadel Pass Trail
Johnston Creek	7/D2	hike, horse	Johnston Creek Trail
Lake Minnewanka	8/C3	hike, bike, horse	Lake Minnewanka Trail
Larry's Camp	7/E2	hike, horse	Mystic Pass Trail, Johnston Creek Trail
Leman Lake	4/D4	hike, horse	Leman Lake Trail
Lost Horse Creek	7/E4	hike, bike, horse	Shadow Lake Trail
Luellan Lake	7/D2	hike, horse	Johnston Creek Trail
Marvel Lake	4/B2	hike	Bryant Creek Trail
Mcbride's Camp	4/B1	hike	Bryant Creek Trail
Merlin Meadows	12/B6	hike	Lake Merlin Trail
Molar Creek	11/G5	hike	Molar Pass Trail
Mosquito Creek	11/F4	hike	Mosquito Creek Trail
Mount Cockscomb	7/G3	hike, bike, horse	Forty Mile Creek Trail
Mount Costigan	8/E3	hike, bike, horse	Lake Minnewanka Trail
Mount Inglismaldie	8/D3	hike, bike, horse	Lake Minnewanka Trail
Mount Rundle	8/B5	hike, bike, horse	Spray River Fire Road, Mount Rundle Trail
Mystic Junction	7/G2	hike, bike, horse	Forty Mile Creek Trail
Mystic Valley	7/F2	hike, horse	Mystic Pass Trail
Norman Lake	16/E4	Hike, horse	Sunset Pass Trail
Paradise Valley	6/G1	hike, horse	Paradise Valley Trail
Pharaoh Creek	7/D5	hike, horse	Pharaoh Creek Trail
Red Deer Lakes	12/B6	hike	Red Deer River Trail, Cotton Grass Pass Trail
Sawback Lake	7/F1	hike	Forty Mile Creek Trail
Shadow Lake	7/D4	hike, horse	Shadow Lake Trail, Gibbon Pass Trail
Siffleur River	11/E2	hike, horse	Clearwater Valley Trail
Stony Creek	8/A1	hike, bike, horse	Lower Cascade Fire Road, Elk Lake Trail
Taylor Lake	7/B2	hike, horse	Taylor Lake Trail, Panorama Ridge Route
The Narrows	8/E3	hike, bike, horse	Lake Minnewanka Trail
Twin Lakes	7/C4	hike, horse	Arnica Lake Trail, Gibbon Pass Trail
Wildflower	12/C7	hike, horse	Baker Creek Trail, Pulsatilla Pass Trail

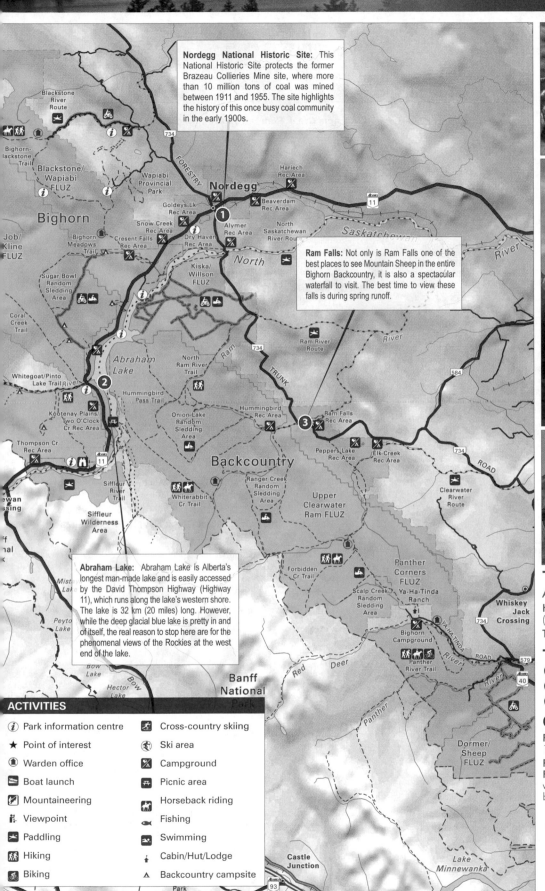

Nordegg National Historic Site: This National Historic Site protects the former Brazeau Collieries Mine site, where more than 10 million tons of coal was mined between 1911 and 1955. The site highlights the history of this once busy coal community in the early 1900s.

Ram Falls: Not only is Ram Falls one of the best places to see Mountain Sheep in the entire Bighorn Backcountry, it is also a spectacular waterfall to visit. The best time to view these falls is during spring runoff.

Abraham Lake: Abraham Lake is Alberta's longest man-made lake and is easily accessed by the David Thompson Highway (Highway 11), which runs along the lake's western shore. The lake is 32 km (20 miles) long. However, while the deep glacial blue lake is pretty in and of itself, the real reason to stop here are for the phenomenal views of the Rockies at the west end of the lake.

ACTIVITIES

- ⓘ Park information centre
- ★ Point of interest
- Warden office
- Boat launch
- Mountaineering
- Viewpoint
- Paddling
- Hiking
- Biking
- Cross-country skiing
- Ski area
- Campground
- Picnic area
- Horseback riding
- Fishing
- Swimming
- Cabin/Hut/Lodge
- ▲ Backcountry campsite

Image © Brian Lang

THINGS TO KNOW

Area: 485, 622 hectares
Highest Point: Mount Cline 3,361 metres (11,027 feet)
Total Vehicle Accessible Campsites: 331

THINGS TO SEE

1 Nordegg National Historic Site
2 Abraham Lake
3 Ram Falls

CONTACT INFORMATION

Parks and Protected Areas:
1-866-427-3582, www.albertaparks.ca
Rocky Mountain House Clearwater Area Provincial Office 403-845-8250
www.srd.gov.ab.ca/fieldoffices/clearwater/bighornbackcountry/default.aspx

BighornWildlandAdventures

The Bighorn Backcountry is a sprawling area just east of Banff National Park made up of six adjoining Forest Land Use Zones. From north to south, these are: Blackstone/Wapiabi, Job/Cline, Upper Clearwater/Ram, Kiska/Wilson, Panther/Corners and Dormer/Sheep. We have also included the surrounding wilderness areas: Siffleur and Whitegoat to cover an area well over 5,000 sq km (1,930 sq miles) that included rugged alpine terrain, low forested valleys and shaggy foothills. While parts of it were to be set-aside as a Wildland Area back in 1986, the area was never officially designated. However, parts of this area are treated like a park in all but name.

The Bighorn contains breathtaking mountainous backcountry terrain and very few facilities or services, so it is best left to the experienced outdoors person to explore. In total, the Bighorn has about 700 km (435 miles) of trails. These trails, which are popular with ATVers, snowmobilers, hikers, horseback riders and cross-country skiers, are mostly old pack trails established in the early 1900s and a number of mineral exploration roads and trails. There are rustic backcountry campsites designated at Landslide Lake, Lake of the Falls, Pinto Lake and Waterfalls Creek as well as many informal sites throughout the area.

The stream fishing for trout is considered the best in the province where as some of the high elevation sub-alpine lakes have been stocked with the unique golden trout. Wildlife, from birds to large mammals, is commonly seen throughout the area. In fact, hunting for trophy bighorn sheep is internationally recognized here.

The main access points are provided along Highway 11, the Forestry Trunk Road (Secondary Highway 734) and Red Deer River Roads. Access off Highway 11, which cuts through the heart of the Bighorn, is limited to mostly trail access. Running up the eastern spine, the Forestry Trunk provides good access tom the many smaller roads that provide access into the Bighorn. Do note that motorized vehicles are prohibited in many areas, including the entire Blackstone/Wapiabi FLUZ and most of the Job/Cline. These two Land Use Zones comprise the majority of the Bighorn found on these maps.

Just to make it interesting, each FLUZ has its own rules and regulations, so if you're going to the Bighorn to snowmobile, note that snowmobiles are not allowed in the Blackstone/Wapiabi or Panther Corners. Other FLUZes have area or timing closures. People heading out with ATVs should also check the regulations regarding closures in the various FLUZes that make up the Bighorn.

CAMPING

People looking for a base to for their outdoor pursuits will find a series of provincial and forestry recreation areas as well as random camping areas around the Bighorn. These sites range from roadside camping areas with little more than picnic tables, fire pits and pit toilets to remote backcountry sits with no facilities. Most camping areas are open from May to October, but some of the recreation areas also have limited camping during the winter months.

Aylmer Recreation Area (Map 30/Inset)
Aylmer Recreation Area is used as a staging area for the Aylmer hiking/equestrian trails (30 km of trails) as well as a boat launch facility for paddlers on the North Saskatchewan River. Fishing and hunting are also popular at the seven unit site.

Crescent Falls Recreation Area (Map 24/E6)
Located next to Crescent Falls on the Bighorn River, this recreation area has 26 camping sites and a picnic area with six tables. There are hiking/equestrian trails nearby as well as river fishing for bull trout, cutthroat and rocky mountain whitefish. The access road from Highway 11 is very steep and narrows in places.

Cutoff Creek Recreation Area (Map 18/G6)
Mostly a parking area for people heading into the Bighorn, people do camp here and a few random, semi-organized sites have been developed. However, there are no services, toilets or fire pits. The site is used mostly by horseback riders and hikers, although some ATVers stage here as well.

Dry Haven Creek Recreation Area (Map 24/G6)
On Highway 11 about 14 km (8.7 miles) west of Nordegg, this recreation area is a popular overnight stop for travellers. There are 14 campsites as well as six tables and a picnic shelter at the day-use area. Visitors can try their luck fishing or hike the trails found nearby.

Eagle Creek Recreation Area (Map 13/B2)
This Forest Recreation Area (one of only a handful of Forestry sites left along the foothills) has a few gravel campsites, equestrian tie facilities, toilets and some fire pits. Very few people camp here, though, as the site is mainly used as a staging area for equestrian trips into the Bighorn. There are occasionally hikers who start here as well.

Elk Creek Recreation Areas (Map 18/G4)
In addition to a fishpond, visitors can explore the number of informal trails in the area. The main site offers room for 13 camping units along with a day-use area.

Fish Lake Recreation Area (Map 30/Inset)
Also called Shunda Lake, Fish Lake is located 8 km (4.8 miles) west of Nordegg on Highway 11. There are 92 campsites as well as a picnic area. The lake is ideal for fishing or paddling, while the trails are enjoyed year round.

Goldeye Lake Recreation Area (Map 24/G5)
Set on the shores of Goldeye Lake, this recreation area has a total of 44 campsites and a day-use area. A series of hiking/cross-country skiing trails provide land based activities while fishing and paddling on Goldeye Lake are possible.

Hummingbird Recreation Area (Map 18/C4)
The Hummingbird Forest Recreation Area is a popular staging area for trips into the Bighorn Backcountry. The site is also a popular destination with campers, with up to 130 groups camping there at one time. While there are plans afoot to formalize the camping area and to expand the parking area to 40 vehicles, the site is currently unimproved.

Kootenay Plains/Two O'Clock Creek Recreation Area (Map 17/D5)
Found next to Kootenay Plains Ecological Reserve, Two O'Clock Creek Campground has 24 campsites together with a day-use area, while nearby Cavalcade Campground is for group camping only. The river offers good fishing and the surrounding trails are used by hikers, mountain bikers and in winter, cross-country skiers.

Peppers Lake Recreation Area (Map 18/G5)
The foothills open up west of Peppers Lake, offering a wonderful view of the front range of the Rocky Mountains. In addition to a hiking trail around the lake, there is an equestrian staging area 2 km (1.2 miles) to the east of the lake. But the real reason people come to Peppers Lake is to fish for brook trout. There is a launch for electric motor boats only at the east end of the lake.

Ram Falls Recreation Area (Map 18/E4)
Located next to popular Ram Falls, this recreation area has 54 campsites as well as a large day-use area. The highlight of the area is the falls. However, it is also a good wildlife viewing area and a good staging area for a variety of outdoor pursuits. The Forestry Trunk Road reaches the recreation area, about 64 km (39.8 miles) south of Nordegg.

Siffleur Wilderness Area (Map 11, 17)
This 255 square kilometre wilderness area contains picturesque valleys, high peaks, alpine meadows and an abundance of wildlife. It offers backpacking, climbing and camping in the summer as well as snowshoeing and backcountry skiing in the winter. There are no vehicles or pack animals allowed in the wilderness area and no fishing in the river. Access is best from the Siffleur Falls Trail near Abraham Lake.

Snow Creek Recreation Area (Map 24/G6)

This group campsite is open year-round and is used as a staging ground to the local attractions such as the Crescent Falls, Bighorn Dam and Goldeye Lake. Campsite reservations can be made by calling (403) 721-3975.

Thompson Creek Recreation Area (Map 17/B5)

Located just outside the gates of Banff National Park on Highway 11, this recreation site has 55 campsites as well as a day-use area with two picnic shelters and picnic tables. Thompson Creek provides fishing for brook trout.

White Goat Wilderness Area (Map 16, 17, 23)

Another large wilderness area bordering on the Bighorn proper, this remote 445 square kilometre area contains hanging glaciers, alpine meadows, waterfalls and beautiful mountain lakes. The area offers backpacking, climbing and camping in the summer as well as backcountry skiing and snowshoeing during the winter. No vehicles or pack animals are allowed within the wilderness area, which is also closed to hunting and fishing to help protect the active wildlife corridor.

Wild Horse Recreation Area (Map 13/D4)

Located next to Wild Horse Creek, as it flows into the Red Deer River, this group recreation area is open from May–September. The area has hiking and equestrian trails as well as snowmobile trails in the winter.

Ya Ha Tinda Ranch (Map 13/A2–12/G3)

The Ya Ha Tinda Ranch is a privately run ranch owned by Parks Canada to winter and train horses for use in the National Parks in the area. It covers 3,945 hectares, running 27 km along the north bank of the Red Deer River. It is home to the rustic Bighorn Campground, which has limited facilities and is free to use. The area is used mainly by horseback riders accessing Banff, although hikers and hunters do visit the area. Large animals, such as bear, wolf, elk, moose, deer, and bighorn sheep, also call this area home. Because of this, campers are required to clean their sites and be bear aware. The Ya Ha Tinda Ranch area was formerly within the boundaries of Rocky Mountains National Park before the present day Banff National Park boundary was established.

FISHING

There are many rivers that flow out of the Bighorn Backcountry; many of these are also found in the Forestry Trunk Area where access is easier. However, those willing to put in that extra effort will find some very good options with few visitors. There are also some very remote mountain lakes and a few stocked options (noted with the 🐟 symbol). If we missed a stream, be sure to check the Forestry Trunk section.

Abraham Lake (Map 17/D2)

Abraham Lake is Alberta's longest man-made lake and is easily accessed by the David Thompson Highway (Highway 11), which runs along the lake's western shore. The lake contains brook trout, cutthroat and rocky mountain whitefish (to 1 kg/2 lbs) as well as some large bull trout (to 5 kg/10 lbs). The odd lake trout and rainbow can also be caught. The best time to fish is in fall through to ice up and the best places to try are near the Bighorn Dam at the north end of the lake or at one of the creek estuaries. Keep in mind that there is a size restriction for the cutthroat and rainbow trout and a bait ban on both the lake and its tributaries.

Allstones Lake (Map 17/D1) 🐟

This small lake is accessed by the Allstones Lake Trail, a 2 km (1.2 mile) one-way trail leading from Highway 11 near the shores of Abraham Lake. The lake contains stocked brook trout that are best taken by spincasting a lure with bait. A two trout limit is in effect.

Bighorn River (Map 24/B7–F7)

The Bighorn River, which is open from June 16 to October 31, drains a large area of the Bighorn Backcountry into the North Saskatchewan River north of Abraham Lake. It is best accessed along most of its length by trail from Crescent Falls. The river contains brown and cutthroat trout as well as rocky mountain whitefish (all to 1 kg/2 lbs) and bull trout (to 2.5 kg/5 lbs) below

Crescent Falls. Above the falls, smaller cutthroat inhabit the waters so it is difficult to catch fish that you can keep (greater than 30 cm/12 inches). Below the falls, the cutthroat must be a minimum of 35 cm (14 inches) to keep. Camping is offered at the Crescent Falls Recreation Area.

Brazeau River (Map 16, 23, 29, 30)

The Brazeau River forms the boundary between Jasper National Park and the Bighorn Backcountry. To reach the headwaters, you must hike from Highway 93 on the Nigel Creek and South Boundary Trails for at least 20 km (12 miles) one-way. As a result, there are few fishermen that sample these fast waters. There are only a few small cutthroat and bull trout near the headwaters. Note that where the river forms the boundary of Jasper, a national park fishing licence is required.

Clearwater River (Map 11, 12, 18, 19)

The short stretch of this river that is found in the Bighorn is rarely fished. Anglers should also note that Tributaries upstream of Timber Creek (Map 18/G6) are permanently closed to fishing. See the Forestry Trunk Road section for more details on this stream.

Cline River (Map 16/F3–17/D3)

The Cline River drains Pinto Lake into Abraham Lake. The river is accessed by the Pinto Lake and the Whitegoat Trails along most of its length. It contains bull trout (to 2 kg/4 lbs), rocky mountain whitefish (to 1 kg/2 lbs) and brook trout (to 0.5 kg/1 lb) below the canyon and cutthroat (to 1 kg/2 lbs) above the canyon. The cutthroat must be 30 cm (12 inches) to keep and the river and its tributaries are closed to fishing from November 1 to June 15.

Coral Lake (Map 16/G1)

A long hike up from Highway 11 near Abraham Lake along the Coral Creek Trail brings anglers to this tiny sub-alpine lake. The lake is seldom fished because of its difficult access, but it does contain the highly sought after golden trout. There is a bait ban in affect at the lake as well as a limit of one trout over 40 cm (15 inches).

Entry Creek & Lake (Map 17/C4) 🐟

This small creek and lake are found just north of Landslide Lake. The lake contains a few stocked cutthroat to 30 cm (12 inches), while the creek also offers small bull trout.

Goldeye Lake (Map 24/G5) 🐟

Goldeye Lake is accessed off Highway 11 west of Nordegg and offers camping. The lake is stocked annually with rainbow, which can grow to 2.5 kg (5 lbs) in size. There is an electric motor only restriction at the lake.

Hummingbird & Onion Creeks (Map 18/A5–C4)

These two creeks join to flow into the Ram River at the Hummingbird Recreation Area. They hold small cutthroat and are accessed by the Onion Lake Road and a series of trails in the area.

Joyce River (Map 18/C1)

Joyce River is a short river that drains into the North Ram River. It is accessed by hiking the Joyce River Trail off the Forestry Trunk Road. The river has good numbers of small cutthroat. However, fishing is catch and release.

Lake of the Falls (Map 17/B4)

This remote lake sees few anglers as it is about a 20 km (12.4 mile) one-way hike in. Those that venture in will find plenty of small cutthroat and some large bull trout, taken primarily on lures. You cannot keep bull trout and the possession and size limit of cutthroat is two fish, which must be 30 cm (12 inches). There is a bait ban in affect.

Michele Lake (Map 16/G4)

Few fishermen sample the waters of Michele Lake because it can only be reached by a long, difficult hike up the Cline River and then bushwhacking up Waterfalls Creek. The lake is said to have good fishing for golden trout that reach 1 kg (2 lbs) in size. However, there are many restrictions on the lake to help this rare fish survive.

North Saskatchewan River (Map 16, 17, 24)

The glacier fed North Saskatchewan River is one of the largest rivers in Alberta. It begins in the northern section of Banff National Park and flows in a south-easterly direction past Rocky Mountain House, through Edmonton and into Saskatchewan. Above Abraham Lake, the river is silty and fishing can be slow. Below Abraham Lake, the river provides a good fishery for brook, brown, bull and cutthroat trout as well as rocky mountain whitefish. There are also a number of restrictions in this area.

Obstruction Lakes (Map 23/F6)
These high elevation lakes are found in the Bighorn Backcountry and are seldom fished due to their remote location. The lakes are stocked semi-annually and hold cutthroat to 1.5 kg (3 lbs) taken by fly-fishing or spincasting. There are a number of restrictions to note on the lakes.

Panther River (Map 12/E6–13/D4)
Although the headwaters of the Panther River are in Banff National Park, most of the fishing occurs outside the park near its estuary with the Red Deer River. The estuary is next to the Forestry Trunk Road where spincasting and fly-fishing for bull trout (to 1.5 kg/3 lb), cutthroat (to 0.5 kg/1 lb) and rocky mountain whitefish (to 1 kg/2 lbs) can be productive.

Peppers Lake (Map 18/G5)
Peppers Lake offers a nice campground and a series of trails to explore. For the angler, it contains stocked brook trout that are best caught by spincasting a lure with bait in the spring. There is an electric motor only restriction on the lake.

Ram & North Ram Rivers (Map 17, 18)
Access into the headwaters of the Ram River is extremely limited except by a long trail (South Ram River Trail). The river has some big cutthroat, some of which are rumoured to grow to a monstrous 60 cm (24 inches) upstream of Ram Falls.

The North Ram River begins to the east of the Kootenay Plains Natural Area and drains into the Ram River further east. Like the Ram itself, the North Ram is known for its great cutthroat trout fishing. It is a catch and release only freestone river, with cutthroat up to (and greater than) 50 cm (20 inches), although those are certainly the exceptions. The river is 50 km (31 miles) long and the section above the Forestry Trunk Road is only accessible by trail.

Red Deer River (Map 12, 13, 14)
The Red Deer River is a big river, with its headwaters at Red Deer Lakes in Banff. The river flows in a northeastern direction, draining a large area east of Banff including a section of the Bighorn. Good fishing for brown trout is offered in the upper reaches of the river west of the Forestry Trunk Road. Other species in the river include rocky mountain whitefish (to 1.5 kg/3 lb) and some walleye. Please note the river is heavily regulated.

Shunda [Fish] Lake & Creek (Map 30 Inset)
Shunda Lake has fair fishing for stocked rainbow (to 2 kg/4 lbs) best caught by fly-fishing or spincasting. Home of the Fish Lake Recreation Area, there is an electric motor only restriction on the lake. Due to the easy access, ice fishing is also popular. The creek actually runs along the highway north of Nordegg and provides brown trout and whitefish.

Tershishner Creek (Map 24/E7)
Tershishner Creek drains into the north end of the Abraham Lake. It has brook trout to 0.5 kg (1 lb) as well as rocky mountain whitefish to 1 kg (2 lbs) and bull trout to 2 kg (4 lbs).

PADDLING

Flowing out of the Rockies, there are some roaring whitewater streams to test. However, those interested in flatwater or lakes will only find a few alternatives, such as pretty Abraham Lake. For each river, we have included a brief description, the put-in and take-out locations and have graded the rivers using a modified version of the International River Classification System. Please remember that river conditions are always subject to change and advanced scouting is essential. You should always obtain more details from a local merchant or expert before heading out on your adventure.

Abraham Lake (Map 9/D7)
Abraham Lake is a big lake at the edge of the mountains that was formed by the damming of the North Saskatchewan River in 1972. It is the largest man-made lake in Alberta. It is a beautiful lake that is easily accessed off Highway 11 and on the rare day when the wind isn't blowing, it can be a marvelous paddle. Don't get too far out, though, as the wind can pick up in minutes.

Bighorn River (Map 24/E6)
From Crescent Falls, this paddle stretches 6 km (3.7 miles/3.5–5 hours) to Highway 11. The paddle is a tough Grade III route in low water and Grade IV in high water. It leads through a V-shaped canyon with one waterfall that must be portaged and five others that can be paddled, but only by experienced kayakers.

Cline River (Map 16/F3–17/D3)
Highway 11 crosses the Cline just before the river flows into Abraham Lake and that's it for road access. The entire Cline is seldom paddled because of the 10 km (6.2 mile) carry up and over Sunset Pass to Pinto Lake. If the hike does not discourage you, then be prepared for a 30 km (2–3 day) Grade III/IV paddle, with nearly continuous rapids. Near the end at the Highway 11 Bridge, the Coral Creek Canyon provides the biggest challenge and is rated Grade IV/V. The canyon can be portaged around. Most paddlers just run the river from the Coral Creek Canyon, as it is the easiest accessible run on the river. You will still have to hike up about 3 km (1.8 miles) to the top of the run and then paddle down through a very narrow, steep-walled canyon leading to the Cline River and the take-out at the bridge on Highway 11. Sweepers and other debris often block the route, so it is imperative that the whole creek is scouted before attempting this Grade IV route. Most people take at least three hours to paddle this section, which attests to the difficulty of the route.

Hummingbird Creek (Map 18/C4–D4)
Take the Onion Lake Road off the Forestry Trunk Road to the put-in located downstream of the gorge and waterfalls on Hummingbird Creek. A short hike down a steep gully from the road brings you to the start. From there, it is a short (3 km/1.8 mile) 1–2 hour Grade II paddle in high water and Grade III paddle in low water. The first half of the paddle brings you through a steep-walled canyon of the creek with several short drops before breaking out onto the Ram River and the take-out, which is located at the end of a short trail on the Onion Lake Road approximately 3.5 km (2.3 miles) from the junction with the Forestry Trunk Road.

Ram River: Upper South Ram Canyon (Map 18/D4)
This paddle begins where the Hummingbird Creek paddle ends (approximately 3.5 km/2.2 miles along the Onion Lake Road). From there, this Grade II paddle extends 8 km (5 miles/1–2 hours) to the take-out near the Ram River Bridge on the Forestry Trunk Road (reached by a short road leading upstream from the bridge). The paddle begins on a gravel bar before entering a short, exciting canyon and soon breaks out into a wider section of the river with few rapids. Don't miss the take-out, as the 30 metre (100 foot) high Ram Falls are downstream.

Red Deer River (Map 13/B2–E4)
The Red Deer River is considered one of the best paddling rivers in Alberta with some challenging paddling in the foothills between Bighorn Creek and Coalcamp Creek. The furthest upstream most people put in is near the Bighorn Creek confluence near the campsite at the Ya Ha Tinda Ranch. Paddlers will have to walk about a kilometre from the campsite to the put-in on the Red Deer River. From here, it is a 26 km (16.2 mile/6–8 hour) Grade II paddle through an open valley. The first 5 km (3 miles) of the paddle is heavily braided, with lots of shallow channels and the occasional sweeper, logjam and boulder garden. Below this, the river stays in a single channel and picks up speed offering a series of ledges and small rapids.

Siffleur River (Map 17/E7–D4)
The Siffleur River is a challenging, remote wilderness paddle, which can only be reached by a strenuous 7 km (4.3 mile) portage along the Siffleur Falls Trail. If the hike does not discourage you then the challenging 6 km (3.7 mile/4–5 hour) Grade IV/V paddle might. The run takes you through a series of canyons with very challenging whitewater sections, particularly in the canyon below the lower falls. Portions of these canyons must be portaged depending on your skill level. After reaching the confluence with the North Saskatchewan River, a short paddle brings you to the take-out at the south end of Abraham Lake.

TRAILS

Butting up to the National Parks to the east, there is a tremendous variety of hiking, biking and equestrian trails to explore in this area. Although OHV and snowmobile systems have many restrictions, you will still find some of the best riding in the province here. Adding to the mix are many longer trails that lead into wilderness areas few people ever get to.

Allstones Lake & Creek Trails (Map 17/E1)
The sharp walls of the gorge provide the backdrop for the hiker as the All-stones Creek Trail leads upstream. There are numerous stream crossings, making the footing quite tricky. This 5.5 km (3.4 mile) trail gains 80 m (260 ft) in elevation en route to the 6 metre (20 foot) high waterfall. The Allstones Lake Trail is 12 km (7.4 miles) long and requires a full day if the hiker stops to admire the spectacular view during the steady 560 m (1820 ft) gain in

elevation. Camping is possible around the crystal clear lake. The trails can be accessed through the campsites on the east side of Highway 11 or along a gravel road south of the causeway across the creek.

Aylmer Trail (Map 30/Inset–24/F7) 🥾🏇

Hikers also enjoy this popular equestrian trail. It begins from the Forestry Trunk Road at the Aylmer Recreation Area. The moderate day hike leads 19 km (11.8 miles) one-way along the North Saskatchewan River to the David Thompson Highway. There is minimal elevation gain of 55 m (179 ft). A less developed route leads west along the North Saskatchewan, eventually meeting a series of undeveloped trails near Abraham Lake.

Bighorn River Trails (Map 24/E6) ⛺🥾🏇🏊ℹ️

The Crescent Falls Recreation Area provides access to several excellent trails. The Bighorn Canyon/Crescent Falls Trail is an easy 3 km (1.8 mile) one-way hike through the Bighorn Canyon to some gorgeous falls. The Bighorn Meadows Trail leads to a sub-alpine meadow. You gain 270 m (878 ft) over the moderate 18 km (11.2 mile) route. There are a couple of creek crossings along the way. The Bighorn River Trail is a 23 km (14.3 mile) route that should take seven hours to hike. It leads through a mountain forest and terrace meadows, with scattered campsites along the way. The true highlight of this trail is the scenic alpine lakes, which require some bushwhacking through steep terrain. In all you will gain 1,130 m (3,673 ft). If this is not enough, you can continue on to the Littlehorn Creek Valley along a seldom-used trail.

Bighorn–Blackstone Trail (Map 24/B3–E5) ⛺🥾🏇

This is a 47 km (29.2 mile) trail that links the Wapiabi Creek area with the Blackstone River from the Crescent Falls Road. Because of the flat terrain, it is great for horseback riding. It leads through forested land and valleys with a few creek crossings. Campsites can be found along the way.

Blackstone Gap Trail & Chungo Gap Circuit (Map 24/E3–A2)
⛺🎣🥾🚴🏇🏍️ℹ️

A series of trails are found along the Blackstone River west of the recreation area. ATVs are no longer permitted past the Blackstone Gap and this is a popular horseback riding area due to the gentle terrain. The actual Blackstone Gap Trail begins 21 km (13 miles) west of the recreation area (at the end of the ATV accessible road). This moderate trail follows the river for about 13 km (8 miles) and past the gap. Side trails lead through an open meadow to reach the three Mons Lakes, climbing a total of 220 m (715 ft) and along Opabin Creek. The Blackstone/Chungo Gap Circuit travels 46 km (28.6 miles) as it heads up through Chungo Gap and through the spectacular front range of the Rockies.

Brazeau River Trail (Map 23/E6–29/F7) 🥾🏇ℹ️🏍️🏊

The Brazeau River Trail is one of only three trails in the Job/Cline FLUZ that is open to motorized traffic. This is in addition to non-motorized use throughout the year. It enters the FLUZ from the north, following the Brazeau River. Outside the FLUZ, there are a number of cutlines and old roads that converge on the trail, but from the trailhead near Brazeau Canyon Wildland Provincial Park to the forestry patrol cabin at Whisker Creek, where off-road access ends, the trail is about 64 km (40 miles) long. This is as far as ATVs and snowmobiles can travel, but horseback riders can continue to Job Lake or along the Job Creek Trail to hook up with the MacDonald Creek Trail in the White Goat Wilderness or to the Coral Creek Trail. The Brazeau River Trail passes through some extremely scenic country, with Tarpeian Rock to the east and the mountains of Jasper across the river to the west. Despite the vertical topography of the area, this trail is quite flat as it makes its way along the river. The trail is open to off-highway vehicles from July 1 to March 15 and to snowmobiles from December 1 to April 30. The trail has long muddy stretches, which keeps most hikers out.

Bridge Creek Trail (Map 17/D4) 🥾ℹ️

Accessed on the north bank of Bridge Creek (Off Highway 11), this is a moderate 6 km (3.7 mile) return hike. Bushwhacking and many stream crossing are necessary when hiking this trail. However, you will be rewarded with a very pretty waterfall.

Canary Creek Trail (Map 18/B5) 🥾🏇ℹ️🏍️🏊

A difficult, 20 km (12.5 mile) multi-use route begins at the Hummingbird Creek Recreation Area off Onion Lake Road. To start, you must ford Onion Creek. From here the route leads through meadows and climbs into the Ram Range. It ends at a junction, where you may continue to either Ram River or along Hummingbird Creek. Mid-June to mid-October is the best travelling time for the trail. The trail is closed to off-highway vehicles from March 16–June 30 and to snow vehicles from May 1–June 30.

Cline Canyon & Coral Ridge Trails (Map 17/D3) 🥾🏇ℹ️

The trail to Cline Canyon is an easy 7.7 km (4.8 mile) loop along well-maintained trails that leads down Cline River and loop north to Coral Creek. There is an elevation gain of 155 m (504 ft). A side trail leads up to Coral Ridge where numerous fossils can be found. It is a difficult (13.5 km/8.4 mile) side route that requires some bushwhacking as you gain 1,025 m (3,330 ft) in elevation.

Cline Fire Lookout (Map 17/D4) ⛺🥾ℹ️

The 19 km (11.8 mile) journey to the lookout is a three or four day excursion best undertaken in the fall when the bush is less lush. After crossing both the North Saskatchewan and Siffleur River footbridges, you need to bushwhack north (through dense Wolf Willows) to the ridge. At the 10 km mark you will encounter the turquoise coloured waters of Abraham Lake. Skirt the lake to eventually meet the old road leading to the scenic lookout. The lookout is manned from May until September.

Coral Creek Trail (Map 17/C3–23/G7) ⛺🥾🏇ℹ️

The Coral Creek Trail heads northwest form the Cline Canyon/Pinto Lake Trail across a pass to Job Valley, where it is possible to access Job Lake. This difficult 42 km (26 mile) trail takes two or three days one-way and gains 600 m (1,950 ft). The best time for this trail is late summer to mid-fall, when the water is lower for the numerous creek crossings. To avoid a lot of the creek crossings, you can access the trail from the cutline that runs alongside Whitegoat Creek to a pass north of Mount Stelfox.

Dormer Mountain Circuit Trail (Map 13/B4) ⛺🥾🏇ℹ️

This is a 44 km (27.3 mile) hiking/horseback trail, or rather series of trails, that will take a couple of days to travel. Due to the many tricky river crossings of the Panther and Dormer Rivers, it is best travelled in late summer and autumn. The elevation gain is 835 m (2,714 ft), but the views are fabulous. The trailhead is located at the Mountain Aire Lodge off the Forestry Trunk Road.

Dormer/Sheep Trails (Map 13/C5) 🥾🏇ℹ️🏍️🏊

The trails in the Dormer/Sheep FLUZ are open to off-highway vehicles and snowmobiles year round, as well as hikers, horseback riders and mountain bikers.

Fish [Shunda] Lake Loop (Map 30/Inset) 🥾🚴🎿

A 5 km (3 mile) stroll along the shoreline of Shunda Lake can be accessed from the Fish Lake Recreation Area. At the 2 km (1.2 mile) junction, a 4.5 km (2.8 mile) side trail leads to Goldeye Lake.

Forbidden Creek Loop Trail (Map 12/D2–18/G6) ⛺🥾🏇ℹ️

A long 78 km (48.5 mile) backcountry route takes you through the beautiful alpine of the Bighorn Wildland. From the end of the Cutoff Creek Road, a trail takes you over to the Clearwater River. Continue south to the Forbidden Creek Trail. Eventually, you will loop back along the Clearwater River Trail. Due to the river crossings, the four-day hike is best left until late summer or early fall.

Goldeye Lake Trail (Map 24/G5) 🥾🚴🎿🎣

This is an easy 5 km (3 mile) walk or ski around Goldeye Lake, which is at the centre of a series of interconnecting trails. An alternate, starting point is found at the Dry Haven Recreation Area, along a 2 km (1.2 mile) trail. A 4.5 km (2.8 mile) trail connects this lake with nearby Shunda (Fish) Lake.

Hoodoo Creek Trail (Map 17/D2) 🥾ℹ️

This 5 km (3 mile) return trail begins off Highway 11 at Hoodoo Creek. It gains 400 m (1,300 ft) in elevation, providing you with spectacular views of some Hoodoos. The trail leads into a ravine and up to a shallow cave.

Hummingbird Creek Trail (Map 18/C4–17/G4) ⛺🥾🚴🏇🏍️🏊

Onion Creek Road is the starting point for this 28 km (17.4 mile) trail along the creek to Hummingbird Pass. After reaching the pass, you can continue to the headwaters of the North Ram River via the Hummingbird Pass Trail. A great view of the surrounding area can be seen off a high column above Hummingbird Creek. The trail is closed to off-highway vehicles from March 16–June 30 and to snowmobiles from May 1–June 30.

Hummingbird Pass Trail (Map 17/F5) ⛺🥾ℹ️

Farley Lake, which is found about 32 km/20 miles from the nearest road access, provides camping and a starting point to this 14 km (8.7 mile) trail that gains 365 m (1,186 ft) in elevation. The trail is very scenic as it runs through beautiful meadows, past a waterfall and provides inspiring views from the pass itself. The difficult trail, which can be muddy, requires you to cross the North Ram River.

BighornWildlandAdventures

Icefall Trail (Map 17/D4)
This trail begins across the highway from the Siffleur Falls Staging Area, at a gate about 200 metres up an old road. This 7 km (4.3 mile) trail offers an easy scramble to an icefall, climbing 205 m (665 ft) along the route.

Joyce River Trail (Map 18/B1–17/F1)
This is an easy, but long 28 km (17.4 mile) hike or ride that leads to a pass between Joyce River and Kidd Creek. The views are limited from the summit, but further exploration up nearby knolls will provide better viewpoints. It is possible to continue on down Kidd Creek, 15 km (9.3 miles) further to Bighorn Dam. The trailhead is located on the Forestry Trunk Road, 4 km (2.5 miles) north of the North Ram Recreation Area.

Kiska/Willson Trails (Map 17/F1–18/B2)
The Kiska/Willson FLUZ is open year-round to all users, from hikers to ATVers and from snowmobilers to skiers, with the exception of the North Ram Trail, which is only open to OHVs from July 1 to August 15. Many of the trails in this FLUZ follow cutlines making them more exciting for riders.

Kiska Creek Lookout Trail (Map 18/A1–17/G1)
Branching from the North Ram Ridge Trail, this 13 km (8 mile) trail follows an old road that has seen its bridges burned. It is a moderate route that takes you to the site of a former fire lookout, where views are quite spectacular. Be sure to keep your eyes open for mountain sheep, which are quite numerous in the region.

Kootenay Plains Trail (Map 17/E4)
This is a 27 km (16.8 mile) moderate bike and horseback ride along an old road that will take you crashing through forested uplands and then down to the grasslands of the Kootenay Plains. Access to this trail on the east side of the North Saskatchewan is from the Siffleur Falls Staging Area. The route can be confusing as there are several side roads and trails, including a popular side trail to Survey Hill. On the west side of the river, the **Figure Eight Trail** is a 3 km (1.8 mile) trail that takes you through meadows up to a rocky viewpoint.

Lake of the Falls Trail (Map 17/B4)
Access to this trail is off of Pinto Lake Trail west of Entry Creek. Scenic views of a waterfall, a serene lake and a thick canopy of conifers, make this a worthwhile three-day trip. The distance from the trailhead off Highway 11 (33 km/20.6 miles return) and the elevation gain (765 m/2,486 ft) make this a challenging trail. A trail continues south of Lake of the Falls through a shallow gorge and up the summit overlooking the lake.

Landslide Lake Trail (Map 17/C4)
Famous for cutthroat trout, this is a popular fishing destination despite the difficult journey to get there. From Highway 11 just south of the Cline River Bridge, it is a 34 km (21 mile/) return trail that gains 640 m (2,080 ft) in elevation. Allow the better part of two days to hike in. An alternate, but more difficult trail begins from the south at Wildhorse Creek. This scenic 11 km (6.8 mile) return trail is shorter, but steeper, climbing 1,140 m (3,705 ft).

Littlehorn Pass Meadows Trail (Map 17/C2–B1)
Accessed at the Waste Transfer Site on Highway 11, this is a 27 km (16.8 mile) hiking trail. The route passes the Whitegoat Falls on Whitegoat Creek and later, the Littlehorn Falls on Littlehorn Creek. There are a couple stream crossings before climbing through meadows to the alpine pass. In the winter, it is one of the two trails that are used to access the Sugar Bowl Riding Area by snowmobiles. The trail is open to off-highway vehicles from December 1 to March 15 and to snowmobiles from December 1 to April 30.

McDonald Creek Trail (Map 17/A3–23/G7)
This is a long 72 km (45 mile) journey, which takes between four to six days from the Pinto Lake trailhead at Cline River. Although very challenging, it is well worth your effort as you enjoy spectacular alpine meadows and several mountain views including the Columbia Icefields to the southwest. It is best to attempt in late summer when the streams are more easily crossed and there is less bush to impede travel. The trail also links up with the Coral Creek Trail, Cataract Creek Trail and the South Boundary Trail in Jasper.

North Cripple Creek Trail (Map 18/B3)
An 11 km (6.8 mile) trail begins off the Forestry Trunk Road between the North and South Ram Rivers. It gains 440 m (1,430 ft) in elevation, while running through meadows and valleys to reach a narrow, but scenic pass. Give yourself about four hours to hike this route.

North Headwaters Trail (Map 17/F2)
A 26 km (16.2 mile) hike begins at the Bighorn Dam parking lot off Highway 11 and takes you into the Rockies timberland. There are several game trails that stray away from the main trail, making it hard to find your way along. Allow a couple of days to hike the trail.

North Ram River Trail (Map 18/B1–17/F4)
This 19 km (11.8 miles) trek takes the hiker on a journey along the North Ram River (and beyond as a myriad of trails link to this trail system). You can locate the trail at an outfitting camp, which is 7.5 km (4.7 miles) west of the North Ram River Recreation Area. The muddy Farley Lake, which offers camping, is a popular destination.

Onion Creek Trail (Map 18/C4–17/G4)
A 33 km (20.5 mile) multi-use trail leads along an old road next to the cascading creek and through the Ram Range to Onion Lake. Mid-June to mid-October is the best time to travel the trail. It is possible to continue on to the North Ram River or the Canary Creek Trails. The trail is closed to off-highway vehicles from March 16–June 30 and to snowmobiles from May 1–June 30.

Peppers Lake Trail (Map 18/G5)
This 16 km (10 mile) trail runs west, then south from Peppers Lake to connect up with the Esker Trail. This trail can also be accessed from the end of a side road off the Forestry Trunk Road.

Pinto Lake Trail (Map 17/C3–16/F4)
This is a long 32.5 km (20 mile) hike that leads from Highway 11 to Pinto Lake. There are waterfalls, river crossings, camping spots and muddy spots to keep the hiker busy. At the lake, a 7 km (4.3 mile) loop takes you around the lake, while trails continue south to an alternate trailhead on the Icefields Parkway via Sunset Pass. The trail also connects with the Whitegoat Trail as well as a difficult route up Waterfalls Creek.

Ranger Creek Trails (Map 18/C4–C6)
The Ranger Creek Trail leads from an outfitters camp south of Hummingbird Recreation Area to a small mountain lake, set in a colourful meadow. This difficult 26 km (16.2 mile) trail gains 515 m (1,674 ft) in elevation and takes two days to hike. Expect wet and boggy terrain, especially after a rainfall. It is possible to combine this trail with the **Lost Guide Canyon Trail** at a left turn after 15.5 km (9.3 miles). The hiker will reach Lost Guide Lake after following this route along a creek for 6 km (3.7 miles). Yet another option is to follow the 11 km (6.8 miles) trail to Clearwater River. This area is ideal for exploring during the summer through to mid-fall and is a popular snowmobile destination.

Scalp and Skeleton Creek Trails (Map 13/A2–12/F1)
See Ya Ha Tinda Ranch Trails below.

Saskatchewan River Trail (Map 17/D5–A6)
This is a long, moderate 48 km (29.8 mile) trail from the Siffleur Falls Staging Area to the Saskatchewan River Crossing. It provides fine views, with minimal elevation gain, but requires crossing Spreading Creek is required about halfway. Many simply follow the old road to Loudon Creek for a 14.5 km (9 mile) journey that passes a ravine. Allow for a full day and be prepared for some bushwhacking.

Siffleur Falls Trail (Map 17/E5)
This is probably the most popular trail in the area. It starts at the suspension bridge over the North Saskatchewan River and is a relatively easy, 12 km (7.4 mile) trail with views of the Siffleur River Canyon. There is a viewpoint overlooking the titular falls.

Siffleur River Trail (Map 17/D5–E7)
A challenging 30 km (18.6 mile) route connects with the Dolomite Pass Trail and the Clearwater Valley Trail. It pushes through forest and dangerously crosses rivers while offering a scenic traverse of the Siffleur Wilderness Area. Bushwhacking routes to Escarpment Lakes and Porcupine Lake are accessible off the main trail. These trails are best done later in the year, when the river crossings are easier. In the winter, it is the domain of snowshoers and backcountry skiers.

South Ram River Trail (Map 18/C4–A6)
This 54 km (33.5 mile) trail gains 345 m (1,121 ft) in elevation and will take hikers at least two days to hike. From Hummingbird Recreation Area, the trail skirts South Ram River and has a few challenging river crossings that are best attempted in the fall. The scenic trail does offer numerous campsites for the weary traveller.

Stelfox Loop (Map 17/C2)
This difficult 22 km (13.7 mile) hike incorporates sections of the Whitegoat Creek and the Coral Creek Trails, joined by a connecting trail just north of Mount Stelfox. If you do not want to walk an extra 10 km (6 miles) or so down Highway 11, you will need two vehicles. There are several creek crossings and a 560 m (1,820 ft) climb to Whitegoat Pass, which offers a view of the Coral Creek Valley below.

Two O'Clock Ridge Trail (Map 17/D4)
The name Two O'clock is named after a common phenomenon that occurs in mountain streams from late spring to early summer. Melt water from the mountains is at its highest level around two o'clock in the afternoon, making creek crossings dangerous during that time. This trail offers a difficult 9 km hike from the recreation area to an alpine area with a beautiful view. It takes a full day to complete this trail that gains 1,150 m (3,738 ft) in elevation.

Vision Quest Trail (Map 17/C2)
Found off Highway 11 at the Cline Solid Waste Transfer Site, this 5 km (3 mile) hike climbs steadily (765m/2,486 ft) along an unmarked trail through pine trees to an open slope where the route is obvious. You pass through an old native Vision Quest Site to a panoramic ridge overlooking Abraham Lake.

Viewpoint Trail (Map 17/D3)
This 4 km (2.5 mile) loop trail is a refreshing hike that takes you to Abraham Lake with minimal elevation gain along the way (15m/49 ft). The trail is accessed at the David Thompson Resort.

Whitegoat Trail (Map 17/C3–16/F4)
This trail stretches over 32.3 km (20 miles) from Highway 11 to Pinto Lake and requires at least two days to hike one-way. It branches north from the Pinto Lake Trail to follow the north side of Cline River. The challenging trail crosses Coral, Boulder, McDonald and Cataract Creeks and is best left to more experienced hikers. There is an elevation gain of 415 m (1,349 ft) along the way. This trail is also used by ATV's and snowmobiles in winter (from December 1 to March 15 or April 30 respectively) to access the Sugar Bowl Snowmobile Area. However, if there is snow on the ground, travel by ATV is extremely difficult.

Whitegoat Creek & Falls Trail (Map 17/C2)
From the Cline Solid Waste Transfer site, an easy 2.5 km (1.6 mile) hiking trail climbs 45 m (146 ft) to the gorgeous Whitegoat Falls. Beyond the falls the trail becomes poorly defined and troublesome creek crossings make it more difficult to continue along the creek to Crescent Falls. Your rewards are found in the variety of vegetation and the views of the North Saskatchewan River Valley. The best season for this 19.5 km (12.1 mile) trail is late spring to early fall.

Whitegoat Lakes Loop Trail (Map 17/C3)
This 9 km (5.6 mile) loop is an easy hike for seeing some of the local points of interest. The trail starts at the David Thompson Resort and heads south to Abraham Lake. It then follows the shore of the lake to Little Indian Falls and continues along a creek to the Whitegoat Lakes and back to the resort. It is possible to connect to Whitegoat Falls Trail, shortly after Little Indian Falls.

Whiterabbit Creek Trail (Map 17/E4–18/A6)
This is a moderate 42 km (26 mile) return trail, perfect for the backpacker prepared for a two or three day excursion. It provides a large variety of terrain linking Kootenay Plains to the North Ram River. This section of the trail gains 610 m (1,983 ft). Another option is to head to Ram River. Choosing this trail requires three or four days to complete the 54 km (33.6 mile) trail, which gains 760m (2,479 ft). Travel on wet, boggy ground and bushwhacking is required, therefore appropriate footwear is recommended.

Ya Ha Tinda Ranch Trails (Map 13/A2–12/G3)
The Ya Ha Tinda Ranch is run by Parks Canada offering trail enthusiasts a base from which to access the southern reaches of the Bighorn Backcountry and Banff National Park. Popular with horseback riders, there are several trails to explore from the staging area at Bighorn Campground. Snowmobilers need special permission to use the Scalp Creek Trail in winter:

Banff Park Trail (Map 13/A2–12/G3)
The main access to Banff National Park, this is a popular trail that follows the north side of the Red Deer River, heading west. It is about 13 km (8 miles) to the park boundary along an old road that is closed to cyclists. A popular stop is Scotch Camp, which rests in a beautiful meadow area. Travellers can continue on the Upper Cascade Fire Road and the Red Deer River Trail in Banff National Park.

Bighorn Creek/Eagle Creek Loop (Map 13/A2)
This easy trail loops from the Bighorn Campground up Bighorn Creek to the ranch boundary fence, then back along Eagle Creek. Riders can choose to take the easy low route or the more difficult high route. Even lower is the Eagle Viewpoint Trail.

Eagle Lake/James Pass (Map 13/A2)
This trail heads up Eagle Creek to Eagle Lake and to James Pass, beyond. It is about 7.5 km (4.5 miles) to the pass.

Hidden Falls (Map 13/A2)
Starting along the Banff Trail, this trail starts about 4.5 km (3 miles) from the Bighorn Campground at the Hidden Falls Ford. From here, a trail on the east side heads up to Hidden Falls.

Scalp Creek Trails (Map 13/A2–12/E2)
The Scalp Creek Trail heads west from the Bighorn Campground and crosses Bighorn and Scalp Creeks before following the west side of the creek northwest to the park boundary. The farther you travel, the more difficult it gets. It is also used by snowmobilers in winter. Closer to the campsite, the Scalp Creek Water Slide is a relatively easy trail leading to a natural waterslide. Be prepared to get wet as the trail crosses the creek four times before reaching the waterslide.

Sheep Mountain Loop (Map 13/A2)
This trail heads north from the Bighorn Campground to Sheep Mountain along a blazed trail. It is possible to descend along an old cat trail, which joins up with the Clearwater Trail. This difficult route will take riders at least eight hours.

Skeleton Creek Trail (Map 13/A2–12/F1)
This 27 km (16.8 mile) route follows an old exploration road north from the ranch to the Forty Mile Patrol Cabin on the Clearwater River. It is a difficult route that climbs 450 m (1,463 ft) along the way. The trail follows the start of the Scalp Creek Trail before branching north. Several side routes, including Bighorn Pastures and Scalp Creek, are worth exploring.

Well Site Trail (Map 13/A2)
This easy trail follows Scalp Creek from the Bighorn Campground to where it crosses the old Banff Trail. Take the old Banff Trail, then, when it forks just a few hundred metres along, take the northwest branch of the trail to an old well site.

Wolf Creek/Labyrinth Mountain Loop (Map 13/A2–C3)
Heading south, this trail follows Wolf Creek back to the Red Deer River and past the Eagle Lake Campground before returning to the start. The difficult loop is about 20 km (12 miles) and will take riders about eight hours to do.

WILDLIFE VIEWING

Outside of the National Parks, the Bighorn area is perhaps one of the best areas in the province to see large animals. In fact, it is a rare trip into the Bighorn where you don't see some form of wildlife. The Kootenay Plains also provides birders with a chance to see a good variety of birds. Listed below are a few of the better viewing areas:

Kootenay Plains Ecological Reserve (Map 17/D5)
The Kootenay Plains Ecological Reserve is a popular destination for bird-watchers, but it was set aside to protect both the fauna and flora found in the area. The open grassland is home to over 60 species of birds and 14 species of mammal, including elk, deer, mountain sheep and moose. A good viewing area for birds is at Windy Point.

Ram Falls Recreation Area (Map 18/E4)
Bighorn sheep can be seen on the slopes of the Ram Range throughout the year. The Ram River Canyon also offers a dramatic view of eroded shale and sandstone and golden eagles may be seen soaring on the canyon air currents. In the fall, bald eagles, merlins and American kestrels wing south along the eastern slopes of the Rocky Mountains. Red squirrels are abundant in the pine and spruce forests and black bears may be seen from mid spring to late fall.

Siffluer Wilderness Area (Map 11, 17)
The Siffluer Wilderness is a large wilderness area located just east of Banff. There is no road access into the area; instead, you will have to explore this area on foot. If you stay in the valleys, expect to see ungulates such as moose, elk and deer. You may also see predators, such as grizzly bear, cougars, wolves and wolverines. If you venture higher into the alpine, watch for mountain goats, woodland caribou, golden-mantled ground squirrels, bighorn sheep, hoary marmots and pikas. Hikers should be experienced and well prepared for wilderness travel before setting out on any of the several access trails.

White Goat Wilderness Area (Map 16, 17, 23)
Similar to Siffluer above, access into this wild area is on foot and requires proper planning and experience to get here. Large mammals inhabit the valleys and the lower slopes of this wilderness area. Watch for moose, elk, white-tailed and mule deer, black bears, and coyotes. Less common, and therefore more exciting to spot are grizzly bears, cougars, wolves and wolverines. In alpine areas, watch for mountain goats, woodland caribou, golden-mantled ground squirrels, bighorn sheep, hoary marmots and pikas, as well as white-tailed ptarmigans, gray-crowned rosy finches, water pipits and horned larks.

Ya Ha Tinda Ranch (Map 13/A2–12/G3)
This private ranch is run by Parks Canada and is home to a mix of grassland and forest. This productive montane has an abundance of wildlife including grizzly bear, wolf, cougar, moose, deer and bighorn sheep. The area is also a major winter range for elk, with about 1,000 elk wintering in the area.

WINTER RECREATION

For skiers and snowshoers, the area has no groomed trails, but there are nearly 700 km (430 miles) of trails, exploration roads and old pack trails to explore. Alpine touring or telemark skis are recommended as there's a good chance you will be breaking trail.

For snowmobilers, the Bighorn is one of the largest and most scenic riding areas in the province, especially if you count all the random riding areas around the actual backcountry. Although some of the FLUZes are now closed to snowmobiling, there is still well over a thousand kilometres of trails to explore. Most of those trails are low elevation and riding is limited by snowfall. But there are also some hardcore alpine riding areas, although caution is needed as avalanche danger is quite real.

Goldeye Lake Recreation Area (Map 24/G5)
Linking with nearby Shunda Lake, there are a lot of ski trails to explore in the Goldeye Lake area. The trails are not groomed, but usually track set by previous skiers. If snowshoeing please stay off the cross-country tracks. Ice fishing on Goldeye Lake is also possible.

Onion Lake Random Sledding Area (Map 17/G4)
The Onion Lake/Hummingbird Creek area is one of the best-known and most popular riding areas in the Bighorn. Like the other riding areas, access can be sketchy in low snow years, as the lower sections of trails often don't have enough snow to cover the rocky ground. It is open December 1 to April 30. There are three trails open to snowmobiling in the area: the Onion Creek Trail (which takes riders to the actual riding area), the Hummingbird Creek Trail and the Canary Creek Trail.

Peppers Lake Area (Map 18/G5)
A number of old logging roads in the Peppers Lake area become a popular snowmobile destination in winter. Since the trails follow old logging roads and seismic trails in the area, you can probably ride for a few hundred kilometres. The lake is also a popular place to ride when it is frozen.

Ranger Creek Random Sledding Area (Map 18/B6)
The Ranger Creek area is open to sledding from December 1 to April 30. Like most of the random riding areas in the Bighorn, access depends on the snow levels. Once you get to the riding area (by the Ranger Creek Trail), there is usually lots of snow.

Scalp Creek Random Sledding Area (Map 12/F2)
This popular play area for sledders has the same closures and suffers the same issues as the other riding areas: access. Snowfall in recent years has been thin, often not covering the trail for more than a few weeks in the heart of winter. The area is open December 1 to April 30 and is accessed along the Skeleton Creek Trail or (by written permission only) along the Scalp Creek Trail from the Ya Ha Tinda area.

Sugar Bowl Random Sledding Area (Map 17/B1)
The Sugar Bowl can be hard to get to, as the trails in are frequently bare except for a few weeks in the heart of winter. This area is open December 1 to April 30. The two trails that are used to access this area are the Littlehorn and the Whitegoat Creek Trails, which are both also open to ATVers. So if the snow is not their, bring along the Quad.

ElkLakesAdventures

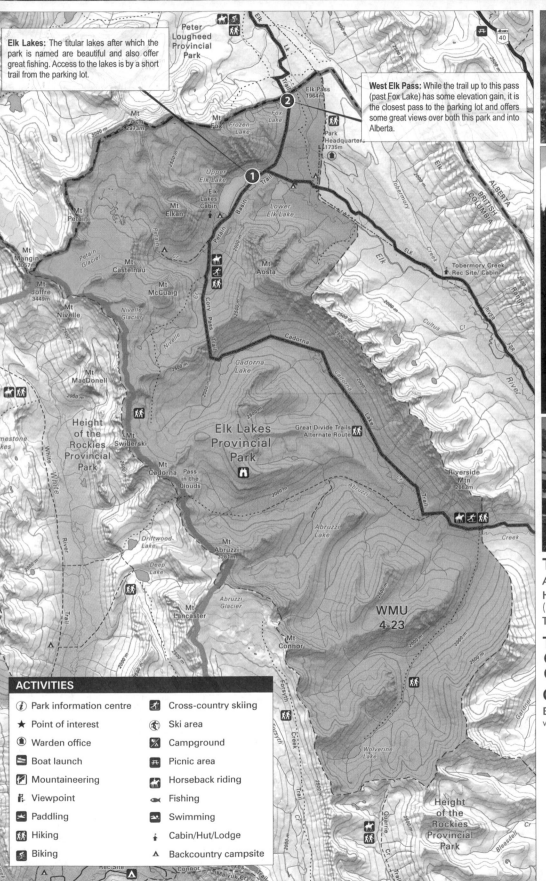

Elk Lakes: The titular lakes after which the park is named are beautiful and also offer great fishing. Access to the lakes is by a short trail from the parking lot.

West Elk Pass: While the trail up to this pass (past Fox Lake) has some elevation gain, it is the closest pass to the parking lot and offers some great views over both this park and into Alberta.

Image © Vanessa Vallis

THINGS TO KNOW

Area: 17,245 hectares

Highest Point: Mount Joffre 3,450 metres (11,319 feet)

Total Vehicle Accessible Campsites: 0

THINGS TO SEE

1 Elk Lakes

2 West Elk Pass

CONTACT INFORMATION

BC Parks: (250) 489-8540
www.bcparks.ca

ACTIVITIES

- (i) Park information centre
- ★ Point of interest
- Warden office
- Boat launch
- Mountaineering
- Viewpoint
- Paddling
- Hiking
- Biking

- Cross-country skiing
- Ski area
- Campground
- Picnic area
- Horseback riding
- Fishing
- Swimming
- Cabin/Hut/Lodge
- △ Backcountry campsite

ElkLakesAdventures

The main attractions of this 17,245 hectare park are the rugged peaks, delicate sub-alpine, mountain lakes and glaciers. The two largest lakes of the park are Upper Elk Lake at 1,800 m (5,905 feet) and Lower Elk Lake at 1,700 metres. Both lakes are glacier-fed lakes that are ice-free from mid-June to November and offer fishing for small whitefish, cutthroat or bull trout. Fishing is also provided in the Elk River and Cadorna Creek and there is a wide variety of wildlife in the park.

The park is an extremely popular destination for hikers, horseback riders and anglers and the park's management plan is an attempt to balance this use with the need to conserve and protect the wilderness and wildlife habitat of the area. There are also many mountaineering and rock climbing routes but limited winter activities due to the avalanche potential and the fact that the road to the park is not plowed. Rugged peaks, mountain lakes, glaciers and an abundance of wildlife are a few of the attractions of this provincial park. There are significant fossil deposits in the area. However, commercial and/or personal collecting is prohibited.

The first documented non-native person through this area was David Thompson in 1811, who established a trading post near Invermere. The area is part of the Ktunaxa First Nations traditional territory, but was also used by the Stoney First Nations in the late 19th century. In 1902, WD Wilcox wrote about the area in National Geographic Magazine. After World War I, the area began to attract mountain climbers and by 1919 the three highest peaks in the area had been climbed.

The area was first established as a game reserve in the 1920s, to protect the number of large animals found in this area, including, as you might expect, an abundance of elk, but also one of the highest concentrations of mountain goats in the world. In 1955, a 1,555 hectare reserve for recreation was established around Elk Lakes. In 1973, the area was designated a Class A park. That was changed in 1977 and the area became a recreation area in 1982. In 1995, the part was designated a Class A park again.

The park is a backcountry park and as such remains relatively undisturbed. For wilderness seekers, the park offers a chance to get away into a dramatically beautiful area. However, because the area is so scenic, it is rare to have an area to yourself for too long. There are four ways to accesses to the park. The most common is via a good quality Forest Service road that runs up the Elk Valley to the park boundary at Lower Elk Lakes. Access to Cadorna Creek is via an old seismic road that branches from the Elk River Forest Service Road. The first three kilometers of this old road have become a trail and are on Forest Service land outside the park. Access from Alberta is from a trailhead at Kananaskis Lakes which goes through Elk Pass to Upper Elk lakes. The last access to the park is from Height of the Rockies Park through a high elevation pass near Mount Cadorna. There are also a couple stocked lakes to help ensure a consistent fishery.

CAMPING

Although there are no vehicle accessible campsites in the park itself, the Elk River Forest Service Road does provide good access to several recreation sites. There are also several backcountry campsites to look for in the park.

Cadorna Creek Watershed (Map 2/A1)
Camping is permitted in the Cadorna Creek Watershed area, with the main site being located at Abruzzi Lake. Here you will find a pit toilet, fire ring and two tent pads. Elsewhere through the valley, you will find rock rings where you can set up camp.

Elk Lake Cabin (Map 5/A7)
This cabin sleeps 10 and is easily accessed by a 3 to 4 hour hike. In winter, the cabin is a popular backcountry ski destination.

Lower Elk Lake Campground (Map 5/A7)
The Lower Elk Lake site is a backcountry site with several tent pads, a food cache, fire pits and a toilet.

Park Headquarters Campground (Map 5/A7)
This campground is located in the parking lot at the park entrance and has no facilities.

Petain Basin Campground (Map 4/G7)
Mountaineers use this campground as a bivouac site. It is located near Petain Glacier and above Petain Falls. There is no bridge across Petain Creek and campers are asked to stay on the gravel flats beside the creek since the basin is a fragile alpine environment. Fires are not permitted.

Petain Creek Campground (Map 5/A7)
Located 1 km (0.6 miles) past the south end of Upper Elk Lake, this site has a toilet, a food cache, tent pads and group fire rings. The actual site of the campground has been relocated, as the creek has a habit of switching channels.

Outside of the Park, a few popular camping areas are found at various recreation sites. The sites are all quite small and provide access to both the river and the trail systems leading into the park. Near Tobermory Creek there is also a cabin that can be used on a first-come first-serve basis.

Riverside Recreation Site (Map 2/B1) 🥾🚴🏍🎣🎿
Riverside is a small (three unit), partially treed site next to the Elk River. The Elk River Forest Road is part of the Trans Canada Trail and fishing is popular on the river.

Weary Creek Recreation Site (Map 2/C2) 🥾🚴🏍🎣🎿
This is a small (two unit) site located next to the Elk River Road and can be accessed by trailers and RVs. Fishing and hunting are popular pastimes in the area.

FISHING

Certainly one of the main attractions to the park is the fantastic fishing. Due to the high elevation there is a limited ice-free season, which usually lasts from mid-June until November. This makes the fish that much more feisty and generally easy to catch.

Abruzzi Creek (Map 2/B1)
A trail accessed creek in Elk Lakes Provincial Park, this stream does not see heavy fishing pressure. This is partly due to the difficult trail access as well as the heavy restrictions that are placed on the creek. It is closed to fishing from September 1 to October 31, there is a bait ban and it is catch and release only for all trout and char from June 15 to August 31.

Aosta Lakes, Upper and Lower (Map 5/A7) 🐟
The Aosta Lakes are a pair of very small lakes found near Upper Elk Lake. Access to these lakes is along the Carol Pass Route. Both lakes are small, totalling less than 10 hectares combined and both are high elevation lakes (over 1,700 m/5,525 feet). This means that the fishing season is short, but the stocked cutthroat will voraciously attack anything that looks edible.

Cadorna Creek (Map 2/B1–5/A7)
Cadorna Creek drains Cadorna Lake in Elk Lakes Provincial Park. It is accessed by the Cadorna Lake Trail and does not see much action. Rumour has it the fishing is fairly steady for cutthroat trout to 45 cm (18 inches).

Cadorna Lake (Map 2/A1) 🐟
A beautiful, remote 13.7 hectare lake found in the Elk Lakes Provincial Park, Cadorna offers good fishing for cutthroat that average 25–35 cm (10–14 inches). Because of its remoteness, the lake sees little pressure. Shore fishing produces well, which is good, because hauling in a float tube along the 15 km (9.3 mile), rugged trail is difficult, to say the least. Spring is the best time to fish here, especially during the chironomid hatches, but the ice stays pretty late on the high elevation (1,905 m/6,191 ft) lake.

Elk Lakes, Lower and Upper (Map 5/A7)
These beautiful alpine lakes make a popular Rocky Mountain hiking destination. These lakes offer good fishing for whitefish (average 20 cm), cutthroat (to 25 cm) and bull trout. Although ice-free from mid-June to November, fishing is best towards the end of the summer after the water has begun to clear. The Upper Lake is 100 m (325 feet) higher than the Lower, which is at 1,700 m (5,525 feet) in elevation. It is also bigger, at 67.5 hectares, compared to 25, and deeper at 52.3 m (170 feet), compared to 6.8 m (22.1 feet).

Frozen Lake (Map 5/A6) 🐟

Yes, the name is a pretty good description of this high elevation (2,226 m/7,235 feet) lake that has a very short ice-free season. As a result, the small stocked cutthroat trout are voracious eaters and most tackle will work. The 6.9 hectare lake is found on an easy trail leading north from Lower Elk Lake. The lake is set at the base of a sheer rock wall and there are a few trees around the edge of the lake.

Tobermory Creek (Map 5/B7)

There is a forest service site where Tobermory Creek flows into the Elk River. From there, a rustic angler's trail provides access to the creek that contains cutthroat trout to 45 cm (18 inches). The creek sees little fishing pressure.

PADDLING

In order to paddle either of the Elk Lakes, you're going to have to carry a canoe or kayak into the park; the shortest carry, to Lower Elk Lakes, is a distance of about 1 km (0.6 miles). To get to the upper Lake, you'll have to carry the canoe another kilometer. However, those who go to the effort of carrying a canoe into the lakes will most likely have the scenic mountain lakes all to themselves. In addition to spectacular scenery and abundant wildlife, the lakes offer good fishing and wilderness camping opportunities.

TRAILS

Most of the trail activity takes place around the Elk Lakes and the West Elk Pass but there are also many mountaineering and rock climbing routes to explore. Winter activities are limited due to the avalanche potential and the fact that the road to the park is not ploughed. No mountain biking is allowed in the park, but the Trans Canada Trail allows bikers to follow the powerline road along the park border up to Elk Pass and over the Great Divide to Alberta. In addition to the marked trails, there are many more unmarked game trails and routes that crisscross the park. These routes, however, should be left to experienced backcountry travellers.

Cadorna Lake Trail (Map 2/B1–3/A7) 🔺🥾🏇🛶🎣⛷🏕

The main route to Cadorna Lake starts from the Elk Valley Bighorn Outfitter's Lodge off the Elk River Road. It is a 13 km (7.9 miles) 6–8 hour one-way hike through the valley bottom to the good fishing lake. The trail is best hiked in the summer to avoid the fall hunting season and the wet, soggy conditions in the spring. Many windfalls and wet areas impede your travel in the valley and it is necessary to scramble up a slide to the pass where superb views can be had. From there, it is an easy descent to the beautiful lake set in a cirque basin. This route also accesses the climbing opportunities at Mount Aosta. You can also take a side trip to Abruzzi Lake by following the fork up Abruzzi Creek (5 hours one-way).

Coral Pass Route (Map 5/A7) 🧗🏕

From Upper Elk Lake Campsite, there are a number of routes for expert mountaineers only. Like many, the route to Coral Pass requires traversing over treacherous snow in the Nivelle Creek drainage (ropes use of ropes.

Elk Lakes Trail (Map 5/A7) 🔺🥾🏇⛷🎣🏕

From the park headquarters, it is an easy 2 km (1.2 km) 40 minute one-way walk past Lower Elk Lake to Upper Elk Lake. The hike leads through old growth spruce forests, meadows and rock slopes gaining 30 m (100 ft) along the way.

Fox Lake Trail (Map 5/A7) 🥾🧗🏕

From the east side of Upper Elk Lake, this 3.9 km (2.4 mile) 1.5–2 hour one-way trail gains 250 m (820 ft) crossing several open avalanche chutes and offering great views of the Elk Valley and Neville Basin. The trail continues past Fox Lake to the West Elk Pass.

Frozen Lake Route (Map 5/A7) 🥾🏕

From Lower Elk Lake, this moderate hike follows either of the trails to West Elk Pass. About 100 m (300 ft) west of the pass, there is a cutline that can be followed to Frozen Lake. It is a short, but steep 2 km (1.2 mile) hike gaining 300 m (985 ft) in elevation. This trail is best hiked in August or September when the lake is no longer frozen. From Frozen Lake, it is possible to scramble to the top of Taiga Viewpoint, at 2,360 m (7,740 ft), where you get a fantastic view of Frozen Lake and its surrounding talus slopes. The latter hike is 2 km (1.2 miles) one-way gaining 225 m (738 ft).

Kananaskis Lakes to Lower Elk Lake (Map 5/A6) 🔺🥾🏇⛷🎣🏕

The Elk Lakes are often accessed from hikers in Peter Lougheed Provincial Park in Alberta. The trail is found at the south end of Kananaskis Lake and initially climbs for 1.5 km (0.9 miles) gaining 50 m (163 ft) to West Elk Pass. It then descends to a trail junction at the park boundary. The left fork takes you to the Elk Lakes Park Headquarters and the right fork takes you to the Lower Elk Lake. Along the trail, you cross Elkin Creek several times and a swampy meadow on a long boardwalk. Views of Mount Aosta are offered on route. Overall, the hike is 4 km (2.4 miles) 1.5 hour one-way, descending 240 m (785 ft).

Pass In the Clouds Route (Map 1/G2–2/A2) 🥾🏕

A rough route leads up to Pass in the Clouds, an area that was severely damaged by fire in 2003. While people can still probably make it up and over the pass into the Height of the Rockies Provincial Park, new growth after a forest fire in 2003 is making this area difficult to traverse.

Petain Creek Waterfall & Basin Trail (Map 5/A7) 🔺🥾⛷🏕

This easy trail is 3 km (1.8 mile) 1–1.5 hours one-way from Upper Elk Lake and takes you to a view of the waterfall and the Castineau Hanging Glacier west of the lake. The trail straddles the banks of the Upper Elk Lake before following a bench above Petain Creek to the falls. If you want to continue onward, try the scramble up the steep slopes to Petain Basin, which is another 4 km (2.4 mile) 4 hours, return gaining 520 m (1705 ft) in elevation along a sporadically marked trail.

Viewpoint Trail (Map 5/A7) 🥾⛷🏕

This 1.2 km (0.7 mile) trail climbs 122 m (400 ft) to a viewpoint over the Elk Lakes area. The trail starts on the west side of the Upper Elk River where it flows into Lower Elk Lake. The trail is short but strenuous and follows the edge of some steep cliffs. Stay well back from the edge.

West Elk Pass Area (Map 5/A6) 🥾🏇⛷🎣🏕

From the park headquarters, it is a 4 km (2.4 mile) 1.5 hour one-way moderate hike through a spruce forest and meadows gaining 240 m (785 ft) to the pass. When you reach the park boundary, you can access the old powerline road into Peter Lougheed Park or make a circuit back to the park headquarters via Upper Elk Lake on the Fox Lake Trail. Other popular destinations include Frozen Lake and the Taiga Viewpoint.

WILDLIFE WATCHING

While there are no formal wildlife watching areas in the park, the area provides very high quality habitats for mountain goat and grizzly bear. In fact, the park has one of the highest concentrations of mountain goats in the world. The park also protects habitat for black bear, bighorn sheep, mule deer, white-tailed deer and moose, along with a variety of small mammals, birds and fish. The park plays an important role in the representation of the Southern Rockies ecosystem.

WINTER RECREATION

In winter, Elk Lakes Provincial Park is a relatively popular wilderness destination. There are no groomed trails for skiing, but backcountry skiers do visit the park fairly regularly. Most of the trails in the park can be skied in winter, but only one is open to snowmobiles.

The park is also becoming a hotbed for ice climbing. There are several waterfalls around the Elk Lakes themselves, which freeze in winter.

The main route to Cadorna Lake is the only route in Elk Lakes Provincial Park that is open to snowmobile. The trail starts from the Elk Valley Bighorn Outfitter's Lodge off the Elk River Forest Service Road. It is 13 km (7.9 miles) one-way to the lake. Backcountry skiers prefer the Elk Lakes area due to the easy ski in and the fact there is a cabin at the lake. Outside of the park, Weary Creek and Mount Bleasdell are other popular snowmobile areas.

ForestryTrunkAdventures

Image © Greg Scratchley

THINGS TO KNOW

Highest Point: Obstruction Mountain 3,205 metres (10,516 feet)

Total Vehicle Accessible Campsites: 1,500+

THINGS TO SEE

1 Cadomin Cave
2 Whitehorse Creek Wildland
3 Cardinal Divide

CONTACT INFORMATION

Parks and Protected Areas:
1-866-427–3582, www.albertaparks.ca
Grande Cache Ranger Station:
(780) 827–3626
Hinton Ranger Station: (780) 865-8267

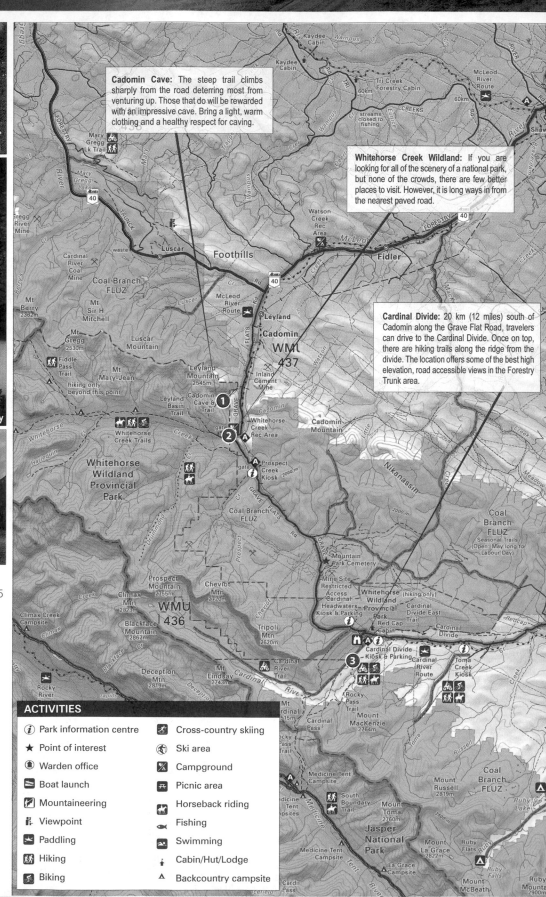

Cadomin Cave: The steep trail climbs sharply from the road deterring most from venturing up. Those that do will be rewarded with an impressive cave. Bring a light, warm clothing and a healthy respect for caving.

Whitehorse Creek Wildland: If you are looking for all of the scenery of a national park, but none of the crowds, there are few better places to visit. However, it is long ways in from the nearest paved road.

Cardinal Divide: 20 km (12 miles) south of Cadomin along the Grave Flat Road, travelers can drive to the Cardinal Divide. Once on top, there are hiking trails along the ridge from the divide. The location offers some of the best high elevation, road accessible views in the Forestry Trunk area.

ACTIVITIES

ⓘ Park information centre	🎿 Cross-country skiing
★ Point of interest	⛷ Ski area
🏛 Warden office	📛 Campground
🛶 Boat launch	🎋 Picnic area
🚣 Mountaineering	🐎 Horseback riding
🎋 Viewpoint	🐟 Fishing
🚣 Paddling	🏊 Swimming
🥾 Hiking	🏠 Cabin/Hut/Lodge
🚴 Biking	⛺ Backcountry campsite

Forming the backbone of backcountry travel in Alberta, the Forestry Trunk Road runs about 1,000 kilometres (610 miles) from the Crowsnest pass in Southern Alberta to Grand Prairie in the north. In this book we are focusing on the area around the Forestry Trunk from the Red Deer River north to Grand Cache. Part of the southern stretch of road is covered in our Bighorn Backcountry, Kananaskis Country and Ghost FLUZ sections of this book, while the southern and northern stretches of this often lonely road are found in our Southern or Northern Alberta Backroad Mapbooks respectively.

The Forestry Trunk is a unique road that is not only one of the few north south roads west of Calgary and Edmonton, but it also falls under several different highway-numbering systems. Some sections are paved, such as the Highway 40 stretches between Hinton and Grand Cache, though most of it remains a gravel road that bumps it way across the foothills of Alberta. Branching from this main artery are roads and trails of all shapes and sizes.

Unlike the parks to the west, this is an area that is open to virtually any type of recreation, especially motorized recreation. This is not to say that people do not enjoy exploring on foot, bike, horse or ski. They do. The area is also as busy during the fall hunting season, as it is when the fishing is good in the spring and early summer.

As you head north along the Forestry Trunk, there are a few significant east west off shoots. Around Nordegg, the David Thompson Highway (Highway 11) crosses the Forestry Trunk Road. This is outdoor recreationists dream highway with access endless trails, parks and fishing holes. The Forestry Trunk is still running as the 734 when the Grave Flats or Cardinal Divide Road branches west. This is popular backroad that leads to the beautiful divide and past Mountain Park. North of here, the road gets a bit confusing to follow as it heads north to Hinton. The actual Forestry Trunk remains a gravel road as it rejoins Highway 40, but at Coalspur the 40 turns south to meet the paved road leading south from Hinton. The Forestry Trunk, however, jogs north then west again to bump along a gravel road into Hinton. Hear the Yellowhead Highway takes travellers west to Jasper or east to Edmonton. Forestry Trunk travellers can continue north along the smoother, but still windy Highway 40 that leads to Grande Cache, near the northern boundaries of this book.

The Forestry Trunk was created to serve industry and it still serves that purpose today. Highway travellers will still need to be alert for big logging or oil and gas trucks that bomb up and down the road. However, if you are cautious and follow the rules of the road, you should have no trouble navigating this, or any other backroad. The fun of course, is finding what lies around the next corner…

CAMPING

The Forestry Trunk area is a recreational hot spot of Alberta. Aiding people in their outdoor pursuits are a series of provincial parks, recreation areas and Forest Land Use Zones. These sites range from roadside camping facilities to remote backcountry parks with no roads, no facilities and, if you're lucky, a few developed trails.

Most camping areas are open from May to October but some of the parks and recreation areas also have limited camping during the winter months. Picnic tables, pit toilets, fire pits, pump water and firewood are found at most recreation areas, while parks often offer a few more amenities including running water and on occasion showers. Camping fees vary, based on services provided. Since many of the provincial park campgrounds are very busy in the summer, a reservation system is in place for a fee. We have included the numbers to these parks. Alberta Parks has a new central reservation site, at https://reserve.albertaparks.ca/, though only a few sites are currently part of that system. In this section, only the Gregg Lake Campground at William A. Switzer Provincial Park is currently tied into that system, but expect more to be added in the next few years.

Athabasca Ranch Forest Land Use Zone (Map 35/C5)

The Athabasca Ranch FLUZ is one of the smaller Land Use Zones at 40 sq km (15.4 sq miles). The area was established to minimize conflicts between motorized access and elk breeding season. The main trail system is the Athabasca Ranch & River Trails just off the Hinton/Entrance Airport Road and open to hiking, biking, skiing and snowshoeing. Outside of these trails, it is mostly old roads that are open to highway vehicles. Note that some of these trails are only open the May long weekend and from June 25 to the end of the Labour Day long weekend.

Big Berland Recreation Area (Map 39/A6)

The Big Berland Recreation Area is an 18 unit site on the shores of the Berland River, just off Highway 40. Although far enough from the highway to escape that noise, the campsite is built almost directly beneath a railway bridge. Fortunately, the tracks don't see that much traffic, but it can be a bit jarring when a train flies over top your tent at 3:30 in the morning. This site is popular with anglers and is also used as a staging area for trips into the Willmore Wilderness, which is found 8 km (4 miles) down the road. Equestrian users please note: there is a corral 4 km (2 miles) down the road for horses.

Blackstone River Recreation Areas (Map 24/F3)

This secluded ten unit campsite is found on the shores of the Blackstone River, west of the Forestry Trunk Road along the Chungo Road. ATVs and snowmobilers frequent the area, as do hikers, horseback riders and canoeists going out onto the Blackstone River. A little further north on the Forestry Trunk Road, the Blackstone Viewpoint Recreation Area is little more than a pullout with a nice view of the valley. Following a difficult trail upstream brings hikers to Wapiabi Caves. The caves should not be explored without proper equipment (the cave is on the list of the 30 deepest caves in Canada) and experience. However, the difficult climb to the caves brings you above treeline to stunning views over the valley.

Brazeau River Recreation Area (Map 30/B6)

This is a small, seven unit site on the shores of the Brazeau River, just off the Forestry Trunk Road, 72 km (43 miles) north of Nordegg. You can hand launch a canoe or kayak here or fish from shore. Most of the other activities in the region are land-based: hiking, horseback riding, cycling, and in the winter, snowmobiling.

Brown Creek Recreation Areas (Map 24/E1)

Found off the Forestry Trunk Road, 42 km (25 miles) north of Nordegg, Brown Creek is a popular fishing creek. The recreation area has nine campsites. There are also unmaintained trails in the area for everything from ATVing to backcountry skiing in winter. Further north on the Forestry Trunk Road there is a nice picnic area with a good view over the valley.

Brule Lake Forest Land Use Zone (Map 35/A7)

The Brule Lake Forest Land Use Zone is a mere 15 sq km, making it the smallest FLUZ in Alberta. Established in 1999 to protect elk populations in the area, there are no developed camping areas. Trail enthusiasts will find several old roads that are open to off highway vehicles and 4wd vehicles, but the main trail in the area is the Brule Lake Sand Dunes Trail. This 24.2 km (14.8 mile) multi-use trail continues beyond the FLUZ as it follows an old railbed on the eastern shore of Brule Lake. The trailhead is on Highway 16, 200 metres west of Overlander Lodge.

Cartier Creek Recreation Area (Map 14/D3)

For a fee, you can use one of 19 campsites at this relatively remote recreation area on the Red Deer River. The recreation area is located about 22 km (13 miles) southwest of Sundre and is open from May through September. Kayaking, fishing and rafting on the Red Deer River are the main attractions to the recreation area.

Coal Branch Forest Land Use Zone (Map 23, 28, 29)

South of Hinton, the Forestry Trunk Road passes through an area where a number of Coal Mines have been built, both past and present, earning this section of the Forestry Trunk the name "Coal Branch". The Coal Branch FLUZ covers 571 sq km (220.5 sq miles) and was developed to mitigate environmental impacts on sensitive areas, as well as protect and properly manage reclaimed mine sites. The area is best known for its OHV riding areas, but there are hiking and horseback trails as well. In winter, the trails are open to skiing and snowmobiling. There are no developed camping areas inside the FLUZ, although it is open to random camping with many informal hiking and riding trails. Fishing is found in Mystery Lake, while the main trails in the area are the Folding Mountain, Mystery Lake and Rocky Pass Trails.

Coalspur Recreation Area (Map 29/D1)
From 1909 until 1962, the Coalspur Mine operated in the area. Today little remains of this ghost town. Visitors will find a mostly open site 8 unit recreation area near the old townsite. This site is popular with people exploring the old ghost town, as well as anglers looking to drop a line in the Embarras River.

Deer Creek Recreation Area (Map 13/G4)
This recreation area is a group use only site. It is located next the Red Deer River and Red Creek which offer fishing as well as canoeing and rafting. It is opened from May through September.

Fairfax Lake Recreation Area (Map 30/B4)
Located off the Highway 40 section of the Forestry Trunk, 50 km (30 miles) southeast of Robb, this 39 unit campsite is a popular spot for anglers. The sites are grouped together and there is a boat launch and even a dock to fish from. The lake's small size makes it a great place for canoeists as well. To reserve a site call 780-865-2154.

Fallen Timber Recreation Area (Map 14/E4)
Located 25 km (15.5 miles) northwest of Cremona, this recreation site has 20 campsites. Canoeists and anglers on Fallentimber Creek, as well as ATV and snowmobile riders use it.

James-Wilson Recreation Area (Map 13/F1)
Found on the Forestry Trunk Road (Highway 734) west of Sundre and north of the Red Deer River, this recreation area has 32 campsites and is open from May through September. There is also a day-use area with picnic tables and a picnic shelter. There are hiking trails as well as ATV/snowmobiling routes in the area, while James River and Wilson Creek provide fishing.

Lovett River Recreation Area (Map 29/F3)
This 18 unit site is carved into the mostly lodgepole pine forest that blankets this part of Alberta. Located 40 km south of Robb on Highway 40, visitors can go canoeing, mountain biking, hiking or fishing. There is a snowmobile staging area two kilometres south of the recreation area.

Mason Creek Recreation Area (Map 38/C3)
This site offers little more than a couple pit toilets for area anglers and paddlers.

McLeod River Recreation Area (Map 35/G6)
Found halfway between Hinton and Robb on the McLeod River, this site boasts a 22 unit campground with fire pits, firewood, washroom and water. The McLeod Group Campsite is also nearby.

Pembina Forks Recreation Area (Map 30/B5)
This 10 unit vehicle access site has four separate tent-only sites. The camping area is located 63 km (37.5 miles) southeast of Robb on the Forestry Trunk. The primary users are anglers but there are some unmaintained hiking trails in the area, too.

Pierre Grey's Lakes Provincial Park (Map 38/F4)
There are 83 campsites in this park, which was developed on the site of an historic trading post. This site is located in rolling foothills but if you look west across the lakes, you can see the Rockies rising in the distance. Three of the five lakes in the park are stocked with rainbow and eastern brook trout. One lake sports a boat launch. In winter, there are 24 km (14.5 miles) of cross-country ski trails; in summer, visitors can hike 9 km (5.5 miles) of those trails. There is also a 10 unit group campground. To reserve a site, call 780-827-1382.

Prairie Creek Recreation Area (Map 19/E1)
East of the Forestry Trunk on Secondary Road 752, this site is found about 41 km (25.5 miles) southwest of Rocky Mountain House. The recreation area

has a 50 unit campground and a group area. There is also a day-use area. Visitors can try their luck fishing, walk the interpretative trails or enjoy cross-country skiing and snowmobiling in winter.

Red Deer River Recreation Area (Map 13/E4)
Set on the shores of the Red Deer River, there are a total of 64 campsites as well as a day-use area with a picnic shelter and picnic tables. The river provides rafting and fishing, while a number of hiking and equestrian trails are found nearby. Campsite reservations can be made by calling 403-637-2229.

Rock Lake-Solomon Creek Wildland Park (Map 34/B4–F5)
Bordering Jasper's northeast boundary, this area is a popular spot for recreation. In addition to 93 campsites and a boat launch at the lake, there are a number of trails in the area, many of which hook up with Jasper and Willmore. The surrounding parkland is home to one of the most diverse habitats in Alberta, ranging from dense lodgepole pine forests to open grasslands and most everything in between. To reserve a site here, call (780) 865-2154.

Seven Mile Recreation Area (Map 19/D5)
Found along the Forestry Trunk west of Caroline, this campground is located on Seven Mile Flats, a well known elk habitat alongside the Clearwater River. The recreation area has 36 campsites as well as a day-use area. The Clearwater River provides canoeing, rafting and fishing.

Sheep Creek Recreation Area (Map 38/A1)
Located 25 km (15 miles) north of Grande Cache on Highway 40, this 9 unit campground is found on the Smoky River, a kilometre south of its confluence with Sheep Creek. Hiking, horseback riding and fishing are the main activities in the area.

Smoky River South Recreation Area (Map 37/F4)
Located just before the Blue Bridge over the Smoky River, when driving north from Grande Cache along Highway 40, this recreation area sports 22 sites. They are set well back into the forest from the river.

Strachan Recreation Area (Map 19/F1)
Found just west of Strachan on Secondary Highway 752, this site area 27 campsites along with a picnic area. Prairie Creek provides fishing, while snowmobilers frequent the area in winter.

Sulphur Gates Recreation Area (Map 37/F4)
This six unit site is located near the dramatic Sulphur Gates gorge on the Smoky River. The site is mostly used by people as a staging area for trips into the Willmore Wilderness. A short hiking trail leads to a viewpoint over the gorge, while a much longer trail takes you to the furthest reaches of Willmore.

Swan Lake Recreation Area (Map 19/F3)
Fishing and water based activities are the main attraction to this well developed area. There are 16 RV accessible campsites, a boat launch and dock (for smaller boats), as well as a large picnic area.

Tay River Recreation Area (Map 19/G4)
There are 34 campsites at this recreation area, which is located off Highway 591 southwest of Caroline. There is also a day-use area that is open year round.

Watson Creek Recreation Area (Map 29/A3)
This 38 unit campground is found 30 km (18 miles) southwest of Robb on Highway 40. Most of the people at this site are here to fish, in either Watson Creek or the nearby McLeod River. To reserve a site, call 780-865-2154.

Whitehorse Creek Recreation Area (Map 28/G4)
South of Cadomin, this is a popular staging area for trips into the nearby wildland park and Jasper. In fact, it is possible to access Miette Hot Springs in from here. Campers will find 26 sites in a very scenic area, including eight sites equipped with horse corrals. The site can be busy on long weekends, which means the 26 camping units are full up. To reserve a site, call 780-865-2154.

Whitehorse Wildland Provincial Park (Map 28/F4)

There are no developed facilities at this park, but informal camping is allowed for overnight hiking/biking/horseback trips. The Cardinal Divide, a treeless ridge that stretches east and west, is popular with hikers, while Whitehorse Creek is also known for the great views into the Rockies and the foothills. Cadomin Cave is also found here.

Wildhorse Lake Recreation Area (Map 35/A6)

There are actually two separate recreation sites here, one at Kinky Lake and one at Wildhorse Lake. The two are a study in contrasts. The Kinky Lake Recreation Area is little more than a big clearing on the shores of the lake, while Wildhorse is a pretty group use campground with mostly private sites. Both lakes sport great views of the sunset over the front range of the Rocky Mountains, while a 4 km trail circles Kinky Lake. To reserve a site here, call (780) 866-2231.

William A. Switzer Provincial Park (Map 35/A3)

Capturing 2,600 hectares (6,000 acres) of the Alberta upper foothills region, this is a popular local get away. Much of the park's recreational opportunities are built around the chain of five lakes—Blue, Cache, Graveyard, Gregg and Jarvis—that are linked by Jarvis Creek. Fishing is a popular activity, as is canoeing, swimming (Kelly's Bathtub is probably the best beach in the park) and windsurfing. There are 220 campsites divided among the park's four campgrounds. Switzer Park is only slightly less popular in the winter, with activities including cross-country skiing, ice fishing, snowmobile staging, snowshoeing and even ice-skating. Cross-country ski trails in the park link up with other trails outside the park, including a linking trail to Black Cat Ranch. To reserve a site here, visit www.reserve.albertaparks.ca or call (780) 865-5152.

FISHING

The Eastern Slopes of the Rockies offer anglers the chance to experience some truly magical angling. From pristine streams to high alpine lakes, there is some truly glorious scenery in this region that serves as a spectacular backdrop to some great fishing. The best fishing is usually found in the rivers and streams and there are literally thousands upon thousands of kilometres of water to test. Because of this, we have not listed every single stream and creek but chances are if there are fish in the main artery, there are fish in the small tributaries.

If you don't see a lake or stream listed here, check the Bighorn Backcountry section or the regulations for closures. Of course, it may also just be barren since there are many lakes that are too shallow and too high to support fish. The lakes that are stocked are marked with the ⬛ symbol.

A La Peche Lake (Map 38/C5)

Accessed by trail only, A La Peche Lake is a fine destination trout lake. The lake contains bull trout to 1.5 kg (3 lbs), rainbow and brook trout. Please note that the trail crosses native land and permission must be obtained to cross.

Athabasca River (Map 15, 21, 22, 27, 34, 35)

The Athabasca is the longest river in Alberta, winding 1,538 km (938 miles) through mountains, prairies, forests and muskeg to Lake Athabasca in Wood Buffalo National Park. It is also home to the only species of native rainbow trout in any river east of the Rockies. The river holds grayling, brook trout, bull trout, burbot, flathead chub, goldeye, lake chub, lake whitefish, longnose dace, longnose sucker, mountain whitefish, pike, pygmy whitefish, rainbow trout, slimy sculpin, spoonhead sculpin, spottail shiner, trout, perch, walleye, white sucker, yellow perch…basically if it swims in a river, you will probably find it somewhere along the Athabasca. In the upper reaches closer to the Rockies, bull trout (to 5 kg/10 lbs), grayling and rainbow (to 1 kg/2 lbs) as well as rocky mountain whitefish to 1.5 kg (3 lbs) are more prevalent.

Beaverdam Creek (Map 29/C2–F3)

Beaverdam Creek flows into the McLeod River 5 km (3 miles) south of Mercoal. There is good access to the upper reaches via an oil road. Rainbow, brook trout, bull trout to 0.5 kg (1 lb) and rocky mountain whitefish to 1 kg (2 lbs) are all found in the creek.

Berland River (Map 38, 39)

A major tributary of the Athabasca River, the Berland itself has dozens of excellent tributaries. Anglers will find grayling and rainbow trout to 1 kg (2 lb), bull trout to 7 kg (14 lbs) as well as rocky mountain whitefish to 2 kg (4 lbs). Access to the upper reaches of the river is gained about 75 km (46 miles) north of Hinton on Highway 40. The Big Berland Recreation Area is a popular spot for folks looking to access the trails leading along the upper stretch of this fine river.

Blackstone River (Map 24, 30)

Running past the Forestry Trunk and Chungo Roads, this river has steep banks that make access rather difficult. The river and its tributaries are limited to catch and release fishing to preserve the stocks and upstream from Mons Creek (Map 24/A3), the river is closed to fishing. This river contains bull trout to 2.5 kg (5 lbs) as well as cutthroat and rocky mountain whitefish to 1 kg (2 lbs). You might also find a few brook trout in smaller tributaries like Lookout Creek.

Blue, Cache & Graveyard Lakes (Map 35/A3)

Part of the chain of lakes in William A. Switzer Provincial Park, these lakes can be accessed via a hiking trail or by canoe. They all support pike to 2.5 kg (5 lbs) and whitefish to 1 kg (2 lbs), although reports of larger pike in Graveyard Lake are common.

Brazeau River (Map 16, 23, 29, 30)

The Brazeau is a major tributary of the North Saskatchewan River, starting in the high peaks of Jasper National Park and flowing nearly a third of the way across the province, with a brief stop in the Brazeau Reservoir, before flowing into the North Saskatchewan. Above the reservoir the Brazeau is big and fast and can be difficult and dangerous to fish. If you can find that perfect hole, some big fish can be caught. Bull trout, rocky mountain whitefish, cutthroat and pike all roam the system.

Brown Creek (Map 23, 24, 30)

Brown Creek is found about 35 km north of Nordegg off the Forestry Trunk Road. About a kilometre south of this, a logging road heads west along the Brown Creek Valley, providing good access for most of its length. You will find bull trout to 2 kg (4 lbs), cutthroat and brook trout to 0.5 kg (1 lb) as well as rocky mountain whitefish to 1 kg.

Cabin Creek (Map 38/F6–39/A6)

Cabin Creek feeds into the Upper Berland River, just a short distance north of where both creeks are crossed by Highway 40. On the south side of the highway, a trail follows the creek all the way to the Willmore Park border. You will find rainbow trout to 0.5 kg (1 lb) as well as bull trout and rocky mountain whitefish to 1 kg (2 lbs) in the creek.

Cadomin Pond (Map 28/G4)

Cadomin Pond is a difficult place to fish, due to steep banks and a 4 km (2.5 mile) bushwhack along Cadomin Creek. For your efforts, you will find rainbow to 1 kg (2 lbs).

Cardinal River (Map 28, 29, 30)

The Grave Flats Road provides the best access to the Cardinal, a fast flowing river that spills into the Brazeau River. The river is divided into two by a set of falls about 10 km downstream of Grave Flats. The upper river used to have an outstanding natural population of bull trout but they were fished to near extinction. The river, and tributaries such as the Russell and Toma, is now a catch and release fishery for cutthroat and bull trout. Below the falls, you will also find whitefish.

Clearwater River (Map 11, 12, 18, 19)

This large river drains a large area northeast of Banff National Park and eventually flows into the North Saskatchewan River near Rocky Mountain House. The river contains a wide variety of sport fish including brook trout (to 0.5 kg/1 lb), brown trout (to 1 kg/2 lbs), rocky mountain whitefish (to 1 kg/2 lbs), bull trout (to 3 kg/6 lbs) and pike (to 5 kg/11 lbs). This section of the river is easily accessed by highways or good logging roads. Many fishermen work the lower reaches of the river by floating down the river in a float tube, sampling the various pools and rapids along the way.

Cold Creek & Pond (Map 35/D6)

Cold Creek Pond is located just off Highway 40, 400 metres south of the Cold Creek Bridge. The shallow pond is stocked annually with rainbow and brook trout since it suffers from frequent winterkill. The best fishing on Cold Creek is found between where the creek crosses Highway 40, south of Highway 16 and the confluence with Maskuta Creek. You will also find small brook trout and some native rainbow trout here.

Cripple Creek (Map 18/C3–D1)
Cripple Creek is a main spawning tributary of the North Ram River. Accessed off the Forestry Trunk Road, the creek contains lots of cutthroat, which are smaller but easier to catch than in the Ram.

Cutoff, Elk & Limestone Creeks (Map 18/G6–19/B5)
Tributaries of the Clearwater River, these small creeks offer brown trout and bull trout. Limestone Creek also offers rocky mountain whitefish. Elk Creek is open from April 1-October 31 and offers fishing on a catch and release basis.

Drinnan Creek (Map 28/C2–E1)
Drinnan Creek contains rainbow trout, bull trout and rocky mountain whitefish, all too about 0.5 kg (1 lb). The creek is easily accessed off a backroad that leaves Highway 40 just south of the Gregg River Road turnoff.

Fairfax Lake (Map 30/B4) 9
It is not uncommon to pull a 1.5 kg (3 lb) brook trout from this lovely lake, which is also stocked annually with rainbow trout. Access is a long drive south of Coalspur off the Forestry Trunk Road.

Fall Creek (Map 19/A2)
Fall Creek has cutthroat above the falls and brown and cutthroat trout as well as rocky mountain whitefish below the falls. The Ram River Trail and several mining roads provide access to the creek.

Flapjack Creek & Lake (Map 23/B1)
You will have to hike 5 km (3 miles) up Ruby Creek to access Flapjack Creek. The catch and release stream contains cutthroats and bull trout. Flapjack Lake is a small muskeg lake, accessed by a 7 km (4.25 mile) trek, either by foot, horseback or ATV. The lake contains bull trout and some cutthroats.

Grande Cache Lake (Map 37/G4) 🐟
Highway 40 skirts the shores of Grande Cache Lake, which is found just east of Grande Cache itself. Every year it is stocked with rainbow trout and despite the heavy fishing pressure the lake sees, it has been known to yield rainbow up to 2.5 kg (5 lbs).

Gregg Lake (Map 35/A3)
A larger William A. Switzer Park lake that offers fishing for pike and whitefish. You might even find some walleye, which were stocked in 1992. The limit on walleye is currently zero.

Gregg River (Map 28/E2–35/G6)
Highway 40 and Gregg River Road skirt, cross and otherwise follow Gregg River for almost its entire length, providing easy access to this good rainbow and bull trout stream. You might also find brook trout, grayling and rocky mountain whitefish here. Tributaries like the Drinnan and Warden are worth testing too.

Hardisty Creek (Map 35/D5)
The Hardisty flows through Hinton, then into the Athabasca River. The creek contains some native rainbow trout.

Hinton Borrow Pit (Map 35/D5) 🐟
A small, unmarked lake, 3 km (2 miles) south of Hinton on Highway 40, the Hinton Borrow Pit has been stocked with rainbow and brook trout. Look for the lake on east side of the highway.

James River (Map 13/C3–G1)
The James River flows eastward from the boundary of the Bighorn Wildland into the Red Deer River north of Sundre. It has brown trout and rocky mountain whitefish that reach 1.5 kg (3 lbs) in size, but average much smaller. There are also the occasional bull trout to 2.5 kg (5 lbs) in the larger pools as well as northern pike and rainbow trout. The best fishing is found west of Secondary Highway 584.

Jarvis Creek & Pond (Map 35/A3–B1) 🐟
Jarvis Creek stitches together a chain of lakes in Switzer Provincial Park. You will find rainbow and brown trout and graylings here. The creek is an excellent place to fish from a canoe. The pond is found on the Graveyard/Cache Lakes Road and is regularly stocked with rainbow. It is fairly heavily fished and the trout remain small.

Jarvis Lake (Map 35/A3)
Jarvis is a typical William A. Switzer Park lake that provides fishing for pike, whitefish and walleye. Although pike were stocked back in the early 90s, the current possession limit is zero.

Joyce River (Map 18/C1)
Joyce River is a short river that drains into the North Ram River. It is accessed by hiking the Joyce River Trail off the Forestry Trunk Road. The river has good numbers of small cutthroat. However, fishing is catch and release.

Kinky Lake (Map 35/B6) 🐟
Located in the shadow of the front range of the Rockies, this pretty, stocked lake is mostly a brook trout lake. There are walleye but, as with most of the lakes in the area, the walleye limit is currently zero. A trail circles the lake allow for good shore access.

Little Berland River (Map 34/A2–39/C6)
The Little Berland is a good rainbow trout stream and a pretty good grayling stream, with some bull trout and rocky mountain whitefish to boot. Easily accessed along Highway 40, about 10 km (6 miles) further south than the Berland River.

Lone Teepee Creek (Map 38/E3)
Lone Teepee Creek skirts the boundary of Pierre Grey's Lakes Recreation Area, then crosses Highway 40 and into the Muskeg River. There are rainbow, bull and brook trout here.

Lovett River (Map 29/F3–30/A4)
The Lovett is a tributary of the Pembina River that flows parallel to the Forestry Trunk Road. The river contains rainbow and bull trout, rocky mountain whitefish and grayling.

Luscar Creek (Map 28/F3)
This catch and release creek is crossed twice by Highway 40 just south of the CRC Luscar Coal Mine as it flows towards the McLeod River. The creek is home to rainbow and bull trout as well as rocky mountain whitefish.

Lynx Creek (Map 18/F3)
This Lynx Creek is found north of Ram Falls on the Forestry Trunk Road. It has cutthroat to 2 kg (4 lbs), but most of the fish tend to be much smaller. However, the cutthroat must be greater than 40 cm (16 in) to keep.

McLeod River (Map 28, 29, 35)
The McLeod winds its way across a fair bit of landscape before finally emptying into the Athabasca River. A complete list of species in this river is basically a list of species in this area: grayling, brook trout, bull trout, burbot, finescale dace, goldeye, lake chub, longnose dace, longnose sucker, mountain whitefish, pike, rainbow trout, spoonhead sculpin, spottail shiner, perch, walleye, white sucker and perch. The river is closed to fishing above Whitehorse Creek (Map 28/G4). Look for pike, walleye and rocky mountain whitefish around Whitecourt, while brook trout are found upstream of Edson. The best grayling fishing is reported between the Highway 32 crossing and Medicine Lodge. As with most large rivers, there is a consumption advisory, due to pollution in the water.

Mary Gregg Lake & Creek (Map 28/E2) 🐟
The area around the stocked lake has been strip mined, making this a starkly dramatic, if not somewhat ugly place to fish. The lake contains rainbow and brook trout. Upstream the creek offers some small rainbow and bull trout, but beaver dams near the confluence of the McLeod River make it difficult for fish to move up the river.

Maskuta Creek (Map 35/B6)
The Maskuta runs parallel to Highway 16 for a few kilometres, just past the Highway 16 Forestry Trunk Road (Highway 40) junction. The creek contains rainbow trout and rocky mountain whitefish to 0.5 kg (1 lb) and is home to a recreation area.

Mason Creek (Map 38/B4)
Highway 40 crosses Mason Creek 17 km (10.5 miles) east of Grande Cache, just before the creek flows into the Muskeg River. Mason Creek is home to bull trout and rocky mountain whitefish to 1 kg (2 lbs), rainbow trout and some grayling.

Moberly Creek (Map 34/C2–F2)
The easiest place to access Moberly Creek is off the Rock Lake Road just north of the Wildhay River Bridge on Highway 40. A trail follows the creek northwest, all the way into Willmore Wilderness Park. Chances are you won't have to walk all the way upstream to find a good hole to catch rainbow or bull trout, grayling or rocky mountain whitefish.

Moosehorn Lake (Map 34/D4)
Best accessed by trail from the Rock Lake Road, this high elevation lake does not see many anglers now that access is closed to ATV's. Those willing to

make the trek will find cutthroat that were once stocked. Along the way, you will also pass by a small waterbody called Busby Lake. This unmarked lake contains bull trout.

Moose Lake (Map 30/A4)
A small lake that is found west of the more popular Fairfax Lake, Moose Lake contains pike, some of which might even be over minimum size 63 cm (25 inches).

Mumm Creek (Map 34/C3)
The Mumm flows into the Wildhay River about 5 km (3 miles) from where the Wildhay flows out of Rock Lake. Rainbow, bull trout and rocky mountain whitefish are the three most common catches here.

Muskeg River (Map 37, 38)
The Muskeg drains north out of Willmore Park, crosses Highway 40 26 km (16 miles) east of Grande Cache, then heads northwest into the Smoky River. The Muskeg is home to some monster bull trout, which are usually found upstream of a set of falls that divide the river into two distinct areas. The falls are a few kilometres northwest of the highway. The upper reaches also host some feisty rainbow, while below the falls grayling and rocky mountain whitefish are added to the mix.

Muskiki Lake (Map 29/F6)
Muskiki Lake lies next to the Grave Flats Road, 23 km (14 miles) west of its junction with the Forestry Trunk Road. Muskiki features stocked brook trout.

Mystery Lake (Map 28/C2)
Located near the Jasper Park boundary, there is only trail access into Mystery Lake. This fine lake makes a popular backcountry destination for anglers interested in bull trout. Rumour has it that fish up to 5 kg (10 lbs) are caught annually, but your average sized catch is closer to 2 kg (4 lbs).

Pembina River (Map 29/D5–30/E3)
The Pembina's claim to fame is its grayling and brook trout but if you want to take one home with you, go early in the season, as most legal-sized fish are quickly caught. In the upper river bull trout (to 2.5 kg/5 lbs), mountain whitefish (to 1 kg/2 lbs) and grayling (to 0.5 kg/1 lb) rule. The river is a major tributary of the Athabasca River.

Pierre Grey's Lakes (Map 38/F4)
A series of lakes, contained within the boundaries of Pierre Grey's Lakes Provincial Recreation Area. For anglers, the stocked lakes are divided into three distinct groups, lower, middle and upper. The Lower Lakes have rainbow to 1 kg (2 lbs) and bull trout to 2.5 kg (5 lbs). The **Middle Lakes** have rainbow to 2 kg (4 lbs) and bull trout to 2.5 kg (5 lbs) and the **Upper Lakes** have brook trout to 1.5 kg (3 lbs).

Prairie Creek (Map 19/B3–G2)
Prairie Creek is a large, slow-moving creek that flows into the Clearwater River south of Rocky Mountain House. The creek and its tributaries offer fairly good fishing for brook trout (to 0.5 kg/1 lb), brown trout (to 2 kg/4 lbs), bull trout (to 2.5 kg/5 lbs) and rocky mountain whitefish (to 1 kg/2 lbs). Between Vetch and Swan Creeks (Map 19/D2), Prairie Creek is closed from September 1 to March 31 and catch and release during the rest of the season. Other notable tributaries include Lick & Dry Creeks (Map 19/F1).

Ram River (Map 18, 19)
The river has some big cutthroat, some of which are rumoured to grow to a monstrous 60 cm (24 inches). The big cutthroat reside upstream of Ram Falls. Below the falls, you will find bull trout, cutthroat trout and rocky mountain whitefish (all to 2 kg/4 lbs or more). Various sections of the river (and its tributaries) are catch and release so check the regulations before you head out.

Red Deer River (Map 12, 13, 14)
The Red Deer River is a major river, with its headwaters at Red Deer Lakes in Banff. The river flows in a northeastern direction, draining a large area east of Banff. Good fishing for brown trout is offered in the upper reaches of the river southwest of Sundre. Other species in the river include rocky mountain whitefish (to 1.5 kg/3 lb) and some walleye. Please note the river is heavily regulated.

Rock Lake (Map 34/B4)
Sitting near the border of both Jasper National Park and Willmore Wilderness Park, this is a beautiful spot to lay down a line. Rock Lake is home to some monster lake trout, some as large as 8 kg (17 lbs). Other species in the lake include bull trout to 2.5 kg (5 lbs), rocky mountain whitefish to 1.5 kg (3 lbs) and pike.

Ruby Creek & Lakes (Map 29/C7–E6)
Both Ruby and Little Ruby Lakes were recently stocked with cutthroat, adding to brown (to 2.5 kg/5 lbs) and bull trout (to 3 lbs) already present. The lakes are a 13 km (8 miles) hike or horseback ride up an often-wet trail that passes through a muskeg. The current limit on cutthroat and bull trout is zero. The creek is a fast flowing creek, especially in lower reaches near the Cardinal River. This means that fish do not have many places to rest, feed and live. Still, there are a few nice holes that hold cutthroat and bull trout.

Silkstone & Lovett Lakes (Map 29/G3)
These small ponds are found on the Luscar Sterco Mine site, about 20 km south of Coalspur on the Forestry Trunk. The lakes are stocked with rainbow.

Smoky River (Map 25, 32, 37, 38)
The Smoky is a big river that drains most of the Willmore Wilderness before meeting Grand Cache. From here towards Grand Prairie access is much more readily found off Highway 40. The river contains some big pike and bull trout, along with whitefish grayling and rainbow.

Solomon Creek (Map 34/F4–35/A6)
The first major stream to join the Athabasca River outside of Jasper, Solomon Creek is an okay place to chase rainbow and bull trout to 0.5 kg (1 lb) or rocky mountain whitefish to 1.5 kg (3 lbs). The creek is crossed by the road to Brule, 8 km (5 miles) after the turnoff on Highway 40. Two kilometres past the Solomon Creek Bridge, a road heads up the valley.

Southesk River (Map 23/B2–F1)
A tributary of the Brazeau River, this remote stream requires some good navigational skills and preferably and ATV or horse to access it from the north. It is also possible to reach this river, which contains grayling, bull trout and pike, from the South Boundary Trail in Jasper. A good holding area is at the mouth of Neilson Creek. Note that portions of this river form the boundary of Jasper National Park and a national park fishing licence is required to fish these sections of the river.

Swan Lake (Map 19/F3)
To the west of the Forestry Trunk, Swan Lake still holds the Alberta record for the largest brown trout, an 8.2 kg (17 lb, 9 oz) fish caught in 1991. In addition to big browns, the lake holds large lake trout (to 5 kg/11 lbs) and pleasantly plump pike (to 10 kg/22 lbs). To help offset the relatively low numbers of fish, the lake is stocked regularly. The lake offers camping at the recreation area, but is subject to many restrictions.

Tershishner Creek (Map 24/E7)
Tershishner Creek drains into the north end of the Abraham Lake. It has brook trout to 0.5 kg (1 lb) as well as rocky mountain whitefish to 1 kg (2 lbs) and bull trout to 2 kg (4 lbs).

Thunder Lake (Map 30/A6)
Although the lake is stocked annually with pike and perch, fishing is not very good in this wide, shallow lake. You might also find brook trout here, but the lake is prone to winterkill. The lake is found 10 km (6 miles) west of the Forestry Trunk Road junction along Grave Flats Road.

Victor Lake (Map 37/F4)
Victor Lake is adjacent to Highway 40 and is found between Grande Cache, the town and Grande Cache, the lake. The lake is stocked annually with brook trout, but the real catch here is rainbow trout, some up to 4 lbs (8 lbs).

Warden Creek (Map 28/D1)
A road splits off from Highway 40 where it crosses the Gregg River. This road heads west and follows Warden Creek part of the way upstream. Small rainbow and bull trout exist in this catch and release stream.

Watson Creek (Map 29/A3)
Watson Creek crosses Highway 40 near the Watson Creek Recreation Area. The creek flows into the McLeod River just downstream. The creek is home to rainbow trout and rocky mountain whitefish.

Whitehorse Creek (Map 28/F4)
The best fishing on Whitehorse Creek is near its confluence with the McLeod River. Unfortunately, this is also where the Grave Flats Road crosses the Whitehorse and the creek sees a lot of pressure here. Fortunately, there is a trail that follows Whitehorse Creek west, deep into the front range of the Rockies. A popular hole is found at the mouth of Drummond Creek. Whitehorse Creek has bull trout, rocky mountain whitefish and rainbow trout.

Wildhorse Lake (Map 35/A7)
Wildhorse Lake is a lovely lake in the shadows of the front range of the Rockies. You will find stocked rainbow trout and grayling here.

Wildhay River (Map 33, 34, 35)

The upper reaches of the Wildhay are easily accessible. Highway 40 crosses the Wildhay River 35 km (21 miles) north of Hinton and the Rock Lake Road follows the river for much of the way between the lake and the trunk road. Above Rock Lake, into Willmore Park, there is good trail access. Farther downstream, however, is more challenging to reach, along long, lonely and sometimes difficult backroads. There is some good fishing for rainbow and bull trout, rocky mountain whitefish and grayling, especially along the Rock Lake to the Forestry Trunk Road section. The Wildhay is catch and release only.

Yara Creek (Map 13/E3)

Yara Creek is easily accessed of the Forestry Trunk Road north of the Red Deer River Recreation Area. It has brown trout and rocky mountain whitefish.

PADDLING ROUTES

From roaring whitewater to gentle flatwater stretches, the rivers and creeks of the Forestry Trunk area offer a tremendous variety of options. Generally speaking, the streams around the Rocky Mountains are much more challenging. The streams further east often provide gentler routes that can be enjoyed by canoe trippers. Those interested in exploring lakes only have a few alternatives, most notably the canoe route along Jarvis Creek in William Switzer.

For each river, we have included the put-in and take-out locations. The length of each run, the season and general comments are also provided. To grade the rivers, we have used a modified version of the International River Classification System. Please remember that river conditions are always subject to change and advanced scouting is essential. The information in this book is only intended to give you general information on the particular river you are interested in. You should always obtain more details from a local merchant or expert before heading out on your adventure.

Bighorn River (Map 24/E6)

From Crescent Falls, this paddle stretches 6 km (3.7 miles/3.5–5 hours) to Highway 11. The paddle is a tough Grade III route in low water and Grade IV in high water. It leads through a V-shaped canyon with one waterfall that must be portaged and five others that can be paddled, but only by experienced kayakers.

Blackstone River: The Gap to Old Bridge (Map 24/C3–D3)

The toughest part of the Blackstone, this section features no rapids above Class III, but has some interesting technical paddling through a narrow canyon that constricts to about 1 metre before widening up again. This section is 30 km (18 miles) long and should take paddlers about 5 hours to complete.

Blackstone River: Old Bridge to the Blackstone Recreation Area (Map 24/D3–F3)

While not as constricted as earlier sections, the Blackstone continues through narrow, canyons over this 11 km (6.8 mile) section. Although the river has only Class II+ rapids in this section (Class III at high water levels), it features lots of technical manoeuvring through a narrow canyon. Give yourself an hour or two to complete this section.

Blackstone River: Blackstone Recreation Area to the Lower

Bridge (Map 24/F3–30/G7)

This 41 km (26 mile) section of the Blackstone sees the river leave the canyon that defined the upper regions and start to widen out. There are some Class II+ rapids formed by ledges, channel constrictions and boulder gardens. This is a popular spot for whitewater canoeists.

Brazeau River: Four Point Creek Campground to Smallboys Camp (Map 16/C1–29/F6)

Hardcore paddlers can carry their boats for 14.5 km (9 miles) along the Nigel Creek Trail to Four Point Creek Campground, where the Brazeau River is finally deep enough to float a boat. This upper section is about as challenging as you can get, with Class VI drops (including a series of 3-7 metre falls). This is an epic 60 km (36 mile) journey with no margin for error. At the end of the trip, there is a 1.5 km portage to the village.

Brazeau River: Smallboys Camp to the Forestry Trunk Road (Map 29/F6–30/C6)

Most people who are doing the Brazeau from Four Point Creek also do this 15 km (9 miles) stretch too avoid the portage. This section has some Class III rapids, but is mostly a scenic float. Beyond the road, it is a 38 km (23 mile) stretch of river to the junction of the Blackstone River. The river continues to mellow in this area and posses few challenges.

Cardinal River (Map 29/A6–30/B6)

The Cardinal is a short, but lively river flowing south from the north/south Cardinal Divide. The river is Class II-III (or Class IV at high water levels) for most of the 42 km (25.5 miles) down from the put-in near the Cardinal Divide parking area to the bridge on the Forestry Trunk Road, just before it flows into the Brazeau River. The river was blocked by a mudslide a number of years ago, forming a small lake just before the take-out and the rapid over the slide is one of the most difficult on the entire run. Give yourself a full day (7-8 hours) to run the river.

Clearwater River: Elk Creek Recreation Area to Cutoff Creek (Map 18/G5–19/B5)

The Clearwater River is a medium sized river that starts in Banff, runs through the Bighorn Backcountry and meets the Forestry Trunk. This section of the river is a 21 km (4 hour) Grade II paddle that gets quite braided as it flows through the foothills. There are some small rapids, sweepers and logjams along the run, particularly around the corners. Towards the end of the run, the river drains into a single channel with the occasional small rapid.

Clearwater River: Cutoff Creek to Forestry Trunk Road Bridge (Map 19/B5–F6)

Paddlers looking to cherry pick the exciting bits of this run may wish to take-out at the Seven Mile Recreation area, 8 km (5.6 miles) from the put-in. The first half-dozen or so kilometres offer a number of exciting, although not terribly challenging Class II features. But the majority of this run is an easy float to the take-out, 20 km (12.4 miles) from where you put-in. It will take about an hour to get to the Seven Mile Recreation Area and about three to get to the Forestry Trunk Road Bridge. Beyond here the river is full of logjams that can block the river.

Gregg River (Map 28/E1–35/G6)

Highway 40 and Gregg River Road skirt, cross and otherwise follow Gregg River for almost its entire length. The usual put-in is where Highway 40 crosses the Gregg for the first time, heading south (Map 28/E1). From here, the river wanders to and fro through an open valley with some easy rapids. The river begins to tighten up and there are some good play spots at about the 15 km (9 mile) mark. The entire run into the McLeod River is 22 km (13 miles) and will take about four hours to complete.

Jarvis Creek Canoe Route (Map 35/A3)

There are five lakes in William A. Switzer Provincial Park that are all linked by Jarvis Creek. It is possible to canoe from one end of the park to the other along the creek. The canoeing is easy (Grade I). In fact, the only difficult part of the journey is hauling your canoe over the occasional beaver dam. The creek is so slow that you can paddle upstream almost as easily as down.

McLeod River (Map 28/G5–35/G7)

Another major river that meanders through the heart of Alberta, the McLeod finally joins up with the Athabasca River at Whitecourt. Below the junction with Whitehorse Creek (Map 28/G4), the McLeod is lively, but not too difficult (Class II-II+). Above the Whitehorse, this is a technician's paradise, with narrow chutes and canyons and waterfalls up to 9 metres (that's just under 30 feet). Most people looking for the Class V+ and VI rapids above Whitehorse Creek Bridge put in 4.2 km (2.6 miles) south of the Whitehorse Creek Bridge. Chutes and drops like Just Plain Crazy (Class V+), Pincushion (Class V), Maelstrom (Class VI) and Hammer Time (Class VI) can be deadly with drops up to 9 metres (24 feet). But if you've got the gall, this is a run that'll blow your mind.

For people looking for something a little easier, the run from the old Steeper Recreation Area to the McLeod River Recreation area is 36.7 km (22.4 miles) Grade II paddle with some Class III rapids and a high possibility of log jams, sweepers and other obstructions. The river just above the put-in is slightly more challenging, but is prone to logjams. Scout this area before attempting. The whole run can be done in a day, but if you like to get out and explore or simply admire the scenery, it is best done as an overnight trip.

Muskeg River (Map 37/G2–38/C3)

The Muskeg is a small river, suitable for whitewater canoes and kayaks only. Because it is so small, even a little rain can swell the river significantly, making this a swift, difficult river From the Muskeg River Bridge to the Mason Creek Recreation area it is a fun, easy paddle that is easily accessible along Highway 2. This is a great place to practice with easy access. The rapids top out at Grade II at low to mid water levels and there are a number of good surfing spots to play in. You can follow the river past Mason Creek for just over a kilometre, but you want to beware of Muskeg Falls. This is a 13 metre (43-foot) cascade that should not run. Below Muskeg Falls, the 22 km (13.4 mile) paddle along the Muskeg River runs through a mostly untouched wilderness before reaching the Smoky River. While the paddling is fairly easy, there are a couple of ledges that span the river that will mess you up if you are not careful. The first is about 1.5 from the put-in and the second is near the halfway point. You will have to carry your craft for 1.5 km from Highway 40 to below the falls.

Ram River: South Ram (Map 18/E4–19/B1)
Remote. Dangerous. Beautiful. These are just a few of the adjectives that describe the South Ram. Road access into this area is almost non-existent as the river cuts across a mostly untouched wilderness from Ram Falls on the Forestry Trunk Road to the North Fork Road Bridge. All paddlers must be self-sufficient. Getting down to the river below Ram Falls can be a bit of work, but is not impossible. The Grade III/IV paddle leads some 54 km (33.5 miles/2–4 days) and while there are long sections of easy paddling, there are also several canyons, numerous waterfalls and lots of ledges, rapids and boulder gardens. There are two major waterfalls that will need to be portaged–Tapestry Falls and Table Rock Falls. Getting down these falls is similar to getting down Ram Falls–steep, scree slopes with sometimes perilous footing. Successfully running the waterfalls is beyond the abilities of most mere mortals. Also of note is Sulfur Canyon, downstream of the confluence with the North Ram, where the river is funnelled through a narrow canyon. The lower section of the canyon is Class V+/VI series of falls, rapids and chutes. After all this excitement, the last section of the river is an easy float. To shorten the float, there is a difficult to find take-out on a road that heads west a few kilometres north of the Prairie Creek Recreation Area. The pipeline leads from the end of that road to the river. In wet weather, this area is impassable. The Upper Ram is described in the Bighorn Backcountry section.

Red Deer River: Forestry Trunk Road to Deer Creek Rec Area (Map 13/E4–G4)
Considered one of the best paddling rivers in Alberta, the Red Deer River offers some challenging paddling in the foothills between Bighorn Creek and Coalcamp Creek. The main access route into the area is the Forestry Trunk Road. The furthest upstream most people put in is near the Bighorn Creek confluence at the Ya Ha Tinda Ranch. See the Bighorn Backcountry for this section. Below the Forestry Trunk, a 12.5 km (7.8 mile/2–4 hour) section of the river is rated Grade II/III. The main feature of this section is Gooseberry Ledge, a Class III drop. There is a series of small rapids leading to the ledge as the river flows over a gravel bed with a few large boulders. Below the ledge, the river becomes more difficult and there is a series of Class III drops and rapids.

Red Deer River: Deer Creek Recreation Area to Cache Hill (Map 13/G4–14/A4)
Finding the take-out at Cache Hill will probably be the most difficult part of this 11.5 km (7.1 mile/1.5–2 hour) Grade II paddle through a wide valley. There are some large surfing waves that develop during high water and some large rapids towards the take-out in both low and high water.

Red Deer River: Cache Hill to Williams Creek (Map 14/A4–B3)
This is an easy 8 km (5 mile/1–3 hour) Grade I paddle in low water and a Grade II paddle in high water. The route takes you through a wide valley where the river flows over a continuous gravel bed with few boulders and obstacles. There are several rapids, a few narrow channels and some sweeping corners that add challenge to the paddle.

Red Deer River: Williams Creek to Coalcamp Creek (Map 14/B3–D3)
More challenging than the previous stretch of river, this 9 km (5.6 mile/1–2.5 hour) Grade II/III route leads through an open valley with some challenging rapids and drops. Double Ledge, towards the middle of the run and the Coalcamp Ledge, near the Coalcamp Creek take-out, are a couple of classic drops to lookout for.

Smoky River (Map 25, 32, 37, 38)
It is possible to paddle the Smoky River from Grande Cache to Grande Prairie, a distance of 219 km (136 miles), which would take the average paddler a week or more to complete. Shorter trips include a 10 km (6 mile) section from the Sulphur Gates Staging Area to the Blue Bridge near Grande Cache. This short, easy run is best done by staying left on the main channel when the river divides. Expect to take two hours to paddle this Grade I+ section. An old road to the left just before you enter the staging area leads down to the river.

From the Blue Bridge, there is another short run to the Smoky River Coal Mine. There is a short Class III rapid, about 0.5 km past an old cable crossing that can be run (stay left to avoid the ledge on right) or portaged around, depending on skill level. The rest of the run is Class I/I+. If you miss the mine, you can take-out at the Sheep Creek confluence or paddle the rest of the way to Grande Prairie.

Sulphur River (Map 37/F4)
The Sulphur River is a wild ride (Class I/III+) from the Sulphur Gates Staging Area south of Grande Cache to 104 St (off Hoppe Ave) in town. This is a great way to experience the spectacular Sulphur Gates, where the river flows through a canyon with 70 metre (230 foot) cliffs right before it flows into the Smoky. There are lots of nice holes and standing waves to play in.

Wildhay River (Map 34/E3–35/B1)
The Wildhay is a small river, with some fun Class II rapids. The river is a great training river for people looking to make the jump from flatwater to whitewater. From the Old Bridge to the Group Camp is a 10 km (6 mile) section of the Wildhay, which has some great little rapids and standing waves for surfing. The Group Camp is found about 5 km upstream from Highway 40. Below the group camp is a 5 km (3 mile) section of river down to Highway 40. This section has fewer rapids than farther upstream, but more than downstream and is a good introduction to whitewater for neophytes. From here, there is a 24 km (14.5 mile) paddle down to near the Jarvis Creek confluence. To get to the take-out, travel about 12.4 km (7.5 miles) down the Hay River Road to a turnoff on your left, just past the foundations of an old ranger station. It is about 200 metres to the river. Learn it well, because if you miss it, it is a long walk back from the next take-out point, near the Pinto Creek confluence. This section is 24 km (14.5 miles) long and has a couple fast drops, but no really tricky rapids.

TRAILS

The Forestry Trunk Road frames the area east of the bigger parks and offers access to a great variety of activities and trails to explore. To help you select a trail in the area, we have provided brief descriptions, including information about length, location and difficulty, of most of the formal and many informal trail systems in the area. Time and distance given is for a return trip, unless otherwise noted. Also included in each description is a symbol to indicate what the trail is used for–mountain biking, hiking, horseback riding, etc. Multi-use trail descriptions are written from a hiker's point of view.

A La Peche Lake Trail (Map 38/C5–E4)
About 32 km (20 miles) south of Grande Cache, across from Pierre Gray Lakes is a large gravel pit. This is the start of the A La Peche Trail, a 25 km (16 mile) multi-use trail that takes people to a popular fishing lake. Now that there is a new road here, this trailhead is more popular with ATVers, especially since there are a number of cutlines in the area that can be explored as well. Hikers and horseback riders can hook up with Cowlick Creek Trail and the Muskeg River Trail, both of which enter Willmore where ATV's and snowmobiles are not allowed. The route also connects in two places with the Mahon Creek Trail.

Allenby–Ram Falls Trail (Map 18/E4)
The trail begins along a well-defined cart track at the Ram Falls Recreation Area. The initial 1.5 km (0.9 mile) stage of the trail allows for good views of the narrow and rugged Ram Canyon. For those more adventurous types, follow the old ranger patrol route for some 15 km (9.3 miles). This later route does require creek crossings.

Ambler Mountain Trail (Map 37/E3)
An easy 4 km (1 hour, 2.5 miles) stroll up the aptly named Ambler Mountain. Okay, so maybe it isn't that easy since there are a few steep pitches, but the trail gets you into the alpine meadows with only 381 metres (1,238 feet) of elevation gained. If you want to catch the wildflowers in bloom, it is best to go in July or early August. Beaverdam Road, which you must follow for about 7 km, can be rough for 2wd vehicles. The trip can be extended another couple kilometres by hiking to the second summit of Ambler. The trailhead is unmarked; watch for a quad trail that crosses the road.

Athabasca Lookout Trails (Map 35/B4)
Although it is possible to drive up to this lookout via the road to the Nordic Centre, it is a much more interesting trip to hike up. The trailhead is found along the Jarvis Lake Road, 2 km (1.2 miles) north of the turnoff to the Nordic Centre. The trail follows an ATV trail along a cutline part of the way up, then heads right and follows a trail to the edge of the ridge. It is 4.6 km (2.9 miles) to the top, gaining 416 metres (1,352 feet) along the way. In the summer, the 33 km (20 miles) of trails around the Nordic centre are taken over by hikers and bikers. The trails are signed with distance markers so that you can choose the length of trail appropriate to your skill level.

ForestryTrunkAdventures

Athabasca Ranch & River Trails (Map 35/C5) 🥾🚴⛷️🏃🎣
The ranch offers a series of looping trails, totalling 12 km (7.32 miles). They are located just off the Hinton/Entrance Airport Road and open to hiking, biking, skiing and snowshoeing. On the north side of the bridge on Highway 40, the River Trail follows the shoreline northeast for 8 km (4.9 miles) towards the Athabasca Ranch. Outside of here, it is mostly old roads that are open to off highway vehicles. Note that some of these trails are only open the May long weekend and from June 25 to the end of the Labour Day long weekend.

Baseline Lookout Trail (Map 19/C3) 🥾🚴🏇🏍️🎣
At the lookout gate off Forestry Trunk Road, a 4 km (2.5 mile) hike climbs through dense fir and alder forests. It is an easy 410 m (1333 ft) ascent to the lookout, which sports panoramic views of the area.

Beaverdam & East Bush Falls Trails (Map 30 Inset) 🥾🏇🏇🎣
The Beaverdam Trail is a loop trail that starts along the Canadian Northern Railway in Nordegg. The gentle trail (elevation gain 40m/130 ft) and the orchids that are abundant at Beaverdam make this a popular 13.8 km (8.6 mile) hike. Leading south is the East Bush Falls Loop Trail. The 6 km (3.7 mile) trail gains 90 m (293 ft) in elevation and cuts across a couple of creeks as it makes its way to some pretty waterfalls. There are a number of old roads in the area that can make finding the falls rather tricky.

Berland River Trail (Map 33/E2–39/A6) 🏕️🥾🚴🏇🏍️🎣🎣
This is one of the main access points into Willmore and only the first 5.5 km (3.4 miles) of the trail is open to ATVs. Beyond here horsepackers and backpackers can ramble as long as they like. It is a 32.8 km (20 mile) return trip from the recreation area to the junction with the Adams Creek Trail.

Bighorn Recreation Trail (Map 35/D5–F7) 🥾🚴🏇🎣
Built in the early 1900s by the Dominion of Canada Forestry Service as a pack trail, this route was originally known as the High Divide Ridge Trail. It is a difficult 22.5 km (13.7 mile) one-way trek that is best done over two days. The trail climbs 523 metres (1,700 feet) in 6 km (3.6 miles) and then follows the ridge for 12 km (7.3 miles), before dropping slowly to the Gregg River Valley. The northern trailhead is 0.5 km along the Cold Creek Road, just off Robb Road, while the southern trailhead is near the bridge at km 38 of the Gregg River Road. You will need a shuttle, unless you plan to trek back the way you came or follow the roads back.

Black Canyon Creek Trail (Map 30/Inset) 🥾🚴🎣
An 18.5 km (11.5 mile) hike or bike takes you through meadows and forests and up steep slopes. Two viewpoints along the way provide views of the North Saskatchewan River Valley and the Black Canyon Creek. The trailhead is located at the Fish Lake Recreation Area.

Black Cat Ranch Trails (Map 34/G5–35/A6) 🥾🏇⛷️🏃🎣
Maintained by the folks at Black Cat Guest Ranch, but open to the public (the trails are on Crown land, after all), there is a grand total of 77.5 km (47.3 miles) of trails in this scenic valley. The trails are highlighted by the dramatic Black Cat Mountain and the front range of the Rocky Mountains. In winter, the trails are groomed on an ad hoc basis. Be sure to call (780) 865-3084 for information on snow conditions before heading out.

Black Cat/Jarvis Link Trail (Map 34/G5–35/A4) 🥾🏇⛷️🏃🎣
There are almost 80 km (49 miles) of trails in the Black Cat Ranch area and over 20 km (12 miles) of trails inside William A. Switzer Provincial Park. Linking the two systems is this moderate 30 km (18.3 mile) trail. This is a popular trail in winter with cross-country skiers.

Blackstone Fire Lookout Trail (Map 30/F7) 🥾🚴🏇🏍️🎣
The Blackstone Fire Lookout trailhead is located 500 metres north of the Brown Creek Recreation Area on the Forestry Trunk Road. The easy 5 km (3.1 mile) route follows the road up to the old fire lookout and entails an elevation gain of 250 metres (813 feet).

Blue Hill Lookout Trail (Map 13/F3) 🥾🚴🎣
Off the Forestry Trunk Road, this easy trail follows a steep, forested old road to the scenic lookout. It is an 8 km (5 mile), half-day hike or bike that gains about 580 m (1,885 ft).

Brazeau Lookout Trail (Map 30 Inset) 🥾🚴⛷️🎣
This is a 23 km (14.3 mile) hike or bike from Nordegg that will take at least a day. With a graveyard and two abandoned coalmines along the way, you are provided with a little history. The climb to the lookout is tough and confusing in spots, but the views near the top are very rewarding.

Brazeau River & Brown Creek OHV Area (Map 30/C6–E7) 🏍️🚵
The Brazeau River Recreation Area is found about 72 km (44 miles) north of Nordegg on the Forestry Trunk Road, while the Brown Creek site is found about 20 km before that. Both areas offer a series of informal off highway vehicle or ATV trails to explore. Most riders stay at the recreation areas, but remember that operation of OHV's is not allowed in the recreation areas themselves.

Brown Creek Area (Map 30/E7)
The Brown Creek Recreation Area is used as an overnight camping area for riders, but OHV's are not allowed off-trailer within the recreation area itself. There are no formally designated ATV trails in the area, but there are lots of informal trails.

Brule Mine Trail (Map 34/G6) 🥾🚴🏇🎣
This 15 km (9.2 mile) trail runs north from Brule, just northwest of the road to the old Brule Mine and then loops back. This is a fairly easy hike, though a little long for the tenderfoot.

Brule Lake Sand Dunes Trail (Map 34/G7–35/B5)
🥾🚴⛷️🏃🏍️🎣
The Sand Dunes Trail is a 24.2 km (14.8 mile) multi-use trail that follows an old railbed on the eastern shore of Brule Lake. The most notable feature is the desert-like sand dunes, but the trip will also take you to the remains of an old railway station. Many people mark this site as the terminus to the trip, but it is possible to make it into a 56 km (34.1 mile) one-way trek by continuing past the old station and following the old railbed to Highway 40. The trailhead is on Highway 16, 200 metres west of Overlander Lodge.

Cache Percotte Forest Trails (Map 35/E5) 🥾🚴⛷️🏃
Cache Percotte Forest is located southeast of Hinton and has 40 km (24.4 miles) of trails within its boundaries. Trails in the network range from easy to moderate, although most mountain bikers and cross-country skiers will find some of the ascents and descents fairly technical.

Cadomin Cave Trail (Map 28/G4) 🥾🎣
Climbing 350 metres (1,138 feet) in about 2 km, the majority of hikers on this trail are actually cavers heading for the Cadomin Cave. Remember, caves are both dangerous and extremely fragile. Do not enter unless you know what you are doing and have proper equipment—the cave is almost 3 km (1.8 miles) long and there are a number of passages to get lost in. The caves are closed from September to the end of April when the bats hibernate.

Canyon Creek Trail (Map 35/F3) 🥾🚴🎣
A scenic 3 km (1.8 miles) loop along Canyon Creek offering spectacular views of the canyon and hoodoos along the creek. The trail runs to the Athabasca River along one side of the creek and returns on the other. There is a 100 metre (325 feet) elevation loss down to the Athabasca. On a warm day there is a swimming hole along Canyon Creek. The trailhead is just past the A16 km sign on your right when travelling east on Emerson Creek Road.

Cardinal Divide East Ridgewalk (Map 29/B5) 🥾🎣
From the Cardinal Divide parking area, you can head northeast along an old road cum trail to the ridge that divides the Alberta drainage neatly in two. This area is usually a riot of wildflowers during the summer. There are few alpine ridges in Alberta that are this easy to access.

Cardinal River Trail (Map 28/G6–29/A5) 🥾🚴🏇🏍️🎣
There are a couple of sections on this moderate trail that aren't very pleasant—poorly drained and well-rutted by too many ATV tires. For those that persevere, it is 9 km (5.5 miles) to the base of Prospect Mountain and the headwaters of the Cardinal River, climbing just over 200 metres (650 feet).

Caw Ridge Trail (Map 37/C1) 🥾🏇🏍️🎣
The ridge is home to an impressive number of wildlife, including the largest mountain goat and mountain caribou populations in Alberta. The Caw Ridge turn-off is found 30 km down the 4wd vehicle only Beaverdam Road. Follow the old road to the top of the ridge, a distance of 8.1 km (4.9 miles) to the top. Once on top of the ridge, hikers can wander while ATVers should stick to the main trail.

Collie Creek Trail (Map 34/D2) 🏕️🥾🚴🏇🎣
A 30 km (18.3 mile) trail that follows Collie Creek across the easternmost corner of Willmore Wilderness. The trail hooks up with Evans Trail, Mumm Creek Trail and about 1,000 km of other trails in Willmore, Jasper and even across the border into BC.

Cowlick Creek Trail (Map 37/G4–38/B5)

Part of the much longer Mountain Trail that takes visitors through the heart of Willmore, the Cowlick Creek section on touches on the fringes of Willmore from just east of Grande Cache. The 13 km (7.9 mile) trail also hooks up with the A La Peche Trail. It is a popular staging area for horseback riders and there is a corral at the trailhead.

Esker Trails (Map 18/D3 & 18/F5)

A moderate, 14 km (8.7 mile) hike begins off the Forestry Trunk Road at Lynx Creek. It gains 260 m (845 ft) in elevation as it runs north through an open valley with views of the Front Ranges. The trail can be hard to follow in places. A second trail can be accessed further south at the Elk Creek Bridge. This 16 km (10 mile) option passes Peppers Creek and the Clearwater River in the Bighorn area.

Folding Mountain Trail (Map 28/C2–35/B7)

This difficult 15.6 km (9.5 mile) slog up 980 metres (3,185 feet) takes the determined hiker to the top of Folding Mountain. The grunt is well worth the effort as there are great views south and west, into Jasper and north and east, over the foothills. Past the top of Folding Mountain, the trail continues another 17 km (10.4 miles) to hook up with roads in the Drinnan Creek area. If you really want to, you can get to the Miette hot springs by foot. The Folding Mountain Trail hooks up with the Mystery Lake Trail here, which in turn leads into Jasper Park and to the hot springs. The trailhead is on Highway 16, just west of Folding Mountain Resort; park at the resort, then walk along Highway for about 5 minutes and watch for trail heading into the bushes.

Goat Cliffs Trail (Map 37/F2)

A difficult trail to access with an even more difficult climb makes the Goat Cliffs one of those trails that doesn't see many tourists. The 3.5 km (2.1 mile) one-way trail gains 820 metres (2,665 feet), making this a pretty relentless hike. It follows a (surprise, surprise) goat trail up a ridge to the top. The trailhead is a little tricky to get to, turning right at the Smoky River Coal/ATCO Electric site, then right again to cross the river and right yet again once you are across. Take the right fork (oddly enough) when the road branches and finally turn left, just before the sawmill, into a parking lot. Many people find the steep cliffs near the top too exposed and stop at the base.

Grande Cache Trails (Map 37/F4)

Located between the town of Grande Cache and the Sulphur River to the south and the Smoky River to the west is a maze of trails and old roads to explore. These trails are mostly easy and there are more than 20 km (12 miles) of them weaving across the countryside. One of the most popular leads down to Fireman's Park before continuing onto Sulphur Gates. The Home Trail is a short 1.5 km (0.9 mile) linking trail on the east side of town that hooks up with the Mineshaft Trail as well as the southeast trailhead to Grande Mountain. The Mineshaft Trail climbs for 4 km (2.4 miles) to an old mine shaft.

Griffith Trail (Map 37/F4)

It is possible to make a 12 km (5 hour; 7.4 mile) loop of the townsite via the Griffith Trail. The actual distance walked or cycled will vary. There are a number of access points, although the most convenient is near the south end of Hoppe Avenue.

Grande Mountain Trail (Map 37/G3)

Although Grande Mountain is not an imposing mountain, the views offered from the summit are indeed grand. On a clear day, you can see all the way to Mount Robson. The moderate 4.8 km/2.9 mile (90 minute) trail gains 730 m (2,373 ft) to the summit of the 2,000 m (6,500 ft) Grande Mountain. The trailhead is north of town near the cemetery. Mountain bikers can make it to the summit along the access road for the radio tower, located east of town on Highway 40.

Happy Creek Trail (Map 35/D5)

Located south of the town of Hinton, the Happy Creek Trail is an easy 5 km (3.1 mile) loop up Happy Creek to near its headwater, then back down the other side. Although the trail is easy to follow on foot, riding it on bike is fairly technical and should be left to the experts or people who don't mind pushing their bike a lot.

Hinton Trails (Map 35/D5)

If laid end to end, the trails in Hinton would stretch 15.2 km (9.3 miles). But they are not laid end to end. Rather, they are spread out across 18 short, mostly interconnected trails, the longest of which is only 2 km long.

Huckleberry Tower OHV Trails (Map 38/G5–39/D3)

This popular ATVing area is found south of Grande Cache on Highway 40. Drive 42 km (26 miles) south to the Huckleberry Tower Road turn-off. From here, it is 35 km (22 miles) to the tower, but there are plenty of random trails in the area that can be followed, too.

Hoff Siding OHV Trails (Map 38/G5)

This popular ATVing area starts from the same location as the Huckleberry Tower Trails. From the Huckleberry turn-off, head 5 km (3 miles) to the main cutline, which then heads 18 km (11 miles) southwest to the boundary of Willmore Wilderness. ATVs aren't allowed in Willmore, but there are other cutlines and trails that intersect the main trail.

James Pass Trail (Map 13/C2)

This moderate 11 km (6.8 miles) trail will take you along the James River to James Pass and Eagle Lake in the Bighorn Backcountry. The trailhead is located north of the Mountain Aire Lodge on the Forestry Trunk Road.

Kakwa Provincial Park Trails (Map 36)

The heart of Kakwa is found north of this book around the Kakwa Falls. This book only touches on a few remote trails that see few visitors each year. The Famm/Trench Creek Trail starts 27 km (16.5 miles) from the nearest trailhead, breaking off the South Kakwa Trail and heading southeast into Willmore Wilderness Park. It is 10 km (6.1 miles) from where the trail leaves the South Kakwa River Trail to the Willmore/Kakwa boundary (and about double that to the nearest trailhead on the Willmore side of things). The South Kakwa River Trail picks up where the Kakwa River Trail left off (17 km/10.4 miles from the nearest trailhead). It follows the South Kakwa River southwest for another 15 km (9.2 miles).

Limestone Lookout Trail (Map 19/C6)

This trail follows the south ridge of Limestone Mountain to the summit. There, the hiker can enjoy an incredible view from the Clearwater River area out to the prairies. This moderate 6 km (3.7 mile) return hike takes half a day and gains 150 m (488 ft) in elevation.

Silkstone and Lovett Lake Trails (Map 29/G3)

If you look closely at these lakes, you may notice something different about them. Something…unnatural. That would be exactly right, as the lakes were created as part of the reclamation process of Luscar's Coal Valley Mine. As part of that process, they also developed a trail system through the young forest. Of course, most people who visit here are heading for the lakes, which are stocked with rainbow trout.

Luscar Lookout Trail (Map 28/F3)

Although the surrounding scenery is affected by open pit mining, the front range of the Rockies looms in the background. This fairly easy uphill hike is 6.4 km (3.9 mile) return, climbing 275 metres (894 feet).

Mary Gregg Lake Trail (Map 28/E2)

Found between Cadomin and Hinton, Mary Gregg Lake is most popular with the angling crowd. More than that, it is a popular winter destination for ice fishing. The trail can be skied or snowmobiled, but the low snow levels mean that most people hike or quad in, even in winter.

Moberly Lookout Road (Map 34/E3)

Just north of the Wildhay River Bridge on Highway 40, a logging road heads west. From the intersection about a kilometre up the road, a rough road heads southwest to the Lookout. This road is usually gated, so you don't have to worry about traffic. It is an 8 km (4.9 miles) return trek, gaining 360 metres (1,170 feet).

Moosehorn Lake Trail (Map 34/D4)

A 15 km (9.1 mile) trail climbs from Rock Lake Road to Moosehorn Lake on the boundary of Jasper National Park. The trails beyond are quite rugged and wet as they hook up with the North Boundary Trail system to the west and Miette to the south.

Mount Hammel Trail (Map 37/E3)

Mount Hammel rises across the Smoky River Valley from Grande Cache, on the edge of the front range of the Rockies. The hike up is a difficult 7.5 km (3.5 hour) climb, most of it along an old logging road. On a clear day from the summit, you can see Mount Robson in BC. A second trail to the top–actually a goat trail–follows the mountain's northeast ridge. Hikers can, of course, link the two into a 15 km loop, while mountain bikers should stick to the road. Also in the area is the short trail to Twin Falls.

ForestryTrunkAdventures

Mount Louie Trail (Map 37/G4) 🥾🐎
From the Cowlick staging area, it is a 5.5 km (3.4 mile) trip to the top of Mount Louie, which is located south of Grande Cache Lake.

Mount Stearn/Lightning Ridge Trails (Map 37/E4) ⛺🥾📷
It is a 20 km (8 hour, 12 mile) return hike to Lightning Ridge, gaining 1,480 metres (4,855 feet) to the high mountain ridge. Many people opt instead for the summit of Mount Stearn, which is only 6.5 km (and 1,000 vertical metres) from the trailhead. Either way, this is a fairly difficult trail, especially doing Lightning Ridge as a day hike. For those looking for a multi-day trip, the **Stearn Highcountry Route** is a challenging backpacking trip that continues past Lightening Ridge and into Willmore. Once over the pass below the ridge, the trail heads down through a lush sub-alpine forest that is usually overgrown with nasty dwarf birch (wear pants). The trail descends to Kvass Flats and then follows the main trail back to the Sulphur Gates Staging Area. The total distance varies; depending on the route and number of side trips, but it is usually a safe bet to allow for two days and a minimum 24 km (15 miles). This is a difficult trip, gaining at least 960 metres/3,120 feet depending on your route.

Mumm Creek Trail (Map 34/C3–B1) ⛺🥾🚴🐎🐟📷
The Mumm Creek Trail starts where Mumm Creek crosses the Rock Lake Road and heads northwest into Willmore. You will eventually meet Little Berland River, where the trail ventures northeast and follows the Little Berland to a junction with the Evans Trail on the boundary of Willmore. This is a moderate 30 km (18.3 miles) one-way trail. You can either return the way you came, hook up with the Willmore network of trails, head out via Evans Creek or return via the Collie Creek Trail.

Muskeg Falls Trail (Map 38/B3) 🥾📷
From Highway 40, an easy 1.5 km (30 minute) one-way hike with minimal elevation gain accesses the falls. There is a fork in the trail, one path leading to the top of the falls, one to the bottom. Both can be wet and slippery.

Mystery Lake Trail (Map 28/C2) ⛺🥾🚴🐎🏍
This moderate 30 km (18.3 mile) return trail to Mystery Lake hooks up with the trail system in Jasper National Park. Past the lake, you can follow the trail for another 10.5 km (6.4 miles) to Miette Hot Springs along one of Jasper's less pleasant trails. The trail is known for stiff climbs with lots of bushwhacking.

Nordegg Mines Ridgewalk (Map 30 Inset) 🥾🚴📷
Although this trail can be followed from the town of Nordegg, it is better accessed off the Forestry Trunk Road south of town. This moderate, 8 km (5 mile) trail follows a series of roads, past three abandoned coal mines, to a ridge full of great viewpoints of the North Saskatchewan River Valley and Brazeau Range. The trail, which follows part of the Brazeau Lookout Trail, gains 340 m (1,105 ft) in elevation.

Ogre Canyon Trails (Map 34/G7) 🥾🚴🐎📷
The trail to the canyon is an easy 16 km (9.7 mile) trip along a mostly deserted road. Because the road is drivable (by 4X4s), many hikers only hike the last little section into the canyon, while bikers and horseback riders take the longer trip. For hikers looking to stretch their legs more, the difficult **Bedson Ridge Trail** continues 14 km (8.5 mile) to the ridge. This trail switches back and forth as it climbs up, then down to Bedson Ridge. This is a historic packhorse trail and is not for the faint of heart or the acrophobic (afraid of heights). There is some scrambling and climbing gear may be needed in some places, as you make your way to the top of this popular climbing destination.

Old Entrance Trail (Map 35/B5) 🥾🚴🏍🐟📷
The trailhead for the Old Entrance trail is on the road to Brule, about 2 km (1 mile) from the Highway 40 junction. The trail runs down to the Athabasca River, then east and west along the river. East will take you to Old Entrance. If you were to walk both east and west along the river, you would cover about 15 km (9.3 miles) by the time you got back to the trailhead.

Overlander Trails (Map 35/A7) 🥾🚴🐎❄🏍
While the historic Overlander route passes through this area, it is developed into something much greater. This area was once logged and there are a number of old logging roads and other trails here. There are more than 20 km (12 miles) of trails tucked in the nook formed by Highway 16, Brule Lake and Jasper National Park. This maze of trails is popular with most every type of recreationist–bikers, hikers and ATVers in summer and cross-country skiers, snowshoers and snowmobilers in the winter.

Peppers Trail (Map 35/B4) 🥾❄
An easy, but long trip along an old logging road that runs past Peppers Lake and along Peppers Creek to William Switzer Provincial Park. The route is 26 km (15.9 miles) return.

Pine Management Trails (Map 35/F7) 🥾🐎🏍❄🚴🏍📷
Starting at the Gregg Cabin Day Use Area, there is a series of five interpretive trails, totalling 6 km (3.6 miles) that can be hiked in about 2.5 hours. The trails are all easy, with little to no elevation gain and open to ATVs.

Ranger Station Walk (Map 30 Inset) 🥾❄
The trailhead for this easy 7 km (4.3 mile) trail is found at the Coliseum Trail parking lot near Nordegg. It is an easy walk to Shunda Creek and its beaver dams. Some bushwhacking may be required.

Rock Lake Trails (Map 34/B4) 🥾🐎❄🏍🐟📷
There is a network of trails around Rock Lake that can be used to hook up with trails in both Jasper and Willmore. The Rock Lake Lookout Trail follows an old road (along the start of the Mountain Trail) and trail to a lookout with views that are as impressive as any in Jasper itself. The moderate 9.7 km (6 mile) trail sees little use. The **Willmore Overlook Trail** is found at the southwest end of Rock Lake. Although the actual trail is only 3 km (1.8 miles) return, it hooks up with other trails in the area.

Rocky Pass Trail (Map 28/G6–29/A6) ⛺🥾🐎📷
The second to last kilometre to the Rocky Pass is very steep as it climbs out of the Cardinal River Valley and up into the alpine meadows of the pass itself. Most don't bother unless they are planning on carrying on into Jasper, hooking up with the South Boundary Trail and the trailhead at Medicine Lake (a 69.3 km/42.3 mile one-way trip). To the pass itself, it is 6.7 km (4.1 miles) or 13.4 km (8.2 miles) return. This is a moderate trip, with three crossings of the Cardinal River.

Ruby Creek Trail (Map 29/D7) 🥾🐎🚴🐟
The Ruby Creek Trail is a moderate 12.5 km (7.6 mile) anglers' trail along Ruby Creek. It is possible to access the small lakes or even the falls further upstream.

Shunda/Baldy Mountain Lookout Trail (Map 30 Inset) 🥾🐎🚴📷
This trail is best accessed from the old Upper Shunda Creek Recreation Area. The 6.5 km (4 mile) trail is rough and rocky and has limited views along the way. Is it worth it? Yes. Once at the lookout, you are provided with panoramic views of Nordegg and the surrounding Front Ranges. Hikers will need about three hours to complete the moderate hike.

Spruce Management Trails (Map 35/B3) 🥾🐎❄🚴🏍📷
Formerly a popular cross-country ski area, it has fallen out of favour with the winter crowd, due in no small part to the creation of the Athabasca Nordic Centre along Highway 40. The site is still used and maintained by "the Friends of Camp 29" (as the trail is alternatively known). There are good views of the Jarvis Creek and Wildhay River Valleys to the north. In all there are 18 km (11 miles) of trails laid out in a series of loops. In summer, the area is open to hikers, bikers and ATVers. In winter, the area is restricted to cross-country skiing only.

Sulphur Rim Trail (Map 37/F4) 🥾🚴🐎🏍📷
An easy 7 km loop trail leading from the southwest end of Hoppe Avenue in Grande Cache. This trail skirts the breathtaking Sulphur River Canyon and requires little (30 metres loss) elevation change. The trail is also used by ATVers. Some hikers might find the lack of scenery between the townsite and the gorge outweighs the gorge itself, but mountain bikers will find this an easy ride. There are a number of trail junctions, but the trail to Sulphur Rim is well signed.

Surveyors Benchmark Trail (Map 30 Inset) 🥾🐎🏍📷
More a road walk than an actual hike, this 15 km (9 mile) route starts from the Nordegg Heritage Centre. It follows 12 Level Road up past a pair of abandoned mines to the Surveyors Benchmark, a 1,770 m (5,807 ft) peak south of Nordegg. The hike is easy but long. Expect to take the better part of a day to hike as you climb 340 m (1,115 ft) in total.

Thistle Creek Trail (Map 23/C1–29/E7) 🥾🐎🏍
Just past the Muskiki Lake Natural Area, a cutline-cum backroad heads southwest for about 9 km (5.5 miles). There are a number of trails in this area, but the main Thistle Creek Trail is a moderate 17.5 km (10.7 mile) return trail.

Upper Cascade Fire Road (Map 13/A3–12/G3)
The 11 km (6.8 miles) road to Scotch Camp is closed to cyclists, but offers an enjoyable route for horseback riders and hikers. Scotch Camp is a beautiful meadow area. Travellers can continue on the Upper Cascade Fire Road and the Red Deer River Trail in Banff National Park.

Whitehorse Falls & Fiddle Pass Trails (Map 28/F4)
A moderate 10 km (6.1 mile) one-way trip up the Whitehorse Creek Valley leads to a sheer wall of rock, which the falls cascade down. The 5 metre (16 feet) high falls are located at the end of an ever-narrowing valley and the pair of towering peaks that frame the falls may cause concern for claustrophobics. The trail to Fiddle Pass on the boundary of Jasper National Park is 14 km (8.5 miles). Both are popular with horseback riders and mountain bikers as they follow an old access road. The Fiddle River Trail (as it is known on the Jasper side of the boundary) continues another 26 km (15.9 miles) to Miette Hot Springs.

William A. Switzer Park Trails (Map 35/A5)
A network of trails, some interconnected, some not, run through this provincial park. Two of the trails, the 4 km long Gregg Lake Trail and Jarvis Lake Trail, are open to mountain bikes. The Jarvis Lake Trail starts at Kelly's Bathtub parking lot and loops 10 km (6 miles) through the southwest corner of the park. The other trails are much shorter.

WILDLIFE VIEWING
Similar to the Bighorn Backcountry to the south, the Forestry Trunk Area is very popular with wildlife enthusiasts. In fact, this road accesses some of the best viewing (and hunting) areas in the province. From countless woodland birds to those big ungulates that always get the heart racing, birds and animals can be seen almost anywhere. Outside of the park areas, there are a few notable viewing areas such as Caw Ridge below.

Caw Ridge (Map 37/C1)
Caw Ridge is one of Alberta's best-known wildlife viewing spots and chances are good that you will see bighorn sheep, elk, moose, mule deer, white-tailed deer, grizzly bear, black bear, lynx, wolf, coyote and/or other smaller creatures. The ridge is home to the largest mountain goat population in Alberta and is the primary spring and fall migration corridor for 250 caribou. This is the largest remaining mountain caribou population in Alberta. Access to the 21 sq. km (12.8 sq. mile) alpine ridge is along the 4wd vehicle only Beaverdam Road and then the old road to the top of the ridge. The ridge also boasts one of the most spectacular sets of dinosaur tracks in the Rockies.

WINTER RECREATION
Below we have provided write-ups on the more popular snowmobiling areas and designated cross-country skiing areas around the Forestry Trunk Road. More options are found in the trails above. These areas range from formalized, club areas to unmaintained trail systems. You will need a trail pass to ride or ski the club trails in order to help maintain the trails and develop new areas. You can get a trail pass from the local club or the Alberta Snowmobile Association. For more information, check out www.altasnowmobile.ab.ca.

As always, avalanches are a hazard when travelling through the mountains in the winter. Always carry an avalanche beacon and never travel alone. When in doubt, stick to groomed routes.

A la Peche Lake (Map 38/E4–C5)
Access to this area is from the large gravel pit across from the Pierre Gray Lakes turn-off, 32 km (20 miles) south of Grande Cache on Highway 40. It is 25 km (15.5 miles) to the lake. There is an 8 km trail that partially circles the lake, or, if the lake is frozen, head out onto it. There are also numerous cutlines in the area. Remember, snowmobiles are not allowed into Willmore Wilderness Park.

Athabasca Lookout Nordic Centre (Map 35/B4)
The Athabasca Lookout Nordic Centre is located just north of the Highway 40/Highway 16 junction in the William Switzer Park, about 13 km (8 miles) from Hinton. The centre is becoming one of the most popular winter sport areas in the province. In addition to 33 km (19 miles) of ski trails, there is a biathlon range, a telemark hill, a small ski jump and a luge run.

Blue Lake Adventure Lodge (Map 35/A3)
The Blue Lake Adventure Lodge in Switzer Provincial Park, located about 20 minutes north of Hinton on Highway 40, maintains 22 km (13 miles) of groomed trails. They also rent equipment and offer ski lessons. Also in the area is the Black Cat/Jarvis Link Trail.

Bluehill Snowmobile Trails (Map 13/G1–14/B1)
The staging area for this riding area is found 5 km (3 miles) due west of Bearberry. There are three ungroomed loops, with a total of 90 km (56 miles) of trail, maintained by the Olds Snowmobile Club. The area is sometimes inaccessible due to logging.

Caw Ridge (Map 37/C1)
Found 30 km (18.6 mi.) along Beaverdam Road is the Caw Ridge turn-off. Head left. An old road leads up the mountainside. It is 8.1 km (4.9 miles) to the top and the ridge area is a big, wide, open place to play. Remember, this is a sensitive alpine area, so please do not ride here unless there is enough snow to protect the alpine flora.

Lovett River Snowmobile Area (Map 29/F3)
From this staging area, there are over 1,000 km (600 miles) of ungroomed but well travelled snowmobile trails to explore. These trails travel along oil and gas roads, along seismic lines and along creek beds. The future of the area is currently in flux, as a mine expansion is cutting into the area. The staging area will be relocated and some–though certainly not all–of the riding in this area will be affected. Check with the Edson Snow Seekers before heading here.

Marv Moore Campground (Map 37/F4)
In the summer, this is a popular Grande Cache Campground; in the winter, the Smoky River Nordic Ski Club takes over. They groom about 5 km (3.1 miles) of trails, 1 km of which is lit for night skiing.

Pierre Grey's Lakes Recreation Area (Map 38/F4)
There area boasts 16 km (10 miles) of mixed trails that are groomed for classic technique, with a separate, smaller section groomed for skating. Currently, there is no charge for using the trails. The forest service trails are located 40 km (24 miles) east of Grande Cache off Highway 40.

Skidoo Valley (Map 35/E7)
The Skidoo Valley Staging area is located south of Hinton on Highway 40, near Wigwam Creek. This staging area gives snowmobilers access to a series of trails, which can be followed up to a high alpine area. Aggressive riders can climb to about 2,150 metres (7,000 feet), although most of the (safer) riding happens about 1,000 metres (3,250 feet) lower.

Spruce Management Trails (Map 35/B3)
Maintained by "the Friends of Camp 29" (as the trail is alternatively known), this area offers good views of the Jarvis Creek and Wildhay River Valleys to the north. There are 18 km (11 miles) of trail laid out in a series of loops that are only open to cross-country skiing.

GhostFluzAdventures

THINGS TO KNOW

Area: 150,000 hectares

Highest Point: An unnamed location found along a ridge near where the boundaries of Banff, the Bighorn Backcountry and the Ghost meet.

Total Vehicle Accessible Campsites: 385

THINGS TO SEE

1. Waiparous Viewpoint
2. Eau Claire Logging dams
3. Blackrock Lookout Site

CONTACT INFORMATION

Parks and Protected Areas:
1-866-427-3582, www.albertaparks.ca
SRD Southern Rockies Area Office:
403-297-8800

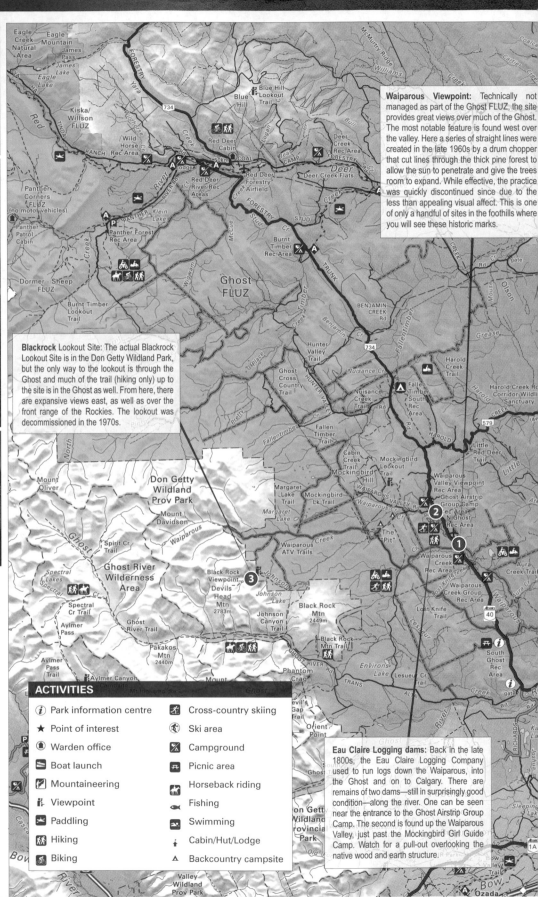

Waiparous Viewpoint: Technically not managed as part of the Ghost FLUZ, the site provides great views over much of the Ghost. The most notable feature is found west over the valley. Here a series of straight lines were created in the late 1960s by a drum chopper that cut lines through the thick pine forest to allow the sun to penetrate and give the trees room to expand. While effective, the practice was quickly discontinued since due to the less than appealing visual affect. This is one of only a handful of sites in the foothills where you will see these historic marks.

Blackrock Lookout Site: The actual Blackrock Lookout Site is in the Don Getty Wildland Park, but the only way to the lookout is through the Ghost and much of the trail (hiking only) up to the site is in the Ghost as well. From here, there are expansive views east, as well as over the front range of the Rockies. The lookout was decommissioned in the 1970s.

Eau Claire Logging dams: Back in the late 1800s, the Eau Claire Logging Company used to run logs down the Waiparous, into the Ghost and on to Calgary. There are remains of two dams—still in surprisingly good condition—along the river. One can be seen near the entrance to the Ghost Airstrip Group Camp. The second is found up the Waiparous Valley, just past the Mockingbird Girl Guide Camp. Watch for a pull-out overlooking the native wood and earth structure.

ACTIVITIES

- (i) Park information centre
- ★ Point of interest
- Warden office
- Boat launch
- Mountaineering
- Viewpoint
- Paddling
- Hiking
- Biking
- Cross-country skiing
- Ski area
- Campground
- Picnic area
- Horseback riding
- Fishing
- Swimming
- Cabin/Hut/Lodge
- Backcountry campsite

GhostFluzAdventures

Weighing in at 1,500 sq km (579 sq miles), the Ghost FLUZ was established to address the growing demand for motorized off-road recreation in the area, as well as to mitigate potential conflicts with other resource values and stakeholders in the Ghost-Waiparous area. The area was established in May 2006 and is one of Alberta's 19 FLUZes. In addition to recreation, there are forestry, oil and gas and grazing activities occurring in the area.

The Ghost FLUZ is part of a large, interconnected series of parks and Forest Land Use Zones connecting to Banff National Park to the west, the Ghost Wilderness Area to the southwest, Don Getty Wildland Park to the south and the Bighorn Backcountry to the northwest. The infamous Forestry Trunk Road runs through the heart of the Ghost FLUZ making it an easily accessible and popular recreational destination for people from Canmore and Calgary. In fact, it is one of the closest designated ATV areas for Calgary natives.

The area first became popular with off-highway vehicles in the 1960s. The many roads and seismic trails built during oil and gas exploration and development help open up a seemingly endless array of trails and areas to explore. Although not that exciting on foot, these cutlines can be a real joy to ride.

Back in 1978 when the Alberta government established Kananaskis Country and started to limit OHV use in that area, the Ghost area saw a dramatic increase in off-highway vehicle activity. Because of the new pressure, 170 km (105 miles) of trails were upgraded for summer and winter use and a campground was built at Fallentimber Creek. In the late 1980s, an access management plan was proposed for the Ghost to address the impact of unregulated OHV and ATV use had on the area.

In the late 1990s and early 2000s, planning and consulting began amongst the general public and user groups, and in 2006, the area was designated as a Forest Land Use Zone.

Today, visitors will find well-established and even designated trails throughout the area. Work is ongoing by volunteers to monitor and improve these areas, including the recent construction of a 24 metre (80 foot) bridge near Bar C on the Trans Alta Road. Although all of the recreation areas are technically not part of the Ghost FLUZ, there are several sites in the area. Random camping, fishing and hunting and countless other activities are also possible.

CAMPING

There are several recreation areas along the Forestry Trunk Road and within the boundaries of the Ghost. However, these sites are not part of the FLUZ and are governed by different rules and regulations. Further, camping is not allowed in the Camp Chamisol and Camp Howard areas. Outside of these areas, random camping is allowed, but please remember to practice of no-trace camping. It is also recommended that campsites not be established within 30 metres (100 feet) of any watercourse to avoid erosion around the waterbody.

Burnt Timber Recreation Area (Map 13/G5)
This recreation area, which is located 65 km southwest of Sundre on the Forestry Trunk Road, has 22 vehicle campsites on the north side and 8 walk-in sites on the south side of the creek. Activities include hiking, paddling and creek fishing.

Fallen Timber South Recreation Area (Map 14/A6)
There are a total of 179 km (111.2 miles) of ATV and snowmobile trails in the area, while the creek offers fishing as well as swimming and paddling. The actual recreation site offers 62 campsites complete with a day-use area.

Ghost Airstrip Recreation Area (Map 9/A1)
One of the largest recreation areas in the province, you will find 170 RV accessible campsites as well as group camping areas. Fishing is provided in Waiparous Creek and in nearby Margaret Lake, while trail enthusiasts can enjoy the good trail network year-round. The Ghost Airstrip Group Camp, The North Ghost Campground and the North Ghost Group Camp are all part of the Ghost Airstrip Recreation Area.

Ghost River Wilderness Area (Map 8, 13)
Bordering on Banff National Park, we included this wilderness area here since it is mainly accessed from the western reaches of the Ghost FLUZ. The remote area protects the rugged mountain terrain that forms the headwaters of the Ghost River. Here you will find peaks to 3,353 m (10,900 ft).

South Ghost Recreation Area (Map 9/C2)
Located 43 km (26.7 miles) northwest of Cochrane on Highway 40, this recreation area is open year-round and has several picnic tables but no campground. It is used as a staging ground for snowmobilers in the winter and ATV riders in the summer.

Waiparous Creek Recreation Areas (Map 9/B1)
Next to Waiparous Creek on the Forestry Trunk Road (Highway 40) is a multi-use recreation area. There are a total of 56 campsites, a group camping area and a small day-use area. The campground is open from May to mid-October, whereas the group camping area is open year-round. The main attraction to the recreation area is hiking in the summer and snowmobiling in the winter. Waiparous Creek also provides reasonably good trout fishing. To the north, the Waiparous Valley Viewpoint offers a scenic viewpoint towards the Rockies.

FISHING

The Ghost area isn't exactly ground zero for fishing opportunities since there are only a few places that people tend to fish. That said, the rivers that flow through here offer some great fishing. As always, check the Alberta Fishing Regulations for up-to-date information. A link to the regulations can be found at www.mywildalberta.com.

Burnt Timber Creek (Map 13/C7–14/A4)
Burnt Timber Creek has brown trout, bull trout and rocky mountain whitefish that grow to 1 kg (2 lbs). There are also smaller brook and cutthroat trout found in the creek. Camping is available at the Burnt Timber Recreation Area.

Fallentimber Creek (Map 13/G6–14/F2)
Fallentimber Creek starts west of the Forestry Trunk Road in the Ghost FLUZ and continues northeast to the Red Deer River near Sundre. The creek offers fishing for brook and brown trout (to 1 kg/2 lbs), bull trout (to 1.5 kg/3 lbs) and rocky mountain whitefish (to 1 kg/2 lbs). Check current regulations for closures and size restrictions.

Harold & Turnbull Creeks (Map 14/B6–E6)
These creeks join to meet the Little Red Deer River outside of Water Valley on Secondary Highway 579. They offer stocked brown trout, which must be released if caught.

Ghost River (Maps 8/C1–9/F3)
Just upstream of Devil's Gap, most of the Ghost's flow is diverted through the diversion canal into Ghost Lakes, then into Lake Minnewanka in Banff National Park. Below the diversion, the river goes subsurface for some distance and then reappears to eventually draining into the Ghost Reservoir on the Bow River. The river contains bull trout, cutthroat trout, brook trout, brown trout and rocky mountain whitefish, which can all grow to 1 kg (2 lbs) but are generally under 30 cm (12 inches). Please note that fishing is closed in the Ghost River Wilderness Area.

Little Red Deer River (Map 14/B7–G5)
From its beginnings near the Forestry Trunk Road, the Little Red Deer River drains in a northeast direction to Highway 22 near Cremona. In the upper reaches, this catch and release river contains brook trout, brown trout, bull trout and rocky mountain whitefish.

Margaret Lake (Map 8/F1)
An OHV trail along the north side of Waiparous Creek accesses this small, shallow lake. The lake is subject to winterkill, so it may be hard to catch a rainbow after a cold long winter.

PADDLING

Covering such a small area, and with virtually no lakes in the area, the Ghost is not home to many paddling opportunities. In addition to the streams listed below, you can also explore the Red Deer River, which is described in the Forestry Trunk Road section of this book. Remember to scout ahead or, better yet, go with someone familiar with the area.

Burnt Timber Creek (Map 13/G5–14/A4)
From the Burnt Timber Creek Bridge on the Forestry Trunk Road to the last bridge over Stud Creek on the Stud Creek Road, kayakers will find a 10 km

(6.2 mile/1.5–2 hour) Grade II paddle. The run is a small volume paddle highlighted by many boulders, bends and small drops.

Panther River (Map 13/D4–E4)

The put-in for this run is found about 9.5 km up the Panther River Road. From there, the Grade II route leads 8.5 km (5.3 miles/1–2.5 hours) to the Forestry Trunk Road Bridge over the Red Deer River. In high water, the many rocks and boulders are covered, creating some challenging standing waves and small holes. In lower water, the exposed rocks offer some technical challenge while the many bends in the river provide some rapids. Towards the confluence, the river valley opens up and it is an easy paddle to the bridge.

TRAILS

There are over 400 km of trails, most designated as multi-use/OHV trails. These trails are no longer being named, but instead are being mapped by their GPS coordinates. While this is effective, it is not very poetic. We've used some of the old names in the write-ups below (and on our maps), but don't expect to find these trail names on the official maps. Also note that many of the trails are closed to OHV traffic at certain times of the year.

Aura Creek Trails (Map 9/C1)

There are two routes leading to Aura Creek. The first route begins 9 km (5.6 miles) north of the Waiparous Creek Bridge on a grassy road. This 7.5 km (4.7 mile) easy trail follows the road and crosses Cow Lake Creek before ascending through a dry forest to a cutline that runs in a northeast direction. The second route begins at the Ghost Ranger Station. The trail runs along the road through four gates before crossing Waiparous Creek. The trail continues through a coniferous forest and crosses the creek one more time before reaching the aforementioned cutline. Here the two routes converge, to head down a dirt road and onto a sandy trail.

Black Rock Mountain Trail (Map 8/G2)

This trail leads 5.5 km (3.4 mile) one-way to the old lookout on Black Rock Mountain. Expect a strenuous hike as you gain 890 m (2,893 ft) over the steep route. Be careful as you walk this rough trail and keep your eyes on the horizon for the tremendous view of Devil's Head Mountain, which stands to the west.

Devil's Gap Trail (Map 8/G2)

This trail runs 7 km (4.3 miles) to the Devil's Gap, which marks the Banff National Park boundary. You can stretch this trail into a multi-day trek, depending on how far or long you want to hike. The trail eventually joins the Lake Minnewanka Trail, which runs another 29.5 km/18.3 miles past Ghost Lake to the Minnewanka parking lot. There is camping at Ghost Lakes, in Banff.

Fallen Timber Bridge Trails (Map 13/F6–14/B5)

From the staging area at Fallen Timber Bridge near the Fallen Timber South Recreation Site, ATVers and snowmobilers can follow a mess of trails in basically any direction, which will connect with all the rest of the trails in the Ghost FLUZ. While all the trails eventually interconnect, the Fallen Timber Bridge staging area is fairly close to the middle of the area, making it one of the most popular points to begin exploration of this area.

Ghost River Trail (Map 8/F2-C1)

The Ghost River Trail follows the Ghost River for 25 km (15.5 miles) to the base of Mount Oliver, near the Banff park boundary. There are several river crossings and it is likely you will need to bushwhack near the headwaters of the river, so the hike is best left for August or September. It will take two or three days to do this scenic route unless you try sampling one of the side trails including the Spectral Creek Circuit, which is a 15.5 km (9.3 mile) loop that is best done over two days. This route requires considerable bushwhacking and several creek crossings on the way to Spectral Lakes, Spectral Pass or Aylmer Pass. Further along the Ghost is the Spirit Creek Trail, which leads through the flat and dry upper valley.

Indian Springs and Environs Lake Trail (Map 8/G2–9/A2)

This is a relatively easy 12 km (7.4 miles) loop that passes through meadows and pine trees and involves some road travel. The highlights are Environs Lake, with its lime green and turquoise waters and the presence of Devil's Head and Black Rock Mountain in the distance.

Johnson Canyon Trail (Map 8/F2)

Beginning from the Ghost River Road, this trail leads to two waterfalls, and natural pools. The 11 km (6.8 miles) trail gains 350 m (1,138 ft) as it follows the ridge above Johnston Creek.

Lesueur Creek Trail (Map 9/A2)

The Lesueur Creek Trail is an unmarked trail that leads through a series of beaver ponds to Meadow Creek. This 8 km (5 mile) trail gains 95 m (309 ft) and takes half a day to complete on foot. There are a number of creek crossings, so the hike is best left until late summer. The multi-use trail starts at the end of an exploration road off Trans Alta Road.

Line Heater Area (Map 14/B4)

This area is not the most popular ATVing area in the Ghost, but provides access to the few trails in the northeast corner of the Forest Land Use Zone. A new trail connects to the Fallen Timber South Recreation Area and the trails in that area.

Margaret Lake Trail (Map 13/F7)

One of the most popular destinations in the Ghost is Margaret Lake. The stocked lake is accessed by a 13 km (7.8 mile) trail and is a popular fishing destination. The trail follows Johnson Creek from the random camping area north of Ghost Airstrip past the four corners.

Mockingbird Lookout Trail (Map 14/A7)

This steep 3.2 km (2 mile), half-day hike can be reached from Waiparous Valley Road. The climb to the lookout is a steady uphill journey through dense Lodgepole pine with an abundance of berry bushes (raspberries, black currents and strawberries). At the summit, Devil's Head to the southwest or Calgary to the southeast can be seen.

South Ghost River Trail (Map 8/F3–9/A3)

This trail is accessed off the Trans Alta Road, 700 metres past Lesueur Creek. The trail runs along what should be the South Ghost River to South Ghost Pass. However, once spring run-off is over, there is no actual river, only a few stretches of water every now and then. It is a strenuous climb to the pass, but views of the meadows and trees below make the climb worthwhile. It is possible to bushwhack to Carrot Creek or Cougar Canyon.

Waiparous Creek Trails (Map 8/F1–9/B1)

From the Waiparous Valley Road, a picturesque 13.5 km (8.4 miles) one-way trail leads to a dramatic gorge on the creek. It is a popular off-roading area, and other users (hikers, bikers and equestrian users) should be careful. The trail to the gorge climbs 305 m (991 ft) but most visitors sample one of the many other options in the area. These include the trails south past Devil's Head Meadows to the Johnson Canyon Trail, the route up to Black Rock Viewpoint or the trail to Margaret Lake. The trail to the lake is a popular 17 km (10.6 mile) return trip that offers spectacular views of the Ghost River Wilderness Area.

WILDLIFE WATCHING

Connected with Banff and the Bighorn Backcountry, you might expect some good wildlife viewing opportunities. You are correct in that assumption, however, there are no formal wildlife watching areas. Since most of this area is foothill country, keep your eyes peeled for everything from bear, coyotes, deer, moose and grouse.

WINTER RECREATION

The good news is that trails that are open to 4wd vehicles and ATVs in the summer are open to snowmobiling in the winter. The bad news, the trails are also open to 4wd vehicles and ATVs as well. That's not a big problem when there's lots of snow, but generally in the Ghost, there isn't enough snow to keep the ATVs off.

Fallen Timber Creek Area (Map 13/F6–14/B5)

Located 70 km northwest of Cochrane off the Forestry Trunk Road, the Fallen Timber South Provincial Recreation Area is a popular staging area for snowmobilers. There is a total of 183 km (113.7 miles) of trails that link Burnt Timber, Fallentimber and Waiparous Creeks.

Ghost Airstrip Snowmobile Area (Map 9/C2–14/A6)

This is one of the main staging areas for trips in the Ghost. The recreation area is open for winter camping. From here, riders can connect to most of the trails in the Ghost. The North Ghost Recreation area is also popular with cross-country skiers and snowshoers.

Hamber Adventures

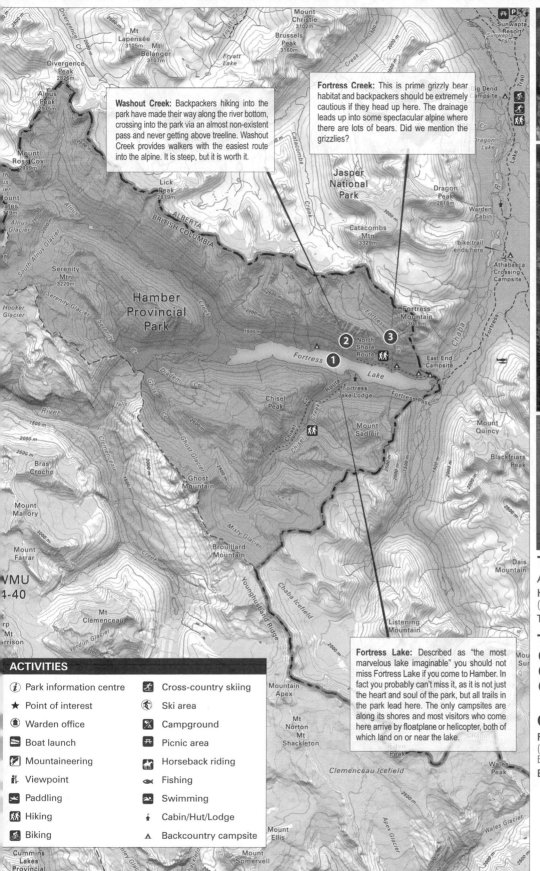

Washout Creek: Backpackers hiking into the park have made their way along the river bottom, crossing into the park via an almost non-existent pass and never getting above treeline. Washout Creek provides walkers with the easiest route into the alpine. It is steep, but it is worth it.

Fortress Creek: This is prime grizzly bear habitat and backpackers should be extremely cautious if they head up here. The drainage leads up into some spectacular alpine where there are lots of bears. Did we mention the grizzlies?

Fortress Lake: Described as "the most marvelous lake imaginable" you should not miss Fortress Lake if you come to Hamber. In fact you probably can't miss it, as it is not just the heart and soul of the park, but all trails in the park lead here. The only campsites are along its shores and most visitors who come here arrive by floatplane or helicopter, both of which land on or near the lake.

ACTIVITIES

- ⓘ Park information centre
- ★ Point of interest
- Warden office
- Boat launch
- Mountaineering
- Viewpoint
- Paddling
- Hiking
- Biking
- Cross-country skiing
- Ski area
- Campground
- Picnic area
- Horseback riding
- Fishing
- Swimming
- Cabin/Hut/Lodge
- ▲ Backcountry campsite

Image © Brian Lang

THINGS TO KNOW

Area: 24,000 hectares
Highest Peak: Mount Scott 3,300 metres (10,827 feet)
Total Vehicle Accessible Campsites: 0

THINGS TO SEE

1. Fortress Lake
2. Washout Creek
3. Fortress Creek

CONTACT INFORMATION

Fortress Lake Wilderness Retreat: (403) 346 1698, www.fortresslake.com, Email info@fortresslake.com
BC Parks: (250) 566-4325, www.bcparks.ca

Hamber Provincial Park is a 24,000 hectare park tucked into a nook carved into Jasper National Park. It is located in BC, but is surrounded on three sides by Jasper and shares much the same scenery. There is no road access into the park; the only way in is by air or via a 22 km (13.7 mile) hike from the Icefields Parkway in Jasper along the Chaba River.

The heart of Hamber is Fortress Lake. Fortress Lake is one of the largest and visually spectacular lakes in the Rockies and is the heart and soul of this park. The only trail in the park skirts its shores, and the main draw to the area is a fishing resort on the southern shores of the lake.

A.P. Coleman first visited the area that is now Hamber Provincial Park in 1892. He called Fortress Lake "the most marvelous lake imaginable." In 1930s, National Park biologists crossed over into this area and stocked Fortress Lake with a strain of Lake Nipigon brook trout, forever changing the area. The trout thrived in the lake, and these days, the lake is considered one of the finest brook trout fishing destinations in North America.

The area was designated a provincial park in 1941 and named after the outgoing Lieutenant Governor of BC, Eric Hamber. At the time, it was BC's largest provincial park, stretching along the Rockies from Mount Robson to Yoho and covering 1,009,112 hectares. However, in 1961, the boundaries were radically cut back to less than 3% of its former size. These reductions were made to open up large areas of the Columbia River Valley to forestry, as well as to make way for the hydroelectric developments. In 1962, the park borders were adjusted up slightly to its current size.

Until the bridge over the Athabasca River was built, the park was nearly inaccessible, and saw less than 100 visitors a year. These days, that number has quadrupled to 400. Even so, many of those people are fly-in guests, usually anglers looking to experience one of the most storied brook trout fisheries on the continent.

In 1991, the park was designated as part of the Canadian Rocky Mountain World Heritage Site.

CAMPING

There are a few designated backcountry campsites in Hamber, all located along the north and east shores of Fortress Lake. Each site is small, with space for only one tent, a pit toilet and a bear pole. The three most popular sites are Fortress Creek, the Burn and East End. There is a fourth campsite at Washout Creek that does not have an actual trail to it. In fact, the Washout Creek site is typically only accessed from the water since it is about an 8 km bushwhack from the end of the trail. The campsite at East End is the only site that has been developed and maintained. The other sites are user maintained, so please respect the area and pack out what you pack in.

At the end of the Chisel Creek Route is the Fortress Lake Retreat. Resort symbol Primarily a fishing lodge, it is available to other users. Reservations are needed, please contact Fortress Lake Lodge at (403) 346 1698, or by email at info@fortresslake.com.

FISHING

Hamber is a remote park, and has only one lake and one river that are fish bearing. But what it lacks in quantity, it makes up for in quality, with what is arguably the best brook trout fishing lake in North America.

Fortress Lake (Map 22/A7)
Canadian Fly Fisher Magazine has said that Fortress Lake has the best brook trout fishing in North America, and who are we to argue? The fishing is strong, due to its remoteness, the short season, and the catch-and-release policy of the only fishing lodge on the lake. Typical catches are in the 2 kg (4 lb) range, but the lake record is 5.2 kg (11.5 lbs). For those that know brook trout fishing, that is a mighty big fish. The lake is not designated catch and release, but the catch and release policy practiced by the lodge helps keep the retention levels on the lake down and the fish sizes up.

Wood River (Map 21/G7)
The Wood River drains Fortress Lake. It is located at the western end of the lake, which is by far the most scenic part of the park. Brook trout inhabit the first couple kilometres of the river as it flows out of the lake. Along with good structure, anglers will find the river has some small fly hatches to work with.

PADDLING

While it would be nearly impossible to haul a boat in via the long trail up the Chaba River, there are boat rentals available for guests of the Fortress Lake Lodge. Mostly it is anglers use these rentals, but the spectacular scenery of the lake would make it a fine place to drop a paddle.

TRAILS

There is only one official trail in Hamber Provincial Park, a rough trail that runs along the north side of Fortress Lake. Of course, to get to the lake, you have to hike in from the Icefields Parkway in Jasper. While the route in has been shortened, you still follow the Chaba River Valley to an unbridged river crossing. This crossing should not be attempted at high water levels.

The main trails in and around the park include:

Fortress Lake Lodge Trails (Map 22/A7)
For visitors to the lodge, there are a couple short trails to explore behind the lodge. Being a fly-in lodge, accessing these trails by foot is nearly impossible.

Fortress Lake Trail (Map 22/B7)
After about 6 km (3.7 miles), the trail along the north side of the lake peters out. It is possible to bushwhack your way to the campsite at Washout Creek (about 4 km/2.5 miles past where the trail stopped being a real trail) and even up into the alpine, though it is quite difficult.

Sunwapta Falls–Fortress Lake Route (Maps 22/C4-22/A7)
Warning: Although there is now a bridge across the Athabasca River, eliminating one of the most dangerous water crossings in the Rockies, getting across the Chaba River is still a relatively dangerous proposition except during low water (late summer and fall). The river crossings keep the majority of backpackers off this difficult but rewarding 24 km/14.6 mile (8 hours) one-way trail. But for those who endure, Fortress Lake is one of the largest, most beautiful lakes along the great divide. The trail begins from the Sunwapta Falls parking lot on the Icefields Parkway in Jasper.

WINTER RECREATION

Hamber Provincial Park is open to winter recreation and some people do make the trip in to the park, but this is quite rare. Winter camping, ice fishing and ski touring are among the possible activities here.

WILDLIFE VIEWING

The park is home to a population of both grizzly and black bears. Sightings are fairly common, especially in the alpine areas above Windfall and Fortress Creek. In fact, the lodge reports that in early fall, the park is home to one of the highest concentrations of grizzly bears in the Rockies. Visitors are asked to take precautions when in bear country.

Height of the Rockies Adventures

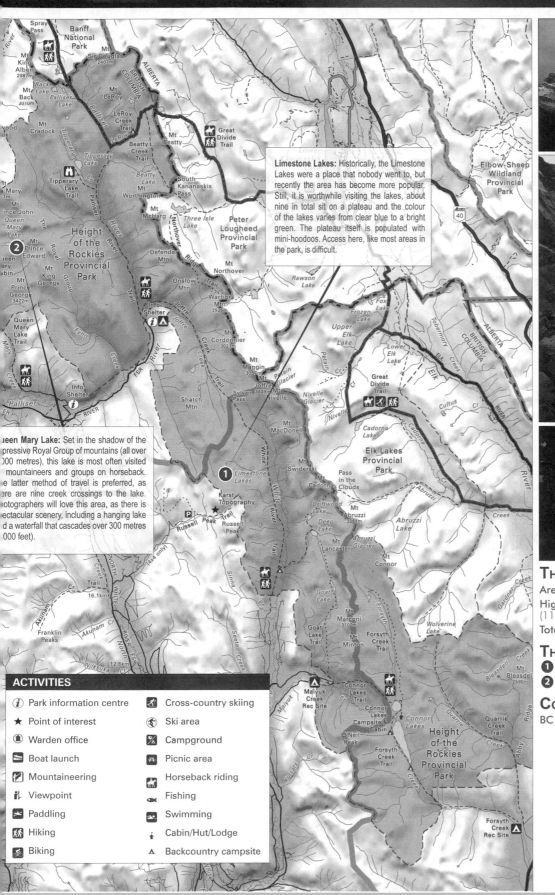

Limestone Lakes: Historically, the Limestone Lakes were a place that nobody went to, but recently the area has become more popular. Still, it is worthwhile visiting the lakes, about nine in total sit on a plateau and the colour of the lakes varies from clear blue to a bright green. The plateau itself is populated with mini-hoodoos. Access here, like most areas in the park, is difficult.

Queen Mary Lake: Set in the shadow of the impressive Royal Group of mountains (all over 3000 metres), this lake is most often visited by mountaineers and groups on horseback. The latter method of travel is preferred, as there are nine creek crossings to the lake. Photographers will love this area, as there is spectacular scenery, including a hanging lake and a waterfall that cascades over 300 metres (1000 feet).

ACTIVITIES

ⓘ Park information centre	🎿 Cross-country skiing
★ Point of interest	🎿 Ski area
🏢 Warden office	🏕 Campground
🛶 Boat launch	🎋 Picnic area
🧗 Mountaineering	🐎 Horseback riding
📷 Viewpoint	🐟 Fishing
🚣 Paddling	🏊 Swimming
🥾 Hiking	🛖 Cabin/Hut/Lodge
🚴 Biking	⛺ Backcountry campsite

THINGS TO KNOW

Area: 54,170 hectares

Highest Point: Mount Joffre 3,449 metres (11,316 feet)

Total Vehicle Accessible Campsites: 0

THINGS TO SEE

① Limestone Lakes

② Queen Mary Lake

CONTACT INFORMATION

BC Parks: (250) 489-8540, www.bcparks.ca

Height of the Rockies Adventures

Originally established as a Forest Service Wilderness Area in 1987, Height-of-the-Rockies Provincial Park was created in 1995. The area has one of the highest densities of mountains over 3,000 metres (9,800 feet) high in the province, with 26 peaks over 3 km tall in an area of 542 sq km (209 sq miles). The area is also home to a variety of wildlife, including the world's highest densities of mountain goats.

The Ktunaxa People used the North Kananaskis and Palliser Passes to get down to the plains to hunt, but, like most of the Rockies, this area saw no year-round settlement. The first non-natives in the area were probably British army Lieutenants Henry James Warre and Mervin Vavasour. The two men were sent as spies from Montreal to Fort Vancouver, travelling by canoe and then by horse, covering the distance from Fort Garry to Fort Vancouver in less than two months. However, Warre—a pretty good artist—had time to draw a series of sketches, which were later published in a book. The second group of non-natives was a group of families being lead by James Sinclair that also passed through to settle down in Washington. The first real exploration of the area was done by the Palliser Expedition in 1858–59.

With development of the new National Park System, this area was proposed for a national park in the early 1900s, but that didn't happen. Later, in 1936, the White River Game Reserve was established to protect the sheer amount of wildlife in the area. However, the area was still open to logging and other resource extraction. With logging knocking on the doorstep of the park, environmentalists pressed hard to see this area protected, and in 1987, BC's first Provincial Forest Wilderness Area was created. The area was closed to resource extraction, but was open to grazing and trapping. Today, the area is now a Class A park, but grazing and trapping are still permitted.

Considering that this area was originally set aside for wildlife habitat, you would think it would be fairly easy to see wildlife here. And it is. In fact, the park is so heavily used by wildlife that some of the wildlife trails are 2.5 metres (8 feet) wide and 30 centimetres (1 foot) deep.

There are no roads that enter into Height of the Rockies Provincial Park, but there are seven trailheads and four mountain passes that are used to access the park. The main trailhead is located at Forsyth and Quarrie Creek and begins close to the Elk River Forest Service Road. No trailhead facilities have been developed here. Access to the Middle Fork is via logging road along the White River beyond Whiteswan Lake. To the north, the Palliser and Albert River Forest Service Roads provide rough access to trailheads here.

CAMPING

There are no vehicle accessible campsites in the park, although there are a few recreation sites just outside the park. However, inside the park, wilderness camping is allowed. Although many of the sites throughout the park are not designated or even maintained, visitors will find a good selection of random, informal camping areas. The include sites at Connor Lake, Ralph Lake, Palliser River, the Middle Fork of White River, Deep Lake and Driftwood Lake.

There are also two cabins inside the park for public use available on a first-come, first-serve basis. There is a six-person cabin, complete with wood stove and a pit toilet nearby at the north end of Connor Lake. At Queen Mary Lake, the eight-person log cabin has a wood and white gas stove.

Outside of the Park, a few popular camping areas are found at these recreation sites:

Forsyth Creek Recreation Site (Map 2/C4)
This six unit recreation site is used mainly as a staging area for hikers entering the Height of the Rockies Provincial Park. There is a corral for the horses and lots of parking space.

Maiyuk Creek Recreation Site (Map 1/G3)
This busy site is used as a staging ground for hikers/horseback riders into the park. There are three campsites to choose from and the corral is popular with horse owners.

Palliser-Albert Recreation Site (Map 4/B7)
This is a medium sized (six unit), open site next to the bridge over the Palliser River. The site is accessed by the rough Palliser River Forest Service Road and is found at the junction of the Albert and Palliser Rivers. Both rivers are very scenic and worth exploring.

FISHING

Connor Lakes is the main fishing destination in the park and for good reason. The fish are big and with a limited open water season the fishing is usually fast and furious. A few streams also begin in the park and provide a good place to cast a line for generally small trout.

Connor Lakes (Map 2/A3)
The lakes, which are actually a chain of three water bodies, can be accessed by trail and there is a campsite and cabin on the main lake. The fishing for cutthroat, which reach 4 kg (9 lbs) but average 30–40 cm (12–15 inches), can be unbelievable at times. In recent years, however, fishing success has declined as rumor of these large, easy to catch fish has increased pressure on the lake. The high alpine lake is closed to fishing from May 1–June 30 to protect the spawning area. The lake is actually the only source of brood stock for Westslope cutthroat trout in the province.

Forsyth Creek (Map 2/A3–C5)
Mainly a trail access creek, Forsyth Creek contains good numbers of cutthroat trout to 40 cm (16 inches). You may also find bull trout to 65 cm (26 inches). The 2 km (1.8 mile) section below Conner Lake (basically to the border of Height of the Rockies Provincial Park) is closed to angling.

Palliser River (Map 4/E5–A7)
The Palliser River flows through the Height of the Rockies to the Kootenay River. Along the way, good numbers of cutthroat to 45 cm (18 inches), bull trout to 4 kg (9 lbs) and whitefish to 40 cm (16 inches) can be found. Try bait or a fly in one of the many pools found in the river after high water (late June).

White River (Map 4/G7–1/C7)
The section of the White River in the park is closed to fishing. Outside of the park, the river produces cutthroat, bull trout, rainbow and whitefish. The fish are found primarily in the larger pools.

PADDLING

Although it is possible, and indeed some anglers do, lugging a canoe into any of the lakes is not the easiest task. Connor Lake is probably the only lake worth the effort.

TRAILS

Hikers/backpackers, horseback riders, hunters, mountaineers and backcountry skiers will find several trails, in various states of repair, leading up many of the river and creek drainages to the alpine. The trails are user maintained and most are difficult, with muddy and brushy sections. None of the trails are marked or open to biking and moderate scrambling is sometimes required. A topographic map and compass are essential. However, the main trails are generally easier to follow and the rewards are sights that few have seen.

For horse packers, there are trailhead corrals at the start of some trails. Grazing is limited and feed should be packed in if you are heading into the Sylvan Pass, Queen Mary Lake or the Middle Fork of the White River meadow areas.

Visitors will find cabins at Connor Lakes and Queen Mary Lake as well as wilderness campsites. Remember, this area has more grizzly bears than BC's grizzly bear sanctuary, so travel with caution.

Connor Lakes [Maiyuk Creek] Trail (Map 1/G3–2/A3)

This trail initially follows a seismic line before reaching a pass and descending to the north end of Connor Lake. The trail is 7 km (4.3 miles) 4 hours one-way.

Forsyth Creek Trail (Map 2/B4)

The trail along Forsyth Creek begins on a seismic road before climbing through a second growth forest to the north end of Connor Lakes and eventually to the cabin. You can continue past the lake but the route becomes hard to follow as you traverse open terrain, eventually leading to the headwaters of Forsyth Creek and the foot of Abruzzi Glacier. Conner Lake is a beautiful sub-alpine lake with a hanging glacier. It is 7 km (4.3 mile), 2.5–3.5 hours from the Forsyth Creek Recreation Site to Connor Lakes.

Goat Lake Route (Map 1/G3–2/A3)

From the Maiyuk Creek Recreation Site, this 9 km (5.5 miles), 4–5 hour one-way hike gains 400 m (1,310 ft) to Maiyuk Pass before dropping 125 m (406 ft) to tiny Goat Lake. The remote mountain lake does offer good fishing for small but feisty trout. The route was badly burned in 2003 and there is not much of a trail to follow anymore. In fact, much of the route passes through a burnt forest and into the sub-alpine.

Joffre Creek Trail (Map 4/E7–F7)

The easiest way into the Sylvan Pass area and the beautiful Limestone Lakes is from the north along Joffre Creek. It is 11 km (6.7 miles) one-way to the pass. The trail continues beyond on a rugged horse trail that follows the White River (see below) to the Maiyuk Creek Recreation Site.

LeRoy & Beatty Creek Trails (Map 4/E5)

From the Palliser River Route a pair of routes lead in an eastward direction to Peter Lougheed Park in Alberta. The LeRoy Creek Trail is 5 km (3 miles) 4 hour one way from the river to the North Kananaskis Pass. The Beatty Creek Trail branches south past Beatty Lake and on to the South Kananaskis Pass. These are rough routes and sometimes difficult to follow.

Palliser River Route (Map 4/E7–C2)

Linking the Palliser River with the Spray River in Banff National Park, this trail begins at the end of the Palliser River Forest Service Road. The southern portion of the hike involves bushwhacking through thick alder or walking along the creek bank and crossing the river channel on numerous occasions. As you climb past the outfitter cabin to Palliser Pass, the trail improves. The trail to the pass is a 20 km (12.2 mile) one-way day jaunt. Many continue north to Spray Lakes Reservoir in Alberta or visit Tipperary Lake and North Kananaskis Pass via side trails.

Pass In the Clouds Route (Map 1/G2–2/A2)

A rough route used to lead up to Pass in the Clouds, but this area was severely damaged by fire in 2003. While people can still probably make it up and over the pass into the Elks Lake area, new growth is making this area difficult to traverse.

Quarrie Creek Trail (Map 2/B3)

An old guide outfitter horse trail leads up Quarrie Creek for about 14 km (8.5 miles) one-way. The trail is not maintained and the trailhead is difficult to locate. There are also lots of bears in the area to be wary of.

Queen Mary Lake Trail (Map 4/C6)

The Queen Mary Lake Trail begins on the Palliser River Forest Road and soon crosses the Palliser River. The well defined but muddy horse trail leads northward eventually climbing to Queen Mary Lake. The difficult day hike is 12 km (7.3 miles) one-way and involves 17 tough creek crossings but the fishing is excellent. To cut down on the number of creek crossing, it is possible to follow logging roads that parallel the creek on the east side. However, there is no actual trail and hikers will have to bushwhack to connect to the trail.

Ralph Lake Trail (Map 4/C5)

Ralph Lake is a beautiful emerald colored lake set in a scenic alpine basin. The unmaintained 5 km (3 mile) 3 hour one-way trail is steep, gaining 850 m (2,790 ft) to the good fishing lake. Mountaineers can continue on to Queen Mary Lake.

Russell Lake and Peak Trail (Map 1/F1)

This trail begins where a bridge has been removed on the North White River Forest Road west of Invermere and well outside the park. From there, hike up the old road 3.5 km (2.1 miles) to a cut block and the start of the marked trail. The 4.5 hour trail continues up the North White River drainage to Russell Lake, gaining 50 m (1,640 ft) over 8 km (4.9 miles) one-way. Alternate routes from here are to scramble to the summit of Russell Peak on a poorly defined trail or continue on to the Sinna Pass at the boundary of the park.

Tipperary Lake Route (Map 4/E5)

Branching from the Palliser River Route is a short but steep and rough side trail, which climbs up to Tipperary Lake. The trail is 2 km (1.2 miles) one way and will take about two hours to hike.

White River Trail (Map 1/G3–G1)

A long rough horse trail follows the middle fork of the White River from the Maiyuk Creek Recreation Site up to Sylvan Pass. This is a difficult trail, with lots of mud and plenty of rough sections. Add in a number of river crossings and you have a trail better left to horseback riders, although backpackers still head this way. The route was burnt in the 2003 fire and while the trail is in okay condition, young lodgepole pine are starting to grow here, which will make the route even harder to follow unless they are cleared, which probably won't happen for a while. For now, it is 21.5 km (13.1 miles) to the pass, gaining 645 m (2,096 feet). Along the route, you can take side trips to any one of five sub-alpine lakes (Deep Lake, Limestone Lakes or Driftwood Lake). For those people who don't like retracing their footsteps, an interesting two or three-day trek can be planned by continuing down the Joffre Creek Trail in the northern reaches of the park.

WILDLIFE WATCHING

There are no formal wildlife watching areas in the park. However, the area provides very high quality habitats for mountain goat and grizzly bear. In fact, between Height of the Rockies and Elk Lake Provincial Parks, this are has one of the highest concentrations of mountain goats in the world. The park also protects habitat for black bear, bighorn sheep, mule deer, white-tailed deer and moose, along with a variety of small mammals, birds and fish. The park plays an important role in the representation of the Southern Rockies ecosystem and is considered to have some of the highest wildlife values in the Canadian Rockies.

WINTER RECREATION

There is no formal development for winter activities in this park, but that doesn't mean that it doesn't happen. Winter ski touring is informal and relatively unpopular, as you need a snowmobile just to get to the park boundary. Do note, however, that snowmobiles are not allowed within the park itself.

The two most common destinations for ski tourists are Queen Mary Lake and Connor Lakes, for the simple fact that there are cabins at these two locations. From here, groups make day-trips out into the backcountry, following trails, or climbing the nearby slopes with skins for a day of backcountry skiing. Note also that most of the trails pass through avalanche terrain and people who visit here should be experienced and well prepared.

Connor Lakes [Maiyuk Creek] Trail (Map 1/G3–2/A3)

This trail initially follows a seismic line before reaching a pass and descending to the north end of Connor Lake. The trail is 7 km (4.3 miles) one-way.

Queen Mary Lake Trail (Map 4/C6)

The Queen Mary Lake Trail begins on the (likely) unploughed Palliser River Forest Road and soon crosses the Palliser River. The difficult trail is 12 km (7.3 miles) one-way. In the winter, the 17 creek crossings are frozen, but care needs to be exercised, as the ice may be thin.

JasperAdventures

Miette Hot Springs: Although they have been commercially developed, the springs are still a great place to visit. The springs produce a daily flow of 568,245 litres (125,000 gallons).

Jasper Information Centre: Sure, this is where you will go to find out information about the park, but the centre was built in 1913 and has influenced the design sensibility of the entire nation.

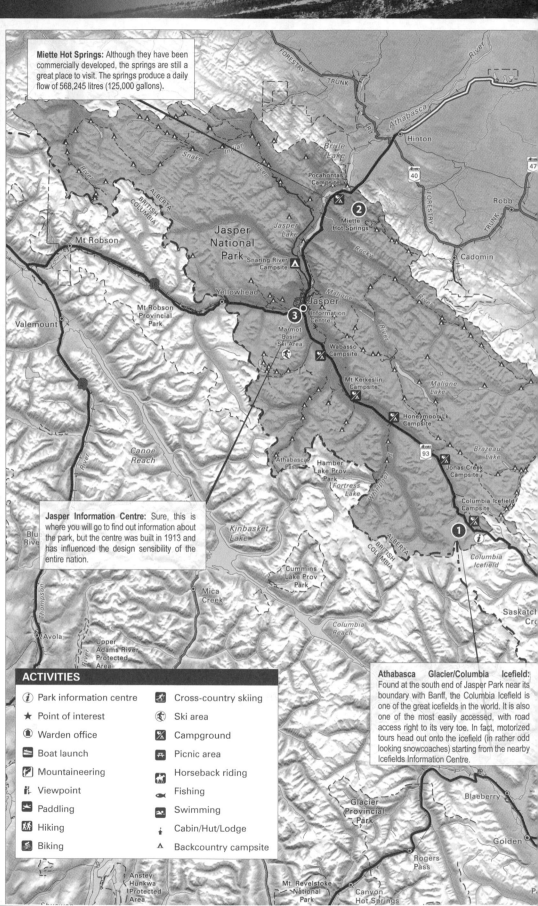

THINGS TO KNOW

Area: 1,080,000 hectares

Highest Point: Mount Columbia 3,747 metres (12,293 feet)

Total Vehicle Accessible Campsites: 1,772

THINGS TO SEE

1. Athabasca Glacier/Columbia Icefield
2. Miette Hot Springs
3. Jasper Information Centre

CONTACT INFORMATION

Campground Reservations:
1-877-737-3783 (International callers
1-905-426-4648) www.pccamping.ca

Backcountry Trail Reservations:
(780) 852-6177

Parks Canada: (780) 852-6176,
JNP_info@pc.gc.ca, www.pc.gc.ca/jasper

Jasper Visitor Centre: (780) 852-6176

Icefield Visitor Centre: (780) 852-6288

Miette Hot Springs: (780) 866-3939

Warden Office: (780) 852-6155

Athabasca Glacier/Columbia Icefield: Found at the south end of Jasper Park near its boundary with Banff, the Columbia Icefield is one of the great icefields in the world. It is also one of the most easily accessed, with road access right to its very toe. In fact, motorized tours head out onto the icefield (in rather odd looking snowcoaches) starting from the nearby Icefields Information Centre.

ACTIVITIES

- ℹ️ Park information centre
- ★ Point of interest
- Warden office
- Boat launch
- Mountaineering
- Viewpoint
- Paddling
- Hiking
- Biking
- Cross-country skiing
- Ski area
- Campground
- Picnic area
- Horseback riding
- Fishing
- Swimming
- Cabin/Hut/Lodge
- ▲ Backcountry campsite

The largest of all the Canadian Rockies Parks, Jasper is also one of Canada's biggest tourist destinations. It is best known for towering mountains, pristine lakes and vast icefields. In addition to the world famous Columbia Icefield, Alberta's highest Mountain (Mount Columbia) is located in Jasper. There are many peaks over 3,000 metres (10,000 feet) high and an abundance of wildlife that stop tourists travelling on the main highway corridors.

Two of the three main access points into the park are via the Athabasca River Valley. The Icefields Parkway enters the park from Banff in the south at the Columbia Icefield and follows the river drainage to its junction with Highway 16. Highway 16 enters the park from the east along the Athabasca River. It continues west through the park, eventually passing into Mount Robson Provincial Park via Yellowhead Pass. There is no road access to the northern portion of the park. Near the junction of the two highways is the Jasper town site, with 4,000 residents.

One of the first Europeans through this area was David Thompson, who arrived in 1813. Seven years later, what would soon be known as Jasper House was built on the shores of Brule Lake. The name comes from the Clerk of the North West Company who was stationed there, Jasper Hawes. The trading post was abandoned in 1884 as the fur trade declined. The park was established in 1907 as Jasper Forest Park. It original boundaries covered 13,000 sq. km, but the park size was reduced in 1930, when the National Park Act was passed and Jasper was officially declared a National Park. In 1911, the Grand Trunk Pacific Railway built a station called Fitzhugh, which later came to be known as Jasper Station. Two years later the park superintendent's residence was built. This building is still standing and is being used as the Information Centre. The station quickly became a thriving community and in 1928, the road to Edmonton opened, allowing easier access to the park.

No matter what draws you to the outdoors, chances are you will find it in Jasper. The 10,898 sq km (6,649 sq. mile) park is home to a 1,200 km (700 mile) trail system, ranging from short strolls around the townsite to some terrific long distance trails. There are great places for climbing and mountaineering, kayaking for all skill levels, river rafting and trails for horse packing and mountain biking. In winter, there is cross-country skiing, ice climbing, ski touring, lake skating, snowshoeing and almost anything else a self-propelled recreationalist could desire. This last point is an important one. There are no ATVs or snowmobiles allowed in the park and none of the watercourses or lakes is opened to gas-powered boats.

A popular destination is Miette Hot Springs, located about 63 km (37.8 miles) east and north of the townsite. The hot springs are the hottest in the Canadian Rockies and have been a popular destination ever since this area was opened up. Miners used to hike about 20 kilometres (12 miles) from Luscar just to spend a few days relaxing in the pools. These days, there is road access to the springs, which is closed during the winter.

Visitors entering the park will find it is governed by a strict set of rules to balance the extremely heavy pressure put on it by humans with the need to conserve and protect the environment. All groups entering the park are required to pay a fee (on top of any accommodation or camping fees) and are given a parks guide outlining the basic rules.

HOT SPRINGS

Miette Hot Springs (Map 28/B2)
While the hot springs at Banff launched the entire National Parks movement, the hot springs in Jasper remained almost unknown until about 1932, when a road was built to the springs. These may be the only hot springs in Jasper, but they are the hottest spring in the Rockies, at a scalding 55°C (131°F). Commercially developed, the bathing pools are kept at a much nicer 40° (104°F). There are two soaking pools here, both about 20 metres (60 feet) long and 10 metres (30 feet) wide. The springs are closed in the winter; the actual date of the closures depends on snowfall; always check with Parks Canada before heading out during the shoulder season. There is a short trail to the source of the springs, where visitors can see the old aquacourt that was closed in 1984. The springs see about 100,000 visitors a year, which is a fraction of the visitors to the Upper Springs in Banff.

CAMPING

There are 1,772 vehicle-accessible campsites spread out across ten separate campgrounds in Jasper, ranging from the giant Whistlers Campground near the townsite to the relatively tiny Columbia Icefields Campground. Campground reservations have recently been introduced in the park and sites can be reserved at Whistlers, Wapiti, Wabasso and Pocahontas Campgrounds. To make a reservation, visit www.pccamping.ca or call 1-877-RESERVE (1-877-737-3783). International callers can call 1-905-426-4648.

Columbia Icefields Campground (Map 16/A2)
This is a tenting only site with room for 33 groups at the southern end of the park. The campground is located near the dramatic Columbia Icefield, one of the most spectacular bits of scenery anywhere. Because of its high elevation, it can get cool at night. The campground is open from mid June until October.

Honeymoon Lake Campground (Map 22/C4)
Honeymoon Lake is located along the Icefields Parkway, just north of Sunwapta Falls. The rustic 35 unit site is open from mid June until early September.

Jonas Creek Campground (Map 22/F6)
Located in the high country that is accessed by the Icefields Parkway, Jonas Creek is a small, rustic area with 25 campsites. It is open from mid June until early September.

Mount Kerkeslin Campground (Map 21/G3)
Located 36 km from the Jasper townsite, Mount Kerkeslin is open from late June until September. There are 42 sites and limited facilities here.

Pocahontas Campground (Map 27/F1)
One of the larger campgrounds in Jasper National Park, there are 140 sites at Pocahontas, which is the first campground entering from the east. The site has flush toilets and firepits and can be reserved. It is often used as a base camp for exploring the Fiddle River Valley, including the ever-popular Miette Hot Springs from mid May to early October.

Snaring River Campground (Map 27/E4)
This rustic campground is located near the Snaring River/Athabasca confluence, 13 km east of Jasper townsite. It is open from mid May to mid September and offers 66 rustic sites.

Wabasso Campground (Map 27/F7)
Located just off the Icefields Parkway, about 15 minutes south of the Jasper townsite, this is a large 228 site campground. Wabasso is open from the end of June to September and can be reserved. A playground, kitchen shelter, flush toilets and a sani-dump make this one of the more developed campgrounds in Jasper.

Wapiti Campground (Map 27/E6)
Located near the Highway 93/93A junction just south of Jasper townsite, the Wapiti Campground is open from mid May to September and then again in winter, from mid October to May. There are 362 sites, making it the second largest campground in Jasper. Of these, 93 sites are open in winter and 40 sites have electrical hook-up. Showers, a kitchen shelter and a sani-station are available.

Whistlers Campsite (Map 27/E6)
Located 3.5 km south of Jasper townsite, Whistler's Campground is the largest camping area in Jasper, with nearly half of all the campsites in the park located here. Of the 781 sites, 77 offer full hook-ups and 100 sites have electric only hook-ups, making it popular with the RV crowd. It is one of two campgrounds with showers and the only area with an interpretive program. A playground, kitchen shelter and sani-station are also available. It is open from May until October.

Wilcox Creek Campground (Map 16/B2)
A rustic campground with 46 sites, this site is located near the Jasper/Banff border. The campground is open year round except late May with no water or firewood on site in the winter season (mid October to mid May).

BACKCOUNTRY CAMPSITES

In addition to these front country campsites, there are over 100 backcountry campsites scattered throughout the park. Our maps show all of these rustic sites, which range from semi-primitive to primitive and may or may not have privies, bear poles or other amenities depending on the site. You are required to have a Wilderness Pass if you are planning on staying at any of these sites and reservations are encouraged. You can reserve space by calling (780) 852-6177.

If you are camping in the backcountry, please practice no trace camping. If you packed it in, you can pack it out. Do not throw garbage or food down pit toilets (because this can attract bears) and camp only on designated sites. Be sure to leave natural and historic objects where you found them and if fires are allowed, please keep them small. Fires are allowed at many campsites, but certainly not all. Fires are not allowed along the Skyline Trail, in the Tonquin Valley, or at Geraldine Lake, for instance. Check out the end of this section for a list of backcountry campsites.

BACKCOUNTRY HUTS

If your interest lies in exploring some remote regions, the Alpine Club of Canada maintains a few alpine huts that can be reserved. These sites range from rustic shelters to cosy log cabins. They serve as a base for hikers, climbers and backcountry skiers to explore remote mountainous areas. Call (403) 678-3200 or visit www.alpine-clubofcanada.ca for more information on location and cost. There are also a few backcountry lodges and even hostels in the area.

Fryatt Hut (Map 21/G5)
Also known as the Sidney Vallance Hut, this hut requires a full day of skiing to reach. It sleeps 12.

Lloyd MacKay Hut (Map 15/E1)
The Lloyd MacKay Hut is found on the shoulder of Mount Little Alberta in one of the most spectacular areas in the entire Rockies. But its beauty is protected by a long, difficult route via Woolley Creek and Woolley Shoulder, a 30 km (18.6 mile) slog that will take one extremely long day or two fairly long days worth of hiking just to reach the hut.

Mount Colin Centennial Hut (Map 27/E4)
The Mount Colin Hut is set beneath the Southwest Face of Mount Colin and is used mostly by climbers heading out onto Colin or CR6 next door. Scrambling and hiking opportunities are limited, but the area is very secluded and pretty. The hut sleeps six comfortably and is reached by following the Overlander Trail along the Athabasca River before turning up the Garonne Creek drainage. The trail to the hut is steep but in good condition and should take about six hours to reach the hut, less if you bike the first 7 km. This area should be left to people with scrambling experience and ropes may be needed in certain sections.

Wates-Gibson Hut (Map 21/B2)
In the popular Tonquin Valley, it will take two days to reach this hut in winter. En route, most overnight in the Edith Cavell Hostel. The hut sleeps 24.

FISHING

If there is one image that defines fishing in Alberta, it is that of the lone fly fisher, standing knee-deep in a sparkling stream, soaring snow-capped peaks rising behind. This is fishing in Jasper National Park.

While most anglers will not hike more than four or five kilometres from the nearest road elsewhere, in Jasper, some people hike for four or five days, just to find that perfect trout stream. Not everybody is willing to trek that far but do not worry, there are a number of lakes, streams and rivers that are easily accessible from the few roads in the park. Angling in Canada's national parks is managed differently from other areas. Current management emphasizes increased protection for the park's native fish while continuing to offer a wide variety of angling opportunities. Ensure that you are familiar with the regulations and have a national park fishing license prior to angling.

Amethyst Lakes (Map 21/B2)
Located more than 22 km (13 miles) from the nearest road, getting to Amethyst Lakes (by horse or on foot) is half the fun. These idyllic lakes are set in the spectacular Tonquin Valley and hold rainbow trout and eastern brook

trout. The biggest rainbow caught here was over 5.5 kg (11 lbs), although the average is closer to 1.5 kg (3 lbs). There is a pair of fishing lodges on the lake. Please note that the tributaries of Amethyst Lake and a 180 metre radius of the lake itself, around the southeast outlet stream, are closed to fishing.

Astoria River (Map 21/B2–27/E7)
The Astoria contains rainbow and bull trout. You may also find a few brook trout here. The lower reaches of the river run alongside Mount Edith Cavell Road, while a trail follows the river into the upper reaches. Please note that 400 metres of the Astoria River, starting at Amethyst Lake, is closed to fishing.

Athabasca River (Map 15, 21, 22, 27, 34, 35, 36)
The Athabasca drains most of Jasper Park and, as a result, it is already a large river by the time it flows out of the park. Actually, it is a large river almost from its headwaters. The river contains rainbow, brook and bull trout, rocky mountain whitefish and maybe a few pike near the eastern borders of the park. The best fishing is between the Athabasca River Falls (Map 21/G2) and the Sunwapta River confluence (Map 22/B4).

Beaver Lake (Map 28/B6)
A short hike from Maligne Lake Road leads to this aptly named lake. Please note that the outlet stream flowing into Medicine Lake is closed to fishing.

Blue Creek (Map 33/A4–E6)
A gorgeous river in a spectacular mountain setting, if you really want to fish this river, you are going to have to work for it. It is located several days by foot or a couple days by horseback from the nearest road. The remote creek contains rainbow and bull trout as well as rocky mountain whitefish.

Brazeau Lake (Map 23/C6)
Brazeau Lake is found within the southern reaches of Jasper National Park and is accessed by a long hike along the Nigel Creek Trail. Overall, the hike (one-way) from Sunwapta Pass off the Icefields Parkway (Highway 93) is about 19 km (11.8 miles). A number of wilderness campsites are located near the lake, including Brazeau Lake Campsite at the south east end of the lake. The lake contains a fair number of small rainbow best taken by spincasting or fly-fishing.

Brazeau River (Map 16, 23, 30)
The Brazeau River forms the boundary between Jasper National Park and the Bighorn Wildland Recreation Area. To reach the headwaters, you must hike from Highway 93 on the Nigel Creek and South Boundary Trails for at least 20 km (12 miles) one-way. As a result, there are few fishermen that sample these fast waters. Also, given that the river is dammed, there are only a few small cutthroat and bull trout near the headwaters making fishing less than inviting above the reservoir.

Cabin Lake (Map 27/D6)
Currently closed to angling but if proposed regulation changes take effect, the lake will be re-opened from July 1 to October 31. The lake is found just outside of the Jasper townsite.

Caledonia Lake (Map 27/D6)
A 4 km (2.5 mile) hike from the Jasper townsite brings you to this picturesque lake, which contains rainbow and brook trout. It is best to lug in a small boat or float tube.

Celestine Lake (Map 27/E1)
This medium sized lake is located by trail off the Celestine Lake Road. The lake offers fishing for rainbow trout and burbot as well as a place to pitch a tent.

Christine Lake (Map 27/B6)
Part of the Dorothy, Christine and Virl Lake chain, Christine Lake contains rainbow trout. The trail into the chain is found 11 km (6.5 miles) west of the Icefields Parkway along Highway 16, just past the Meadow Creek Bridge.

Deer Creek (Map 33/F5)
Warning! If you want to fish Deer Creek, it will require a serious investment of time and effort, as the creek is a four to five day hike from the nearest road. For your effort, you will be rewarded with the creek all to yourself. While it is not worth the effort to head here simply to fish the creek, hikers who bring a fishing rod with them will find the creek fairly productive. Bull trout inhabit this high mountain stream.

Dorothy Lake (Map 27/C6)
The trailhead to Dorothy Lake is 11 km (6.5 miles) west of the Icefields Parkway along Highway 16, just past the Meadow Creek Bridge. The lake itself is located about 3 km (2 miles) down the trail (before Christine Lake) and is home to rainbow trout.

Jasper Adventures

Edna Lake (Map 27/E3)
Edna Lake lies just off the east side of Highway 16. The lake is home to pike (for the most part quite small) and whitefish.

Fiddle River (Map 28/D3–34/G7)
The Fiddle River runs alongside the Miette Hot Springs Road making the lower reaches easy to access. The river contains rainbow and bull trout as well as rocky mountain whitefish.

Geraldine Lake (Map 21/F3)
It is a 6 km (3.5 mile) hike to the second Geraldine Lake from the trailhead, which is itself 6 km along the Geraldine Fire Road. The trail is difficult, but the reward is big brook trout. The lake is open from June 30 to October 31 and also contains rainbow.

Horseshoe Lake (Map 21/G2)
Horseshoe Lake lies adjacent to Highway 93, 27 km (16.5 miles) south of Jasper and contains rainbow trout. The tiny lake is open June 30 to October 31.

Iris Lake (Map 27/C6)
Iris lake lies about a kilometre south of Dorothy Lake (which means you will have to hike in about 2 km (1 mile) to get to the lake) and, like Dorothy, Iris Lake is home to rainbow trout.

Kerkeslin Creek (Map 21/G2–22/B3)
Highway 93 crosses Kerkeslin Creek, 30 km (18 miles) south of Jasper. The creek contains bull and rainbow trout and is paralleled by a rough foot trail.

Kerkeslin Lake (Map 22/A2)
A tiny lake, located after a gruelling 10 km (6 mile) slog up from Highway 93. Needless to say the bull trout in this lake rarely see a lure.

Lake Annette (Map 27/E5)
Located next to the Japer Park Lodge, Lake Annette is home to rainbow and brook trout.

Leach Lake (Map 21/G1)
The name does not make one want to stand in these waters with bare legs for a long period of time, does it? This lake is just off Highway 93A, 2 km (1 mile) south of the Whirlpool River Bridge and is home to rainbow.

Lorraine Lake (Map 22/C1)
Lorraine Lake is a tiny lake containing brook trout and is a 2 km (1 mile) hike from the Maligne Lake parking lot.

Maligne Lake (Map 22/D2)
Maligne Lake is the biggest lake in Jasper Park and contains some of the biggest rainbow and brook trout in the park as well, up to 2.5 kg (5 lbs). The biggest rainbow ever caught in Alberta–9.1 kg (20 lbs, 4 onuses)–was pulled from Maligne Lake. If you do not have a boat, we recommend you rent one since you will need to cover water to find them.

Maligne River (Map 22/C1–27/E5)
Between Medicine Lake and Maligne Lake, the Maligne River contains rainbow and brook trout. Currently, this section is open to fly-fishing only from August 1 to October 1. Below Medicine Lake, you will find brook and bull trout as well as rocky mountain whitefish.

Medicine Lake (Map 28/B6)
There is good fishing in the fall, when Medicine Lake is at its lowest levels and the rainbow have returned. Medicine Lake is only open to fly-fishing, a boat or float tube is recommended.

Meadow Creek (Map 21/B1–27/B6)
Meadow Creek drains Moat Lake, which is located in the Tonquin Valley and flows down to the Miette River. You can hike the 24-plus kilometres (14 miles) in to fish the headwaters or you can fish the lower reaches, which are crossed by Highway 16, 15 km (9 miles) west of Jasper. The creek contains rainbow and maybe a few brook or bull trout in the lower section.

Miette River (Map 26/E4–27/E6)
The Miette is a good fishing river, containing rainbow, brook and bull trout as well as rocky mountain whitefish. Highway 16 crosses the river just south of the Jasper townsite and then parallels the river for several kilometres westbound. The upper reaches are accessed by a rugged trail. The river is open to angling year-round.

Mile 16.5 Lake (Map 21/F1)
A small lake located just east of the Whirlpool River Bridge on Highway 93A. The lake contains rainbow and is open May 19 to September 3.

Minaga Creek (Map 27/A5)
The trail to Dorothy and Christine Lakes provide the best access to this creek, which flows into the Miette River near Highway 16. The creek contains rainbow and brook trout.

Minnow Lake (Map 27/C5)
Minnow Lake is a 9 km (5.5 mile) hike from the Jasper townsite, or rather, from the gate on the Alberta Power Road. The small lake contains brook and rainbow trout.

Moab Lake (Map 21/F2)
You will have to hike about 1.5 km (1 mile) from the end of the Whirlpool River Fire Road to Moab Lake, which is home to rainbow and lake trout. There are boat rentals available through area tackle shops.

Moat Lake (Map 21/A1)
Moat Lake is located 2 km (1 mile) past Amethyst Lake in the Tonquin Valley. This stunning little lake is a 24 km (14.6 mile) hike or horseback ride from the nearest road and even if you do not catch any of the rainbow trout that inhabit this lake, you will not be disappointed. Boat rentals are available, as well as accommodations at a pair of fishing lodges on Amethyst Lake.

Mona Lake (Map 22/B1)
There are brook trout in this small lake, located 3 km (2 miles) by trail from the Maligne Lake parking lot.

Princess Lake (Map 27/E1)
Princess Lake is located a stone's throw from Celestine Lake and is home to rainbow trout and burbot.

Pyramid Lake (Map 27/D5)
Pyramid Lake is a good size lake just outside the Jasper townsite. The lake contains rainbow trout, lake trout, rocky mountain whitefish and longnose suckers. A boat launch is available.

Ranger Creek (Map 22/C4)
A tributary of the mighty Athabasca River, this small creek is only open from May 19 to September 3. Due to the highway access, it is best to bushwhack upstream to find the better pools holding trout.

Riley Lake (Map 27/D5)
It is a 2.5 km (1.5 mile) hike to Riley Lake, located just outside the Jasper townsite. The lake contains rainbow trout.

Rocky River (Map 22, 27, 28)
Highway 16 crosses the Rocky River 35 km (21 miles) east of Jasper and is the only easy access point to the Rocky. For those willing to bushwhack, some fine pools holding rainbow, brook and bull trout are found.

Snake Indian River (Map 27, 33, 34)
The Snake Indian River flows through a lot of Jasper's remote backcountry and there is a trail that follows it all the way to its headwaters. It would take about a week to hike or a few days to horseback to the headwaters. If you are not willing to put in quite so much legwork, the lower reaches of the river are easily accessed from Celestine Lake Road. The river contains bull trout and rocky mountain whitefish.

Snaring River (Map 26/D3–E4)
Highway 16 crosses the Snaring, 17 km (10 miles) north of Jasper. The best fishing, at least for rocky mountain whitefish, is actually downstream of here, between the highway and where the Snaring flows into the Athabasca River. The river also contains rainbow and bull trout. It is open to angling year round.

Southesk River (Map 23/B2–F1)
A tributary of the Brazeau, this remote stream flows out of Southesk Lake and for a short ways forms part of the Jasper Park boundary. The river can be accessed from outside of the park by ATV or horse, hooking up with the South Boundary Trail and the Southesk Lake Trail. ATVs are not allowed within the park boundaries. Hikers can also access the river from along the South Boundary Trail. The river contains grayling and pike.

Sunwapta River (Map 15, 16, 22)

The Sunwapta is a high mountain river that runs next to Highway 93 for most of its length. The highway is both a blessing and a curse, as it provides easy access for you but also for the gazillion tourists who will gawk and take pictures as you lay down a line to catch the rainbow, brook and bull trout that inhabit these waters. The river is open to angling year-round.

Talbot Lake (Map 27/F2)

Talbot Lake lies just off Highway 16, 32 km (19 miles) north of the Jasper townsite. The warm-water lake contains pike and whitefish. It is open to angling year-round and best fished from a boat.

Topaz Lake (Map 33/B5)

It is about 100 km (60 miles) from the nearest trailhead to Topaz Lake via the North Boundary Trail. Expect to take at least a couple of days by horse and four or five days by foot to make it to this remote mountain lake, which is home to rainbow trout.

Valley of the Five Lakes (Map 27/E7)

You will have to hike in to the Valley, which is 2 km (1 mile) off Highway 93. There are boat rentals on the Fifth Lake, which is one of the best places to catch one of the rainbow or brook trout that inhabit this lake chain. The First Lake is also a good bet. Third, Fourth and Fifth Lakes are open from May 19 to September 3, while the first two lakes are open June 30 to October 31.

Wabasso Lake (Map 27/F7)

Wabasso Lake is located 18 km (11 miles) from Jasper on Highway 93, then a 3 km (2 mile) hike along an easy hiking trail. Wabasso is not really a lake; it is an old beaver pond (you can see the dam in the northeast corner of the lake). The lake contains rainbow trout and is open from June 30 to October 31.

Whirlpool River (Map 21/C6-F1)

A long, lonely trail follows the Whirlpool up to its headwaters near the BC/Alberta border but you can access the lower reaches off Highway 93, 22 km (13.5 miles) south of Jasper townsite. The outlet stream from Moab Lake (Map 4/E7), including a section of the river, is closed to fishing.

PADDLING ROUTES

Jasper is known for its natural beauty and pristine wilderness. What better way to explore the peace and tranquillity of the mountains than by paddling one of the small wilderness lakes or a meandering river? Of course, some people prefer the adrenaline rush of conquering some of the world's greatest whitewater, which can also be found within Jasper's boundaries. These are rivers that whitewater kayaking videos were made for and if you don't think you're up to it, you probably aren't. Fortunately, the park offers a little bit of something for everyone, with routes from Class II to Class VI+.

For each river, we have included the put-in and take-out locations. The length of each run, the season and general comments are also provided. To grade the rivers, we have used a modified version of the International River Classification System. Please remember that river conditions are always subject to change and advanced scouting is essential. The information in this book is only intended to give you general information on the particular river you are interested in. You should always obtain more details from a local merchant, detailed guidebook or expert before heading out.

Astoria River (Map 21/E2-27/E7)

The Astoria River doesn't move much water, but that which it does move it moves quickly. There is a lot of whitewater on the 12 km (7.3 mile) section from Cavell Creek to where the Astoria flows into the Athabasca River and there are some awful long sections that are continual Class IV or Class V, including the Canyon. The sheer excitement of the Astoria is interrupted near Highway 93A by a dam and most people chose to take-out here, rather than continue down the last 3.5 km (2.2 miles) to the Athabasca (you will have to paddle another 2 km on the Athabasca to get to the next convenient take-out). The last section is slightly steeper, but lacks the really big ticket features that define the upper section.

Athabasca River (Map 15, 21, 22, 27, 34, 35, 36)

It is possible to follow the 1,538 km (938 miles) long Athabasca River all the way to where it flows into Lake Athabasca, and from there, on to the Arctic Ocean via the Slave River, Slave Lake and the Mackenzie River. That trip would take at least two months of hard paddling, possibly three and

most of it is well outside the scope of this mapbook. Don't despair: you can do shorter sections, ranging from a few hours to a few days. Outside of the often fatal Athabasca Falls, there are no rapids rated higher than Class III for the entire length of the Athabasca covered by this mapbook. Although it is possible to carry your craft farther upstream along a hiking trail, the farthest upstream most people put-in is at the Big Bend picnic area, 15 km above the falls. Unlike most of the rivers that tumble off the Front Range, the Athabasca rolls briskly through its large, wide valley behind the Front Range and then plugs up in a series of broad, shallow lakes and shallow, braided sections, interspersed with some Class II waters. Beyond Brule, the river makes its lazy way toward the arctic, passing through Hinton, Whitecourt and Fort Assinaboine before flowing off our maps.

Athabasca River: Big Bend to Athabasca Falls (Map 22/B3-21/G2)

It is a 15.5 km (9.5 mile) stretch between the put-in at Big Bend, just below Sunwapta Falls and the take-out above Athabasca Falls, and you do not want to miss the take-out. Only one person has ever survived the drop, and you could be the second, but why run the risk? You can take-out at the portage trail on the west (left) bank of the river or where Highway 93 parallels the river, a kilometre or so above the falls. This section contains some Class II/II+ rapids caused by the river narrowing.

Athabasca River: Athabasca Falls to Old Fort Point Bridge (Map 21/G2-27/E6)

Most of the rapids in this section (which can be rated as high as Class II+/III) are at the start, nearer to the falls and at the end, between Mile 5 Bridge and the take-out. The middle of the run is long, calm sections punctuated by short stretches of rapids.

Athabasca River: Old Fort Point Bridge to Hinton Bridge (Map 27/E6-35/D4)

This section is 89.6 km (54.7 miles) long and will take at least a couple days unless you push yourself. If you are planning on camping inside Jasper Park, note that there are only two campsites on this section, on an island just above Jasper Lake and just above the Fiddle River confluence. Make sure you book your campsite early. Once out of the park, there are campsites on Brule Lake along the east shore. There are some Class II rapids in this section.

Beauty Creek (Map 22/G7)

Beauty Creek exists for one reason: to show off, preferably in front of a camera. If you are looking for an exhilarating ride down a wild white river, there are other places wilder and whiter. If you are looking for a great picture of you dropping off a 12 metre (39 foot) high waterfall...well, here's your chance. It could be your last, considering the nasty recirculation and undercut rocks. There is not much point in starting higher than the 1.5 km (1 mile) mark (you will have to hike your boat in all the way) from the Icefields Parkway (Highway 93). The short but challenging creek boasts Class V and VI features, and there is at least one portage, maybe more depending on water levels.

Fiddle River (Map 28/B2-A1)

A ridiculously technical river, with lots of Class V or VI rated drops and chutes along the 18 km run. You have to hike about 3.5 km (2.2 miles) past Miette Hot Springs to the put-in and be warned: even slight changes in water levels can change certain rapids from nothing to roaring. There are points where getting out of a canyon would be near impossible, so you don't want to go into this one unprepared.

Jacques Creek/Rocky River (Map 28/B5-27/F2)

Be forewarned: if you want to run the 9 km (5.5 mile) Jacques Creek you are also going to have to run the Rocky River. An alternate access between your put-in and take-out is nonexistent. And, quite frankly, Jacques Creek is an alternate and easier way onto the Rocky. Highway 16 crosses the Rocky River 32 km (19.5 miles) east of Jasper. This is your take-out. Your put-in is in Jacques Lake, which is found at the end of a 13 km (8 mile) hike. There are a number of difficult logjams in the middle section and it is only the last five or so kilometres where the creek gets really interesting, including a 5 metre drop called the Sweet Spot. The Rocky is a larger river with a couple classic Class V drops.

Maligne Lake (Map 22/C1-F3)

Maligne Lake is the biggest lake in Jasper and it will take paddlers the better part of a day to make it from one end of the lake to the other. It is 22 km (13 miles) to Coronet Creek, at the southeast end of lake, which sports 8 tent pads and a trail up towards a glacier. There are also 8 tent pads at Samson Narrows (Fisherman's Bay). Due to the decline in the Harlequin duck populations, the Maligne River is closed to all watercraft.

Miette River (Map 27/B6–E6)

The Miette is a small volume river with some Class III rapids. The paddling gets progressively easier as you head downstream towards Jasper. From Gieikie Siding to the Highway 16 Bridge near the Jasper townsite (Map 4/C3) is 16.5 km (10 miles). The first couple of kilometres are Grade II/III but beyond this, the river is never rated higher than Grade II. There is one boulder garden, at about the 10 km (6 mile) mark, that is Class II+/III but it is easily portaged. The river flows parallel to Highway 16 and you can break the river into smaller sections if you want to. The most obvious alternate take-out/put-in is a picnic site 3.5 km (2.2 miles) from Gieikie Siding.

Poboktan Creek (Map 22/F5)

It is a 5 km (3 mile) grunt up a trail to the start of this run, which is, surprisingly enough, 5 km (3 miles) long. Listen for the sound of a waterfall as you enter the canyon after the gravel flats, then head off the trail to the creek. This run is Grade IV+/V, with a number of Class IV and higher features.

Rocky River (Map 28/G7–27/F2)

This is a classic Rocky Mountain run through the remote backcountry of Jasper National Park. Wild and white (up to Class V+), once you are on the river there is no easy way off until the end (at Highway 16). This is a 62 km (38 mile) paddle, which should take you at least four days to complete. You will have to carry your craft 10 km (6 miles) from the Grave Flats Road to the Medicine Tent River (Map 29/A5), which you will follow for 8.5 km (5 miles) to the Rocky. The Medicine Tent is a shallow river, often not deep enough to float a boat. The Rocky is. And from here to the take-out, it is a mix of lazy and the psychotic–up to Class V+ rapids. Watch out for Rocky Falls, near the 7 km (4 mile) mark; a tributary enters the river from the right about a kilometre above the falls, which don't plunge straight down, but bounce from exposed rock to exposed rock and would not be fun to go over.

Snake Indian River (Map 34/B5–27/E1)

The Snake Indian River is a medium sized river that flows through the remote northern end of Jasper Park. Most kayakers (and that's who usually heads up the river) make the 14.5 km (9 mile) hike to the put-in near where Willow Creek flows into the Snake Indian. It will take a day to hike up the river, then a couple more to float down. From the put-in to the Celestine Lake Bridge, it is 39 km (29 miles) of mostly Class II paddling, with two notable exceptions. The first is the 25 metre (81 foot) high Snake Indian Falls. You do not want to go over the falls. You will find the falls within the first five kilometres (3 miles), after a sharp left and then, 150 metres (500 feet) beyond, a sharp right. The falls are about 150 metres past this corner and are tough to see from above. Beyond the falls, there is a Class IV ledge into a Class II/II+ canyon.

Sunwapta River (Map 22/G7-C4)

Rafting companies run 8 km (5 miles) of the Sunwapta, from about a kilometre south of Bubbling Springs to just above the Sunwapta Falls. This section is rated Grade II/III, with some Class II+/III+ rapids. However, you can make a day on the river by putting in 23 km (14 miles) upstream, at Grizzly Creek. This section is mostly Grade II, with one major Class III+/IV rapid caused by a rockslide on the right side of the river. This section can be portaged via a 2 km (1.2 miles) to get past the falls. From here to the end of the Sunwapta is another 11 km (6.8 miles). This section contains some Class III waters right at the put-in, but gets easier as it goes along. It is a 2 km (1.2 mile) paddle from the Sunwapta/Athabasca River confluence to the take-out.

Whirlpool River (Map 21/F2)

The Whirlpool is an open run, noted more for its scenery than for its whitewater. Near the put-in at the horse corrals on Moab Lake Road there are a few Class II+/III drops in the first few kilometres of the run before the river tames. From the corrals to the Athabasca River confluence, it is 9.5 km (5.8 miles) or about four hours. It is possible to hike another 2 km upstream from the corrals, which adds 3 km (1.9 miles) and a Class III+/IV drop onto the trip.

TRAILS

Trying to choose between the five national parks located in the Canadian Rockies is a nearly impossible decision between a family of beauties. All of them are beautiful, all of them are charming and all are worth spending time with.

But for the hiker and especially for the long distance backpacker, the wilds of Jasper prove to be most alluring. Home to possibly the most breathtaking and easily one of the most popular backpacking trips in the Canadian Rockies, the Skyline Trail comprises only 44 km (26.8 miles) of Jasper's 1,200 km (732 miles) of trails. And at 10,898 sq. km it would take even the most hearty backcountry traveller several lifetimes to see all there is to see in Jasper.

Horse packing is also an extremely popular pursuit in Jasper. Some trails are best suited to horses, due to numerous river crossings or thick, low brush that horses can step over but hikers have problems with. There are nine holding corrals maintained by Parks Canada and are available free of charge. Keys can be accessed at the Park Trail Office (780) 852-6177. Corrals are found at: Portal Creek Trailhead on Marmot Basin Road, Sunwapta near the Warden Station on Highway 93 Kilometre 72, Beaver Lake Trailhead at the south end of Medicine Lake, Maligne Lake, Whirlpool River Trailhead near Moab Lake parking lot, Camp Parker at Nigel Creek Trailhead, Dorothy Lake Trailhead at Geike Siding, Miette Lake Trailhead at Decoigne Warden Station and the Miette Hot Springs Corral.

There is a quota on backcountry camping and some of the most popular trails are almost constantly full during July and August. You can reserve space by calling (780) 852-6177.

Astoria River Trail (21/D2) 🏕 🥾 🐎 🎿 🐟 🚻

This is the easiest route into one of the premier backpacking destinations in Jasper, the Tonquin Valley. The Astoria River Trail is a moderate 16.9 km (10.3 miles) hike from the trailhead on Mount Edith Cavell Road to Clitheroe Campground (add an hour or so to hike the extra 3.4 km /2.1 miles to Amethyst Campground). This route has less elevation gained (and lost) as it makes its way into the Tonquin than via Maccarib Pass. While it is not as pretty as the other route, the whole area is a slice of heaven on earth and is one of the most photographed areas in the park. There are several alternate routes and day hikes through the Tonquin Valley and into the Eremite Creek Valley, so give yourself a few days (or even better, weeks) to explore.

Athabasca Glacier Forefield (Map 16/A2) 🥾 🚻

Although this is a short trail (2 km/1 mile or half an hour return), it can be a little tricky hiking this close to the Athabasca Glacier. In summer, meltwater runs across portions of the rocky trail, soaking the feet of many. The area is a popular stopping point for people passing through along the Icefields Parkway and access to the trailhead is located at the end of a road across from the Icefields Centre.

Athabasca Pass Trail (Map 21/F2–C6) 🏕 🥾 🐎 🎿 🐟 🚻

Before highways, before the railways, there was the Athabasca Pass, first traversed by David Thompson in 1811. The pass became an important trade route for the next few decades or so. Although those heady early days of exploration are long gone, it is sometimes hard to remember that nearly two hundred years have passed since this unspoiled wilderness was first discovered. From the Moab Lake parking area the trail begins on the Whirlpool Fire Road before becoming a much more difficult route. This difficult 98.2 km (59.9 mile), 4-6 day return trek follows the Whirlpool River for much of the way to the pass. Unlike more popular backpacking routes, the Athabasca Pass is often devoid of people. The pass is 545 metres (1,771 feet) higher than the trailhead.

Bald Hills Lookout Trail (Map 22/C1) 🥾 🚻

Trudging the 5.2 km (3.2 miles) to the Bald Hills Lookout from the Maligne Lake Picnic Area along an uninspiring fire road, you might wonder why you are bothering; especially considering the 480 metre (1,560 feet) elevation gain. When you get to the top, you will forget your earlier concerns: the near 360-degree views of Maligne Lake and the surrounding countryside are inspirational. From the lookout, it is possible to wander south for another 2 km (1.2 miles) along an indistinct footpath to a pair of promontories that offer even better views than from the lookout. There are no dogs allowed on the trail.

Beauty Creek Trail (Map 22/G7) 🥾 🚻

Once a popular stop along the old Banff-Jasper Highway (built in 1940), this area has all but been forgotten by modern travellers since the highway was rerouted. It is only 3.2 km (2 mile) return from the trailhead (2 km/1.2 miles south of Beauty Creek Hostel) along an easy trail that takes you along the deep limestone gorge of Beauty Creek (don't get too close, unless you're one of the psycho kayakers who enjoys going over these falls) and past a number of smaller cascades before reaching Stanley Falls.

Blue Creek Trail (Map 33/E6–A3) 🏕 🥾 🐎 🐟 🚻

A 33 km (20 mile) side trip from the North Boundary Trail (NBT), which also connects with the West Sulphur Trail in the Willmore Wilderness Area. It is also possible to venture back into Jasper Park around the Ancient Wall via Hardscrabble Pass and down the Glacier Pass Trail to either the NBT trailhead or Willow Creek Trail. The Blue Creek Trail starts at km 63.3 of the NBT and follows the Blue Creek Valley northwest to Azure Lake, a stunning alpine lake less than an hour below Hardscrabble Pass on the Jasper/Willmore border. Note: Any route to Azure Lake will take you at least a week to hike; this is a difficult place to get to and reserved for experienced backpackers.

Brazeau River Trails (Map 16/C2–23/D6)
See Poboktan-Brazeau-Nigel Route listed later in this section.

Caledonia Lake Trail (Map 27/D6)
It is a brisk 4.2 km/2.6 mile (2.5 hour) up and down hike from the trailhead just off Cabin Creek Road, near the west end of Jasper. The trail leads through mostly dense forests, with the occasional lake providing more open views of the surrounding countryside. Beyond Caledonia Lake, the trail climbs to Minnow Lake, 5 km (3 miles) beyond. If you're going to walk that far, however, it is best just to do the whole Saturday Night Lake Circuit (see below).

Cavell Meadows Trail (Map 21/E2)
Climbing far above the tourist-choked interpretive trails at the base of Mount Edith Cavell (see Path of the Glacier Loop below), the moderate 6.1 km (3.7 mile) trail to Cavell Meadows is an awe-inspiring trip to a verdant meadow at the base of Angel Glacier. While most of the tourists stay low, this trail still sees a lot of use. If you stay right at the trail junction (at the 2.2 km/1.3 mile mark), the 400 metres (1,300 feet) in elevation gain is much more gradual. The meadows themselves are a fairly fragile ecosystem and you can see the damage inflicted by idiots who don't stay on the path. Don't be an idiot. Also, leave the pets back at home, as there are no dogs allowed on the trail. There are early season closures while snow is still on the trail.

Chrome Lake Trail (Map 21/C2)
The trail to Chrome Lake is not as popular as others in the Tonquin Valley/Eremite Valley area, but it is the most direct route to the Alpine Club of Canada Hut. While Maccarib Pass is a soaring walk through acres upon acres of alpine meadow and the Astoria River Trail has its own charms as it climbs the shoulder of Oldhorn Mountain, the difficult 14.7 km/9 mile (7 hour) trail to Chrome Lake is not maintained, narrow and, with a few notable exceptions, accomplished mostly in the confines of a dense forest.

Coronet Creek [Henry MacLeod] Trail (Map 22/F3)
It is a 22 km (13.4 mile) paddle up to the end of Maligne Lake to the start of the Coronet Creek Trail. From here a moderate trail leads up the creek valley, past the Henry MacLeod Campground at km 6 (mile 3.6) towards the glacier from which Coronet Creek flows. It is another 2 km (1.2 miles) one-way past the campground to the Coronet Glacier moraines.

Cottonwood Creek Loop (Map 27/E5)
From the Jasper Activity Centre, this easy 3.5 km/2.1 mile (2 hour) trail runs northwest along the Pyramid Bench, a terrace that rises above the west side of Jasper. The trail accesses Cottonwood Slough, then loops east along the north banks of Cottonwood Creek.

Cottonwood Slough Trail (Map 27/E6)
Despite its uninspiring name, Cottonwood Slough is a pleasant, marshy area home to many species of flora and fauna and it is one of the best birding areas near the townsite. Like most of the trails around the townsite, this 4.1 km/2.5 mile (depending on where you begin; a trailhead along Pyramid Lake Road, or from the Jasper Activity Centre Parking lot are the two most popular starting points) circumnavigation of Cottonwood Slough is an easy hike and should not take more than a couple hours for even the most casual hiker to do.

Devona Lookout Trail (Map 27/E1)
Like all the Jasper Fire Lookout sites, the Devona Lookout has been removed but the trail up still survives, as do the expansive views of the Athabasca Valley. Perhaps the most prominent feature from the lookout is Roche Miette, the flat-topped mountain that stands at the junction of the Miette Valley and the Athabasca River Valley. From the end of Celestine Lake Road (a narrow road with alternating one-way traffic), it is 9.4 km (5.7 miles) one-way to the Devona Lookout, gaining 325 metres (1,056 feet) in elevation. The trail leads past two lakes–Princess and Celestine–to the lookout.

Dorothy, Christine and Virl Lakes (Map 27/C6)
Close enough to the Jasper townsite to be easily accessible but just far enough away to dissuade the crowds of people that haunt the trails immediately around town. This easy 9.6 km (5.9 mile) return hike leads past three

mountain lakes and has the added bonus of a mere 250 metre elevation gain, meaning it can be hiked during the shoulder season, when higher elevation destinations are snowed under. The trailhead is 11 km (6.7 miles) west of the Icefields Parkway along Highway 16, just past the Minage Creek Bridge.

Elysium Pass Trail (Map 27/B5)
This moderate 30 km (18.3 mile) return trail starts out from the same place as the trail to Dorothy, Christine and Virl Lakes (see above) but after 2.7 km (1.6 miles) splits from that trail. This more challenging route heads west up the slope of Emigrants Mountain gaining 805 metres (2,616 feet) along the way. Expect to take about 7 hours to reach the pass. Doing this as a day hike is difficult but not impossible but it is better to spend the night at the campsite near a small stream that flows south from Elysium Pass.

Eremite Valley Trail (Map 21/B2)
A short day trip from the Tonquin Valley (see Astoria River Trail, above, or Maccarib Pass below), it is an easy 8.9 km (5.4 miles) from the Clitheroe Campground to Arrowhead Lake at the head of Eremite Valley. This is a popular day hike from the Tonquin Valley Campgrounds and many people spend a few hours scrambling around on the mountains that surround the small, alpine lake. There are no dogs allowed on the trail.

Fiddle River Trail (Map 28/A2–E4)
Fiddle Pass stands along the eastern boundary of Jasper and is the ultimate destination of this moderate 24.6 km/15 mile (2 day) one-way trek. The trek is best saved for later in the year, as there are a number of river crossings that can be difficult during high water. You will gain 1,025 metres (3,331 feet) from the trailhead at Miette Hot Springs to the 2,135 metre (6,939 feet) high pass. From here you can return the way you came or continue down to the Whitehorse Creek Recreation Area, 17 km (10.4 miles) beyond the park boundaries.

Fortress Lake Trail (Map 22/C4–B7)
Warning: Although there is now a bridge across the Athabasca River, eliminating one of the most dangerous water crossings in the Rockies, getting across the Chaba River is still a dangerous proposition except during extremely low water (in September). The river crossings keep the majority of backpackers off this difficult but rewarding 24 km/14.6 mile (8 hours) one-way trail. But for those who endure, Fortress Lake is one of the largest, most beautiful lakes along the great divide and actually lies in BC's Hamber Provincial Park. The trail begins from the Sunwapta Falls parking lot.

Fryatt Valley Trail (Map 21/G2–G4)
From the parking lot located 2.1 km (1.3 miles) off Highway 93A on the Geraldine Fire Road, this is a difficult slog up a long, tedious hill. Once you proceed to the tiny hanging Fryatt Valley it all proves to be well worth the effort. Mountain bikes are allowed to kilometre 11.6, (mile 7) making day trips feasible, but it is better to accomplish this difficult 46.6 km (28.4 mile) return trip over two or more days to give yourself time to explore the upper valley. Although 820 metres (2,665 feet) gained over 23 km (14 miles) doesn't sound like much, most of that is gained in the last half of the hike, including one prodigious scramble up the Headwall and into Fryatt Valley, gaining 200 metres (650 feet) in less than a kilometre. Most backpackers set up camp at the Headwall or Brussels Campsites below and hike up the Headwall sans pack, especially as there are no campgrounds. The 12 person Alpine Club of Canada Hut, which must be reserved ahead of time, is a popular winter destination for expert skiers. Fryatt Valley itself is a skier's delight, with many possible daytrips from the hut.

Geraldine Lakes Trail (Map 21/F3)
It is an easy, 1.8 km (1.1 miles) one-way hike to Lower Geraldine Lake and the terminus for most people who head up this trail. Beyond this point, 4.2 (2.6 miles) of rough, rugged, difficult kilometres lay between you and the Second Geraldine Lake. The trailhead is found on the Geraldine Fire Road.

Geraldine Lookout Trail (Map 21/F3)
From the end of the Geraldine Fire Road, the Geraldine Lookout Trail climbs 530 metres (1,723 feet) across 2.6 km (1.6 miles) to a limited viewpoint of the Whirlpool and Athabasca River Valleys. The hike up is enclosed in a lodgepole pine forest and it is only at the top that you really can see anything. This used to be a fire lookout but the structure has since been removed. Considering the less than panoramic views offered from here, it is not really a surprise. Still, it is a popular trip with mountain bikers, most of whom start their trip from the bottom of the road.

Glacier Pass Trail (Map 33/G5–C4)
The start of the Glacier Pass Trail is located at km 46.5 (mile 28.4) on the North Boundary Trail (see below); expect to take the better part of two days to reach it. From the junction, head northwest up Deer Creek Canyon to Little Heaven Meadows, then along Mowitch Creek to Glacier Pass. From here, you can hook up with the Blue Creek Trail by hiking around the north end of the Ancient Wall and into Willmore Wilderness or backtracking to the McLaren Pass Trail (see below).

Glacier Trail (Map 22/C1–16/C2)
Well before there was an Icefields Parkway, there was the Glacier Trail, a three-week trek on horseback from Jasper to Lake Louise. Although much of the southern part of this route has been incorporated into the Parkway, it is possible to hike an 89.7 km (54.7 mile) along a series of existing trails, from the parking lot on the northwest shores of Maligne Lake to the Nigel Pass Trailhead in Banff. This is a difficult, weeklong journey up and down the high passes of the east side of the Athabasca Valley. Your highest point—Jonas Shoulder—will be 2,470 metres (8,028 feet), while your lowest point—Maligne Lake—is 1,690 metres (4,518 feet), although you will cross two other passes along the way. Dogs are not allowed on this trail.

Jacques Lake Trail (Map 28/B5)
You expect to climb up and over high mountain passes or along exposed cols and ridges when hiking in Jasper. But for people looking for something a little easier, may we suggest Jacques Lake? At 24.4 km (14.9 miles) return, it is a long day hike from the trailhead at the Beaver Creek Picnic Area (about 8 hours) but you will gain less than 100 metres (325 feet) elevation along the entire route.

Jonas Pass Trail (Map 16/C1–22/E5)
This 53 km (33 mile) trail climbs 555 m (1,820 ft) as it makes its way through Jonas Pass, at 2,470 m (8,103 ft). It is an impressive four day backpack trip that spends more than 13 km (8 miles) above the treeline, offering expansive views of the surrounding mountains. Chances are good you will see mountain caribou and hoary marmot in the alpine. There is no camping in the Pass itself, meaning that you will have to hike the 20 km (12.4 mile) pass section in one day. No dogs allowed.

Lac Beauvert Trail (Map 27/E6)
An easy 3 km/1.8 mile (1 hour) loop around Lac Beauvert, one of the two lakes that surround the Jasper Park Lodge. The trailhead is near the Jasper Park Lodge visitor parking lot.

Lake Annette Loop (Map 27/E5)
A short 2.4 km (1.5 mile) paved, wheelchair accessible trail that circles Lake Annette. The trail is perfect for a short stroll and a picnic at the Lake Annette Picnic Area, where the trail begins and ends.

Lorraine & Mona Lakes Trail (Map 22/C1)
Escape the crowds at the north end of Maligne Lake and take an easy 5 km (3 mile) hike to Mona Lake and back. The trail follows the first 2.5 km (1.5 miles) of the Skyline Trail and skirts past Lorraine Lake along the way. Fishing is possible at the lakes.

Lower Sunwapta Falls (Map 22/C4)
Stopped at Sunwapta Falls along the Icefields Parkway, but not interested in fighting through the swarm of people gathered at the brink for a view? Escape the crowds and take an easy 2.6 km (1.6 mile) hike (about 30 minutes) to the Lower Falls, which few people bother to visit, even though they are arguably the prettier of the two.

Maccarib Pass/Tonquin Valley Trail (Map 27/D7–21/B1)
Starting from along the road to Marmot Basin and leading into one of the premier backpacking destinations in Jasper—the Tonquin Valley—the Maccarib Pass Trail is a bit longer than the other trail into the area, the Astoria River trail (see above). Expect to take about 7 hours to hike the 22.9 km (14 miles) to Amethyst Campground. Add an hour or so to hike the extra 3.4 km/2.1 miles to Clitheroe Campground; remove an hour if you choose to stay at Maccarib Campground, at the 19.5 km/11.9 mile mark. For the extra effort into the valley, you get more scenery, the highlight of which is a 6 km (3.7 mile) long meadow west of Maccarib Pass. From Amethyst Campground, you can access trails to Moat Lake, Arrowhead Lake and the aforementioned Astoria River Trail back to civilization, where you will have to arrange for a

shuttle back to Marmot. Maccarib Pass is 730 metres (2,373 feet) higher than your starting point, while you lose 235 metres (764 feet) of that heading down to Amethyst Lake. Dogs are not allowed on this trail.

Maligne Canyon Trail (Map 27/F5)
A popular trail through an impressive limestone canyon that is best hiked from northwest to southeast. From Sixth Bridge to the Maligne Canyon Parking Area is 3.7 km/2.3 miles (3 hours) one-way; from Fifth Bridge it is only 2.1 km/1.3 miles (2 hours); either way this is an easy hike.

Maligne Pass Trail (Map 21/F5–C1)
It is only 15.2 km (9.2 miles) one-way to Maligne Pass from the trailhead 200 metres south of the Sunwapta Warden Station along the Icefields Parkway. With an elevation gain of 700 metres (2,275 feet) it would be a long, hard day trip. However, many take an extra couple of days to explore the lakes and meadows along the escarpment of the Endless Chain Ridge. Fewer people take the extra day or two to hike to Maligne Lake, another 32.7 km (19.9 miles) one-way beyond the pass. This is partly due to the fact that the trail can be soggy even late into summer. Dogs are not allowed.

McLaren Pass Trail (Map 33/F5)
The McLaren Pass is usually used as an alternate (and more scenic) routing for through-hikers on the North Boundary Trail (NBT). The trail to the pass adds 10.8 km (6.6 miles) on to the total distance hiked. For the extra effort, there is a scenic meadow and big open views of the surrounding terrain, something sorely missing along the NBT proper. The McLaren Pass Trail starts at Little Heaven Meadows via the Glacier Pass Trail, which is located some 55.4 km (33.8 miles) from the NBT trailhead. You climb 350 metres (1,138 feet) up Deer Creek from Little Heaven.

Mary Schäffer Loop (Map 22/C1)
An easy 3.2 km/2 mile (1 hour) interpretive loop starts at the first Maligne Lake Parking Lot. The trail leads along the shores of Maligne Lake, and then loops back through the evergreen forest, providing insight into the flora and fauna of the area.

Miette Lake Trail (Map 26/G5–B3)
A long, muddy slog up to some spectacular scenery along the Miette River and over two high passes before hooking up with the Moose River Trail in Mount Robson Park in BC. The junction is found 43.5 km (26.5 mile) from the trailhead on Decoigne Road and most hikers will need two days to reach the Moose River Trail. Many prefer to hike to Miette Pass and back, a difficult 24.2 km/14.8 mile (8 hour) hike one-way.

Mina Lakes/Riley Lake Loop (Map 27/D6)
From the Jasper Activity Centre parking lot, it is an easy 2 km (1.2 mile) hike to the north shore of Upper Mina Lake. You will gain about 160 metres (520 feet) elevation in the process. From the lake, you can head back down the way you came or follow a popular circuit route past Riley Lake and the Cottonwood Slough, for a 9 km (5.5 mile) loop. A shorter and less scenic route can be constructed by cutting east past Two Sloughs. Once past Riley Lake, the trail connects with a maze of trails on the North side of Cottonwood Creek. Expect to take about 3 hours if you do the circuit route.

Moose Pass Trail (Map 32/G7)
The trail to Moose Pass is located at km 151.3 (mile 92.3) of the North Boundary Trail (see below). Although located inside Jasper, the easiest way to get to it is via Mount Robson Provincial Park's Berg Lake Trail. It is only 28.1 km (17.1 miles) from the Berg Lake parking lot to the start of the 9.5 km (5.8 mile) Moose Pass Trail, which many argue is the most scenic pass in the Northern Jasper area. It will take you the better part of two days to reach the pass via the Berg Lake Trail or the better part of two weeks from the NBT trailhead. From the pass, a difficult 49 km (29.9 mile) trail descends through Mount Robson Park along Moose River to the Yellowhead Highway (Highway 16).

Moose Lake Loop (Map 22/C1)
A 1.4 km loop takes you from the hustle and bustle of the crowds that gather at the Maligne Lake Picnic Area to the peaceful Moose Lake. The trail cuts through a boulder strewn landscape formed by a giant rockslide from the Opal Hills thousands of years ago.

Moosehorn Lake Trail (Map 34/F7)
A difficult, unmaintained and soggy trail climbs up to Moosehorn Lakes, just outside the Jasper Park boundary. The original trailhead has been aban-

doned because a beaver built a dam and flooded it. These days the trail starts and ends at the Ogre Canyon Trailhead and follows the Lower Athabasca River Trail for a few kilometres. Much of the rest of the two day trail is slogging through mud and wading through rivers.

Mystery Lake Trail (Map 28/C2)

Certainly not one of the easiest hikes in the park, this one involves a stiff climb up towards the Sulphur Skyline from the Miette Hot Springs, followed by an even steeper climb down to the Fiddle River, followed by a long bushwhack to Mystery Lake. The trail will feel much longer than 10.5 km (6.4 miles) by the time you reach the lake. Before you reach Mystery Lake, there is another trail heading southeast that connects this trail with the Fiddle River Trail to create a 19.7 km (12 mile) loop.

North Boundary Trail (Map 27, 32, 33, 34)

At 179.4 km (109.4 miles), this is the longest trail in Jasper Park, although the last 22.7 km (13.8 miles) are actually in BC, along the Berg Lake Trail in Mount Robson Provincial Park. This is not a high alpine hike, like the Skyline Trail, but a difficult ten-day-plus hike (some people take up to two weeks to finish) through lower valleys and passes. It is a well-maintained wilderness trails, but most hikers will be deterred by the sheer amount of time needed to backpack from tip to tail. However, the Willow Creek Trail (see below) starting from Rock Lake is used by some to make a shorter trek.

Cyclists can travel from the trailhead at the end of Celestine Lake Road (Map 27/E1) as far as Snake Indian Falls (Map 34/B6), a dramatic cascade found near the 26.5 km (16.2 mile) mark. The trail is easier to hike east to west, as your starting point in Jasper is higher (1,080 metres/3,510 feet) than in Mount Robson (855 metres/2,779 feet) and elevation gains are more gradual. As well, Mount Robson is the scenic highlight of the trip; why not have it at the finale to your trip, rather than at the beginning?

Old Fort Point Loop (Map 27/E6)

The North West Company built a cabin near this prominent roche moutainée–a bedrock knob carved by passing glaciers–in 1811. Although the Henry House is gone, the hill still bears its name. While Old Fort Point is a mere bump compared to the soaring peaks that surround it, its location in the middle of the Athabasca Valley (not to mention the wide open 360 degree views) makes it a popular viewpoint. There is a set of stairs that climb to the top of Old Fort Point in only 700 metres, as well as a 3.1 km (1.9 miles) trail that winds its way to the summit up the back of the mountain. The latter trail is both more scenic and easier on the knees since you can do the stairs on the way down, for an easy 3.9 km (2.4 miles) loop.

Old Fort Point/Maligne Canyon Loop (Map 27/E6–F5)

It might be a bit of a stretch for some people to do the 20.7 km (12.6 mile) loop from Old Fort Point to Maligne Canyon and back in a day. Many arrange for a shuttle so they can do half of the loop from parking lot to parking lot. If you do, choose to hike the Maligne Canyon section on the way back since the views are better. Note that bikes are not allowed between the first and fifth bridges through the Maligne Canyon.

Old Fort Point to Valley of the Five Lakes (Map 27/E6)

An easy 11.5 km (7 mile) half day hike starts from Old Fort Point and shuffles over to the Valley of the Five Lakes Trailhead on the Icefields Parkway. If you can not arrange for a shuttle, it is a slightly more taxing 20 km (12.2 mile) there-and-back day hike. The trail features a handful of lakes, each with a different shade of bluegreen and is popular with mountain bikers looking for a good cardio workout.

Opal Hills Loop (Map 22/C1)

A stiff 460 metre (1,495 feet) climb along the first 3 km (1.8 miles) of this trail can be disheartening, especially if the trail is wet. But the climb gets you to the flowery sub-alpine meadow at the top as quickly as possible. The meadow is a mere 1.6 km from the trailhead at the Maligne Lake Picnic Area.

Overlander Trail (Map 27/E5–D3)

Named after a group of adventurers who made an arduous journey to the Cariboo Goldfields overland in 1862, the Overland Trail follows a small portion of their route. The trail begins at the Sixth Bridge Picnic Area on Maligne Lake Road and follows the river north to Cold Sulphur Spring. This is a moderate 15.2 km (9.3 mile) one-way hike or bike with open views of the Athabasca River Valley.

Palisade Lookout Trail (Map 27/D5)

Accessing the former site of the Palisade Lookout involves a long, grind (840 metres/2,730 feet) up a 10.8 km/6.6 mile (3 hour one-way) access road from the end of Pyramid Lake Drive. For your efforts, you are rewarded with some of the best panoramic views of the Athabasca Valley but the climb up offers very little to recommend it. Most people who head up here do so via mountain bike, which has the added bonus of a fast, easy descent. In winter, part of the road is groomed, but skins are definitely recommended. But for people wanting a taste of ski touring, this trail has all the elevation gain of a Maligne Pass, with almost none of the avalanche hazards.

Path of the Glacier Loop (Map 21/E2)

This short (3.2 km/2 mile return), easy interpretive trail leads from the end of Mount Edith Cavell Road to a tiny lake at the base of Cavell Glacier. Like most of the high country accessed off the Icefields Parkway, this is a truly spectacular little hike. Because of the ease in getting to it, and the shortness of the trail, hundreds of people flow through here on a summer weekend.

Patricia Lake Circle (Map 27/D5)

An easy 6.8 km (4.1 mile) hike from the Jasper Activity Centre–longer, if you choose to link up with one of the other trails in the area–this trail loops past both Patricia Lake and Cottonwood Slough.

Poboktan Creek Trail (Map 22/F5–23/B6)

Built in 1921/22, the trail up Poboktan Pass and on to Brazeau Lake was the first trail into the remote southern reaches of the park. The difficult 21.3 km/13 mile (8 hour) one-way trail splits from the Maligne Pass Trail (see above) after 6.2 km (3.8 miles), to follow Poboktan Creek up to Poboktan Pass. Much of the upper trail is muddy, dreary and often churned up by horses. The trail does hook up with the spectacular Jonas Pass-Brazeau Lake Loop at km 21.3 (mile 13) and is part of the Glacier Trail. There are no dogs allowed on this trail.

Poboktan-Brazeau-Nigel Route (Map 16/C1–22/E5)

Give yourself at least five days to backpack this difficult route that strings together a series of trails in the southeast corner of Jasper. This route gains 750 m (2,460 ft) and is as difficult as it is spectacular. The trail passes though extensive alpine meadows as it makes its way up (and drops down out of) three separate mountain passes. Because of the high elevation, this one is best left until mid-July at the earliest. No dogs allowed.

Pyramid Lake Loop (Map 27/E5)

One of the nicest day hikes from the Jasper Townsite, this 17.4 km/10.6 mile (7 hour) hike gains the most elevation of any trail in the area. You begin by climbing 60 m (195 feet) to the edge of the Pyramid Bench, then another 120 m (390 feet) to the Pyramid Overlook before descending to Pyramid Lake. It is an easy trail but slightly long for the average tourist on foot.

Rocky Pass Trail (Map 28/G6–29/A6)

Most of this trail lies outside of Jasper, but the moderate 11.4 km/7 mile (4 hour) one-way trail is the only access to the South Boundary Trail (see below) without having to hike the entire trail itself. The trail climbs 120 metres (390 feet) to the Rocky (or Cardinal) Pass, at km 7 (mile 4.3), which is also the park boundary, then descends 260 metres (845 feet) to the Medicine Tent Campsite, where many people who hike this trail spend an evening or two. The trailhead is located along the Grave Flats Road at the Cardinal Divide.

Saturday Night Lake Loop (Map 27/C6)

Also known as the Twenty Mile Loop, this easy trip extends over 24.6 km (15 mi) and can be done in one long (7-9 hour) day. Many choose to divide the trip across two days. The trailhead leaves from an unmarked parking lot, just off Cabin Lake Road. Continue past Caledonia Lake and follow the north side of Caledonia Creek to a campsite at Minnow Lake. You can stop here or continue your northeast progression to the High Lakes Campsite, which marks the halfway point of the trail. It also marks the turnaround point, as the trail turns back down the valley half a kilometre beyond after gaining 540 m (1,755 feet). From here the trail continues in a generally downward direction, past Saturday Night and Cabin Lakes, then down to the trailhead.

Skyline Trail (Map 22/C1–27/F6)

Most discussions of backpacking trips in Jasper (and indeed, the Canadian Rockies) don't go far without superlative-drenched ravings about trips along the Skyline Trail. At 44 km (26.8 miles), most people take at least three days to complete this difficult trek, which spends over half its time at or above the tree line, along the crest of the Maligne Range. Conditions along the trail can be difficult if the weather turns inclement and the section between Curator Lake and The Notch is often still under snow late into July. Cyclists are allowed along the final (or first, depending on where you start) 9 km (5.5 miles) at the north end; a tough grind up to the Signal Mountain Fire Lookout. Most hikers start from the Maligne Lake Picnic Area. There are no dogs allowed on this trail.

Signal Mountain Fire Road (Map 27/F6)
A tough, 9.1 km (5.5 mile) grunt 980 metres (3,185 feet) up to an old fire lookout with spectacular views over the Jasper townsite and area. The trailhead is located on Maligne Lake Road and is actually the northern portion of the Skyline Trail.

South Boundary Trail (Map 16, 23, 28, 29)
Eschewing high alpine passes for forested river valleys, the difficult 165.7 km/101 mile (10 day plus) South Boundary Trail is nonetheless one of the best hiking experiences in Jasper. This is not a trail to be attempted lightly; there is only one escape route from the heart of this trail, which spits you out in the middle of a long, lonely, almost always deserted road. Travellers on the South Boundary Trail must be self-sufficient. For your effort, you will be rewarded with a portion of the park that few people have ever taken the effort to see. The trail starts at the Beaver Creek Picnic Area (Map 28/B6) and ends at the Nigel Pass Trailhead (Map 16/C2), in Banff Park.

Southesk Lake Trail (Map 23/D2–A2)
The trail to Southesk Lake might qualify as Jasper's least travelled trail. Veering off the South Boundary Trail at km 88.6 (mile 54), very few South Boundary Trail hikers take the extra two days it takes to hike into and out along the 22.4 km (13.7 mile) one-way trail to Southesk Lake. People who set out to visit the lake itself usually knit together the Rocky Pass Trail, the South Boundary Trail and The Southesk Lake Trail into a difficult 65.5 km (40 mile) one-way (three to four day) jaunt to a remote, romantic lake, far removed from the usual hordes that populate Jasper's easier trails.

Sulphur Skyline Ridge Trail (Map 28/B2)
With an elevation gain of 700 metres (2,275 feet) across 4 km/2.4 miles (1.5 hours), hikers might think twice about this trail. But the views from the top of the Skyline are as impressive as any in a park full of mind-blowing viewpoints. This hike starts and ends at the Miette Hot Springs so bring your bathing suit.

Tangle Falls Trail (Map 15/G1–16/A1)
Following the trail to Wilcox Pass (see below), this poorly defined trail continues beyond the pass and descends along Tangle Creek, finally spitting you out 11 km (6.7 miles) from where you started (10 km/6.2 miles if by road) at Tangle Falls on the Icefields Parkway. Most people who do this route start from the falls (the trail begins just south of creek by the base of the falls) and hike up to the alpine then back along the same route. Expect to take the better part of a day (more if your route-finding skills are poor).

Toe of the Athabasca Glacier (Map 16/A2)
An easy, 1 kilometre interpretive trail starts from the Athabasca Glacier parking lot and gives visitors access to the area right in front of the glacier. You can look and even touch but unless you know how to handle yourself on a glacier, do not actually climb onto it. Even this close to the edge, it can be dangerous to the unaware.

Utopia Pass Trail (Map 28/B2)
This is an easy 5.2 km/3.2 mile (3 hour) return hike from the Miette Hot Springs to Utopia Pass along the Fiddle River Trail (see below). Like many of the passes in the Rockies, Utopia Pass is a riot of wildflowers in early summer, and, with only 275 metres (894 feet) elevation gain, is one of the easier passes to access.

Valley of the Five Lakes (Map 27/F7)
Although there are a couple different ways to get to these bluegreen gems (see Old Fort Point above or Wabasso Lake Trail below), the most direct route is an easy 2 km/1.2 mile (1 hour, one-way) hike in from the trailhead along the east side of the Icefields Parkway. The terrain is rolling, but not strenuous.

Vine Creek Trail (Map 27/D2)
The trailhead to this easy 8.1 km (4.9 mile) trail is located near the halfway point of the Celestine Lake Road.

Wabasso Lake Trails (Map 27/F7)
It is 3.2 km/2 mile (1.5 hour) one-way to Wabasso Lake from the trailhead on the Icefields Parkway; a little longer if you do the half-loop around the lake to where Wabasso Creek flows out. Wabasso Lake itself is a small, picturesque lake that is an easy destination for those with little time or energy. For those with a bit more time and energy, the trail hooks up with trails to the Valley of the Five Lakes Trail. It would be an 11 km/6.7 mile (5 hour) one-way hike. Curator Lake can also be reached from here along the Skyline Trail, but requires an uninspiring climb up (wa-a-ay up) through dense forest. Expect to climb 1,100 metres (3,575 feet) over this exhausting 15.9 km (9.7 mile) one-way extension. However, the views from the valley that Curator Lake is in are spectacular.

Watchtower Basin Trail (Map 27/G6–28/A7)
You can reach the Watchtower Basin from the trailhead on Maligne Lake Road in about four hours and still make it back down the 12.8 km (7.8 mile) one-way trail in time for supper. But we recommend spending the night at the Watchtower Campsite, at km 9.8 (mile 6) and spend the next day exploring. This is the same alpine scenery that the Skyline Trail is famous for but without the crowds. You will climb 985 metres (3,201 feet) to Watchtower Column–but for your efforts you will be rewarded with big, open views of the surrounding countryside. If this hike isn't stiff enough for you, it is possible to connect with the Skyline Trail and hike out that way or via the Wabasso Lake Trail to the south. There are no dogs allowed on the trail.

Whirlpool Fire Road (Map 21/F2)
From Highway 93A, it is an 11.5 km (7 miles) one-way drive to the end of the gravel Whirlpool Fire Road and another 3 km (1.8 miles) beyond to Tie Camp on the Athabasca Pass Trail. Bikes are not allowed past the end of the fire road.

The Whistlers Trail (Map 27/D6)
Why hike up to the Whistlers, other than to save yourself the cost of the tram ticket? It certainly isn't for the remoteness of the peak, as over 200,000 visitors a year see the summit, the vast majority shelling out for the tram. Maybe it is for the sense of accomplishment; gaining 1,250 metres (4,062 feet) over the 9.6 km (5.9 mile) hike up from the trailhead, just off Whistlers Road. Maybe it's to rub it in the noses of all the freshly scrubbed tourists who took the lazy way up. Or maybe it's just because the views from here are superlative; 360 degree views of the surrounding peaks and valleys. One thing is certain, if you are going to hike this 3 hour, one-way trail, save it for a clear day.

Wilcox Pass Trail (Map 16/A2)
A moderate 8 km (4.9 mile) there-and-back hike on a open ridge overlooking some of the most dramatic scenery in Jasper Park: a series of 3,400 metre-plus (11,000 feet plus) peaks, including Mount Athabasca and the world famous Athabasca Glacier, headwaters for the Sunwapta River. While tourists scurry around at the base of the glacier, you will have few visitors other than bighorn sheep as you survey the wonderful views. You can also head up to the North Peak of Mount Wilcox along the ridge that starts at the south end of the pass for a total elevation gain of 940 metres (3,055 feet). Others choose to continue north to Tangle Falls. The trailhead is located 2.8 km (1.7 miles) south of the Icefield Centre.

Willow Creek Trail (Map 34/B4)
An alternate starting point to the North Boundary Trail (see above), this trail runs 13.9 km (8.4 miles) from Rock Lake to where it connects with the NBT. Access to the Snake Indian Falls is a couple kilometres shorter this way, although not much.

Wolf Pass Trail (Map 34/D5)
Okay. So you want to get to Moosehorn Lake but don't relish the idea of hiking 3 km through a swamp (see Moosehorn Lake Trail). This 25.5 km (15.5 mile) trail is no less damp since you must cross Willow Creek at least twenty times over a 3 km (1.8 mile) section of trail called the Notch.

Jasper Adventures

WINTER RECREATION

There are a number of groomed cross-country ski trails in Jasper, plus an almost infinite amount of backcountry terrain (see trails above) that is explored by everyone from the weekend snowshoer to the hardcore telemarker. If you are planning on heading out into the backcountry, be careful, especially in the mountains. Make sure you know what you are doing. Avalanches are only one of many dangers you will face out there. Never travel alone and always carry a beacon, shovel and probe in avalanche country. More importantly, know how to use them. That said, there is nothing that can compare to heading out into the mountains and laying down first tracks on a mountain through two feet of pure powder.

Athabasca/Whirlpool Area (Map 21/F2)
A series of easy to moderate groomed trails, the longest of which is 18 km (11 miles) return to Moab Lake along the Whirlpool Fire Road. The trail is groomed from the Meeting of the Waters (the confluence of the Whirlpool and Athabasca Rivers) picnic area beside Highway 93A. The highway is closed in the winter south of this point allowing for two groomed routes, along Highway 93A to Athabasca Falls as well as the summer road to Moab Falls.

Beaver/Summit Lakes (Map 28/B6)
This is an easy 10 km (6 mile) return trip along the trail to Jacques Lake, although it is only groomed to First Summit Lake. Beyond the summit it is an extra 6 km (3.7 miles) one-way to Jacques Lake.

Cabin Lake Fire Road (Map 27/D6)
Cabin Lake is 3 km (1.8 miles) from the Cottonwood Slough Parking Lot on Pyramid Lake Road. Since the elevation gain is a mere 80 metres (260 feet), it is considered an easy 2 hour round trip.

Fryatt Valley (Map 21/G2–G4)
Accessing the Fryatt Valley and the Alpine Club of Canada (Sidney Vallance) Hut involves a difficult 13 km (7.9 mile) one-way trip gaining 780 metres (2,535 feet) along the way. The headwall, a 200 metre (650 feet) climb in less than a kilometre, near the end of your journey is a difficult obstacle, especially so late in the day. Give yourself plenty of daylight, or be prepared to spend the night outside. Fryatt Valley itself is a skier's delight, with many possible daytrips from the hut. This one is best left to experienced backcountry enthusiasts only.

Jasper Park Lodge Area (Map 27/E6)
There are 25 km (15 miles) of groomed trails around Jasper Park Lodge, groomed and maintained by the lodge itself. You can also skate or snowshoe as well. The longest trail is a 10 km (6 mile) moderate loop around the perimeter of the Lodge property, while the shortest is a loop exactly half that distance, known as the Cavell Trails.

Little Shovel Pass (Map 21/B1)
This ski touring route travels through most of the same area as the famed Skyline Trail. Little Shovel Pass is 20 km (12.2 mile) return, but many choose to extend the outing and explore the high alpine bowls that this area is famous for. You will gain 650 metres (2,113 feet), much of it in the first few kilometres from Maligne Lake. As you get higher up, follow the creek since the summer trail crosses several dangerous slopes. Beware of avalanches and do not venture out alone.

Maligne Lake Area (Map 21/C1)
Most of the summer hiking trails around Maligne Lake were groomed in winter for cross-country skiing, but are not any more. Still, skiers can head out and break trail on routes that include the Lorraine Lake Loop, Upper Moose Lake Loop and Evelyn Creek Loop. You can also ski to the Bald Hills Lookout, but this is a more challenging route.

Mount Edith Cavell Road (Map 21/E1)
In the winter, the road up to Mount Edith Cavell is only ploughed to the Meeting of the Waters where the Whirlpool and Athabasca rivers join. It is an easy 11 km (6.7 mile) one-way trip to the Mount Edith Cavell Hostel. Expect to take 5 hours as you climb 500 metres (1,625 feet). If you chose to do this as a day trip, the trip back down is much quicker.

Palisades Lookout (Map 27/D5)
Most people will find the 890 metres (2,893 feet) gained along this 11 km (6.7 mile) one-way (22 km/7 hour return) trail more than they bargained for. Skins are definitely recommended. But for people wanting a taste of ski touring, this trail has all the elevation gain of a Maligne Pass, with almost none

of the avalanche hazards. The route follows a fire road through forest all the way up and is a breeze on the way down.

Poboktan Creek Trail (Map 22/F5–23/B6)
Built in 1921/22, the trail up Poboktan Pass and on to Brazeau Lake was the first trail into the remote southern reaches of the park. It is a moderate 26 km (15.9 mile) return trip to the Waterfall Warden Cabin for experienced ski tourists, but the 400 metre (1,300 feet) elevation gain might scare some people off. Hardcore ski tourists may choose to continue on along the Jonas Pass-Brazeau Lake Loop.

Pyramid Bench Area (Map 27/E5)
A number of the lower elevation trails between Pyramid Lake and the townsite of Jasper are groomed in winter. These include the Mina/Riley Lakes Loop (6.7 km/4.1 miles return), the Patricia Lake Loop (4.8 km/2.9 miles return) and the Pyramid Bench Loop (4.7 km/2.9 miles return).

Saturday Night Lake Area (Map 27/C6)
The first major stop on the Saturday Night Lake Loop is a 4 km/2.4 miles (1.5 hours) return trip to Marjorie Lake. Caledonia Lake is another 4 km/2.4 miles beyond. The truly adventurous can ski the entire 24 km (14.6 miles) of the Saturday Night Lake Loop, but be prepared to lay first tracks beyond Caledonia Lake.

Sunwapta Falls/Fortress Lake Trail (Map 22/C4)
A 26 km (15.9 miles) intermediate ski trip along what is usually a well trampled trail (although not groomed). The trail crosses the footbridge over the Sunwapta River, then south to the Athabasca Flats. From here it is possible to ski all the way to the confluence of the Chaba and Athabasca Rivers. If you chose to do the entire 26 km route, expect it to take a full day.

Tonquin Valley (Map 21/B1)
A backcountry trip par excellence. Tonquin Valley, which is so popular in summer, is nearly deserted in winter. Although much of the route is up gentle slopes, there is danger of avalanches in the area. Be prepared. You can get to the valley via the Astoria River (14 km/8.5 miles one-way to Wates-Gibson Hut, gaining 150 metres/488 feet) or via Maccarib Pass (28 km/17 miles one-way to the hut, gaining 740 metres/2,405 feet). A good option is ski in via Astoria and out over Maccarib Pass. Eremite Valley, the Fraser Glacier and Amethyst Lakes are all popular day trips from the hut.

Valley of the Five Lakes (Map 27/F7)
This is an easy 4 km/2.4 mile (2 hour) trip along a popular hiking trail. The terrain is rolling, but not strenuous. After just under a kilometre from the parking area on the Icefields Parkway, the trail hooks up with a creek bed, which is easy to follow. Take the left hand fork. Make sure the creek is well frozen before attempting.

Wabasso Lake (Map 27/F7)
There is a fork in the creek that leads to the Valley of the Five Lakes. If you take the right hand fork, you can follow it 6 km (3.7 miles) to Wabasso Lake (actually, you can follow it for about 5 km/3 miles before it gets too difficult to follow; at this point, get onto the hiking trail, which is on your right). Expect to take about 4 hours to ski the 12 km (7.4 mile) return trip.

Whistlers Campground Area (Map 27/E6)
An easy 4.5 km (2.7 mile) loop is groomed around the Whistlers Campground during the snowy season. This trail is lit for night skiing.

WILDLIFE VIEWING

Even more than Banff, Jasper is home to easily seen wildlife. There are elk wandering the streets of the Jasper townsite, bighorn sheep relaxing alongside Highway 16 and moose on the road to Maligne Lake. This means a couple of things. First, slow down. It is common for wildlife to be on the road and if you're going too fast, you might have an accident. Second, it is very easy to get close to the wildlife. Too close, in a lot of cases, resulting in conflicts and even, occasionally, death. Remain at least 100 m (300 ft) from predators such as bears, cougars and wolves and at least 30 m (100 ft) from all other animals.

Highway 16 Corridor (Map 26, 27, 32, 33)
This is the easiest place to see wildlife and it is the rare trip through Jasper indeed where there isn't a herd of elk or a bighorn sheep or two standing next to the road. Make sure you pull well off the road if you stop and do not approach wildlife, especially elk, which have injured more people in Jasper than bears have.

Jasper Townsite (Map 27/E6)
One of the best places to see elk, surprisingly enough, is the Jasper townsite. They like to graze in the large open fields near the two entrances to the town, as well as near the railway station.

Maligne Lake Road (Map 27/E5–22/C1)
There are approximately 150 moose in Jasper Park and the best place to see them is around Maligne Lake. Another good place to see moose is around the Pocahontas Ponds, near the Miette Hot Springs Road.

LIST OF BACKCOUNTRY CAMPSITES

Campsite	Map	Type	Accessed By
Adolphus & Adolphus Horse	25/F1	hike, horse	Berg Lake/North Boundary Trail
Amethyst	21/B2	hike	Maccarib Pass/Tonquin Valley/Astoria River Trail
Ancient Wall	33/D5	hike, horse	Blue Creek/North Boundary Trail
Arête	23/E5	hiker	South Boundary Trail
Astoria	21/C2	hike	Astoria River /Tonquin Valley Trail
Athabasca Crossing	22/C6	hike, bike	Fortress Lake Trail
Athabasca Island	27/D3	canoe	Athabasca River Route
Avalanche	22/F5	hike	Maligne Pass Trail
Big Bend	22/C5	hike, bike	Fortress Lake Trail
Blue Creek	33/E5	hike, horse	North Boundary Trail/ Blue Creek-horse
Boulder Creek	16/C1	hike	Nigel Pass/South Brazeau River Trails
Brazeau Lake	23/C6	hike	Poboktan/Brazeau Trail System
Brazeau River	23/D6	hike	Brazeau Area
Brazeau Meadows	23/D6	hike	Brazeau Trail System
Brulé	34/G7	canoe	Brule Lake/Athabasca River Route
Brussels	21/G4	hike	Fryatt Valley Trail
Burnt Timber	22/F2	horse/hiker	Southesk Lake Trail
Byng	33/A6	hike	North Boundary Trail
Cairn Pass	23/C1	horse/hiker	South Boundary Trail
Cairn River	23/D2	hiker	South Boundary Trail
Calumet	32/F7	horse/hiker	Moose Pass/North Boundary Trail
Caribou Inn	33/B4	hike	Blue Creek/North Boundary Trail
Celestine Lake	27/E1	hike	Vehicle/North Boundary Trail
Chown Creek	32/D5	hike, horse	North Boundary Trail/ Chown Creek-horse
Climax Creek	28/E6	horse/hiker	South Boundary Trail
Cline-horse	16/C1	hike, horse	Nigel Pass/South Brazeau River Trails
Clitheroe	21/B2	hike	Maccarib Pass/Tonquin Valley/Astoria River Trail
Colonel Pass	26/C2	horse/hiker	Snaring River Area
Coronet Creek	22/F3	canoe, hike	Maligne Lake
Curator	27/G7	hike	Skyline Trail
Dean Pass	23/C3	horse/hiker	Southesk Lake Trail
Donaldson Creek	32/D5	hike	North Boundary Trail
Elysium Pass	27/A5	horse/hiker	Elysium Pass Trail
Evelyn Creek	22/B1	hike	Skyline Trail
Fisherman's Bay	22/E3	canoe	on Maligne Lake
Four Point	16/C1	hike	Nigel Pass/South Brazeau River Trails

Campsite	Map	Type	Accessed By
Glacier Pass	33/C4	hike	Glacier Pass/North Boundary Trail
Grizzly	28/C4	horse/hiker	South Boundary Trail
Headwall	21/G4	hike	Fryatt Valley Trail
Henry McLeod	22/F4	canoe, hike	by trail from Maligne Lake
High Lake	27/C5	hike, bike	Saturday Night Lake Loop
Horseshoe	34/B5	hike	North Boundary Trail
Idaleen Lakes	26/D1	horse/hiker	Snaring River Area
Isaac Creek	23/F3	horse/hiker	South Boundary Trail
Jacques Lake	28/B5	hike, bike	Jacques Lake/South Boundary Trail
John John Creek	23/B6	hike	Poboktan/Brazeau Trail System
Jonas Cutoff	23/A6	hike	Poboktan/Brazeau Trail System
Kane Meadows	21/C6	horse/hiker	Athabasca Pass Trail
La Grace	29/A7	hiker	South Boundary Trail
Little Heaven	33/F5	hike, horse	Glacier Pass/North Boundary Trail/ Little Heaven-horse
Little Shovel	22/B1	hike	Skyline Trail
Lower Fryatt	22/A3	hike	Fryatt Valley Trail
Lower Moose-horn	34/G7	horse/hiker	Moosehorn Lake Trail
Maccarib	21/B1	horse/hiker	Maccarib Pass/Tonquin Valley Trail
Mary Vaux	22/E4	hike	Maligne Pass Trail
McCready Horse Camp	23/A6	hike, horse	Poboktan/Brazeau Trail System
Medicine Tent	28/C5	horse/hiker	South Boundary Trail/ Medicine Tent-horse
Middle Forks	21/D4	horse/hiker	Athabasca Pass Trail
Miette Lake	26/E3	horse/hiker	Miette Lake Trail
Minnow Lake	27/C5	hike, bike	Saturday Night Lake Loop
Moosehorn	34/E6	horse/hiker	Moosehorn Lake Trail
Natural Arch	33/B4	hike, horse	Blue Creek/North Boundary Trail
Oatmeal	33/A6	hike, horse	North Boundary Trail
Old Horse	22/E4	hike	Maligne Pass Trail
Poboktan Creek	22/F5	hike	Poboktan/Brazeau Trail System
Portal	21/C1	hike	Maccarib Pass/Tonquin Valley Trail
Rocky Forks	28/F6	horse/hiker	South Boundary Trail/ Rocky Forks-horse
Ronde Creek	34/F7	hiker	Moosehorn Lake Trail
Saturday Night Lake	27/C5	hike, bike	Saturday Night Lake Loop
Schaffer Camp	22/D3	hike	Maligne Pass Trail
Scott Camp	21/D5	hike, horse	Athabasca Pass Trail
Second Geraldine	21/F3	hike	Geraldine Lakes Trail
Seldom Inn	34/B6	hike, horse	North Boundary Trail/ Seldom Inn-horse
Shalebanks	34/C7	hike	North Boundary Trail
Signal	27/F6	hike, bike	Signal Mtn Fire Rd/Skyline Trail
Simon Creek	21/E3	hike	Athabasca Pass Trail
Slide Creek	28/C3	hike, bike	Fiddle River Trail
Slide Creek	28/C3	horse	Fiddle River Trail

SEE A COMPLETE LIST OF CAMPSITE ONLINE ON OUR BLOG.
HTTP://BACKROADMAPBOOKS.COM/BLOG/

JasperAdventures

102

KananaskisCountryAdventures

Image © Aaron Teasdale

THINGS TO KNOW

Area: 425,000 hectares

Highest Point: Mount Joffre 3,450 metres
(11,319 feet)

Total Vehicle Accessible Campsites: 1,220
(+1,000 private sites)

THINGS TO SEE

1 Highwood Pass

2 Kananaskis River

3 Chester Lake

CONTACT INFORMATION

Alberta Parks: (403) 678–5508
www.albertaparks.ca

Backcountry Permits: (403) 678-3136

Barrier Lake Info Centre: (403) 673-3985

**Canmore Nordic Centre Park Visitor
Information Centre:** (403) 678-2400

Elbow Valley Info Centre: (403) 949–4261

Friends of Kananaskis: (403) 678–5593
friends@kananaskis.org www.kananaskis.org

Peter Lougheed Park Info Centre:
(403) 591-6322

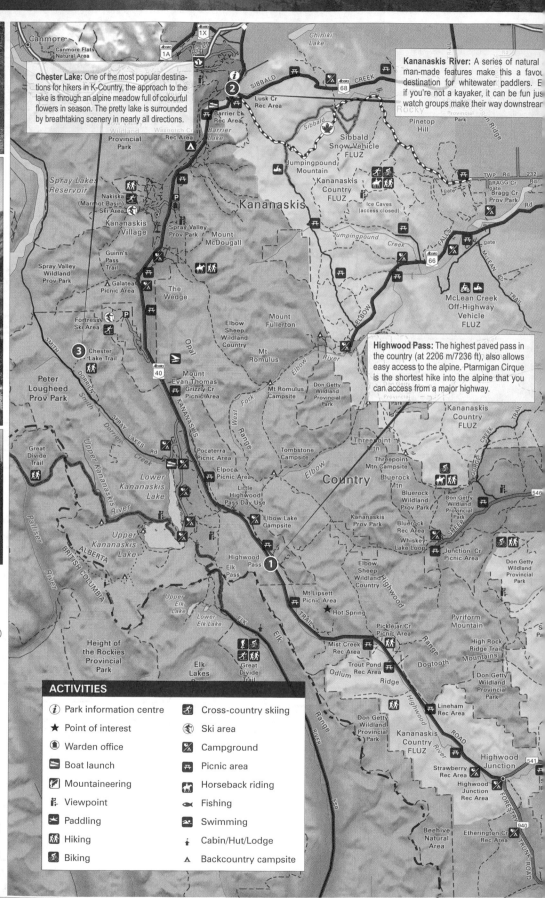

Chester Lake: One of the most popular destinations for hikers in K-Country, the approach to the lake is through an alpine meadow full of colourful flowers in season. The pretty lake is surrounded by breathtaking scenery in nearly all directions.

Kananaskis River: A series of natural man-made features make this a favou destination for whitewater paddlers. E if you're not a kayaker, it can be jus watch groups make their way downstrear

Highwood Pass: The highest paved pass in the country (at 2206 m/7236 ft), also allows easy access to the alpine. Ptarmigan Cirque is the shortest hike into the alpine that you can access from a major highway.

ACTIVITIES

ⓘ	Park information centre	🎿	Cross-country skiing
★	Point of interest	⛷	Ski area
🏛	Warden office	🍴	Campground
🚤	Boat launch	⛺	Picnic area
🧗	Mountaineering	🐎	Horseback riding
🧍	Viewpoint	🎣	Fishing
🚣	Paddling	🏊	Swimming
🥾	Hiking	🏕	Cabin/Hut/Lodge
🚴	Biking	⛺	Backcountry campsite

Located southeast of Banff and southwest of the Stoney Indian Reserve, Kananaskis Country is the name given to this sprawling multi-use area that encompasses a large area of the East Slopes of the Rocky Mountains and foothills. The region gets its name from a pair of lakes, a river and a couple high mountain passes that in turn were named for a legendary First Nations brave who was struck and stunned by an axe, but made a "wonderful recovery." The name has since come to mean "meeting of the waters". Captain John Palliser gave the name to the area in 1858 when he came through on a scientific and geographic expedition sponsored by the British Government.

By 1883, commercial enterprise came to the Kananaskis Valley, as the Eau Claire and Bow Lumber Companies began logging in the area. In 1932, the dam between Upper and Lower Kananaskis Lakes was begun. Surprisingly, the area around Kananaskis was excluded from the National Parks Act in 1930, instead becoming part of the provincially managed Rocky Mountain Forest Reserve. In 1978 the area that would become Peter Lougheed Provincial Park was officially dedicated as Kananaskis Country.

During its formative years in the mid-1970s, the future of K-Country (as those in the know now call this 4, 250 sq km/1,641 sq mile area) was discussed, debated and fought over by members of the public and by governmental policy makers. Many people had different visions for the future of Kananaskis Country. Ultimately, through public consultation, the Alberta Government decided to create Kananaskis Country as a multi-use recreation area, setting aside some areas as parks and recreation areas while maintaining some areas as Forestry Land Use Zones (FLUZes) and Ecological Reserves. This resulted in many areas receiving the highest levels of protection, but maintained the option of providing hunting and even off-highway vehicle use in others.

The area around Kananaskis Lakes was turned into a provincial park, providing it with the highest level of protection available in the Alberta Parks system. Originally named Kananaskis Provincial Park, it was later renamed Peter Lougheed Provincial Park in honour of the former Premier. Farther east is the Elbow-Sheep Wildland Provincial Park which is open to more forms of recreation, like hunting. Further east and south of the Highway 66, which contains some of the most popular recreation areas in the province, is the McLean OHV Area. This area allows for Off Highway Vehicle Use, including quading, 4-wheel drive vehicle and motorcycles. The southern area of Kananaskis Country is known as the Highwood/Cataract district and like other Forestry Lands within Kananaskis Country is still open to logging, mining and oil and gas exploration, but under strict guidelines.

While nearby Banff draws upwards of four million people a year, Peter Lougheed Provincial Park, one of the most popular destinations in K-Country, sees a lot less. The Peter Lougheed Visitor Centre has averaged over 76,600 visitors over the last three years. Many of these visitors are Albertans, although the area is becoming more popular with visitors from around the world, too. For those looking for a Rocky Mountain getaway without the National Park crowds, this is a great destination. While the core areas of the park can seem just as busy as Banff on summer long weekends (around the Kananaskis Lakes, especially), it is not difficult to find a deserted corner for yourself.

HOT SPRINGS

Mist Mountain Warm Springs (Map 5/C7)
A small, cooler spring that is set somewhere on the side of Mist Mountain in Kananaskis. This spring sees little use since there is no real trail to the springs and access is difficult. Many people, including our researcher, have searched in vain to find the springs. If you do happen to find the springs, the soaking pool is about 1 metre (3 feet) across and maybe 30 centimeters (1 foot) deep. Not exactly the most luxuriant soak and the water is luke warm on the best of days. Give yourself the better part of a day to track these down.

—CAMPING, PARKS AND RECREATION AREAS—

Unlike the provincial and national parks described in other parts of this book, K-Country is made up of a series of parks and recreation areas. There are nearly 40 public campgrounds, scattered throughout the various sites of K-Country that are vehicle accessible. These range from small, rustic recreation areas to large provincial parks with power and water. There are also hundreds of day-use areas, backcountry campsites and wildland parks to explore. Please practice "leave no trace" camping while in the backcountry.

Backcountry permits are required at designated backcountry campsites, while random camping is only allowed within wildland parks (with the exception of Sparrowhawk Tarns and Memorial Lake). The parks service recommends contacting one of the areas Visitor Information Centres for details or calling (403) 678-3136. Reservations for vehicle accessible campsites can be made through www.reserve.albertaparks.ca.

Bow/Spray Valley Area

The northern reaches of K-Country border on the Bow River, while the western reaches run next to Banff National Park along the Spray River Valley. Within the area is one of the busiest campgrounds in Alberta. The revamped Canmore Nordic Centre, with the recent Olympic success of some of its athletes, is also worth a visit.

Bow Valley Provincial Park (Map 9/A6)
This popular park is located 28 km east of Canmore along the Trans-Canada Highway. There are two full facility campgrounds, the Bow Valley Campground and the Willow Rock Campground offering nearly 400 campsites in the park. Additionally for larger groups, three group campgrounds are available including Grouse, Owl and Elk Flats. Many of these sites are within earshot of the busy highway, which can make for an unsettled night, especially for tenters. In addition to the campgrounds, there are 11 different day-use areas that help you enjoy the recreation pursuits in the valley. Hiking and biking trails are available in the summer, as is fishing at a number of rivers and lakes in the valley. To reserve a space at Bow Valley or Willow Rock, phone (403) 673-2163 or visit www.reserve.albertaparks.ca.

Bow Valley Wildland Provincial Park (Map 4, 8, 9)
An amalgamation of several former natural areas, including Wind Valley and Yamnuska, this expansive wildland park has been established to protect wildlife habitat to the east of Banff. In addition to several trails, the south face of Yamnuska is a popular traditional climbing destination. There are designated backcountry campsites at Jewell Bay and Quaite Valley near Barrier Lake, as well as vehicle accessible campsites at Lac des Arc, Three Sisters and Bow River.

Spray Valley Provincial Park (Map 4, 8)
Bordering on Banff National Park, the hub of this 26,598 hectare area is found 18 km south of Canmore on a good gravel road called the Smith-Dorrien Spray Trail (Secondary Highway 742). The main camping area is found along the west side of Spray Lake, but the 50 sites are not RV friendly. The road is rough and the sites are not level. There is also a 51 unit camping site at Eau Claire, just off Highway 40 about 38 km south of Highway 1. There is winter camping allowed at Buller Mountain Pond Picnic Area. Within the park there are also several different day-use areas with picnic tables as well as several backcountry campsites including Ribbon Lake, Ribbon Falls and Lillian Lake. At the various creeks, ponds and lakes, fishing and paddling are popular, while the trail systems are enjoyed year-round.

Elbow Valley Area (Map 5, 9)

Found only 30 minutes from Calgary, this area offers a total of 13 different campgrounds ranging from serviced RV sites with hook-ups (McLean Creek) to several hike-in destinations. Fishing, an off-highway vehicle trail system, kayaking and endless trails are some of the highlights of the area. The Elbow Falls Trail (Highway 66) runs through the heart of this stairway to the Rockies and can be accessed by travelling south of Cochrane via Highway 22 or west from Calgary on Highway 22x. We have listed the campgrounds and bigger day-use sites in the area below.

Big Elbow Backcountry Campsite (Map 5/D4)
Best known for its shorter access and equestrian camping, there are 6 backcountry camping sites here.

KananaskisCountryAdventures

Don Getty Wildland Provincial Park (Map 5, 9)
Figuring where to list this rather confusing park is about as challenging as finding all seven pieces that are found in and around K-Country. Each parcel protects a unique feature, but they all share limited (trail) access. Forgetmenot Mountain is a popular hiking destination in the area.

Elbow Falls Recreation Area (Map 5/E2)
Comprised of a 55 site campground at Beaver Flats as well as the popular year-round destination of Elbow Falls Day Use Area, this area is located 13 km past the Elbow Valley Visitor Information Centre on Highway 66.

Elbow River Recreation Area (Map 5/F1)
This day-use area is located 12 km southwest of Bragg Creek on Highway 66. It includes Allen Bill Pond, a favourite with local picnickers and anglers, as well as Paddy's Flat Campground.

Fisher Creek Recreation Area (Map 5/G3)
A fair ways off the beaten trail and just east of our maps, this site is located 27 km (16.8 miles) southwest of Bragg Creek. The 30 site camping area is often less busy than others in the area.

Gooseberry Recreation Area (Map 5/G1)
Located 8 km (6.2 miles) southwest of Bragg Creek on Highway 66, this quiet site has space for 83 camping units.

Little Elbow Recreation Area (Map 5/D3)
One of the bigger sites in the area, there are 94 sites in the main camping area, as well as another 46 sites in an equestrian area. This is a popular staging area for horseback and backpacking trips in the area.

McLean Creek Recreation Area (Map 5/F1)
The primary campground for ATVers and snowmobilers taking trips into the McLean Creek OHV Zone, there are 170 campsites here. Many of the campsites have electrical service, however some do not. This is a huge site located in a lodgepole pine forest, with access to miles upon miles of trails. The McLean Staging Area and McLean Pond (stocked annually) also offer day-use opportunities.

West Bragg Creek Recreation Area (Map 9/F7)
Another day-use only area, this site marks the trailhead for the West Bragg Creek Cross-Country Ski trails. In the summer, intrepid hikers and mountain bikers use these non-maintained trails.

Wildhorse Backcountry Campsite (Map 5/F3)
Accessible by trail only, the Wildhorse Campsite is found at the junction of four trails (Wildhorse, Volcano Ridge, Hog's Back and an alternate route off the Hog's Back).

Highwood Valley/Cataract Area (Map 2, 5)
Located 45 km (28 miles) west of Longview along the Highwood Trail (Highway 541) is the Highwood River Valley. Cataract Creek continues south from the river to meet up with Highway 532 and the foothills. This area of K-Country is home to eight different campgrounds with a total of 240 vehicle sites, the largest of which is Cataract Creek. In addition, there are several day-use areas to help explore the many trails and other features in the area. Below is a sampling of some of the sites in this recreational area. Highway 40, between Peter Lougheed Provincial Park and the Highway 940 is closed from December 1st to June 14th and re-opens to vehicle traffic on June 15th.

Cataract Creek Recreation Area (Map 2/G4)
The largest campground in the Cataract area, this site hosts 102 sites. It is a popular site with trail enthusiasts and is used as a put-in location by paddlers. It is found just east of our maps off Secondary Highway 940.

Cat Creek Recreation Area (Map 2/F2)
A small day-use only site, there are picnic tables plus parking for people using the trail system.

Don Getty Wildland Provincial Park (Map 2, 5)
Within this area are three pieces of this wildland park. Each parcel protects a unique alpine feature, but they all share limited (trail) access. Cataract Creek (just east of Map 2) is the easiest to access and boasts some of the best fishing in the province.

Etherington Creek Recreation Area (Map 2/G3)
In addition to the main campground that offers 61 sites, there is a nearby equestrian site that has room for 10 groups. Both sites are used as staging grounds for the vast trail system in the area, but if you are not camping, you should use the day-use area.

Fitzsimmons Creek Recreation Area (Map 2/G2)
Located alongside the Forestry Trunk Road (Secondary Highway 940), near the confluence of Fitzsimmons Creek with the Highwood River, this is a day-use site. Picnicking, fishing and hiking are the most common pursuits in the area.

Highwood Junction Recreation Area (Map 2/G2)
More like a rest stop than a recreation area, Highwood House is a welcome outpost of civilization after a fairly long drive, especially when heading north along Highway 940. There are indoor washrooms, a concession, pay phones and gasoline.

Lantern and Mist Creek Recreation Areas (Map 2/E1–5/E7)
These small day-use sites are used as staging areas for hikers and horseback riders.

Strawberry Recreation Area (Map 2/F2)
Used mostly by horseback riders, there is space for 18 groups and their horses here, but this site is only open from September to November.

Trout Pond & Picklejar Recreations Area (Map 5/E7)
The Trout Pond site is located, near Odlum Creek and is mostly used as a rest area by travellers along Highway 40. More adventurous anglers accessing the lakes by trail can use the Lantern Creek Recreation Area listed above.

Kananaskis Valley (Map 4, 5, 8, 9)
The Kananaskis Valley, through which the Kananaskis River flows, is found south of the Bow Valley Provincial Park on the Kananaskis Trail (Highway 40). Within the valley are extensive recreation facilities, including a number of public and private campgrounds and day-use areas to help you enjoy the trail systems, fishing, swimming and paddling opportunities available. The Kananaskis Village, Nakiska Ski Area and Elbow-Sheep Wildland Provincial Park are some of the notable features in the valley.

Canoe Meadows & Stoney Creek Group Camping (Map 9/B6)
Two group campsites are found around Barrier Lake at the north end of the valley. Between them, there is room for 65 units.

Elbow-Sheep Wildland Provincial Park (Map 4, 5, 9)
Lying to the east of Highway 40, this large wildland park is only accessible by foot, mountain bike or horse. For the few that make the effort to get here, this is an area of vast lodgepole pine and spruce forests set in the foothills of the Rockies. Backcountry campsites are found below Mount Romulus and Tombstone Mountain.

Eau Claire Recreation Area (Map 4/G2)
Next to the confluence of Kananaskis River and Rocky Creek, campers will find 51 sites here.

Mount Kidd RV Campground (Map 4/G2)
This private site rests just south of the golf course and offers 229 campsites, including 88 sites with electrical hook-ups. Across the highway, Wedge Pond and the Evan-Thomas Creek Trails are worth exploring.

Sundance Lodge (Map 4/G1–5/A1)
In addition to camping in supplied trappers tents and tipis, visitors will find 23 vehicle campsites here. This site is found north of the village turnoff, on the east side of the Kananaskis River

Peter Lougheed Provincial Park (Map 4, 5)
Peter Lougheed Provincial Park was established in 1978 and preserves vast areas of alpine and sub-alpine and contains the Highwood Pass, the highest paved pass in Canada. Within the park are many of the big game species (mountain goats, grizzly and black bears, cougars, big horn sheep, wolves, elk, moose and deer) typical of the Rocky Mountains. The park also provides a wide range of recreation pursuits including hiking, mountain biking, cross-country skiing, fishing and paddling. It has a total of six main campgrounds (Boulton, Canyon, Elkwood, Interlakes, Lower Lake and Mount Sarrail) with 496 camping units. Only Boulton Creek Campground takes reservations. Mount Sarrail Campground is the most rustic with 44 walk-in sites for tenters, while the campground on the Lower Lakes is arguably the most beautiful. The park is open year-round and is accessed by the Kananaskis Trail (Highway 40) or the Smith-Dorrien Spray Trail (Secondary Highway 742). For campsite reservations at Boulton Creek, call 1-866-366-2267 or visit www.reserve.albertaparks.ca.

KananaskisCountry Adventures

Sheep Valley Area (Map 5)

The Sheep River Valley west of Sandy McNabb has been converted to park-land to help protect wildlife in the area. Sheep River Trail (Secondary Highway 546) from Turner Valley is the main road into the area, while trails stretch in all directions linking up with other areas of K-Country. In addition to wildlife viewing, paddling, hiking, biking, cross-country skiing and fishing are popular pastimes in the area. The road is closed beyond the Sandy McNabb Recreation Area in the winter. Also the Gorge Creek Trail (the Road) is closed indefinitely to vehicles due to flood damage from Ware Creek Day Use Area to just north of the Sheep River Trail (Hwy 546).

Bluerock Wildland Provincial Park (Map 5/E5)

This park protects a part of the Sheep River Valley, a natural wildlife corridor for elk, moose, bighorn sheep and grizzly bear, just to name a few. There is fishing in Ware Creek and backcountry camping for six groups at Threepoint Backcountry Campsite.

Sheep River Provincial Park (Map 5/G5)

The area around the Sheep River has been converted to parkland to help protect the bighorn sheep common to the area. Two different drive-in camping areas are found off the Sheep River Trail; Sandy McNabb with 119 sites to the east of our maps and Bluerock with 83 sites. There are also five backcountry camping areas as well as nine different day-use areas scattered along the road. All the day-use sites have picnic tables and pit toilets. The various creeks and rivers within the valley provide paddling and fishing opportunities, while a number of hiking, cross-country skiing and equestrian trails are found within the valley. Secondary Highway 546 is closed beyond the Sandy McNabb Recreation Area in the winter.

Sibbald Creek Area (Map 9)

This popular year-round recreation area is found south of the Trans-Canada Highway on the Sibbald Creek Trail (Secondary Highway 68). It has a number of different campgrounds and day-use sites. In the summer, there are a number of trails including the Jumpingpound Demonstration Forest. Several nearby creeks and lakes provide fishing, while snowshoeing and snowmobiling are popular in the winter.

Dawson Equestrian Recreation Area (Map 9/D6)

Used as a staging area for trips along the Tom Snow or Coxhill Ridge or Eagle Hill Trails, there is space for 17 groups plus their horses.

Lusk Creek Recreation Area (Map 9/B6)Further west, near Barrier Lake on the Sibbald Trail, this picnic area is on Lusk Creek, which can offer pretty good fishing.

Pine Grove Recreation Area (Map 9/E6)

Made up of two large group use campgrounds, there is space for up to 40 camping units here.

Sibbald Lake Recreation Area (Map 9/D6)

The main campground in the area, visitors will find 134 vehicle accessible sites here. Nearby, the Sibbald Viewpoint is worth a look.

Sibbald Meadows Pond Recreation Area (Map 9/C6)

This site sees some use from anglers and day-hikers, but mostly it is used as a rest stop for travellers.

FISHING

The Eastern Slopes of the Rockies offer anglers the chance to experience some truly magical angling. From pristine streams to high alpine lakes, there is some truly glorious scenery in this region that serves as a spectacular backdrop to some great fishing. The best fishing is usually found in the rivers and streams and there are hundreds of kilometres of water to test. Because of this, we have not listed every single creek, but chances are if there are fish in the main artery, there are fish in the small tributaries.

This is not to say there isn't any lake fishing opportunities within K-Country. There are in fact several good locations to test. Of these, the Kananaskis Lakes see most of the lake fishing pressure. The stocked ponds (noted with the symbol) are also good places to try. If you don't see a lake or stream listed here, check the regulations; it may be closed.

Allen Bill Pond (Map 5/G1)

This tiny pond is home of the Allen Bill Pond Recreation Area, a small picnic site. The pond is located next to Highway 66 and each year it is stocked with rainbow trout (between 20–30 cm/8–12 inches). In addition to rainbow, the pond is home to some small brook trout and rocky mountain whitefish. Camping is nearby at the McLean Creek and Elbow River Recreation Areas.

Aster Lake (Map 4/F6)

A remote, high mountain lake near the BC boundary in Peter Lougheed Provincial Park, Aster Lake holds stocked cutthroat to 20 cm (12 inches). The lake is a 10 km (6.2 mile) hike from the parking lot at Upper Kananaskis Lake via an unmaintained route.

Barrier Lake (Map 9/A6)

The shores of Barrier Lake are located off Highway 40 southeast of Canmore. It contains brown trout to 1.5 kg (3 lbs), rocky mountain whitefish to 1 kg (2 lbs) and a few small brook trout. The lake is a man-made expansion of Kananaskis River and is best fished by trolling or spincasting.

Bateman Creek (Map 9/D6)

Bateman Creek has brook, bull, cutthroat and rainbow trout. It drains into the Jumpingpound Creek near Old Buck Mountain and is accessed by Secondary Highway 68.

Canmore Creek (Map 8/D6)

Canmore Creek is a short creek that runs from Grassi Lakes into the Bow River. There has been a recent effort to control brook trout (which are not native to the system) and reintroduce cutthroat, which are. In addition to the cutthroat and brookies, you will find brown trout and whitefish. The fish are small, usually in the 25-30 cm (10-12 inch) range.

Canyon Creek (Map 5/B2–E2)

Canyon Creek contains good numbers of brook trout, plus a few cutthroat and bull trout. An Elbow River tributary, the lower reaches are easily accessible by road while the upper reaches are accessed via trail or bushwhacking.

Chester Lake (Map 4/F3)

Chester Lake contains illegally transplanted Dolly Varden to 4 kg (8 lbs) and is one of the 2 or 3 lakes in Alberta that contains dollies. It is rumoured that some may have made their way downstream to Mud Lake and it is because of this escapement that Northern Dolly Varden are harvestable between July 1st and October 31st. Be sure to check the fishing regulations for any local changes.

Commonwealth Creek & Lake (Map 4/E3)

This lake is occasionally stocked with cutthroat trout. It is not a popular lake since access is by bushwhacking and shore fishing is difficult. But for those willing to bring a float tube, cutthroat to 40 cm (16 inches) await. The creek also holds small, stocked cutthroat.

Coxhill Creek (Map 9/D7)

This creek is best accessed by the Tom Snow Trail. It has brook, bull, cutthroat and rainbow trout.

Crane Meadows Ponds (Map 9/C6)

Found on the south side of Highway 68 on Sibbald Creek, these beaver ponds (too tiny to mark on our maps) hold a fair number of small rainbow and brook trout. Accessing the ponds is difficult without waders and shore casting is nearly impossible.

Dyson Creek (Map 5/G6)

Offering brown and rainbow trout, this creek can be accessed by several trails including the Green Mountain Trail.

Elbow Lake (Map 5/B5)
It is a steep, short hike leads from Highway 40 up to this small lake at the summit of Elbow Pass along a popular hiking trail. The lake contains mostly brook and some cutthroat trout to 30 cm (12 inches). Shore fishers will do best from the north side of the lake.

Elbow River (Map 5/B5–G1)
From its headwaters at Elbow Lake (east of Kananaskis Lakes), the Elbow flows in a northeast direction and is followed by Highway 66, 22 and 8 all the way to Calgary, where it drains into the Bow River. The upper reaches of the river contain small brook trout, brown trout (to 2 kg/4 lbs), bull trout (to 1.5 kg/3 lbs), cutthroat (to 1 kg/2 lbs) and mountain whitefish (to 1 kg/2 lbs). Upstream of Elbow Falls, the trout must be 30 cm (12 inches) to keep if they are caught in the main river or one of the tributaries (except Quirk Creek, which is a catch and release stream, open from June 16 to October 31). From Elbow Falls downstream to Canyon Creek, the river is closed to fishing. Tributaries, such as Cougar, Ford and Prairie Creeks, offer reasonably good fishing.

Evan-Thomas Creek (Map 4/G1–5/A2)
Evan-Thomas Creek has brook, brown and cutthroat trout in the trail accessed upper reaches. In summer, the lower reaches near Highway 40 tend to be dry.

Fortress Lake (Map 4/F2) 🐟
This small, high alpine lake is set in the shadow of the Fortress and is reached via a 4 km (2.4 mile) trail from the Fortress Ski Area to the south. Note that it is necessary to park at the decommissioned bridge that leads to Fortress and walk/bike 8 km up the road to the base of the former ski hill. The lake is not ice-free until July and is home to a fairly good population of stocked cutthroat trout.

Galatea Lakes (Map 4/E2) 🐟
The Galatea Creek Trail takes anglers to Lillian Lake, a distance of 6 km (3.7 miles) from Highway 40. From there, you will see a trailhead pointing the direction to Lower and Upper Galatea Lakes, bodies of water that hold stocked cutthroat up to 40 cm (14 inches).

Gap Lake (Map 8/F6)
This lake is located right next to Highway 1A to the west of the Bow Valley Provincial Park. There is a picnic area and a place to hand launch small craft at the lake. The lake contains brook trout (to 0.5 kg/1 lb), a few brown trout (to 6 kg) and rocky mountain whitefish (to 2.5 kg/5 lbs). At the time of writing this book, the lake holds the world record for the largest rocky mountain whitefish (2.55 kg or 5 lbs 10 oz), which was caught in 1991.

Goat Pond (Map 8/D7)
Goat Pond is found a couple kilometres north of the Spray Lake Reservoir off the Smith-Dorrien Road. It has fair numbers of brook trout, lake trout and rocky mountain whitefish. Trolling, fly-fishing and spincasting all work, although there are a lot of snags and shore fishing can be frustrating.

Grand Valley Creek (Map 9/G2)
This creek drains into the Bow River to the west of Cochrane and provides fishing for small rainbow and rainbow-cutthroat cross. The best fishing is near the creek estuary.

Grassi Lakes (Map 8/D6)
A pair of small lakes found just south of Canmore, the Grassi Lakes contain a few brook trout between them. Access is along a short hiking trail.

Grotto Mountain Pond (Map 8/F6) 🐟
This small pond, (too small to be marked on our maps), is found next to Highway 1A near the Grotto Mountain Picnic Area. The pond offers fly-fishing and spincasting for brook trout, rocky mountain whitefish, rainbow and brown trout. Most of the fish in the pond are small.

Headwall Lakes (Map 4/F3) 🐟
The route to Headwall Lakes starts from the Chester Lake parking lot. After crossing Headwall Creek, an indistinct, easy-to-miss trail branches off to the left and follows the creek up to the small lakes. Both lakes hold stocked cutthroat to 30 cm (12 inches) and are easy to fish from shore.

Highwood River (Map 2/G2–5/E7) 🐟
Highwood River begins in Kananaskis Country near the BC-Alberta border and flows eastward into the Bow River north of High River. The river contains brook, cutthroat and rainbow trout as well as rocky mountain whitefish, which all grow to 1.5 kg (3 lb), but tend to be under 40 cm (16 in). There are also some larger bull trout (to 3 kg/6 lbs) in the big pools. From the

headwaters to the Kananaskis Country boundary, the river and all tributaries (except Storm Creek) are open to fishing from June 16 to October 31 and all trout must be released except brook trout, which have a limit of two. There is also a bait ban (except a limited maggot season). Within 500 m of the Bow River, fishing is open year-round and you can keep up to two trout greater than 40 cm in size from June 1 to March 31 as well as up to five whitefish. Remember, these restrictions are subject to change, so check the regulations before heading out.

Hogarth Lakes (Map 4/E3)
A pair of crystal clear lakes found northwest of Mud Lake (head west along the Burstall Pass Trail, then take a right past Mud Lake), these two lakes contain cutthroat to 40 cm (16 inches). Fly-fishing works well.

Jumpingpound Creek (Map 9/C7–G6)
This creek flows northward and drains into the Bow River at Cochrane. The creek contains fair numbers of small brook, bull, cutthroat and rainbow trout as well as rocky mountain whitefish. To maintain the fish stocks, the creek and its tributaries are closed from November 1 to June 15 and are catch and release only the rest of the year, except for brook trout (limit of two) and rocky mountain whitefish (limit of five from June 16 to August 31).

Kananaskis Lake, Lower (Map 4/G5–5/A5) 🐟
Found in the heart of the Peter Lougheed Provincial Park, Lower Kananaskis Lake is accessible by a good paved road (Kananaskis Lake Trail) and offers several camping and picnic sites. Trolling is the most productive method of fishing this lake, which holds bull trout (to 5 kg/11 lbs), cutthroat (to 1 kg/2 lbs) and rainbow (to 2.5 kg/5 lbs). In fact, the lake holds the record for Alberta's largest bull trout taken in the mid-1980s, a whopping 8.14 kg (17 lbs, 15 oz). Please note that Northwest Bay and Smith-Dorrien Creek are closed to fishing to protect spawning bull trout. Also, there is a bait ban on the lake.

Kananaskis Lake, Upper (Map 4/G6–5/A6) 🐟
Upper Kananaskis Lake is arguably the prettier of the two Kananaskis Lakes. However, the fish are usually smaller, due to fluctuating water levels. The lake holds rainbow, which can get to 2.5 kg (5 lbs). 2001 was the first time the lake was stocked with bull trout and these fish have grown to 45 cm (18 inches). They were stocked again in 2003 along with cutthroat trout (for the first time). Although a trail circles the lake, shore anglers usually fair better near the mouth of the Upper Kananaskis River. Folks with boats have more options and can try trolling the many bays or around the islands.

Kananaskis River (Map 4/G4–9/A6)
Kananaskis River flows northward from the Kananaskis Lakes into the Bow River. The river is easily accessed along most of its course by the Kananaskis Trail (Highway 40). The fishing is fairly spotty, but with patience you may be able to catch a brook trout, cutthroat trout or rocky mountain whitefish (all to 1 kg/2 lbs). For the river and its tributaries (except Smith-Dorrien Creek) from the headwaters to Highway 1, fishing is closed from November 1 to March 31 and all cutthroat and rainbow must be over 30 cm (12 inches) to keep. From Highway 1 to the Bow River, fishing is open year-round, but on a catch a release basis (except for brook trout and rocky mountain whitefish).

Lake Rae (Map 5/C5)
This small lake is found south of the Elbow Pass Trail. The small lake is open year-round, with a catch limit of two…if there are any fish here at all.

Little Elbow River (Map 5/C3)
This small river has fair numbers of cutthroat and rainbow trout (to 0.5 kg/1 lb) and bull trout (to 1.5 kg/3 lbs). The upper reaches of the river are accessed by the Little Elbow River Trail whereas the lower reaches are accessed by the Elbow Falls Road (Highway 66).

Loomis Lake (Map 2/D1)
Loomis Lake is a tiny lake that is reached by the trail off Highway 40. The 11 km (6.8 mile) hike along an old logging road deters many. However, the surprisingly large cutthroat (to 2 kg/4 lbs) makes the lake well worth the effort to visit. A two trout limit applies.

Loomis, McPhail and Odlum Creeks (Map 2/E1)
These small creeks are tributaries of the Highwood River and are catch and release fisheries for brook, brown and rainbow trout. Access is by trail from Highway 40.

Maude Lake (Map 4/E5) 🐟
Located in Peter Lougheed Provincial Park, this seldom-visited lake is reached by a 15 km (9.3 mile) hike along the Maude-Lawson Lakes Trail from the dam on Lower Kananaskis Lake. The small, stocked cutthroat in the lake come readily to most trout flies and small lures (with bait). A two trout limit applies.

McLean Pond (Map 5/F1)
McLean Pond is found next to the McLean Creek Trail (2wd access), just south of Highway 66. The stocked pond offers fair fishing for brook trout and rainbow by spincasting, bait fishing or fly-fishing. A day-use area is located next to the lake (McLean Pond Recreation Area).

Mist Creek (Map 5/D7)
Mist Creek is another catch and release fishery for brown, cutthroat and rainbow trout. The Mist Creek Trail, which begins off Highway 40, provides good access along most of the creek.

Moose Creek (Map 9/E7)
Accessed by the Tom Snow Trail, Moose Creek has brook, bull and cutthroat trout.

Mount Lorette Pond (Map 9/A7)
This tiny, stocked pond is found off Highway 40 south of Barrier Lake. It contains some small brook trout and rainbow that can be caught by bait fish or spincasting from shore. A network of trails has been developed around the lake to allow access to the physically challenged.

Mud Lake (Map 4/E3)
Located just west of the Smith-Dorrien/Spray Trail, this lake contains cutthroat trout to 30 cm (12 inches), bull trout to 50 cm (20 inches) and whitefish to 30 cm (12 inches). There are also rumours that Dolly Varden (the close cousin to bull trout), which were transplanted in Chester Lake, have made their way downstream to this lake. If you do find a dolly here, contact the Fisheries Biologist at the Alberta Sustainable Resource Development office in Canmore at (403) 678–5508 (ext. 263).

Odlum Pond (Map 2/C1)
A tiny tarn at the head of Odlum Creek, this pond produces small cutthroat (the odd one does reach 30 cm/12 inches). A 12 km (7.5 mile) return trail follows the creek up to the lake.

Picklejar Creek & Lakes (Map 5/E7)
A total of four tiny lakes are found at the headwaters of Picklejar Creek in a gorgeous sub-alpine basin. The lakes are reached by a series of trails from Highway 40 and have a self-sustaining population of cutthroat, which can be taken on a fly or with a small lure. Picklejar Creek drains the Picklejar Lakes and offers a catch and release fishery for brook, brown and cutthroat trout. Check the regulations for restrictions on the lakes.

Pigeon & Wind Creeks (Map 8/F6)
The Skogan Pass Trail parallels Pigeon Creek for much of its length, but most of the fishing occurs close to the Trans-Canada Highway. This is a low volume stream that holds a few brook and brown trout as well as whitefish to 30 cm (12 inches). In dry summers, the creek has been known to dry up completely. Nearby Wind Creek also holds a few fish.

Pocaterra Creek (Map 5/A5)
Highway 40 parallels Pocaterra Creek for part of the distance it flows from Highwood Meadows to the Kananaskis River. It holds a fair number of small cutthroat, bull and rainbow trout.

Quirk Creek (Map 5/E2)
An Elbow River tributary, Quirk Creek contains good numbers of brook trout, plus cutthroat and bull trout in much fewer numbers.

Rawson Lake (Map 4/G6)
Rawson Lake is found in the Peter Lougheed Provincial Park south of Upper Kananaskis Lakes. A short trail leads from the Upper Lake Trail to Rawson Lake. It is a 5 km (3 mile) hike to the lake, but with cutthroat getting up to 2 kg (4 lb), it sees heavy pressure. Please note that fishing season runs from July 16 to October 31, all fish must be released and there is a bait ban in affect at the lake.

Ribbon Creek & Lake (Map 4/F2)
Ribbon Lake is located at the headwaters of Ribbon Creek. The lake, which is accessed by a perilous 10 km (6.2 mile) hike up (and we do mean up) from Highway 40, has many small cutthroat. The fish take readily to most small lures and trout flies. The lake is frozen until mid June so it is best to fish from late June until ice up in late October. The stocked lake has a primitive campground on its shores and has a two trout limit in place. The creek holds a few brook, brown and cutthroat trout.

Rocky Creek (Map 4/G2–5/A3)
Rocky Creek has brown trout and flows into the Kananaskis north of the Eau Claire Recreation Area.

Rummel Lake (Map 4/E2)
Found just outside the northern boundary to Peter Lougheed Provincial Park, this tiny lake is accessed by a rough trail up Rummel Creek. The lake offers good fly fishing and spincasting for small cutthroat in the spring and fall. The fishing season runs from July 1 to October 31 and there is a one trout limit (greater than 40 cm/16 inches) and a bait ban.

Running Rain Lake (Map 2/C1)
An undeveloped 2.7 km (1.7 mile) trail begins opposite the beaver dams on Highway 40 and follows the creek to Running Rain Lake. The lake sees few anglers, due to its remote location and as a result offers good fishing for small cutthroat (to 40 cm/15 inches). Spincasting and fly-fishing have equal success. A two trout limit is in affect.

Sheep River (Map 5/C5–G5)
Named after the animals that often grace the slopes of the upper reaches, this river flows through the Turner Valley before draining into the Highwood River. The river offers fishing for brook, cutthroat and rainbow trout as well as rocky mountain whitefish (all to 1 kg/2 lbs). There are also some large bull trout (to 5 kg/11 lbs) in the deeper pools. Within the parks, the cutthroat and rainbow must be greater than 30 cm (12 inches) to keep and the fishing season runs from June 16 to August 31. Downstream, the river is open from June 16 to October 31, the trout limit is two and the whitefish limit is five. The river serves as a major spawning area for bull trout and rainbow from the Bow River.

Sibbald Creek & Lakes (Map 9/D6)
The biggest of the Sibbald Lakes is only 5 metres (15 feet) deep at its deepest, and, as you might expect, is subject to winterkill, which keeps the number and size of fish down. The stocked lakes are located just south of the Trans-Canada Highway and offer slow fishing for small rainbow and a few brook trout. No motorboats are allowed on the lakes. The creek is easily accessed by Highway 68 and offers small brook, brown, cutthroat and rainbow trout.

Sibbald Meadows Pond (Map 9/C6)
On the north side of Secondary Highway 68, this popular stocked pond has lots of room for fly-casting. Expect to find rainbow and brook to 30 cm (12 inches).

Smuts Creek (Map 4/E2)
Okay. Let's get the name out of the way first. General Jan Christian Smuts was Prime Minister of South Africa in the first half of the twentieth century. So the name isn't rude. The creek contains lots of small cutthroat (to 30 cm) and the occasional bull trout or whitefish. There are also worries that stocked, non-native Dolly Varden are making their way into the system from Chester Lake. If you do find a dolly, contact the Fisheries Biologist in Canmore at (403) 678-5508 (ext. 263).

Smuts Lake (Map 4/D3)
This tiny, hike-in lake is found below Mount Smuts. It is open all year, but you can only keep one cutthroat trout larger than 40 cm (15 inches).

Sparrow's Egg Lake (Map 9/A5)
One of a group of lakes that occupy the marshy valley bottom between Highway 40 and the Kananaskis Lakes Trail, this small lake is a 2 km (1.2 mile) bushwhack with route finding through thick forest from the Elkwood Campground. It is not recommended for a casual cast. It contains stocked rainbow to 2.5 kg (5 lbs) and cutthroat to 2 kg (4 lbs). The catch and release only lake is prone to winterkill.

Spillway Lake (Map 4/G4–5/A4)
Spillway Lake is located right beside the Smith-Dorrien/Spray Road just past the north end of Lower Kananaskis Lake. It contains some rainbow trout. The water is shallow and clear, so it is easy to see the fish. They can see you, too and are easily spooked.

Spray Lake Reservoir (Map 4/D2–8/D7)
Spray Lake Reservoir, in Kananaskis Country, is easily accessed by the Smith-Dorrien/Spray Road south of Canmore. The south end of the lake borders Banff National Park and there are a few campgrounds and day-use areas nearby. This is a good-sized lake; over 20 km (12.4 miles) long and is subject to strong winds. It offers reasonably good fishing for lake trout (to 8 kg/18 lbs), cutthroat (to 1 kg/2 lbs) and rocky mountain whitefish (to 1 kg/2 lbs). The lake has a boat launch and is best trolled during the early spring and the late fall.

Spray River (Map 4/C3; 4/D1–8/A4)
Spray River flows north into and out of the Spray Lakes Reservoir, eventually draining into the Bow River at the town of Banff. The river contains brook,

cutthroat and rainbow trout as well as rocky mountain whitefish. Anglers willing to hike above the reservoir will find cutthroat, while below the reservoir, you will start finding a few brown trout in addition to the other fish species. Most of the lower reaches of the river are accessible by the fire access road (hike/bike) linking Banff and the reservoir.

Stenton Lake (Map 8/E4)
Access to this small lake at the head of the South Ghost River involves a rather long drive up and around to the South Ghost Trailhead and then a 10 km (6.2 mile) hike up the South Ghost Trail. Because of this relatively difficult access, few anglers make the trek. Those that do will find stocked cutthroat to 45 cm (18 inches). You can keep one, as long as it is over 40 cm (16 inches).

Talus Lake (Map 5/C4)
Open year-round, there is a limit of two cutthroat at this tiny, hard to access lake.

Three Isle Lake (Map 4/F6)
To reach this small sub-alpine lake, take the Three Isle Lake Trail beginning on the northern shores of the Upper Kananaskis Lake. Because of the 10 km (6.2 mile) one-way hike, the lake sees few fishermen. Fishing is very good for small, stocked cutthroat on a fly or with a lure. Camping is provided at the east end of the lake with a permit and there is a two trout limit in affect.

Three Sisters Creek (Map 8/E6)
The Three Sisters are one of the most prominent landmarks around Canmore. This creek runs up the valley between those mountains and Mount Lawrence Grassi. The lower reaches are accessible by road just east of Canmore, while the upper reaches are not really accessible except by bushwhacking. The creek contains some brook and brown trout.

Threepoint Creek (Map 5/E4–G3)
Threepoint Creek is a spawning tributary for Bow River rainbow and is the largest tributary for the Sheep River. There are also brook, brown and cutthroat trout and even rocky mountain whitefish in the creek. For cutthroat and rainbow trout, the fish must be greater than 30 cm (12 in) in size to keep.

Tombstone Lakes (Map 5/B5)
Named after nearby Tombstone Mountain, which in turn was named for the distinctively shaped rocks near the summit, the lower lake contains lots of small cutthroat to 30 cm (12 inches). It is a 10 km (6.2 mile) hike in to the lake. Nearby Upper Tombstone Lake holds no fish.

Ware Creek (Map 5/G4)
Ware Creek flows into Threepoint Creek and has cutthroat and rainbow trout as well as rocky mountain whitefish.

Wasootch Creek (Map 5/A1–9/A7)
This Kananaskis River tributary has small brown trout.

Watridge Lake (Map 4/D2)
Located a short walk from the Mount Shark Trailhead south of Spray Lake, Watridge Lake contains good numbers of cutthroat to 4 kg (8 lbs). Fly-fishing or spincasting from a float tube works best, as shore casting is difficult.

Wedge Pond (Map 4/G2)
Found right next to Highway 40 north of Limestone Mountain, this small pond was recently stocked with arctic grayling. The pond has a bait ban as well as catch and release restrictions in place.

Whiteman's Pond (Map 8/D6)
This tiny pond has brook and lake trout as well as rocky mountain whitefish. The Smith-Dorrien/Spray Road southwest of Canmore easily accesses the pond.

PADDLING

For such a big area, there are relatively few rivers and lakes to explore. Please remember that river conditions are always subject to change and advanced scouting is essential. The information in this book is only intended to give you general information on the particular river you are interested in. You should always obtain more details from a local paddle sport merchant or expert before heading out on your adventure.

Barrier Lake (Map 9/A6)
Barrier Lake is located next to Highway 40 just south of the Bow Valley Provincial Park. There is a boat launch at the Barrier Lake Day Use Area that is shared with anglers. This is a man made lake, so watch out for submerged hazards.

Elbow River (Map 5/D3–G1)
Highways 66 and 22 follow the Elbow River for part of its length. About 35 km (22 miles) of the river is paddleable, a mixture of flatwater, rapids and some drops. The put-in and take-out area depends on how far you want to paddle. Simply pick your parking spots along one of the highways and start paddling. Runs include the section from Cobble Flats Recreation Area to Beaver Flats Recreation Area. It begins on a fairly easy, braided section of the river. However, the river soon enters a 1.5 km long boulder garden creating many mid-stream obstacles and plenty of pools and rapids. After the boulder garden, the river slows making it an easy paddle to the take-out. This is a 5 km (3 miles/1–1.5 hours) Grade I/II run, with a Class II boulder garden.

From Beaver Flats to Paddy's Flat Recreation Area is a 9 km (5.5 mile/3 hour) section, rated Grade II+ in low water and Grade III+ in high water. The run leads through a series of narrow bedrock canyons with plenty of nice ledges as well as the 5 m (16 foot) high Elbow Falls. Finally, it is 17 km (10.6 miles) of Grade II paddling from Paddy's Flat to the town of Bragg Creek. The most noteworthy rapids are rated a Class II+ and come just before the take-out, at the bridge in Bragg Creek.

Kananaskis Lakes (Map 4/G5–5/A6)
Found in the heart of the Peter Lougheed Provincial Park, the two Kananaskis Lakes are accessible by paved road and both have good boat launches. The Lower Kananaskis Lake is more exposed and subject to higher winds. Canoeists might want to stick to the upper lake, but kayakers should have no trouble. Watch out for submerged trees and rocks.

Kananaskis River (Map 9/B6)
The Kananaskis River drains the Kananaskis Lakes into the Bow River at the Bow Valley Provincial Park. This section is dam controlled and flow rate can vary greatly. Occasionally during low water, the dam will be turned off for a few hours. During these times, the only way to travel the river is to walk up and down the streambed. The uppermost run is from Barrier Lake Dam to Canoe Meadows. Despite being only 4 km (2.4 miles/1 hour) long, this section of the Kananaskis is very popular. On a busy weekend there can be up to 100 paddlers playing in the standing waves, running the short rapids and otherwise having a good time. Because of this, a number of new standing waves were built by constricting the river with boulders, to alleviate the bottlenecks at some of the more popular rapids. Most people put at the Widowmaker Day Use Area (just down from the dam). Widowmaker is the first and most difficult rapid. Other features include Good Humour (a rodeo hole for pulling endos) and the Green Tongue of Death (a great surfing wave). The route is rate Grade II, with some Class II/III+ rapids.

Below Canoe Meadows is a 6 km (3.6 mile/1.5 hour) easy Grade I paddle to the Highway 1 bridge. This section is ideal for canoeists looking for a scenic paddle. The river has few tough spots, except for the occasional logjam or sweeper.

Sheep River (Map 5/F6–G5)
The Sheep River begins in Kananaskis Country and flows eastward into the Bow River. It is a small volume river that is usually divided into two runs. From the end of Secondary Highway 546 to the Indian Oils Picnic Site is a 14 km (8.7 mile/4–5 hour) run best left to expert kayakers. This section is rated Grade III/IV. The put-in is reached by walking the old road upstream from the end of Secondary Highway 546. If you want to reduce the run to 9 km (5.6 miles/2–3 hours), put-in at the Bluerock Recreation Area. The most challenging part of the run is below this recreation area, where you will find three major falls, including the Sheep River Falls, which is the first and easiest, rated a mere Class IV.

Below the Indian Oils Picnic Site, it is possible to paddle down to the Sandy McNabb Recreation Area. This section is much easier than the higher reaches, a fairly easy Grade II paddle through a scenic canyon. However, there are many boulders, ledges and tight bends, which create some challenging Class II/II+ rapids. The paddle extends 11 km (6.8 miles/2–3 hours) from the picnic site to the picnic grounds at Sandy McNabb Recreation Area (east of our maps).

Sibbald Lake (Map 9/D6)
Sibbald Lake is a small shallow, clear lake. Because of its small size, the lake is rarely rough and offers good canoeing, especially for families with smaller children.

KananaskisCountryAdventures

TRAILS

Kananaskis Country has longed served as the outdoor playground for locals looking for an escape from the overcrowded national parks. The area provides endless, year-round opportunities for every type of traveller. There are off-highway vehicle areas, cross-country ski systems, hiking, biking and horseback trails as well as unmarked routes leading to spectacular vistas.

The area has a history of resource extraction activity and many of the trails follow old exploration and logging roads, seismic lines and animal paths. Although they usually provide easy travel, the routes can be somewhat confusing and hard to follow as they interweave with other old roads and trails. The most popular routes are signed, but many are not.

Aster Lake Trail (Map 4/G6)
From the Upper Lakes parking area, this 11 km (6.8 mile) route takes you past Hidden Lake as it makes its way up and down through forests, meadows and across creeks. Spectacular views can be seen along the way. A shorter option would be to turn around at the Waka Nambe Viewpoint.

Baldy Pass Trail (Map 9/B7)
There are a couple ways to reach the pass. The southern route from the Baldy Pass parking area off Highway 40 is a moderate hike or difficult bike ride. This 8 km (5 mile) trail climbs 490 m (1,593 ft) through trees up to the pass (a distance of about 4 km/2.4 miles). From the north, at the Lusk Creek Picnic Area off Highway 68, it is an 11.5 km (7.1 mile) hike to Baldy Pass. It leads through forest and along the Old Mill Road to reach the pass.

Big Elbow Trail (Map 5/D3–C5)
This moderate 26.5 km (16.5 mile) one-way route gains 350 m (1,138 ft) as it follows an old fire road along the Elbow River. Most people who travel this trail, do so as part of the popular Elbow Loop or to explore the surrounding peaks. There is backcountry camping along the route, as well as some great mountain views. Banded Peak can be reached by a difficult 5 km (3 mile) route that takes you 1,015 m (3,300 ft) up to the mountain summit. The **Mount Cornwall Route** is a full-day journey that gains some 1,340 m (4,355 ft). The 12 km (7.4 miles) trek veers off the main trail near South Glasgow Creek. The trek has no steep slopes and provides some glorious scenery including a long ridge of orange shale.

Bill Milne Bike Path (Map 4/G2)
Formerly the Evan Thomas Bike Path, this paved trail stretches 10 km (6.2 miles) one-way from Kananaskis Village to Wedge Pond. It passes Ribbon Creek, the golf course and Mount Kidd RV Park. As the name implies, most people bike this trail, although it can be walked as well.

Black Prince Cirque Trail (Map 4/G5)
Beginning at the Black Prince Day Use Area, this is a moderate hike of 4.5 km (2.8 miles) return. The main trail leads to Warspite Lake while an unmaintained trail continues to Black Prince Lakes, passing the Warspite Cascades along the way. Be warned that it is quite a climb (591 m/1,921 ft gain) to view the Black Prince Lakes.

Bluerock Trails (Map 5/F5)
Accessed at the Bluerock Recreation Area are a series of trails. The **Bluerock Creek Trail** is a moderate, but short 2 km (1.2 miles) trail. The trail provides beautiful vegetation and great viewpoints. Those looking for more of a challenge will find the **Bluerock Trail** fills this bill. It is a difficult 24 km (14.9 mile) hiking and biking trail that gains 750 m (2,438 ft) through the beautiful foothills country. Follow the road up Bluerock Creek to the footbridge. Here, the trail climbs up Bluerock Mountain for a great view, before the steep descent. It is possible to follow Gorge Creek to the Indian Oils Trails. This trail is easier, but still climbs over a dry ridge.

Boulton Creek Trail (Map 5/A6)
An easy 5 km (3 mile) walk through the forest and valley. The trailhead is accessed at Boulton Bridge Picnic Area. As you walk the trail, you will hear, if not see, the rushing water of Boulton Creek.

Bow Valley Trails (Map 9/A6)
The Bow Valley Provincial Park offers a series of easy trails. The **Bow River Trail** is a short 2.5 km (1.6 mile) wheelchair accessible trail that follows the shoreline of the Bow River from the campground. There are fishing opportunities and a possible side trip option to the sand forest. The **Bow Valley Bike Path** links the visitor centre with the campground via a 4.4 km (2.7 mile) one-way trail. The trail follows undulating terrain through forest and meadows. The **Many Springs Trail** is an easy 2 km (1.2 mile) route that follows an access road from the Many Springs parking area through meadows to a series of warm springs. It is only open from mid-May to mid-October, but it is possible to find flowers here while the rest of the valley is still shaking off winter. **Middle Lake Interpretive Trail** provides an easy 2.5 km (1.6 mile) walk around the lake. The trail begins at the Middle Lake parking area and is a good stroll for families as there is plenty of wildlife, including several species of ducks. **Moraine Trail** also begins as the Bow Valley Campground. The 3 km (1.8 mile) trail climbs some rubble to offer fabulous views all around.

Bryant Creek Trail (Map 4/D2–A1)
Accessed from the Mount Shark parking area (off Spray Lakes West Road), this is one of the most popular trails in the Canadian Rockies. It is a 22.5 km (14 mile), moderate trail that gradually climbs 520 m (1,690 ft) to meet up with the Allenby Pass Trail. Most travellers continue on to Mount Assiniboine Park in BC.

Buller Pass Trail (Map 4/E2)
This moderate, 10 km (6 mile) hike begins at the Buller Mountain Picnic Area. It gains 670 m (2,178 ft) in elevation, making the trail quite a steep climb. Hikers get to see a small waterfall and a fabulous view of Ribbon Lake. It's a long day hike, but there is no place to stay, except by hiking through the pass and descending to Ribbon Lake. The scenic Guinn's Pass Trail can be accessed off this trail, 1 km (0.6 mile) west of Ribbon Lake.

Burstall Pass Trails (Map 4/E3)
This 13 km (8 mile) trail begins at the Burstall Pass parking area. It leads past glaciers and across streams to the pass and offers a lot of opportunity for exploration. You can descend to the Upper Spray Valley, access Burstall and Hogarth Lakes or explore the French Creek Trail, which provides access to three beautiful waterfalls. The 7 km (4.3 mile) trail ends at the base of the French Glacier, where further exploration requires an ice axe and rope. It is a popular winter destination for backcountry skiers.

Canadian Mount Everest Expedition Trail (Map 5/A5)
The name of this trail makes it sounds like it should be a difficult trail. It is not. In fact, it is a moderate loop, covering 2.2 km (1.4 mile) as it passes through primarily spruce forest as well as fields of green and pink coloured wintergreens. The trail, which begins off the Kananaskis Lakes Trail at the White Spruce parking area, finishes with spectacular views over the Kananaskis Lakes. The trail was re-named in 1984 after the successful Canadian expedition to Everest's peak.

Canmore Nordic Centre Trails (Map 8/D5)
This area offers 65 km (40 miles) of looping trails, good for all levels of cyclists, hikers or cross-country skiers. The trails vary from wide paths to tricky single-tracks. A few paved trails have even been created for summer training using roller skis. There are trail maps at most major intersections along the trail. Access is off the Smith-Dorrien Spray Lakes Trail or from Canmore at 8th Street and 8th Avenue. The Canmore access requires climbing a 4 km (2.5 mile), steep trail to the Nordic centre. Another option is the Georgetown Trail. This is an easy 8.5 km (5.3 mile) hike to an old coal-mining town.

Carnarvon Lake Trail (Map 2/E2)
From the Cat Creek Picnic Area, this 17 km (10.6 mile) scenic multi-use trail climbs an old road to the foothills of the High Rock Range. To reach the lake, which offers good cutthroat trout fishing, a scramble off the main road is necessary. A ford of the Highwood River limits access to the trail until after spring run-off (late June). The Strawberry Hill Trail, found in between Fitzsimmons and Carnarvon Creeks, can be accessed from the 6 km (3.7 mile) mark of the main trail.

Cat Creek Trails (Map 2/F2)
From the Cat Creek Picnic Area, **Cat Creek Waterfalls Trail** is a popular 4 km (2.5 mile) return trail that leads to the falls. Many people combine this trail with a side trip to the Cat Creek Hills. There is no one route up to the hills, but, unlike many other interweaving trails, it does not matter which route you take. As long as you keep heading up, you will eventually get to the top, where you will find good views west over the Elk Range.

Chester Lake Trail (Map 4/E3)
This is a 5 km (3 mile) hiking trail accessed from the Chester Lake Parking area. It takes you to a beautiful mountain lake, by climbing through forests and meadows. Three Lakes Valley and Rummel Lake can also be accessed via unmaintained routes if you wish to continue past the lake. Alternatively, an 8 km (5 mile) trail leads northeast to The Fortress. Some climbing up loose, exposed, rocky terrain will bring you to the 3,000 metre summit, where you can enjoy the views of both the Spray and Kananaskis Valleys.

110

Cougar Creek Trail (Map 8/E5)
The moderate trail along Cougar Creek can be used for a half hour stroll or a two-day hike. Numerous creek crossings are required on this 11 km (6.8 miles) trail, which gains 640 m (2,080 ft) to Cougar/Carrot Column. Fortunately, the main creek bed usually dries up after the creek forks. However, this makes it difficult for the backpacker to obtain water. Access is found on Benchlands Trail, off the Bow Valley Trail (Highway 1A) just before Cougar Creek crossing. The best season for this hike is mid summer to early fall.

Cox Hill Ridge Trail (Map 9/D6)
Accessed via the Powderface Trail off the Sibbald Creek Trail (Highway 68) at the Dawson Trailhead, this 20 km (12.5 mile) hiking and biking trail shares its beginnings with the Tom Snow Trail before crossing Jumpingpound Creek and becoming Coxhill Ridge Trail. It starts to steeply climb up the hill to the breathtaking view at the top. Jumpingpound Ridge Trail takes you back down to the Powderface Trail. From here you need to either follow the road (Powderface Road) back to the Dawson Equestrian Area or arrange a pick up. The Jumpingpound Ridge Trail comes out on the Powderface Trail 15 km from the end of Highway 66.

Eagle Hill Trail (Map 9/C6)
Accessed at the Sibbald Lake Recreation Area, this moderate 8 km (5 mile) biking and hiking trail climbs 330 m (1,073 ft). It follows a rough road and trail that cuts through a poplar forest, past several clearings to a lookout over looking the Stony Indian Reserve in the Bow Valley. In the meadow en route to Sibbald Lake Campground is the frame for a sweat lodge and Stoney Indian prayer flags. The sweat lodge is not a business or an activity. They are both used in religious ceremonies and are left standing for time weather and return to them to earth. Visitors are asked respect these religious symbols and leave this site undisturbed. The Deer Ridge Trail is a moderate 7 km (4.3 mile) trail that branches west off the Eagle Hill Trail. It climbs to a ridge overlooking Sibbald Creek.

Elbow Pass Trail (Map 5/B5)
Accessed off Highway 40 at the Elbow Pass Trailhead, a difficult 9 km (5.6 mile) trail begins. The trail gains 305 m (991 ft) in elevation and takes about seven hours on foot. If biking, some pushing may be required as there are some steep rises. Elbow Lake is beautiful and great for trout fishing, while Tombstone Backcountry Campground provides a good base for other side trips including continuing to Elbow River via the Big Elbow Trail. Further south, the Piper Creek Trail is a 4 km (2.5 mile) trek into a beautiful valley that strays away from the main trail near Edworthy Falls. It requires a crossing of the Elbow River and Piper Creek. Some may wish to continue 560 m (1,820 ft) up to the passes beyond.

Elbow Valley Trails (Map 5/E2)
A 10 km return trail joins the Elbow Falls and Elbow River Recreation Areas. The forested trail climbs 365 m (1,186 ft) as it winds up and down next to the highway. Canyon Creek must be forded along the way. Branching from the main trail are a couple loop trails. The Sulphur Springs Trail is a 4.5 km (2.8 mile) trail that takes you past the smelly springs, to a great viewpoint. The **Riverview Trail**, which begins at Paddy's Flat and concludes at Elbow Valley Trail and Sulphur Springs Trail junction, is a 4.5 km (2.8 mile) hike that gains 105 m.

Elk Pass Trail (Map 5/A6)
The Elk Pass Trail is part of the Trans Canada Trail that heads over Elk Pass to Elk Lakes Provincial Park in BC. It is easy travelling on an old road until Fox Creek where the trail forks. The upper section is easier, but less interesting. Once on the pass the trail improves. The meadow in Elk Lakes Park offers good camping and a base for some excellent hiking trails. The difficult 19 km (11.8 mile) trail begins at the Elk Lakes trailhead, off the Kananaskis Lakes Trail.

Evan-Thomas Creek Trail (Map 4/G1–5/A2)
A 15 km (9.3 mile) trail (un-maintained after the first 1.4 km) that gains 760 m (2,470 ft) in elevation begins at Highway 40 near Kananaskis Village and leads to the pass. You can also access it from the Little Elbow Trail to the south. Best left for biking or horseback riding in summer, the route is also used by ice climbers. The trail involves a few steep climbs through an open forest that the occasional view of the Northern Opals. There are side trails or routes to explore from the main trail.

Exshaw Pass Trail (Map 8/F5)
A moderate, but long 13 km (8 mile) hike is accessed at the Exshaw Creek Bridge off the Bow Valley Trail (Highway 1A). There are a few stream crossings and over 900 m (2,925 ft) in elevation to gain before reaching the marvellous viewpoints at the pass. It is possible to return via Exshaw Ridge to the east, but this alternative is more difficult.

Flat [Trap] Creek Trail (Map 2/G1–5/G7)
This multi-use trail can be accessed from the Flat (Trap) Creek Bridge (on Secondary Highway 541). It is a moderate, 38 km (23.7 mile) route through meadows and grassy hills with good views of the surrounding area. The elevation gain is 435 m (1,414 ft). Options such as the 9.5 km (5.9 mile) Grass Pass Trail, the 3 km (1.8 mile) Sullivan Pass Trail and the 7.5 km (5.3 mile) Head Creek Trail are all accessible from the main trail, which is best hiked from June through October.

Ford Creek Trail (Map 5/D2)
The Ford Creek Trail is an 18 km (11.2 miles) one-way trail that is usually used to access the trails in the Jumpingpound Valley. The popular multi-use trail climbs 590 m (1,918 ft) along the Nihahi Ridge.

Ford Knoll Trail (Map 5/D3)
This 4 km (2.5 mile) hiking trail begins from the Forgetmenot Pond Picnic Area. It gains 235 m (764 ft) in elevation and is quite strenuous. Your reward comes at the top, with great views of the surrounding mountains and the river valley.

Fortress Lake and Ridge Trail (Map 4/F2)
Accessed from the former Fortress Mountain Ski Area, hikers must park at the decommissioned bridge that leads to Fortress, then hike or bike the 8 km (5 miles) up the road to where the hike begin. Once you finally hit the trailhead, you'll find a difficult 5 km (3 mile) hiking trail that leads to a pretty blue lake. Excluding the road walk, hikers will gain 270 m (878 ft) in elevation as the trail climbs through forest and along the Fortress Ridge, until descending to the lake. Keeping left at the junction is the less strenuous way to reach the lake from the ridge.

Fullerton Loop Trail (Map 5/F1)
A 7 km (4.3 mile), moderate early season hiking trail begins at the Allan Bill Pond Picnic Area. Following along Elbow River, the trail climbs 213 m (692 ft) to the ridge for a view of Moose Mountain. There are a few creek crossings.

Galatea Creek Trail (Map 4/F2)
From the Galatea parking area, a 6.5 km (4 mile) hiking trail climbs 460 m (1,495 ft) to Lillian Lake. You can continue another 1.5 km (0.9 miles) and 155 m (504 ft) to the picturesque Upper Galatea Lake. This is a difficult day hike that is rewarded with waterfalls, canyon views and mountain lakes. The scenic **Guinn's Pass Trail** can also be accessed from the main trail. This 3 km (1.8 mile) trail climbs 457 metres to the Ribbon Creek/Buller Pass Trail allowing hikers to create a two-day round trip hike, rather than the usual out-and-back variety. However, completing this loop means that hikers will have to descent the difficult chained climb above Ribbon Falls, something best left to experienced backcountry travellers. The two trailheads are about 4 km (2.4 miles) apart on the Smith-Dorrien Spray Lakes Road.

Gorge Creek Trail (Map 5/F5)
The Gorge Creek Trail makes its way along the boundary between the Bluerock Wildland and McLean Creek Off-Highway Vehicle Area. As it is mostly in the former, off-highway vehicles are not allowed. It is 14.5 km (9 miles) from the Gorge Creek Picnic Area to the Threepoint Trail/Volcano Creek Trail junction. There is 400 m (1,300 ft) of elevation gained along the route.

Grassi Lakes Trail (Map 8/D6)
This moderate walking trail is 4 km (2.5 miles) long and gains 300 m (975 ft) in height. The trailhead is located at the Spray Residences parking lot, off of the Smith-Dorrien Spray Trail. The trail takes you to two gorgeous blue lakes and provides great views of mountains and waterfalls. From the end of the upper lake you can continue on to see some pictographs.

Grotto Canyon Trail (Map 8/F6)
With rock climbing opportunities, excellent scenery and First Nations Pictographs, this is a popular hike. It is a 6 km (3.7 mile) trail that gains 670 m (2,178 ft) in elevation from the Grotto Mountain Picnic Area. If you cross the creek after the first canyon, be careful of rising water levels, as you may get stuck behind the canyon. Many choose to stop at the canyon, an easy 2 km (1.2 mile) walk that passing by a waterfall en route.

Grotto Mountain Trail (Map 8/F5)
From the Indian Flats Road (off the Bow Valley Trail) at the parking lot of the Alpine Club, is a 10 km hiking trail. The trail should be left to equipped rock climbers, as you must scramble 50 m (163 ft) up a cliff (after climbing a daunting 1,365 m/4,436 ft in elevation). After, as you travel along the ridge, you will be provided with views of the country below.

Ha Ling Peak Trail (Map 8/D6)

This short 1.6 km (1 mile) grind to the summit is located off of the Smith-Dorrien Spray Trail at the Goat Creek parking area. During your climb, do not be surprised to see several other hikers attempting the route, as it is very popular. At the summit you will appreciate the bird's eye view of Canmore and the Bow Valley. Keep to the most beaten path as the trail is poorly defined and fairly braided.

Heart Creek Trails (Map 8/G6)

This 4 km (2.5 mile) interpretive hike takes you through a lush canyon to a rock step and hidden waterfall. The trailhead is located off the off Lac Des Arcs Interchange on the Trans-Canada Highway and requires several creek crossings along the way. The steep Heart Mountain Horseshoe Trail veers off from the main trail and is considered a moderate scramble, accessible to experienced climbers only. Also in the area is the 10 km trail to the Quaite Valley Backcountry Campsite.

Indian Oils Trail (Map 5/F5)

A half-day trail off Sheep River Trail, the Indian Oils Trail covers 7.5 km (4.7 miles), with a moderate elevation gain of 395 m (1,295 ft). It crosses several small creeks, while meandering through a mix of meadow, aspen and pine forest. There are several scenic viewpoints as you trek between Gorge Creek and the Sheep River.

Iron Springs Trail (Map 5/F1)

This moderate 8 km (5 mile) trail can be accessed from the north (Bragg Creek Road) and the south (Elbow Falls Trail). This trail follows several logging roads/ ski trails where one encounters a mill site and can see Moose Mountain to the west. The ultimate destination of this hike, Iron Pond, is located in the valley bottom with flowery meadows and grazing cows. Allow a few hours to enjoy the hike. In the winter, this is groomed as part of the Bragg Creek Trails.

Jewell Pass Trail (Map 8/G6–9/A6)

From the Heart Creek Trailhead, this 10.5 km (6.5 mile) one-way bike or hike gains 280 m (910 ft) in elevation. Follow the rolling trail to the Quaite Valley Trail. Here, you climb to Jewell Pass where the trail joins Stoney Trail. The lower part of the trail offers fine views of a falls, Barrier Lake and Mount Baldy. Many hikers will use the Jewell Pass Trail to create a loop trail on the way down from Prairie View.

Jumpingpound Demonstration Forest (Map 9/E6)

An easy interpretive 10 km (6.2 miles) long trail weaves through the Jumpingpound Demonstration Forest.

Jumpingpound Ridge Trail (Map 9/C7–5/C1)

Following a sandstone ridge, this 22 km (13.7 mile) trail is quite popular with mountain bikers and hikers alike. It can be readily accessed at the Dawson Equestrian parking area of Highway 68. At the top of your trek you reach 2,180 m (7,085 ft) where you are immersed in alpine flowers and experience views of Fisher Range and Compression Ridge. Along your trek, do not miss the summit of Jumpingpound Mountain with its panoramic views.

Junction Creek Trail (Map 5/F6)

Accessed at the Junction Creek Picnic Area, this 11 km (6.8 miles) route passes by Junction Creek and leads to a meadow above the Sheep River. An even less formal route heads east up to the lake.

Junction Mountain Lookout Trail (Map 5/G6)

This 16 km (10 mile) long trail system is open to hikers and mountain bikers. It starts at the Indian Oils parking area and offers several side trails to explore. The hike's primary destination is Junction Lookout, which stands just below Junction Mountain and offers views to Calgary (on a clear day) as well as Bluerock Mountain to the northwest. This trail is essentially one continuous dirt road, with several dips and valleys over many creeks and rocky stretches.

Jura Creek Trail (Map 8/G5)

Following along the creek and through a tight canyon nestled in the Fairholme Range, this 8 km (5 mile) hike gains 670 m (2,178 ft) in elevation. There are a many creek crossings along the way through the canyon, but the hiker is rewarded with views of many rock formations. This unmaintained trail is not recommended in early spring or after heavy rainfall. The trailhead is located off the Bow Valley Trail (Highway 1A) at Exshaw.

Kananaskis Canyon Trail (Map 5/A5)

Found at the Canyon Campground is a short 0.8 km (0.5 mile) loop trail that follows the Kananaskis River into an impressive canyon. Hundreds of years ago it was used by the Kootenay Indians from BC on their annual quest for buffalo meat. This trail is technically moderate, but does require a number of stairs to be ascended when climbing out of the canyon.

Kananaskis Lakes Trail (Map 5/A5)

Families, usually out biking, frequent this paved, multi-use trail. The moderate 24 km (14.9 mile) return route should take most cycling groups about four hours. It starts at the Visitor Centre and follows the rolling asphalt through Lodgepole Pine forests with glimpses of the surrounding peaks. The trail also offers good cross-country skiing in the winter. There are three individually named sections offering different access points and views. The Lodgepole section stretches 4.8 km (2.9 miles) from the Visitor Centre to Elkwood Campground. The Wheeler section continues 4.6 km (2.9 mile) to Boulton Creek. Finally, the Lakeside section, which is the most scenic section, continues another 5 km (3 miles) to the Mount Sarrail Campground.

King Creek Trail (Map 5/A4)

This un-maintained trail found at the King Creek Picnic Area is a short (1.5 km) walk through a scenic gorge. Be careful, as the trail is popular with grizzly bears, too. This easy hike is best undertaken in late afternoon when the western sun illuminates the Opal Range. For more adventuresome types, hike and ford the creek many times for about 2.6 km to a remarkable view of Elpoca Mountain.

Lawson Lake & North Kananaskis Pass (Map 4/F5)

This trail begins at the North Interlakes Picnic Area and climbs 550 m (1,788 ft) over 19 km (11.8 miles) to the North Kananaskis Pass. At the beautiful Lawson Lake, Mount Maude and Haig Glacier make for a spectacular backdrop. Further along and a little off the main trail is Turbine Canyon Campsite, for those seeking an overnight excursion. Please note that a backcountry camping permit is required.

Link Trail (Map 5/G4)

This 10.5 km (6.5 mile) trail connects trails in the east Sheep region to those by the Front Ranges region in the west. You gain 375 m (1,219 ft) as you hike through pine forest and meadows.

Little Elbow Trail (Map 5/D3–C5)

This easy 23 km trail (One way; 14.3 mile) follows a fire road up the Little Elbow River until reaching the Mount Romulus Campsite where it rises steeply to the pass. There are many side trips and alternate routes that can be taken along the way. This half of the Elbow Loop gains 400 m (1,300 ft). A popular option is to join the Elbow Pass Trail, which will take you to the Elbow Pass Picnic Area (off Highway 40). It is a 6 km (3.7 mile) hike or bike up to the pass and then down to the lake.

Little Highwood Pass Trail (Map 5/A5)

This tough jaunt of 3.5 km (2.2 miles) goes to a pass to join with the Pocaterra Cirque and the West Fork of Pocaterra Creek. There is an elevation gain of 396 m (1,287 ft) and a loss of 640 m (2,080 ft). It is rough going with very few views to speak of. Most people, if going through the effort to find a trail here, choose to hike the Pocatarra Ridge Route, also found from the same trailhead.

Lookout Trail (Map 5/A6)

The Kananaskis Lookout can be reached from two directions. If on a mountain bike we recommend starting the trail from the Kananaskis Lakes Trail at the Pocaterra parking area. From here it is 4 km (2.5 miles). If hiking, try starting your 6.5 km (4 mile) journey from the Kananaskis Lakes Trail at the Boulton Creek Campsite. If originating from the campsite, you will find yourself on the Whiskey Jack Trail until it reaches Lookout Trail and continues on to the Fire Lookout. At the summit, take your time to enjoy the panoramic view, which takes in the Kananaskis Lakes, Elk Lakes and Mount Fox. Please respect the Fire Lookout's privacy as this person works and lives here nearly half the year.

Loomis Creek Trail (Map 2/D1)

Loomis Creek can be accessed at the Lineham Creek Picnic Area off of Kananaskis Trail (Highway 40). The multi-use trail is 13 km (8 mile) return and follows a logging road along the Loomis Creek Valley. Hikers will take about six hours to finish the trail, gaining 240 m (780 ft) in elevation. At the midpoint of the trail, hikers can bushwhack to Loomis Lake, a tucked away jewel or continue south to Bishop Ridge. You climb 425 m (1,381 ft) to access the ridge. The trail should be left until July, as you will have to cross the creek a number of times.

Lower Kananaskis Lake Trail (Map 5/A5)

An easy 3.5 km (2 mile) one-way walk around the eastern shore of Lower Kananaskis Lake, this trail begins at the Canyon Picnic Area. Low water levels in early summer reveal unattractive mud flats. However, there are terrific views of the Spray Range from along the trail, which is used by snowshoers in winter.

Lusk Pass Trail (Map 9/B7)
This trail connects Jumpingpound with the Kananaskis Valley. The trail gains 350 m (1,138 ft) over 8.5 km (4.3 miles) one-way as you climb through a thick pine forest with occasional views. Access can be found at Lusk Creek Picnic Area on Sibbald Creek Trail (Highway 68).

McLean Creek OHV Zone (Map 5/G2)
Nearly 200 square kilometres have been set a side for multiple users in the McLean Creek area. While hikers, mountain bikers and horseback riders are allowed in this area, it is truly a domain ruled by 4X4s, ATVs and motorbikes. There are hundreds of kilometres of formal and informal trails winding through this area, ranging from easy cruising to mud bogging. There are two staging areas, one at McLean Creek Recreation Area, one at the Fisher Creek Recreation Area. Some of the major trails to explore include the Elbow Valley Trail, Fish Creek Trail, Fisher Trail, McLean Trail, Quirk Trail and Silvester Trail.

McPhail Creek Trails (Map 2/E2)
The **McPhail Creek Trail** is a 10 km (6.2 mile) day hike, which can be easily accessed at the Cat Creek Picnic Area. The trail is known for the large groups of elk, which graze the hills around the creek. The initial crossing of the Highwood River is tricky and should be left until later in the season. From a rustic creek side campsite near the end of the trail, you can access several exciting options. **Lake of Horns** is a gorgeous alpine lake that requires climbing another 200 vertical metres (650 ft) in 1.5 km (0.9 miles) up a headwall. The **Weary Creek Gap Trail** climbs 4 km (2.5 mile) to a pass between Mount Muir and Mount McPhail. The pass, which marks the southern end of the Elk Range and the northern end of the High Rock Range, was known as the Elk Trail Pass to the Stoney Indians because of the graceful animal that frequents the area. Another option is to climb the **Strachan Ridge Trail**. This 7 km (4.3 mile) trail begins at the 6 km (3.7 mile) mark of the McPhail Creek Trail. There are a few steep hills along the trail, which takes you to the open ridge northeast of Mount Strachan.

Missinglink Trail (Map 5/G5)
This moderate, 8 km (5 mile) trail can be accessed at the Missinglink Trailhead or from the Link Creek Trail. This hike is mostly boring with the only highlight being a view of Missinglink Mountain.

Mist Creek Trail (Map 5/D7)
This 12 km (7.4 miles) trip gains 555 m (1,804 ft) as it climbs to Rickert's Pass and the Sheep Trail junction. It begins at the Mist Creek Picnic Area on Highway 40. For the most part it is an easy route with some route finding required through pine and spruce forests. At the 8.8 km (5.5 mile) mark you will ascend to Rickert's Pass, which offers a tremendous view up Misty Basin to Storm Mountain. Hardcore hikers may wish to try the Mist Ridge Route. This difficult 23 km route climbs 745 m (2,445 ft) and can be walked in a long, hard day. The route is usually travelled in a counter clockwise direction, taking the right-hand branch when the trail splits after about 1 km. Follow this up onto the ridge, which features gorgeous mountain views, before descending into Rickert's Pass for the long walk home along the Mist Creek Trail.

Mist Mountain Route (Map 5/C7)
Random bits of flagging tape are all that mark this rough route up Mist Mountain. If you can find the trail, it begins in a boggy forest before heading nearly straight up. While the views are nice once you get above trees, the route is steep, climbing 1,330 m (4,323 ft). There is a small warm spring (32°C/83°F) located on the east side of the mountain. It should take about six hours to scramble to the top and back, longer if you try to find the springs.

Moose Mountain Trails (Map 5/E2–9/E7)
From the Moose Mountain Road, hikers and mountain bikers will find a popular series of trails. The **Moose Mountain Fire Lookout Road** climbs 470 m (1,528 ft) along a 7 km (4.3 mile) trail that takes you along the spectacular ridge of Moose Mountain. **Moosepackers Trail** is a 22 km (13.7 mile) jaunt with some 500 m (1,625 ft) gained in elevation. It has several locations for good views as it meanders through the forest. Incidentally, Moose Mountain is a huge domed limestone structure, thereby making it a natural reservoir for gas. There are active sour gas wells in the area. Watch for signs.

Mount Allan Trails (Map 8/F7)
The summit of Mount Allan can be climbed starting from 2 different locations. From the north, an 11 km (6.8 miles) journey begins at the Trans-Canada Highway near the Banff Gate Resort. This is a long, difficult hike whereby it is essential to start early and utilize vehicles at either end. But it is one of the most delightful ridge walks in the Rockies. The opposite end of the trail

begins from the Kananaskis Trail (Highway 40) at the Ribbon Creek parking area. It too is a long day requiring you to start early and bring plenty of water. This long outing is well worth your effort when you discover a row of 25 metre (81 foot) high conglomerate pinnacles that are simply breathtaking.

Mount Assiniboine Trail (Map 7/F6–4/D2)
This long 62 km (38.5 mile) trail loops from Alberta into BC and back into Alberta again. It can be done as one long multi-day hike or it can be done in a couple shorter hikes, starting at either end. There are two points from which a hiker can start; the Sunshine Village parking area (near Banff) or from the south, at the Mount Shark Trailhead. There are many features to see and several campgrounds along the route for those looking to camp. The highlights include Mount Assiniboine, one of BC's highest peaks, at 3,618 m (11,759 ft), Lake Magog, as well as the Valley of the Rocks, which was created by one of the world's largest landslides. Once in the Mount Assiniboine Area, there are numerous trails to explore. Grizzly bear sightings are common in the area.

Mount Indefatigable Trail (Map 4/G5)
Formerly a very popular route up a spectacular ridge, this trail is no longer maintained due to traversing through critical grizzly bear habitat. As a result, all signage, bridges and benches have been removed and the area is not recommended. Interested parties will need to have competent map reading and route finding skills and be very familiar with updated Bear Safety Techniques. Those who do go, can expect a moderate climb of 503 m (1,635 ft) over 5 km (5 miles) return that should take two hours to hike from the North Interlakes Picnic Area to a breathtaking viewpoint below Mount Indefatigable. Add another 2 hours for the roughly 2.5 km return trip to the south peak.

Mount Kidd Lookout Trail (Map 4/G1)
From Kananaskis Village and the Nakiska Ski Area (see below), the Terrace Trail heads south to the Kovach Trail junction. Continue on the Kovach Trail for about 1.5 km (0.9 miles) to a faint trail, which may or may not be marked. This trail climbs up onto a ridge, which can easily be followed to the site of the former lookout. The lookout was situated on a grassy slope and it is not uncommon to see sheep, elk and grizzly bears in the area.

Return the same way as the terrain around the back of Mount Kidd is dangerously exposed and does not lead to the true summit of the mountain.

Mount Shark Trails (Map 4/D2)
Accessed off the Smith-Dorrien Spray Trail at Mount Shark Trailhead, there are 20 km (12.5 miles) of ski trails that can be enjoyed by hikers, bikers and horseback riders. The moderate trails range in length from 2-15 km (1.2–9.4 miles) and give access to several other trails in the area. The Commonwealth Lake Trail is found 2 km (1.2 miles) south of the Mount Shark parking area off an old road. The 2 km (1.2 mile) trail to the pretty little green lake gains 183 m (595 ft). Those that wish to go further could loop around Commonwealth Lake, a steep trail which gains 290 m (943 ft) over 6 km (3.7 miles) or continue south to the Smuts Pass. **Karst Spring Trail** is a 9.6 km (5.3 mile) return walk to the north shore of Watridge Lake. Karst Springs is one of the largest springs in North America. **Marushka (Shark) Lake Trail** is a 4.5 km (2.8 mile) hike out to Shark Lake. It follows Marushka Creek until it reaches the sparkling green lake, with Mount Smuts in the background. The **Watridge Lake Trail** is a 7.4 km (4.5 mile) trail, which takes you down a short steep incline to the lake, known for its cutthroat trout fishing. The trail is best hiked from late spring to early fall when the White Bog Orchids are out. It follows old logging roads and portaging a canoe is possible. **White Man Pass Trail** is a six hour 17 km (10.6 mile) trail that climbs 425 m (1,381 ft) to White Man Pass. It is a quiet backcountry trail, full of history and mystique and you will likely find yourself surrounded by the ghosts of the past. The best season for the trail is mid-summer to early fall.

Nakiska [Marmot Basin] Ski Area (Map 4/G1–8/G7)
A popular summer route in the Nakiska Ski Area is the **Aspen Loop**. This easy trail follows the **Terrace Trail** from the west end of the parking lot to the **Kovach Trail**. Turn on this trail, which brings you to the Aspen Trail proper. The loop takes you into the splendour of a flowery meadow, before connecting back up with the Kovach Trail. Another popular option is the 10.5 km (6.5 mile) **Hummingbird Plume Lookout Trail**. The lookout is actually an old shack, dating back to 1941 when there actually was a view. Tall timbers now block the view, but a short trip from the meadows, up a 130 m (423 ft) slope, will provide views of the Kananaskis Valley and Fisher Range. To return, follow the powerline road past Troll Falls. To the north a combination of old roads and trails provide access to **Marmot Basin**. By following the **Skogan Pass Trail**, there are about 7.5 km (5.3 miles) of trails that lead to an area between Mount Allan and Lower Collembola Ridge.

Nihahi Ridge Trail (Map 5/C3)
This is a 5 km (3 mile) hike, which climbs quite steeply (390 m/1,268 ft) up a rocky ridge, providing great views of the Front Range. Summer through fall is the best time to hike the trail.

Northover Ridge Route (Map 4/F6)
Once at Three Isle Lake, this 11 km (6.8 miles) trail leads over the ridge to Aster Lake. The route can be windy and the ridge itself is narrow and exposed, making this traverse the domain of experienced parties. From the ridge, a fabulous view of the Great Divide is available. On your return from the lake, you gain 620 m (2,015 ft). With this in mind, some hikers may choose to begin this trail at Aster Lake.

Odlum Creek Trail (Map 2/D1)
This 9 km (5.6 mile) trail provides access to Odlum Pond and Ridge as well as Bishop Ridge and the Loomis Creek Trail to the south. There are a few creek crossings and some falls along the scenic route. The trailhead is located at the Lantern Creek Picnic Area.

Old Baldy Trail (Map 5/A1)
The Old Baldy Trail gains 860 m (2,795 ft) in elevation as it climbs 8 km (5 mile) to a fabulous viewpoint. It is accessed at the Evan-Thomas Creek parking area. There is an optional return down the west flank or via the left hand fork via very steep grassy slopes: take care if you descend this route. Experienced climbers can continue up to the summit of Mount McDougall, which is considered a difficult scramble.

Ole Buck Trail (Map 9/D6)
A moderate, 2.5 km (1.6 mile) trail takes you up the mountain to an excellent view of Sibbald Lake and Moose Mountain. The vegetation can make the hike quite colourful during the spring and fall.

Old Goat Glacier Route (Map 8/D7)
Topographical maps do not show a glacier here and if global warming keeps on its current trend, perhaps it won't be in a few years. For now, this glacier remains hidden from view behind a rock headwall. People interested in bushwhacking up an open slope to the hanging valley where the glacier resides, can start at the stream cascading down the headwall to the road.

Opal Ridge Scramble (Map 4/G3)
Accessed off the Kananaskis Trail (Highway 40) at the Fortress Junction, a 3 km (1.8 mile) hike/scramble ascends by weaving through steep cliff bands as you climb 1,012 m (3,320 ft) to the south summit. Once upon Opal Ridge, the views of the Opal Range to the east are spectacular. Although not recommended, an optional return follows the Grizzly Creek Trail south by bushwhacking along an unmarked route.

Palliser Pass Trail (Map 4/D2–D4)
Beginning at the Mount Shark Trailhead, this 21 km (13 mile) one-way route follows the unspoiled Upper Spray Valley and passes Leman Lake before climbing to the pass. There are camping areas along the way to help you enjoy this 2-3 day wilderness trip. The Burstall Pass Trail can be used as a shortcut to Palliser Pass.

Phone Line Trail (Map 5/G6)
A 7 km (4.3 mile) hike along old logging roads, runs between the Sentinel Ranger Station and the Bighorn Ranger Station. It gains 180 m (585 ft) in elevation. The trailhead is accessed from the south, along the Junction Mountain Trail and from the north, along the Green Mountain Trail.

Picklejar Creek & Lakes Trails (Map 5/E7)
Accessed off of the Kananaskis Trail (Highway 40) at the Picklejar Creek Picnic Area, this trail leads 4 km (2.5 mile) to the first Picklejar Lake. Travelling another 1.4 km will lead you passed the 2nd and to the 3rd Picklejar Lakes. The route leads between Picklejar and the unmarked Cliff Creeks and is a challenging hike. There is a connecting trail to Picklejar Lakes as well as another access trail from Lantern Creek Picnic Area. It is about 4 km (2.5 mile) to reach the first lake, where the fishing is good. In fact, the name for this area comes from an old saying that the fish were so plentiful here, you could catch them in a...well, you get the picture.

Pocaterra Ridge Trail (Map 5/A5)
This difficult 9 km (5.6 mile) one way route is not marked or maintained, but it climbs steeply up onto Pocatarra Ridge. Most people leave one vehicle at Little Highwood Pass Picnic Area and another at the Highwood Meadows.

Pocaterra Trail (Map 5/A5)
This 10 km (6.2 mile) one-way trail begins at the Pocaterra Hut parking area. It leads through open meadows and forested land, providing views of Mount Wintour and the Opal Range. En route 290 m (943 ft) in elevation is gained as you hike or bike the trail. The Lookout, Whiskey Jack and Rolly Road Trails all join the Pocaterra Trail.

Porcupine Creek Trails (Map 9/A7–5/B1)
Accessed off the Kananaskis Trail (Highway 40) at the Porcupine Creek Bridge, the main trail is a 7 km (4.3 mile) hike. The terrain is mostly easy as you travel alongside Porcupine Creek. Further exploration is possible on the surrounding ridges for those experienced in route-finding and off-trail hiking. It is possible to hike up either fork of Porcupine Creek.

Powderface Trails (Map 5/D2)
Access is found at the Powderface Picnic Area on Highway 66. It is 7 km (4.3 miles) to Powderface Pass along the Powderface Creek Trail. Once at the pass, views of Nihahi Ridge can be seen. If biking, be prepared to do some pushing. To continue, travel north, 2.5 km (1.6 miles) to Powderface Ridge. This route will gain another 130 m (423 ft) in elevation, but provides views of Fisher Range and Belmore Browne Peak. Powderface Ridge Trail can also be reached from the end of Highway 66. This route climbs 640 m (2080 ft) over 7 km (4.3 miles).

Prairie Creek Trails (Map 5/D2)
The Prairie Creek Trail is an 8 km (5 mile) multi-use trail that will take you along varied terrain and past some beaver ponds. The muddy trail climbs 180 m (585 ft) from the Powderface Picnic Area. The **Prairie Link Trail** is a 3 km (1.8 mile) trail connecting to the Powderface Creek. It is found 5 km (3 miles) along the main trail. The **Prairie Mountain Trail** is a popular, but tough 5 km (3 mile) trail climbing 715 m (2324 ft) in elevation. The view from the summit is superb along this good early season hike.

Prairie View Trail (Map 9/A6)
This trail leads to a plateau overlooking Barrier Lake, affording stunning views of Barrier Lake and Mt. Baldy before descending to the treed Jewell Pass.and Jewell Pass. The 13 km (8 mile) trail climbs 420 m (1,365 ft) from east end of the lake. Many also visit the active Barrier Lake Fire Lookout, which sits about 1 km from the main trail.

Ptarmigan Cirque Trail (Map 5/C6)
While the climb through a steadily thinning forest is pretty stiff (214m/683 ft in about 2 km), the alpine scenery is nothing short of breathtaking. The route is 4.5 km (2.8 miles) return and also offers an interpretive brochure. The trail starts in the Highwood Pass, at the 2,206m (7,236 ft) mark, where snow remains until early summer. You will rarely find alpine scenery so accessible, making this a very popular trail in the summer. Fall is a great time to hike this trail, as the larches turn a lovely golden colour. If you wish to avoid the crowds, the nearby **Arethusa Cirque Route** is located just 1 km to the south. The 1.5 km (0.9 mile) trail has been flagged from a point just south of the creek to the treeline. From here you can wander the cirque or hike up to the top of Little Arethusa along un-maintained trail if you are comfortable with off-trail hiking.

Quirk Creek Trail (Map 5/E3)
This 20 km (12.5 mile) return, multi-use trail begins at the Cobble Flats Picnic Area. From here, you ford the river and follow the fairly level road up Quirk Creek. Hikers will find the route uninspiring. Bikers should return on the Wildhorse trail, where a smooth trail offers a more enjoyable downhill ride. Add another 4.5 km (2.8 miles) and a whole lot more elevation by climbing the scenic **Quirk Ridge Trail.**

Raspberry Ridge Lookout Trail (Map 2/G4)
This moderate 4.5 km (2.8 mile) trail gains 650 m (2,112 ft) as it follows a zigzagging fire road to an active fire lookout. Alpine flowers and numerous raspberries and Saskatoon berries can be found along the way. Over time, hikers have created a shortcut, cutting off the switchbacks. This trail goes straight up to the ridge, making it more difficult on the ascent, but it does shorten the descent time by about an hour (if your knees are up to it). Access is found off the Forestry Trunk Road at Cataract Creek Road.

Rawson Lake Trail (Map 4/G6)
Gorgeous views and fishing this mountain lake are the main attractions of this trail. The 8 km return (5 mile) hike is accessed along the Upper Kananaskis Lake Trail. It climbs 550 m (1,040 ft) to a meadow near the southeast end of the lake. Mid-summer to early fall is the best time of year for this trail, especially since no fishing is allowed between November 1st and July 15th.

Ribbon Creek Trails (Map 4/F1)

From the Ribbon Creek parking lot, a 20 km return (12.5 mile) trail leads up the spectacular valley. You pass waterfalls, canyons and cliffs on route to the campsite at Ribbon Falls. From here a difficult scramble is necessary to reach the lakes using chains to climb a steep cliff band. . The route climbs 595 m (1,934 ft), including 255 m (829 ft) after the falls. A short option is the Ribbon Creek Loop. This moderate 6 km (3.7 mile) offers the tranquillity of Ribbon Creek. Others stop at Ribbon Falls, which is an 8.1 km (5 mile) trail that gains 311 m (1,011 ft).

Rummel Lake Route (Map 4/E2)

Rugged beauty awaits those who hike this 5 km (3 mile) trail, which gains 350 m (1,138 ft). The access point lies along the old logging road across the highway from the Mount Shark Road. Hikers may wish to continue toward Rummel Pass (3.5 km from the lake) and Lost Lake (2 km from the pass). From mid-summer to early fall is the best time of year for this trail. Please note that the route from Lost Lake eventually connects with Galatea Creek Trail, albeit it is usually choked with deadfall and obstructions as it is unmaintained.

Running Rain Lake Trail (Map 5/C7)

Never mind that this rough, difficult to find route is mostly an access route for anglers. The fact is that this is a pretty 2.7 km (1.7 mile) hike to a pretty lake that is regularly frequented by grizzly bears. There are some muddy sections and a trio of river crossings, but the hike is not too difficult, gaining 153 m (497 ft) to the lake.

Sheep Trail (Map 5/E6–C5)

Most often accessed at the Junction Creek Picnic Area, this 22 km (13.7 mile) trail begins. It provides views of the Gibraltar Mountain and the Front Ranges as well as beautiful meadows along the way. The trail can also be accessed at the Sandy McNabb Recreation Area. There are many side trips to keep you busy, including the 4 km (2.5 mile) Green Mountain Trail, a tricky, twisting 6 km (3.7 mile) trail to Burns Lake and a 50 km (31 mile) trip on the Big/Little Elbow Trails.

Sibbald Lake Trails (Map 9/D6)

Two easy trails begin at the Sibbald Lake Recreation Area. Beginning on the middle fork, a 5 km (3 mile) hiking trail leads along a forestry exhibit trail to a great viewpoint, featuring the Sibbald Flats below. Beginning on the left fork, a 1 km (0.6 mile) trail loops through trees and meadows to a ridge viewpoint. When returning, the Moose Pond can be accessed off the main trail.

Skogan Pass Trail (Map 8/F6–4/G1)

This 19 km (11.8 mile) trail can be accessed from either the Nakiska (Marmot Basin) Ski Area in Kananaskis or Three Sisters Drive out of Canmore. Whether biking or hiking, you will travel through the Nakiska Ski Area to the less than scenic powerlines. However from the pass, the views include the Three Sisters and the Canmore corridor. From the north access point, the Pigeon Mountain Trail is a 5 km (3 mile) side trip that gains 550 m (1,788 ft) in elevation. The summit provides a splendid viewpoint.

Smith-Dorrien Mountain Trails (Map 4/F3)

This area has 32 km (19.9 miles) of trails, ranging from smooth roads, to rough, steep trails. It offers something for all levels of cyclists, hikers or cross-country skiers. The area is fun to explore, while admiring the rugged Spray Mountains. Branching from this system is the James Walker Creek Trail. It is an easy 4 km (2.5 mile) trail to a mountain lake. From there, you can continue 2 km (1.2 miles) into the scenic Upper Valley.

South Kananaskis Pass–North Kananaskis Pass (Map 4/F5)

This 10.5 km (6.5 mile) trek can be started either from the South Pass via Three Island Lake Trail (13 km from the trailhead) or from the North Pass via the Lawson Lake Trail (19 km from the trailhead). Backcountry sites at Three Isle Lake and Turbine Canyon are used as starting/ending point of this trip and should be booked ahead of time. The hike is a strenuous trip and hikers should bring plenty of water and expect tremendous height gains and loss. Route-finding and good navigation skills are also needed in a couple areas. Near Beatty Creek look for the miniature valley of rocks, which is comprised of trees, boulders, sink holes and blue tarns.

Sparrowhawk Creek Trail (Map 4/E1)

A trail leads to Read's Ridge and even to Mount Sparrowhawk from the Sparrowhawk Picnic Area. The ridge is a fabulous viewpoint and provides access to Read's Tower, after a good climb, gaining 270 m (878 ft) in 1 km (0.6

miles). The harder option, to Mount Sparrowhawk is 5 km (3 miles) and gains over 1,430 m (4,648 ft) in height and is for experienced hikers/scramblers only. The Sparrowhawk Tarns can also be reached from the trailhead. It is a 5 km (3 mile) hike to reach several small lakes.

Stoney Trail (Map 9/B6)

A long 20.5 km (12.7 mile) one-way trail follows the powerline west of Barrier Lake. This popular equestrian route can be accessed at Stoney parking area (access from Kananaskis Village turn-off), Barrier Dam Day Use Area or the Grouse Group Campsite (access off of Trans-Canada Highway).

Terrace Trail (Map 4/G1)

This trail takes you from the Galatea Trailhead across the river and then follows its west bank, north to the Kananaskis Village and/or the Ribbon Creek Trailhead. It is better to bike or ski the 11.5 km (7.1 mile) return trail.

Three Isle Lake Trail (Map 4/G6)

This is one of the most popular trails in the Kananaskis Lakes area. From the Upper parking area, a 13 km (8 mile) trail skirts Mount Indefatigable, crosses the Palliser Rockslide and winds it way through a sub-alpine forest to the mountain lakes. The trail gains 580 m (1,885 ft). For overnight hikers, there is a backcountry campground along the way (reservations made through Backcountry Permit Desk). From here, a 3 km (1.8 mile) trail leads past the north side of Three Isle Lakes to South Kananaskis Pass. The height gain is 125 m (406 ft) to the pass. Beatty Lake is a further 2 km (1.2 miles) away, in BC.

Three Sisters Trails (Map 8/E6)

Providing a spectacular backdrop to the city of Canmore, the Three Sisters have long enticed hikers. Many of the trails follow old roads that provide remnants of logging activities from years ago. The **Three Sisters Creek Trail** ends at a waterfall. Many turn around here, but it is possible to scramble down and across the creek and then up again on the other side. The road soon peters out into a trail, which leads to the ruins of two old cabins. A strenuous climb leads to a viewpoint of the Three Sisters and an even more strenuous climb will take you to Three Sisters Pass. It is possible to hike out via the **Three Sisters Pass Trail** and down to the Smith-Dorrien Spray Lakes Road. Most hikers travel this trail from the Spray Lakes side since you only climb 595 m (1,934 ft) over 3 km (1.8 miles) to the viewpoint. The **Middle Sister Trail** follows Stewart Creek for an 8 km (5 mile) one-way trek. The old road up Stewart Creek seems easy enough, but as you get a glimpse of the Middle Sister, you will realize you are in for a struggle later on. The 1,400 m (4,550 ft) scramble to the summit is strenuous, but not technical. Viewpoints along the way will provide glimpses of Little Sister and the Bow Valley.

Threepoint Mountain Trail (Map 5/D4)

This rough multi-use trail takes you from the Big Elbow Trail to the Volcano Creek Trail. After fording the river, you push your way up the ridge to cross the divide and then descend to the campsite at Volcano Creek. It is a 10 km trail one-way and gains 460 m (1,495 ft) in elevation. A 7 km (4.3 mile) side trip to Upper Threepoint Creek is possible.

Tom Snow Trail (Map 9/E7)

This is a 30 km (18.6 mile) multi-use trail that has several access points. This route is the main connector between the Sibbald Creek Valley (at the Spruce Woods Picnic Area) and the Elbow River Valley (at the West Bragg Picnic Area). The Bragg Creek end climbs 155 m (504 ft) making it the easier access route. This low elevation, easy trail offers an earlier season than most of the trails in the area. It follows old roads through meadows, grasslands and mixed forests.

Tyrwhitt Loop Trail (Map 5/B6)

This difficult 12 km (7.4 miles) hike stitches together five separate trails and routes into a loop that is perfect for the adventurous nature lover, including some or all of the Grizzly Col, Grizzly Ridge, Highwood Ridge, Pocaterra Cirque and Mount Tyrwhitt Trails/Routes. Some of the highlights of this trail include a valley brightly covered with wild flowers, a high column, two ridge walks and a viewpoint on an arch. The trail gains 900 m (2,925 ft) in elevation and can take up to eight hours to complete. The best time of year for trying this trail is mid-July through mid-October. Access is found on Highway 40 at Highwood Meadows parking area.

Upper Canyon Creek Trail (Map 5/C1)

To explore Upper Canyon Creek, begin off the Powderface Trail at Canyon Creek (Mount McDougall Memorial). This trail gains 260 m from east to west. It is also possible to access the Canyon Creek Trail via a 3.7 km (3.4 mile) connector trail from the Prairie Creek Trail.

Upper Kananaskis Lake Trails (Map 4/G6–5/A6)

It is possible to circle Upper Kananaskis Lake via a moderate 16 km (10 mile) trail. The trail can be accessed via the Upper Lake Day Use Area or the North Interlakes parking area. The 4.5 km section along the eastern shoreline is a popular section and connects the two access points. Mountain bikes are only permitted as far as Point Campground, but must access the campground via the Three Isle Lake Trail and then cutting over to Upper Lake Trail using the 100 metre connector through an open rocky area. On the west side of the lake the trail moves inland for a ways, passing Lower Kananaskis Falls.

Volcano Ridge Trail (Map 5/F4)

This trail is a good one to incorporate with others to form a loop. One of which is a 13 km (8 mile) loop that incorporates Gorge Creek, Link Creek and Gorge Link Trails. This loop is accessed via the Gorge Creek Road. Another loop is Volcano Ridge/Threepoint Creek Loop. This is a difficult 41.5 km (25.8 mile) trail that requires about seven hours to complete by bike. This trail starts on the Volcano Ridge Trail at the Gorge Creek access and continues over the ridge and along the road to Threepoint Creek Trail. Follow this smooth trail to the bumpy North Fork Trail. This trail will eventually lead back to closed Gorge Creek Road. The best time of year for this trail is mid-July to mid-October, when the snow is gone. The **Volcano Creek Trail** is an easy 4 km (2.5 mile) extension the follows the north side of Volcano Creek to the Threepoint Mountain and Gorge Creek Trail junction. This trail climbs 120 m (390 ft) while offering fine views of Bluerock Mountain and access to surrounding peaks.

Wasootch Ridge Route (Map 9/A7–5/A1)

The un-maintained Wasootch Ridge Trail can be reached at Wasootch Creek Picnic Area. The trail starts at the far end of the parking lot across from the outhouse and heads steeply through forested slopes to gain the ridge. Less seasoned hikers can follow the trail, gaining elevation on the undulating ridge until their appetite for views is satisfied. More experienced hikers may wish to continue toward the summit which involves an exposed scramble and is not recommended for novice hikers. The trail is 13 km (8.1 mile) round trip gaining 890 m (2,893 ft). It is possible to access the Baldy Pass Trail via a 3.6 km connector from the picnic area to Porcupine Creek. Up Wasootch Creek itself are the Wasootch Slabs, a popular rock climbing area. Mid-summer to early fall is the best time of year for these trails.

West Wind Loop (Map 8/F6)

This is a confusing 13 km (8 mile) route that follows assorted trails, old mining roads and railway tracks. You will visit an old mine site (now being made into a golf course) as you pass Three Sisters Creek, Stewart Creek and later Deadman Flats. The route gains 380 m and offers access to the Wind Valley and Three Sisters Trails.

Whiskey Jack Trail (Map 5/A6)

This rough trail has some steep segments as it climbs 4.5 km (2.8 mile), one-way from the Boulton Creek parking area. The trail connects with the Lookout and Pocaterra Trails.

Whiskey Lake Loop Trail (Map 5/F6)

This loop is accessed from the end of the Sheep River Trail. From there, the trail follows the Sheep Trail and loops around Whisky Lake. It is possible to link up with the Bluerock Equestrian Recreation Area before heading back to the trailhead. This 3.5 km (2.2 mile) hike is best done in the late spring through mid-fall.

Wildhorse Trail (Map 5/E3)

This popular mountain biking trail is found at the Little Elbow Recreation Area. The 15 km (10 mile) one-way trail climbs 355 m (1,165 FT) around Forgetmenot Mountain. A nice loop is formed with the Quirk Creek Trail.

Wind Valley Trails (Map 8/F6)

A series of trails can be found west of the Pigeon Mountain Ski Area. The **Upper Wind Trail** is a short 1.3 km (0.8 mile) trail gaining 35m (114 ft). This route offers a stunning view of the Windtower and Wind Ridge. The **South Wind Hoodoos Trail** is a short, but strenuous 3 km (1.8 mile) hike that takes you to The Obelisk, one of the world's highest hoodoos. The **Wind Pond Trail** is a moderate trail that climbs 825 m (2,681 ft) over 10 km (6 miles) to the pond found near Mount Allan. The **Wind Ridge Trail** leads 7.5 km (4.7 miles) from the West Wind Loop (see above). Your climb of 760 m (2,470 ft) offers incredible views of the Windtower. Beware of grizzly bears in this area.

Windtower Trail (Map 8/E7)

Unlike the Wind Valley Trails which happen in the shadow of the Windtower and which are accessible from the north, this trip starts from the Smith-Dorrien Spray Lakes Road. Why? Silly question, if you have ever seen the Wind-

tower, you would know that three sides of it are sheer cliff and the peak is only approachable from the west. The trail passes through Wind Pass (itself a fine destination), then climbs steeply up along a scree/shale slope. This 2 km (1.2 mile) grunt up to the top features some good views out over the Spray Valley. As you come to the top, the mountain falls away from you on three sides, dropping nearly 750 m (2,438 ft) straight down. Needless to say, this is not a hike for those scared of heights.

Yamnuska Ridge and CMC Valley Trail (Map 9/A5)

A very popular trail is found at the end of Quarry Road off of the **Bow Valley Trail** (Highway 1A). The trail climbs an old gated road and horse trail to the ridge with spectacular views. You climb 435 m (1,414 ft) 3.5 km (2.7 miles) return. For the more ambitious, it is possible to continue an additional 7 km (4.3 miles) to a viewpoint of the CMC Valley and the impressive Ephel Duath Cliff. This trail drops 150 m (488 ft) to the valley bottom where the trail deteriorates before climbing back up to the vantage point.

WINTER RECREATION

Winter visitors will find lots to do within K-Country. Listed below are many of the popular cross-country skiing and snowshoeing areas. We have also noted those few areas that can be used by snowmobiles.

Unfortunately, the following roads are closed in winter: Highway 40 from December 1–June 14; Powderface Trail from December 1–May 14; the McLean Creek Road from December 1–April 30; Highway 940 from December 1–April 30; and the Sheep River Trail from December 1–May 14.

Burstall Pass Trail (Map 4/D3)

It is 7.5 km (4.7 miles) one-way to the pass from the trailhead on the Smith-Dorrien Spray Trail in Peter Lougheed Provincial Park. The trail provides an excellent backcountry ski/snowshoe as it leads past glaciers and across (hopefully frozen) streams to the pass. From here, can you descend to the Upper Spray Valley for further exploration.

Canmore Nordic Centre Provincial Park (Map 8/D5)

The Canmore Nordic Centre is one of the world's premier Nordic skiing centres. It has 72 km (44.7 miles) of cross-country ski trails, including 2.5 km (1.6 miles) of lit trails. The area appeals to both competitive skiers (there are 32 km/19.9 miles of competitive cross-country trails and 20 km/12.4 miles of biathlon trails) and recreational skiers (approximately 50 km of the trails are groomed and track set). Facilities include a day lodge, meeting rooms, biathlon facilities, rentals, repairs and lessons as well as an on site athlete training building.

Chester Lake Trail (Map 4/E3)

Found off the Smith-Dorrien Spray Trail, this 5 km one-way trail leads through the forest up to Chester Lake. It is an occasionally groomed trail that can be used by backcountry skiers, but is shared with snowshoers for the first kilometre; watch for signs that point the way for snowshoers. You will gain 310 metres (950 ft) to the lake.

Goat Creek Trail (Map 8/C6)

This is an interesting backcountry ski/snowshoe trip that is not too challenging. However, it is still a daunting 18.3 km (11.4 miles) from the trailhead on the Smith-Dorrien Spray Trail to the Banff townsite. The first part of this trail is rougher than the last, which follows the Spray River Fire Road into town. You can arrange for a shuttle, return the way you came or do this route in reverse by starting in Banff.

Highway 40 (Map 2/E2)

In the winter and spring, Highway 40 is closed from December 1st to June 14th. However, there is 5 km (3 miles) of the road open for easy snowshoeing in winter.

Hogarth Lakes Loop (Map 4/E3)

This is an easy 4.5 km (2.7 mile) snowshoe trail from the Burstall Pass Trailhead. The route opens up as it makes its way along a series of ponds, offering good views of the mountains.

Kananaskis Lakes Trail (Map 5/A5)

The road leading to the Kananaskis Lakes offers a number of a number of groomed cross-country ski trails. All together, there are more than 75 km (47 miles) of mostly easy or moderate trails to explore. Additionally, K-Country continues to add trails designated for snowshoeing, please stop by the Peter Lougheed Visitor Information Centre for new routes.

Marsh Loop (Map 5/A5)

This easy 1.5 km (0.9 mile) trail starts at the William Watson Lodge and has some gentle uphill and downhill sections. For a longer walk, the Lower Kananaskis Lake or Penstock Trails are popular snowshoe routes in the area.

McLean Creek Snowmobile Area (Map 5/G2)

McLean Creek is one of the biggest and best-known off-roading areas in the province. In the winter, this area becomes a snowmobile haven. Between McLean Creek, Fisher Creek (above) and Sibbald Flats (below) there are 209 km (130 miles) of trails. ATVs are also active in this area in the winter.

Mount Shark Racing Trails (Map 4/D2)

The Mount Shark Racing Trails were developed for organized races, as well as training. When not being used for races, the 18 km (10.8 miles) of trails are open to the public. If a race is in progress, it is possible to follow the Watridge Lake Trail from the trailhead at the end of Mount Shark Road to the lake for a moderate 3.2 km (2 miles) ski.

Nakiska [Marmot Basin] Ski Area (Map 4/G1)

Nakiska is the closest mountain ski area to Calgary and as a result can be quite busy. There are four chair and two surface lifts servicing 28 named trails. The longest run is 3.3 km (2 miles) offering skiing for every skill level, although the majority of the runs appeal to the intermediate skier. The mountain doesn't get as much snow as ski areas farther west, but it makes up for it with snowmaking abilities to ensure consistent conditions, if not spectacular snow, throughout the season.

Penstock Loop (Map 5/A5)

This 5.5 km (3.3 mile) trail starts at the Canyon Picnic Area and follows part of the penstock as it makes its way through the forest to Kent Creek. It is a relatively easy trail.

Ribbon Creek Area (Map 4/F1)

Found 20 km (12.4 miles) south of Barrier Lake Information Centre on Kananaskis Trail (Highway 40), near the Nakiska (Marmot Basin) Ski Area, Ribbon Creek offers a series of ungroomed cross-country ski/snowshoe trails. Ranging from easy to difficult, the 58 km (34.8 miles) of trails that wind their way through the forests and meadows along Ribbon Creek and through Marmot Basin.

Sibbald Flats Snowmobile Area (Map 9/D6)

To reach the Sibbald Flat Staging Area, take the signed turn-off for the Sibbald Creek Trail off the highway about 35 km (22 miles) west of Calgary. Turn south on Powderface Trail and watch for the Dawson Staging area, 3 km (1.8 miles) down. There are ten sites for winter campers. Between McLean Creek, Fisher Creek (above) and Sibbald Flats, there are 209 km (130 miles) of trails. ATVs are also active in this area in the winter.

Smith-Dorrien Trails (Map 4/F3)

There is 33 km (19.8 miles) worth of track set intermediate and difficult cross-country ski trails here. The trails are not recommended for beginners.

West Bragg Creek (Map 9/F7)

Found 10 km (6 miles) west of Bragg Creek, there are about 45 km (28 miles) of mostly easy groomed cross-country ski trails in the area. The longest trail, which is 16 km (10 miles) long, will challenge most skiers.

WILDLIFE VIEWING

Although wildlife can be seen virtually anywhere in this vast playground, there are a few notable areas worth visiting. Visitors can expect big game species (mountain goats, bighorn sheep, wolves, bears, cougar, elk, moose and deer) typical of the Rocky Mountains as well as countless birds and smaller creatures. When travelling in K-Country, you are truly a visitor to the home of many wild animals, so it is important to give them the space and respect they deserve in their natural setting.

Bow Valley/Yamnuska Mountain (Map 9/A5)

Hiking trails at the base of Yamnuska Ridge lead hikers through a mixed forest, meadow and wetland environment. Flower spotters will be delighted at all the orchids, while birdwatchers will tune in to the songbirds. Folks who like watching larger animals should head higher up the mountain, where they stand a good chance of spotting a bighorn sheep or mountain goat. Finally, those with herpetological tendencies can explore the wetlands, where they will find long-toed salamanders, tiger salamanders, boreal toads, wood frogs and spotted frogs.

Peter Lougheed Park (Map 4/G4–5/B6)

A natural mineral lick at King Creek attracts bighorn sheep, deer, elk and moose, making this a great place for watching larger ungulates. Another good spot is Pocaterra Fen, where you will also see a variety of birds. Pikas can also be seen at close range along the Rock Glacier Interpretive Trail near Highwood Pass.

Sheep River Wildlife Sanctuary (Map 5/F5)

A large band of bighorn sheep lives year round in this sanctuary, with its abundant grasslands and convenient escape routes along the river canyon walls. The sanctuary is an excellent place to watch sheep feeding, interacting and on occasion, being stalked by coyotes. During the fall, mature rams can often be closely observed from the comfort of your vehicle. This is also one of the best areas in the province for observing migrating birds of prey, which follow the foothill ridges in spring and fall. Golden eagles are especially prominent. Cougars have occasionally been observed in the area, but more likely are small mammals, like Columbian ground squirrels. The sanctuary is closed to vehicles December 1 to May 15 to protect the winter sheep range.

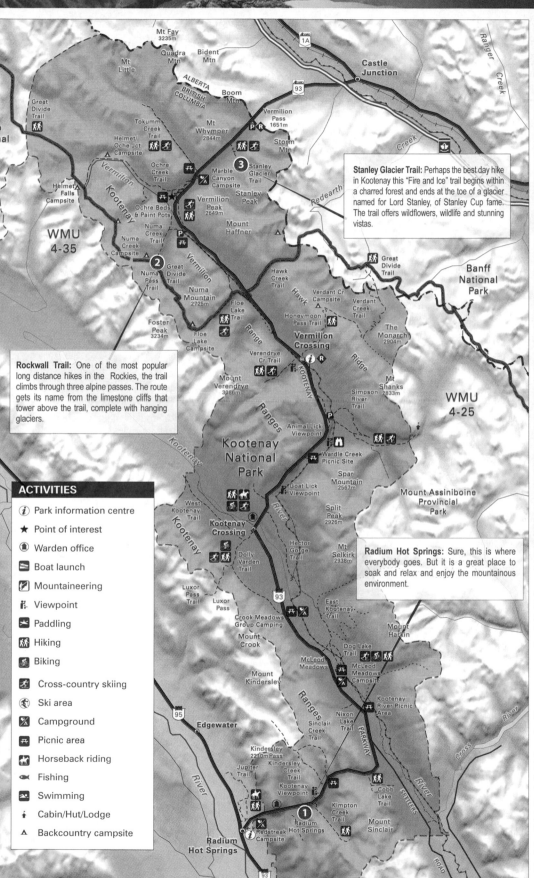

Rockwall Trail: One of the most popular long distance hikes in the Rockies, the trail climbs through three alpine passes. The route gets its name from the limestone cliffs that tower above the trail, complete with hanging glaciers.

Stanley Glacier Trail: Perhaps the best day hike in Kootenay this "Fire and Ice" trail begins within a charred forest and ends at the toe of a glacier named for Lord Stanley, of Stanley Cup fame. The trail offers wildflowers, wildlife and stunning vistas.

Radium Hot Springs: Sure, this is where everybody goes. But it is a great place to soak and relax and enjoy the mountainous environment.

ACTIVITIES

- (i) Park information centre
- ★ Point of interest
- Warden office
- Boat launch
- Mountaineering
- Viewpoint
- Paddling
- Hiking
- Biking
- Cross-country skiing
- Ski area
- Campground
- Picnic area
- Horseback riding
- Fishing
- Swimming
- Cabin/Hut/Lodge
- △ Backcountry campsite

THINGS TO KNOW

Area: 1,406,000 hectares
Highest Point: Deltaform Mountain 3,424 metres (11,233 feet)
Total Vehicle Accessible Campsites: 431

THINGS TO SEE

1 Radium Hot Springs
2 Rockwall Trail
3 Stanley Glacier Trail

CONTACT INFORMATION

Campground Reservations:
1-877-737-3783,
(International callers 1-905-566-4321)
kootenay.info@pc.gc.ca,
www.pccamping.ca,
www.pc.gc.ca/kootenay
Kootenay Visitor Centre: (250) 347-9505
Radium Hot Springs Pools:
(250) 347-9485
Avalanche Information: 1-800-667-1105,
www.avalanche.ca
Emergencies: 911

Kootenay National Park is home to the popular Radium Hot Springs, which is easily the biggest draw to the area. However, the park has much more to offer than the springs. In addition to a variety of trails, fishing holes and paddling routes, wildlife is a common sight along Highway 93 as it cuts through the heart of Kootenay National Park.

Archeological evidence showing this area has been visited in summer by a variety of native groups for nearly 10,000 years. The Ktunaxa (Kootenay) people's oral history tells us that the park has long been an east-west travel route they used to cross into what is now known as Alberta through White Man Pass, Simpson Pass and Vermilion Pass to hunt bison. The Paint Pots, a series of iron-rich springs and the nearby ochre beds, were culturally significant for the Ktunaxa, Stoney and Blackfoot tribes. The brightly coloured earth was used for decoration, ceremonies and trade. In the early 1900s, the ochre beds were actively mined. The ochre was hauled by horse drawn wagon to the CP Rail line at Castle Mountain, where it was shipped to Calgary to be used as a pigment for paint. These sites are still considered sacred by First Nations, so treat them with respect.

The first recorded visit was by Sir George Simpson in 1841. The Governor of the Hudson's Bay Company passed through the area on his round the world trek. The same year James Sinclair led a group of settlers to Walla Walla, Washington from Winnipeg, via this area. Sinclair is thought to be the first non-native person to soak in the hot springs. However, the area was not properly documented until 1858, when James Hector passed through the northern part of the park.

One of the first settlers in the area was John McKay, who staked a homestead in the area of Radium Hot Springs, along the Columbia River. A few years later, Roland Stuart bought the land around the springs. He tried to develop the springs into a health spa and was aided by a road being built from Banff to Vermilion Pass and a grant from millionaire John Harmsworth, a paraplegic who, after soaking in the pool recovers some mobility back in his legs.

Stuart went to England at the start of the World War I, and while he was abroad, the federal government signed an agreement to build a road from Banff to Windermere. He still had not returned by 1920, when the federal government created the Kootenay Dominion Park, which included Stuart's Land. Stuart was paid $40,000 for his original $160 investment, but even at that time, some assessed the property value as high as $500,000. The hot springs remain the most popular tourist destination in the park.

Like all the Rocky Mountain National Parks, the park is governed by a strict set of rules to balance the extremely heavy pressure put on it by humans with the need to conserve and protect the environment. All groups entering the park are required to pay a fee (on top of any accommodation or camping fees) and are given a parks guide outlining the basic rules.

CAMPING

There are five frontcountry or vehicle accessible campgrounds in Kootenay National Park and the Redstreak Campground now has sites that are reservable. To make a reservation, visit www.pccamping.ca or call 1-877-RESERVE (1-877-737-3783). International callers can call 1-905-566-4321. The other sites are available on a first-come first-serve basis.

Crook's Meadow Group Campground (Map 3/C3)
Crook's Meadow is located 34 km from the West Gate entrance and is for group camping only. You must book space with Parks Canada.

Redstreak Campground (Map 3/B6)
This popular campground is 0.5 km from the Highway 93 and Highway 95 junction. There are 242 vehicle/tent sites and offers a sani-station, showers, interpretive programs and trails that link to the popular hot springs. It is open from early May until October.

Marble Canyon Campground (Map 7/A4)
Marble Canyon has 66 sites with flush toilets. The campground is located 17.2 km from the Banff-Kootenay boundary on Highway 93 and is open from late June to September.

McLeod Meadows Campground (Map 3/D4)
Located 26.9 km from Radium on Highway 93, there are a total of 90 vehicle/tent sites with flush toilets and a sani-station here. It is open from late May until September.

Dolly Varden Campground (Map 3/C3)
The designated winter camping area in Kootenay National Park, Dolly Varden Campground is found 35.6 km from the West Gate entrance on Highway 93. The 4 sites are for off-season use only (September to May).

Outside of Kootenay Park
Outside of the Park, a few popular camping areas are found at these sites:

Cross River Canyon Recreation Site (Map 3/F6)
Found near the southeast tip of the Kootenay National Park, this small site has long been a favourite of backroad travellers. For this reason, the Forest Service has created a user maintained recreation site here. The site is RV accessible.

Dry Gulch Provincial Park (Map 3/C6)
This park is located five minutes south of Radium Hot Springs on Highway 3 just outside of Kootenay National Park. The park contains 26 vehicle/tenting campsites in a quiet, shaded pine forest. The campground is offered on a first come first serve basis from May 1- September 15.

Kootenay Crossing Recreation Site (Map 6/F6)
On the Beaverfoot Road, this is a small, semi-open site offering fishing and paddling. The site is located near the headwaters of the Kootenay River in a scenic mountainous area.

BACKCOUNTRY CAMPING

There are six sites in the Kootenay Backcountry, all of which are primitive and offer tent pads for 6 to 18 tenters. Bear poles are provided at all sites except Verdant Creek site, while pit toilets and fireboxes may or may not be provided, depending on the site. These campgrounds are found at Floe Lake (7/A6), Helmut/Ochre Creek Trail Junction (6/G4), Helmut Falls (6/F4), Numa Creek (7/A5), Tumbling Creek (6/G5) and Verdant Creek (7/D6). Unfortunately recent fires have caused the closure of a few sites such as at Kaufmann Lake and the Tokumm Valley Campsite. Also, the ever popular Fay Hut was reported to have burned down in April, 2009.

Camping is only allowed in designated campgrounds. A wilderness pass is needed for anyone planning on making an overnight trip into the backcountry. These passes are available from the Parks Canada visitor centre and you can reserve backcountry campsites up to three months in advance. Call (250) 347-9505 in summer or (403) 522-1264 from September to May.

FISHING

Fishing within Kootenay National Park remains a popular pastime. Even the most obscure lakes seem to receive a lot of fishing pressure and the fish tend to be small. But the natural beauty of the area and the long stretches of isolated streams more than make up for the lack of size. Anglers should also note that National Parks waterbodies are governed under their own regulations and you will need a special license to fish. Regulations can be downloaded from www.parkscanada.gc.ca.

Cobb Lake (Map 3/E5)
It is accessed from Highway 93 along an easy trail that actually descends to the lake. This dark water lake has many brook trout averaging 20–30 cm (8-12 in). Try a wet fly cast past the drop-off or use a lure. Shore casting is difficult due to the tree line.

Dog Lake (Map 3/D3)
It is a popular fishing lake that is accessed by a 3 km (1.8 mile) trail from McLeod Meadows Campground. The lake holds good numbers of small brook trout (average 25–35 cm/10–14 inches). Shore fishing is difficult, as the shallows are weedy.

Floe Lake (Map 7/A6)
Despite the gruelling 10 km hike, the lake receives constant fishing pres-

sure throughout the summer. Fishing for nice sized cutthroat (average 35–40 cm/14-16 in) remains fair at this beautiful mountain lake.

Kaufmann Lake (Map 6/G3)
This is a popular hike-in lake that is accessed via the Tokumm Creek Trail. The lake is found at 2,150 m (6,988 feet) in elevation and provides good fishing for stocked rainbow and brook trout. Some of the brookies reach 40 cm (16 inches) in size. Shore fishing is possible and a good area to try is near the inlet creek.

Kootenay River (Map 3/G7–6/E6)
The Kootenay National Park section of the Kootenay River is a fast flowing, murky river. This section does offer some excellent fly-fishing holes (use attractor patterns) since access is generally limited to logging road and/or bushwhacking (except where Highway 93 parallels the river in Kootenay National Park). A national park permit and fishing license is required when fishing in the park.

Ochre Creek (Map 6/G4–7/A5)
It is a small trail access creek that offers small cutthroat, bull trout and whitefish. Fishing is better in the summer or fall (after the high water recedes) using a fly or bait.

Olive Lake (Map 3/D5)
It is located at Sinclair Pass on Highway 93. The small lake has fair numbers of small brook trout to 25 cm (10 inches). Try casting into the shallows from a boat for best results, as shore fishing is difficult due to the tree line.

Simpson River (Map 7/D7–G7)
It is accessed by trail from Highway 93 and provides good fishing for small cutthroat that can reach 40 cm (16 inches) and bull trout to 4 kg (9 lbs). The fish are primarily found in the large pools in the first 8 km of the river and will take to flies or bait.

Verdant Creek (Map 7/E6)
It is a remote tributary of the Simpson River. The creek has numerous cutthroat and bull trout in the 20–25 cm (8–10 inch) range that readily take to bait or flies.

Vermilion River (Map 3/C3–7/A4)
It is the main fishing stream flowing through Kootenay National Park. Highway 93 provides good access to this river, which provides small cutthroat, rainbow and bull trout (averaging 20–30 cm/8–12 inches). The fishing is slow until the water clears in late summer and fall.

PADDLING

River paddlers come to Kootenay Park in search of challenging, but manageable whitewater. Both the Kootenay and Vermilion Rivers definitely satisfy this need. Please remember that river conditions are always subject to change and advanced scouting is essential. The information in this book is only intended to give you general information on the particular river you are interested in. You should always obtain more details from a local merchant or expert before heading out on your adventure.

Kootenay River: Kootenay Crossing to Settler's Road Bridge (Map 3/B2–F6)
This section of the Kootenay is a 57 km/34.8 mile (day+) Grade II route with the odd sweeper and logjam. To add some distance and challenge to the route, you can start on the Vermilion River. Camping is possible along the route, which ends at the southern tip of the park.

Kootenay River: Settler's Road Bridge to Kootenay Bridge (Map 3/F6–1/A3)
This section is a 49 km/29.9 mile (day+) Grade III route, which contains lots of rapids. The steep-walled canyons, scenery and challenging rapids make it a thrilling route. It is possible to access or camp at Horseshoe Rapids, which is often portaged around due to the tight corner. Expert open canoeists and kayakers all enjoy the route.

Vermilion River: Tokumm Creek to Ochre Creek (Map 7/A4–A5)
Highway 93 follows the Vermilion from Vermilion Pass down to Hector Gorge, where it leaves the Vermilion and follows the Kootenay River down to the confluence of the two rivers. Such close road access means that there are lots of put-in and take-out possibilities. There is a Class V+/VI gorge above the Highway 93 Bridge that can be run by true experts. Most everyone else will want to put-in below the bridge. The first section is the most fun, with Class II/III whitewater for the first little while. The paddling gets easier the farther you get downstream.

Vermilion River: Numa Falls to Floe Creek (Map 7/A5–B6)
Numa Falls are rated Class V+. As a result, most people 'seal launch' from the river right into the canyon below the falls. This 9 km (6 mile) section of river is Grade II/III, with a few ledges and one Class II/III chute to watch out for in the upper section of the run.

Vermilion River: Vermillion Crossing to Hector Gorge (Map 7/C7–3/C1)
At 13 km (8 miles), this is one of the longest runs on the Vermilion. It is also the easiest, with only a few Class II+ features to mix things up. Accordingly, canoeists and beginner kayakers favour this section as it is quite scenic. It is possible to put-in 3.7 km (2.2 miles) upstream from the Crossing, which will add a Class III canyon to the proceedings. You can also add in the Hector Gorge section for a 29 km (17.8 mile), five hour float.

Vermilion River: Hector Gorge to Kootenay River (Map 3/C1–C3)
At higher water levels, this run can be quite exciting; with a major Class III rapid and lots of play waves. At lower water levels, it is an easy float through Hector Gorge, which is actually just a steep-sided valley. This section is 16 km (10 miles) long.

TRAILS

The park has just over 200 km (120 miles) of trails, which pales in comparison to the other national parks in the book. The highest concentration of trails is in the northern section of the park, where you will also find the biggest mountains. Mountain biking is allowed on the fire roads and if you plan to horseback, you must check with park staff before heading out. Backcountry skiing and snowshoeing is a fine alternative during the winter. None of the trails are track set so be prepared to break trail.

Cobb Lake Trail (Map 3/E5)
From the parking lot on Highway 93, the trail initially switchbacks downhill losing 150 m (488 ft) in elevation before crossing Swede Creek at about 1.5 km (0.9 miles). The trail continues through a dense second growth forest and reaches the lake at 3 km (1.8 miles), gaining 50 m (163 ft) in elevation from the creek. The lake provides fairly good fishing and can be accessed from May-November.

Dog Lake Trail (Map 3/D3)
Beginning at the McLeod Meadows Campground, this easy 6.5 km (4 mile) trail initially crosses the Kootenay River on a wooden suspension bridge. The trail is well maintained and has an elevation gain of 60 m (195 ft) before you reach the boggy shoreline of Dog Lake. If you do not want to return the way you came, take the lesser-used and wetter trail to the northwest of Dog Lake. This alternative leads to the East Kootenay Fire Road and back to the suspension bridge. The trail is open year round with the hiking season extending from April-October.

Dolly Varden Trail (Map 3/B2)
From the warden station at Kootenay Crossing, it is an 8.8 km (5.4 mile) one-way hike leading to the Crook's Meadows Group camping site. The trail follows an old fire road and gains 185 m (601 ft) in total but it is up and down terrain the entire distance. The lower elevation trail can be hiked or biked from April to October or skied in the winter. If you employ a two car shuttle system, you can avoid the long trek back to the wardens' stations.

East Kootenay Fire Road (Map 3/C2–F6)
This fire road was constructed in 1926 to service the east side of the Kootenay River Valley. To reach the northern access point, travel 5.3 km (3.2 miles) south of the warden's station at Kootenay Crossing. From there, it is 29.5 km (18 miles) one-way trek to the south end of the road. There is little elevation gain along the way making the day trip a long but easy venture. The road is generally away from the river and passes through a second growth coniferous forest. You can shorten the route by crossing the footbridge near McLeod Meadows Campsite. This is a popular trail that can be skied or snowshoed in the winter.

Floe Lake Trail (Map 7/B6)
A footbridge leads across the Vermilion River and Floe Creek before the steady climb to the sub-alpine. Soon, the trail begins to switchback up Numa Mountain before traversing across several avalanche chutes along Floe Creek. The final 3 km (1.8 miles) involves a steep hike to the lake. It is all worth it as Floe Lake is set beneath a rugged rock wall covered by a cascading glacier. The 20 km (12.2 mile) return hike requires a 700 m (2,275 ft) climb to the lake at 2,500 m (8,125 ft).

Haffner Creek Trail (Map 7/B4)

From the Marble Canyon Campsite, this unmaintained but marked trail leads up the north side of Haffner Creek, approximately 1.5 km (0.9 miles) one-way. It is possible to extend beyond this point but you should expect to bushwhack and straddle windfalls as the trek is little more than a series of game trails.

Hawk Creek Trail (Map 7/C5)

This trail extends 9.5 km (5.8 miles) 3 to 4 hours one-way to Ball Pass gaining 900 m (2,925 ft) along the way. The trail begins on the north side of Hawk Creek, about 350 m (1,138 ft) north of the Floe Lake parking lot on Highway 93. A steep climb through the forest and over avalanche chutes and rockslides leads to the pass. The surrounding snow-capped mountain peaks and the beautiful alpine meadows with wildflowers make the tough climb worthwhile.

Helmet Creek Trail (Map 7/A4–6/F4)

From the Paint Pots parking area, this trail follows the Ochre Creek Trail for about 6.5 km (4 miles) before branching left. The trail up Helmet Creek crosses Ochre Creek on a suspension bridge and then switchbacks uphill before reaching the Helmet Creek Valley and a view of a spectacular 365 m (1,186 ft) high waterfall. It is a 15 km (9.1 mile) one-way trip to Helmet Falls, gaining 750 m (2,438 ft) along the way.

Honeymoon Pass Trail (Map 7/D6)

Beginning at Vermilion Crossing on Highway 93, this popular but difficult 5.5 km (3.4 mile) hike leads up to the 2000 m (6,500 ft) Honeymoon Pass. It begins on a boardwalk over a marshy lowland area before the steep 700 m (2,275 ft) uphill climb through the forest to the pass. Continuing on takes you down into the Verdant Creek Valley and Banff National Park (see below).

Kimpton Creek Trail (Map 3/D6)

Beginning about 7 km (4.3 miles) from the western park gate on Highway 93, this trail initially crosses Sinclair Creek and then travels up the east side of Kimpton Creek for 5.5 km (3.4 miles). The trail deteriorates into little more than a game trail past the sign marking the end of the maintained route. There is a 150 m (488 ft) elevation gain. The best time to take this hike is in April to October.

Kindersley Pass Trail (Map 3/C5)

Beginning just north of the Kootenay Viewpoint on Highway 93, this 10 km (6.1 mile) hike leads to the scenic pass. At 8.5 km (5.2 miles), you pass through Kindersley Pass at 2,210 m (7,183 ft). From there, the trail climbs steadily to 2,395 m (7,784 ft) and the open alpine, which provides spectacular views of the surrounding valleys. It is possible to hike into the Sinclair Creek Valley and return to Highway 93 without retracing your steps.

Luxor Pass Trail (Map 3/B2)

The trail to Luxor Pass begins on the Dolly Varden Trail at Kootenay Crossing. The trail branches from the fire road at 4.1 km and is a steady 4.3 km (2 hour) climb up a steep, densely forested mountainside to the pass at 1,900 m (6,235 ft) in elevation. It is not a highly recommended route since the trail is not maintained and offers few viewpoints.

Nixon Lake Trail (Map 3/D4)

The signed trailhead for this 2 km (1.2 mile) trail is found about 2.8 km (1.7 miles) south of McLeod Meadows Campsite. The easy trail leads through a second growth forest full of wildflowers in the spring to the shores of marshy, Nixon Lake.

Numa Creek Trail (Map 7/A5)

Beginning at the Numa Picnic Area on Highway 93, this trail crosses the Vermilion River and then Numa Creek before ascending up a narrow forested valley for 6.4 km (3.9 miles) to a fork in the trail. The trail gains about 120 m (390 ft) in elevation and can be hiked any time from early June to late October.

Ochre Creek/Ottertail Pass Trail (Map 7/A4–6/G4)

From the Paint Pots parking area, this trail follows Ochre Creek for about 6.5 km (4 miles) to a campsite at Helmut Creek. Continuing northwest results in hiking the difficult to follow Ottertail Pass Trail that stretches into Yoho National Park. That trail has not been maintained for years and is overgrown.

Paint Pots/Marble Canyon Loop (Map 7/A4)

Natives and commercial ventures once used the Paint Pots for painting purposes. A popular trail leads past the pots, to the Ochre Creek Trail and the Marble Canyon Loop. The canyon loop brings you through a narrow gorge with a number of natural rock bridges. Allow 3 hours for this 9 km (5.5 mile) return hike gaining 100 m (325 ft) in elevation.

Redstreak Trail (Map 3/C6)

This trail begins 4.4 km (2.7 miles) from the western park gate on Highway 93. You immediately cross Sinclair Creek on a small wooden bridge and then begin the ascent up the Redstreak Creek Valley through a lush second growth forest of Douglas-fir and Lodgepole pine. The trail ends below Redstreak Mountain about 2.4 km (1.5 miles) from the start. The elevation gain is 150 m (488 ft).

Redstreak Restoration Trail (Map 3/C6)

This new 1 km (0.6 mile) interpretive loop trail begins at the Redstreak Campground and follows the edge of the bench overlooking the Columbia Valley. Learn why grasslands and open forests are so important for wildlife and see how this habitat is being restored. An interpretive brochure is available at park facilities.

Rockwall Trail (Map 7/B6–6/F4)

The Rockwall Trail is one of the best-known multi-day hikes in the Kootenays. The route gets its name from the limestone cliffs that tower above the trail, complete with hanging glaciers. The trail climbs through three alpine passes. Access onto the trail is from the Floe Lake Trail from the south and from Helmet Creek in the North. The trail also hooks up with the Numa Creek and Tumbling Creek Trails for people not wanting to hike the entire 55.6 km (34.5 mile) route.

Simpson River/Mount Shanks Lookout Trail (Map 7/D7)

North of the Simpson River an easy trail system begins at the wooden bridge crossing over the Vermilion River. The old lookout road past the gates branching left leads to a scenic lookout tower and an old cabin on the south side of Mount Shanks. This hike is 9.5 km (5.8 miles) 4 hours return, gaining 365 m (1,186 ft) to the tower at 1,645 m (5,346 ft). The right branch leads 16 km (9.8 miles) up the Simpson Valley to the boundary of Kootenay National Park, gaining 120 m (390 ft) along the way. From here, difficult routes access the Surprise Creek Shelter in Mount Assiniboine Provincial Park (2 km/1.2 miles), or follow the river up through the Simpson Pass and down into Sunshine Village in Banff. This is a popular backcountry skiing destination.

Sinclair Canyon/Juniper Trail Circuit (Map 3/C6)

This popular 6.5 km (4 mile) return hike combines several shorter trails in the most commercial part of Kootenay National Park. The best place to start is at the Redstreak Campground. The trail begins in an open Douglas-fir forest, continues east on the south side of Highway 97 with views of the canyon before reaching the Aquacourt. From the Aquacourt, take the pedestrian tunnel crossing under Highway 93 and head up the road to the Juniper Trail. This trail switchbacks up the forested slopes before heading west to the canyon and then Sinclair Creek. Eventually, you will have to cross Highway 93 and return to the campground entrance kiosk. The well-maintained route provides excellent views of Sinclair Canyon and has an elevation gain of 190 m (618 ft).

Sinclair Creek Trail (Map 3/D5)

Across from the radio tower on Highway 93 just below Sinclair Pass, this hike climbs steadily up Sinclair Creek Valley into the alpine meadows below Brisco Range. Once in the meadows, the trail becomes hard to follow but it does continue past Sinclair Meadows to Kindersley Pass at 2,200 m (7,150 ft), where you can descend back to Highway 93. To reach Sinclair Meadows involves a hike of 5 km (3 miles) 2-3 hours one-way gaining 550 m (1,788 ft) in elevation. The total circuit is 16 km (9.8 miles) 3-4 hours.

Stanley Glacier Trail (Map 7/B4)

This popular 8.5 km (5.2 mile) trail leads to the foot of the steep rock wall upon which Stanley Glacier lies. The best views of the glacier come when you reach the open talus slopes near the foot of the glacier. The trail gains 300 m (975 ft) over 6 hours return and is used in the winter by backcountry skiers.

Tokumm Creek Trail (Map 7/A4–6/G3)

This difficult trail climbs 580 m (1,903 ft) to Kauffman Lake from the Marble Canyon parking lot, a distance of 15 km (9 miles).

Tumbling Creek Trail (Map 7/A5–6/G5)

This is a 22 km (13.4 mile) 1–2 day hike, which begins off Highway 93 on the Ochre Creek Trail. The Tumbling Creek Trail makes five creek crossings, with two of them on suspension bridges and another on a log bridge over a narrow canyon. The trail also passes by a 100 m (325 ft) high waterfall and ultimately culminates at a sub-alpine camping area below the Tumbling Glacier. The elevation gain along the way is 450 m (1,463 ft) to a high point of 1,900 m (6,175 ft). From the camping area it is possible to access Wolverine Pass at 2,250 m (7,313 ft) in elevation.

Valley View Trail (Map 3/B6)
This 1.2 km (.7 mile) easy trail begins at the Redstreak Campground entrance kiosk. The trail leads to a viewpoint overlooking the Columbia Valley, where picnic tables are offered. There are also self-guided interpretive signs to help you enjoy the natural beauty of the area.

Verdant Creek/Talc Lake Trail (Map 7/D6)
This difficult trail climbs to Honeymoon Pass, then to Redearth Pass on the boundary of Banff National Park. Many people day hike to Honeymoon Pass, a distance of 5.6 km (3.5 miles) that climbs 715 m (2,346 ft). There is a campground at Verdant Creek, 2.5 km (2.1 miles) past the pass. From Honeymoon Pass to Redearth Pass is another 12.6 km (7.8 miles), gaining another 113m (371 ft). From Redearth Pass, it is possible to hike 320 m (1,040 ft) down to Talc Lake, or continue through the pass to Egypt Lake in Banff National Park. The route continuing through the Verdant Creek Drainage beyond East Verdant Creek is non-existent in places.

West Kootenay Fire Road (Map 3/B2–6/G7)
From Kootenay Crossing, the West Kootenay Fire Road leads to the Beaverfoot Road outside of Kootenay National Park. This is the beginning of a popular mountain biking route that leads all the way to the Trans-Canada Highway at the boundary of Yoho National Park. This mountain biking trek is 66 km long (40.3 miles) 5–8 hours one-way and is best completed by using a two car shuttle system. Outside of the park, the road deteriorates and is extremely rutted and grown-in in places. Allow about 4 hours to walk the 8 km (4.8 mile) one-way trail, which is also shared with horseback riders and cross-country skiers.

Wolverine Pass Trail (Map 6/G5)
The Wolverine Pass Trail is popular backcountry skiing route in the winter that sees a fair bit of activity in the summer. The 30 km (18.3 mile) moderate horse trail follows Dalhard Creek to the pass at 2,250 m (7,380 ft). From there, you can approach the Rockwall Pass or Tumbling Creek Trails in Kootenay National Park.

WINTER RECREATION

Kootenay National Park lacks the development of other national parks. For backcountry skiers and snowshoers, this means that the area is wonderfully wild and often untracked. There are a number of relatively easy, but ungroomed routes for folks looking for an introduction to backcountry skiing.

Chickadee Valley (Map 7/B4)
This moderate route follows the Chickadee Creek Valley for 5 km (3 miles), through an old burn area, to an open area at the head of the valley. The surrounding valley slopes are very open and are good places to practice telemarking.

East Kootenay Fire Road (Map 3/C2–F6)
The East Kootenay Fire Road runs parallel to the Kootenay River for the better part of 30 km (18 miles). There are numerous access points near the northern section of the road, while the southern end of the road hooks up with the Natural Bridge Cross-Country Ski area (see below).

Hector Gorge (Map 3/C1)
This easy 11 km (6.7 mile) trail follows an old fire road as it loops away from, then back to, Highway 93. Overall, you gain 150m (488 ft) in elevation.

Simpson River (Map 7/D7–E7)
It is an easy 16 km (9.8 miles) from where the Simpson River flows into the Vermilion to the boundary of Kootenay National Park, gaining 120 m (390 ft) along the way. From here, it is possible to ski to the Surprise Creek Shelter in Mount Assiniboine Provincial Park (2 km/1.2 miles), or follow the river up through the Simpson Pass and down into Sunshine Village in Banff. This difficult extension is also shown in the Southwestern Alberta Backroad Mapbook.

Stanley Glacier Trail (Map 7/B4)
Take the moderately difficult trail (most people need skins, or at least a good wax), as you climb 275 m/894 ft up the Stanley Creek Valley to the treeline. From here it is possible to head up onto the slopes to put in a few turns, or return to the parking lot, via the creek.

Tokumm Creek Trail (Map 7/A4–6/G3)
The Fay Hut (about 12 km/7 miles) was once the main route here, but it burned down in 2009. Other options are to ski to Kaufmann Lake and back in a long day (30 km/18.3 miles), or to continue beyond to the Eagle Eyre, near Opabin Pass (in Yoho). Another option is to ski beyond Fay to the Neil Colgan Hut. The Kaufmann Lake Route is considered moderate, while all the other routes are difficult.

West Kootenay Trail (Map 3/B2)
From the Kootenay River Crossing Warden Station, this easy 19 km (11.6 mile) route follows an old fire road to the park boundary. There is a bridge that crosses the river and it is possible to return along the less developed trail on the other side of the river.

Outside of Kootenay Park
Just outside of the park are a couple other popular ski & snowshoeing destinations:

Natural Bridge Cross-Country Ski Trails (Map 3/F6)
The parking lot to this remote ski area is 16 km (9.8 miles) from Highway 93 on the Cross River Road. There are four loops, two for beginners and one each for intermediate and advanced skiers. In total, there are 12 km (7.3 miles) of groomed trails with the longest and most difficult being the highlight of the area. This 5 km (3 mile) advanced route crosses the natural bridge at the spectacular upper canyon of the Cross River. A warming hut on the Oochucks Loop overlooks the Kootenay River.

Nipika Cross-Country Centre (Map 3/F6)
At 14 km (8.5 miles) along the Cross River Road is this series of trails and a warm-up hut. These trails are maintained by donations from users and are mostly easy or intermediate. The only exception is where this trail system links up with the Natural Bridge trails by crossing the natural bridge, along a fairly difficult trail.

WILDLIFE VIEWING

You are never guaranteed to see wildlife in Kootenay National Park; they tend to scatter throughout the park. However, park is home to many, many different species of wildlife, and it is a rare trip indeed that you do not see any wildlife, even if you are just passing through.

The best time to see wildlife is in winter, when they come down from the high country. You may see bighorn sheep, elk, moose or even wolves near or on the road, so caution is needed when driving through the park. Remember, it is illegal to approach, feed, or harass wildlife and winter is an especially hard time on animals as food is scarce. One of the best places to see these animals is at a natural mineral lick, located alongside the highway.

Mineral Lick Viewpoint (Map 3/D5)
A natural mineral lick, located just off the highway, is a great place to see large ungulates. They tend to congregate here, especially in winter or in the early morning/early evening.

Mount Wardel (Map 3/C1)
If you're patient enough, and have a good pair of binoculars, you can usually see mountain goats on the slopes of Mount Wardel. They are usually found lower down on the slopes in winter.

Radium Hot Springs Pools (Map 3/C6)
One of the most unique creatures in the park is the Rubber Boa. Yes, it's a snake, but it's not the man eating, neck choking beast of so many Hollywood movies. This snake grows to a maximum of less than 90 cm (36 inches) and is rarely seen. If you do see one, don't disturb it and report the sighting to Parks Canada staff.

Radium Hot Springs Townsite (Map 3/B6)
Radium Hot Springs sits at the junction of the Columbia River Valley and the Sinclair Creek Valley. It is the traditional wintering ground for a band of bighorn sheep numbering more than 150 strong. The sheep are often seen on nearby slopes, or even wandering through town.

MountAssiniboineAdventures

THINGS TO KNOW

Area: 39,050 hectares

Highest Peak: Mount Assiniboine 3,618 metres (11,871 feet)

Total Vehicle Accessible Campsites: 0

THINGS TO SEE

1 Mount Assiniboine

2 Assiniboine Pass Trail in winter

CONTACT INFORMATION

Campground and Cabin Reservations:
Mount Assiniboine Lodge (403) 678-2883
www.assiniboinelodge.com
BC Parks: (250) 489-8540, www.bcparks.ca

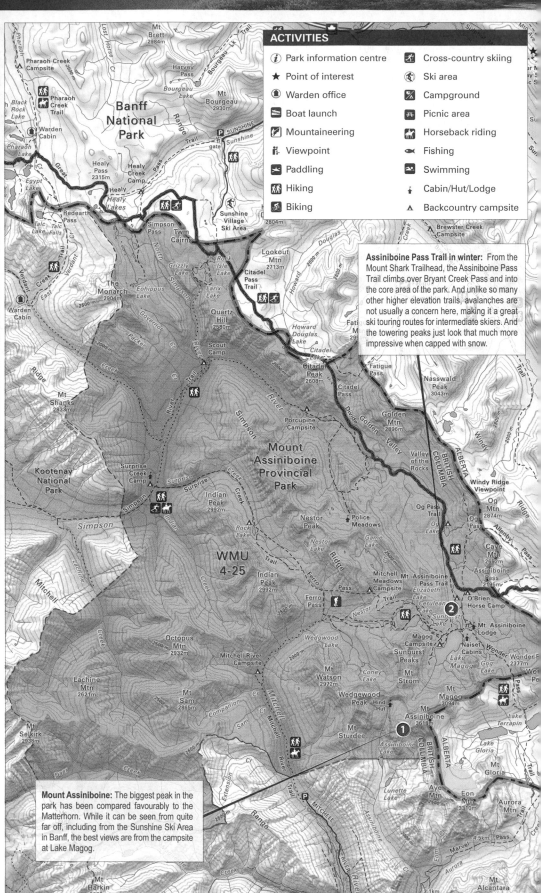

ACTIVITIES

ℹ	Park information centre	🏃	Cross-country skiing
★	Point of interest	⛷	Ski area
🏛	Warden office	🏕	Campground
⛵	Boat launch	⛩	Picnic area
🧗	Mountaineering	🐎	Horseback riding
📷	Viewpoint	🎣	Fishing
🛶	Paddling	🏊	Swimming
🥾	Hiking	🚶	Cabin/Hut/Lodge
🚲	Biking	△	Backcountry campsite

Assiniboine Pass Trail in winter: From the Mount Shark Trailhead, the Assiniboine Pass Trail climbs over Bryant Creek Pass and into the core area of the park. And unlike so many other higher elevation trails, avalanches are not usually a concern here, making it a great ski touring routes for intermediate skiers. And the towering peaks just look that much more impressive when capped with snow.

Mount Assiniboine: The biggest peak in the park has been compared favourably to the Matterhorn. While it can be seen from quite far off, including from the Sunshine Ski Area in Banff, the best views are from the campsite at Lake Magog.

A nearly perfect combination of high elevation lakes and meadows surrounded by snowcapped peaks makes this park a hiker's paradise. Lake Magog, with a campground, cabins and the Mount Assiniboine Lodge, forms the hub of the park and most people who visit this spectacular park stay at Lake Magog and make day trips from here.

Of course, visitors need to get here first. There is no road access into the park and visitors must hike into the core area. Most visitors hike into the park from Spray Lakes in Alberta. Mountain biking is allowed on the Assiniboine Pass Trail, while horseback riding is only possible after approval from the Parks branch. The park is also a popular backcountry skiing destination with the Naiset Cabins, Bryant Creek shelter or Mount Assiniboine Lodge adding comfort to the fantastic scenery. For those with cash to burn, Alpine Helicopters will fly people and/or gear into Lake Magog for a fee.

The area has long been used by the Ktunaxa First Nations and is part of their traditional territory, although they did not inhabit the area year round. The area has also been used by Shuswap and a number of prairie nations, including the Pelgan, Blood and Assiniboines. When geologist George Mercer Dawson visited the area in 1885, he named the most distinctive peak in the area after the Assiniboine, thinking it was part of their traditional lands.

Mount Assiniboine is the seventh tallest mountain in the Canadian Rockies, covering 80 sq km (30.9 sq miles). Because of its resemblance to the Matterhorn, mountaineers flocked to the mountain to climb it. The first successful attempt was by James Outram and Swiss guides Christian Hasler and Christian Bohren in summer, 1901.

5,120 hectares of what is now Mount Assiniboine Provincial Park was set aside in 1922, due in no small part to strong lobbying by the Alpine Club of Canada. It was, by some
odd coincidence, the seventh park in the BC Provincial Park system. In 1973, the park was coincidentally expanded by a factor of seven to its present size of 39,050 hectares.

CAMPING

Because the park is so remote, day hiking is not really an option. There are a few backcountry campsites scattered throughout the park, but the most common place to stay is at Lake Magog.

Lake Magog Campsite (Map 4/A1)
The main campsite in the park, this is also the most beautiful, situated on the shores of Lake Magog. There are 25 designated sites with gravel pads, a water tap and metal storage boxes for food. Open fires are prohibited here; while a group campground is found nearby at O'Brian Meadows (call 250-489-8540 to reserve).

Og Lake Campsite (Map 4/A1)
Found to the north of Lake Magog, this is a smaller site with only one outhouse. There is no water source, save for the lake itself. There is a metal storage box for food.

Porcupine Campsite (Map 7/G7)
Located near Citadel Pass, this campsite is used most frequently by folks hiking in or out via Sunshine Village in Banff.

Mitchell Meadows Campsite (Map 3/G1)
This small campground is located near the Mitchell Meadows Hut and is used most frequently by people who got to the hut too late to get a spot. Mitchell Meadows is located on the trail to Ferro Pass.

Rock Isle Lake Campsite (Map 7/F6)
This campground is located in the northern section of the park, near the Banff boundary.

Simpson River Campsite (Map 3/E1)
A small backcountry campsite that is located along the Simpson River Trail, which begins from Highway 93 in Kootenay National Park.

BACKCOUNTRY HUTS & LODGES

For those looking for a slightly more upscale outdoor experience, you can rent a room at the **Mount Assiniboine Lodge**, in the core of the park. The lodge also maintains five rustic alpine cabins south of Magog Creek. Reservations for both are recommended.

The Alpine Club of Canada maintains a 16 person hut in Assiniboine bowl, which is for experienced climbers only (this is not a hiking route). Reservations can be made through the lodge. There are also cabins found at Surprise Creek, Mitchell River and Police Meadows. Police Meadows Cabin and Surprise Creek Shelter are not open to the public during hunting season.

FISHING

Often lost in the accolades of the park is the fact that it is a fantastic fishing destination. Some very large fish are caught each year and there are periods where the action is none stop, especially in the lakes outside of the core area. The limited ice-free season, which usually lasts from mid-June until November, helps keep the fish quite active.

Cerulean Lake (Map 3/G1)
A spectacular setting and big fish makes the long, tough 20 km (12 mile) hike in worth it. The high elevation (2,213 m/7,192 foot), 25.3 hectare lake is catch and release only. You will find cutthroat and rainbow up to 2.5 kg (6 lbs) with some as large as 7 kg (15 lbs). Shore fishing is tough so you should use a floatation device to cast towards the drop-off and shallows.

Gog Lake (Map 4/A1)
A much smaller counterpart to Lake Magog, this high elevation lake offers hungry cutthroat trout to 1 kg (2 lbs).

Lake Magog (Map 4/A1)
This gorgeous wilderness lake is framed by snow-capped peaks, including Mount Assiniboine and offers fair numbers of cutthroat to 3 kg (7 lbs) that average 35–40 cm (13–15 inches). This is a high elevation lake (2,149 m/7,050 feet) and usually isn't free of ice until late spring or early summer. Shore fishing is possible even during the heart of summer, with the best time to fish being at dawn and dusk.

Mitchell River (Map 3/F2–G4)
The upper reaches are accessed by pack trail. Regardless of your point of entry, the river provides many enticing pools that hold cutthroat to 35 cm (14 inches). There are also some bull trout to 4 kg (9 lbs) and whitefish.

Rock Lake (Map 3/F1)
Found near Ferro Pass to the west of Mount Assiniboine, it is about 11 km (6.6 miles) by foot to access the lake. The difficult access results in very little fishing pressure and the lake holds numerous small cutthroat in the 15–20 cm (6–8 inches) range.

Sunburst Lake (Map 4/A1)
Considered by many to be one of the premier fly-fishing lakes in the Rocky Mountains, Sunburst Lake is found to the west of Lake Magog. This 8.6 hectare lake produces some very large cutthroat, reaching up to 5–7 kg (10–15 lbs). The high elevation (2,219 m/7,212 feet) lake has a relatively short ice-free period and the water remains cold even in the heart of summer. The long, tough hike in deters all but the hardcore angler.

Wedgewood Lake (Map 3/G1)
At the headwaters of Mitchell River, this hike-in lake offers good fly fishing and spincasting for cutthroat. However, shore casting is difficult due to the trees surrounding the lake. The fish can reach 1.5 kg (3 lbs) but average 30–35 cm (12–14 inches) in size.

PADDLING

There are no paddling opportunities in the park.

TRAILS

The combination of high elevation lakes and meadows surrounded by snow capped peaks makes this park a hiker's paradise. While not a huge area compared to the neighbouring Banff National Park, it offers a number of multi-day treks. Most people hike into the core of the park around Lake Magog and do a series of day hikes from here. The park is also a popular backcountry skiing destination with several cabins and the lodge making fine winter destinations.

MountAssiniboineAdventures

Allenby Pass Trail to Lake Magog (Map 4/A1–8/A6)

Beginning in Banff National Park, this route takes you up Brewster Creek to Allenby Pass gaining 1,070 m (3,510 ft) along the way. The trail then dips 500 m (1,625 ft) from Allenby Pass to Bryant Creek before climbing back over Assiniboine Pass for another 216 m (702 ft) elevation gain. Overall, the scenic but challenging hike is 44 km (27 miles) one-way. The maximum elevation is 2,440 m (7,875 ft) at Allenby Pass.

Assiniboine Lakes Loop Trail (Map 4/A1)

This short, three-hour hike provides access to three beautiful lakes. Access to the trailhead is found at the Lake Magog Campsite. Mid-June through September is the best time to hike the trail.

Assiniboine Pass Trail (Map 4/A1)

Accessed from the Lake Magog Campground, this hike is a 3.7 km (2.3 mile) 2 hour round trip. It runs through meadows and forested land to the ridge, before descending into the Bryant Creek Valley.

Bryant Creek Trail to Lake Magog (Map 4/C2–A1)

This is the most popular route into Lake Magog. It takes you from Canyon Dam off the Spray Lakes West Road along Bryant Creek and over Assiniboine Pass to Lake Magog. The first 14.5 km (8.8 miles) follows several dirt roads before 7 km of rough trail leads to the pass. The total distance of the hike is 25 km (15.2 miles) 7–8 hours one-way gaining 520 m (1,700 ft) to the Assiniboine Pass at 2,195 m (7,200 ft). An alternate route is to travel past Marvel Lake to Wonder Pass. That route is 26 km (15.8 miles) 7–8 hours one-way with an elevation gain of 700 m (2,275 ft) to a maximum of 2,378 m (7,800 ft).

Ferro Pass Trail (Map 4/A1–3/G1)

Accessed from the Lake Magog Campground, this hike is 9 km (5.5 miles) 6 hours one-way, gaining 275 m (900 ft) along the way. The trail runs past several lakes and provides an excellent view from the pass, at 2,270 m (7,450 ft) in elevation. Many hikers prefer the higher route towards tiny Elizabeth Lake and Ferro Pass as opposed to the lower route to Ferro Pass.

Mitchell River Trail (Map 3/G3–G1)

Horse packers and every once in a while, a brave (or foolhardy) backpacker will find a seldom used 24 km (14.6 mile) day + horse trail that starts from Bay Mag Mine and leads to Ferro Pass in Mount Assiniboine Provincial Park. Along the way, there are several side routes, camping locations and scenic vistas. Expect to ford the river on several occasions and to do some bushwhacking while gaining 1,100 m (3,610 ft). It is another 6 km to Lake Magog on a much more developed trail.

Moose Bath (Map 4/A1)

From Lake Magog, this hike is 8 km (4.8 miles) 4 hours return and involves an initial climb of 140 m (460 ft) to the pass near Elizabeth Lake. The Moose Bath is 150 m (488 ft) below. On the return to Assiniboine Lodge, the trail climbs about 100 m (325 ft) to a view overlooking Cerulean Lake. The maximum elevation reached is 2,290 m (7,515 ft).

Og Lake Trail (Map 4/A1)

To reach Og Lake from the Lake Magog Campground, it is an easy 11 km (6.7 mile) 4 hour return valley walk gaining 185 m (605 ft) in elevation. The trail leads through a sparse sub-alpine forest and large alpine meadows, including the vast Og Meadows, before reaching the Valley of the Rocks and Og Lake.

Og Pass Trail (Map 4/A1–7/F6)

Og Pass is reached by an 11.5 km (7 mile) 5–6 hour strenuous hike from the Lake Magog Campground, gaining 470 m (1,540 ft) in elevation. The trail is well worn, as it is the main horse trail leading into the park from Sunshine Village, in Banff National Park. Once you reach the pass, you will be rewarded by one of the best panoramic views in the park. Also, the wildflowers below Windy Ridge are spectacular. Mid-June through September is the recommended time to visit this trail.

Sunburst Valley Trail (Map 4/A1–3/G1)

From the Lake Magog Campground, the trail leads in a northwest direction passing by Sunburst Lake after about 1 km (0.6 miles) and Cerulean Lake half a kilometre later. Soon, the trail reaches the height of land at 2,300 m (7,545 ft) and descends north to Elizabeth Lake. From there, you can retrace your footsteps back to Lake Magog, try climbing to Ferro Pass or visiting

Wedgwood Lake. Overall, the trail is 8 km (4.8 miles) 3 hours return gaining 150 m (488 ft). It is one of the most popular routes in Mount Assiniboine Park.

Sunshine Ski Village to Lake Magog (Map 7/F6–4/A1)

From the Sunshine Village in Banff, this hike stretches 27 km (16.5 miles) 8 hours one-way past Og Lake to Lake Magog. The advantage of this route is that although it is longer than other routes, the elevation gain is only 488 m (1,600 ft) to a maximum of 2,408 m (7,900 ft).

Surprise Creek Trail to Lake Magog (Map 7/D7–4/A1)

From Highway 93 in Kootenay National Park, take the Simpson Valley Trail for 9.5 km (5.8 miles) and then hang a right on the Surprise Creek Trail at the hiker's cabin (free to use by all travellers). From there, the trail climbs 825 m (2,705 ft) up the Surprise Creek Valley to Ferro Pass at 2,270 m (7,450 ft) before dropping down to Lake Magog. This seldom used route into Mount Assiniboine Park is 29 km (17.7 miles) one-way leading primarily through a forested setting.

The Nub (Map 4/A1)

This trail is reached off the trail from Lake Magog to Elizabeth Lake about 0.5 km (0.3 miles) south of the tiny lake. The hike leads steadily uphill to Nub Peak gaining 400 m (1,310 ft) to the summit. The latter part of the hike is a scramble to the top on a poorly defined trail. From the top, you get a view of four mountain lakes and the sub-alpine meadows below. Overall, the trail is 3.8 km (2.3 miles) 2 hours one-way.

Wedgewood Lake Trail (Map 4/A1–3/G1)

Starting at Sunburst Lake west of Lake Magog, this moderate trail extends 5.1 km (3.1 miles) one-way. Gorgeous lakes and scenery highlight this trail, which is best done in early summer to early fall.

Wonder Pass Viewpoint Trail (Map 4/B2)

From Lake Magog, this 10.5 km (6.4 mile) 3–4 hour easy hike passes through beautiful sub-alpine meadows with wildflowers and past Og Lake. The elevation gain is 230 m (748 ft) to the pass at 2,400 m (7,875 ft). At the viewpoint, you overlook a couple of turquoise lakes and the spectacular mountain terrain.

WINTER RECREATION

The park has long been a popular backcountry skiing destination as the meadows below Mount Assiniboine offer some good terrain with great scenery and lots of powder. The season runs from early December to mid April with accommodation at Naiset Cabins, Bryant Creek Shelter or Mount Assiniboine Lodge. Most skiers prefer a helicopter ride to Lake Magog and then ski out at the end of the trip.

Assiniboine Pass (Map 4/A1)

The most popular and easiest route into the park, this route starts at the Mount Shark trailhead in Peter Lougheed Provincial Park and climbs into BC via the Assiniboine Pass. The trail has an extremely low risk of avalanches (as long as you stay on the trail), making it a great way to experience the spectacular terrain at a time when fewer people visit. Once in the park, there are many low risk, light touring destinations around the lodge.

Rock Island Lake (Map 7/F6)

Sunshine Village maintains a groomed trail to Rock Island Lake in the winter, a distance of 2.5 km (1.5 miles).

WILDLIFE VIEWING

The park offers a diversity of habitats and attracts large populations of mountain goat, bighorn sheep, moose, elk, deer, grizzly and black bear, wolves, coyote and wolverines. The park is also home to 93 species of birds. Keep your eyes and ears open while out on the trails and you will be surprised by what you can see and hear. Of course, if bears are in the area, you are encouraged to make noise to scare them off before you come face to face with these generally shy creatures.

MountRobson Adventures

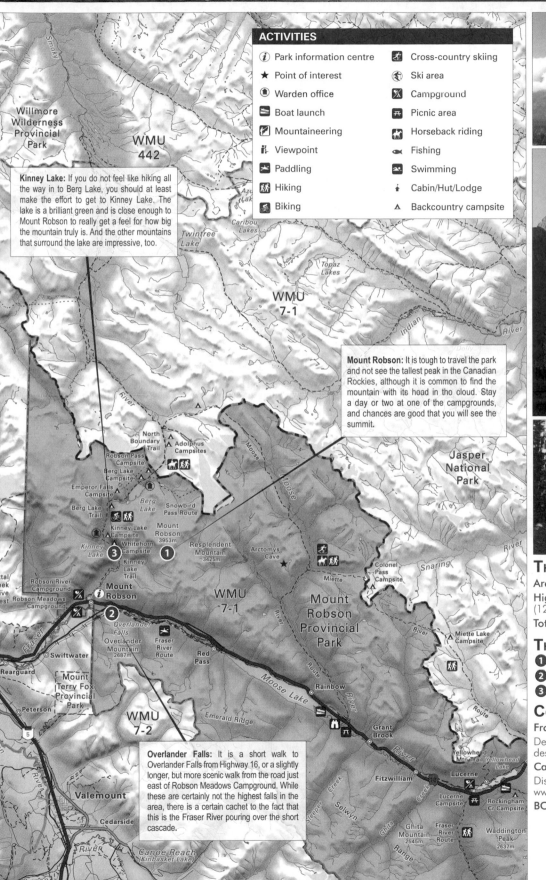

ACTIVITIES

- ℹ️ Park information centre
- ★ Point of interest
- 🛡️ Warden office
- 🚤 Boat launch
- 🧗 Mountaineering
- 📷 Viewpoint
- 🛶 Paddling
- 🚶 Hiking
- 🚴 Biking
- ⛷️ Cross-country skiing
- 🎿 Ski area
- ⛺ Campground
- 🎪 Picnic area
- 🐎 Horseback riding
- 🎣 Fishing
- 🏊 Swimming
- 🛖 Cabin/Hut/Lodge
- ⛰️ Backcountry campsite

Kinney Lake: If you do not feel like hiking all the way in to Berg Lake, you should at least make the effort to get to Kinney Lake. The lake is a brilliant green and is close enough to Mount Robson to really get a feel for how big the mountain truly is. And the other mountains that surround the lake are impressive, too.

Mount Robson: It is tough to travel the park and not see the tallest peak in the Canadian Rockies, although it is common to find the mountain with its head in the cloud. Stay a day or two at one of the campgrounds, and chances are good that you will see the summit.

Overlander Falls: It is a short walk to Overlander Falls from Highway 16, or a slightly longer, but more scenic walk from the road just east of Robson Meadows Campground. While these are certainly not the highest falls in the area, there is a certain cachet to the fact that this is the Fraser River pouring over the short cascade.

THINGS TO KNOW

Area: 224,866 hectares

Highest Point: Mount Robson 3,954 metres (12,972 feet)

Total Vehicle Accessible Campsites: 180

THINGS TO SEE

1. Mount Robson
2. Overlander Falls
3. Kinney Lake

CONTACT INFORMATION

Frontcountry Information:
Design By Nature (250) 566-4811
designbynature@telus.net

Campground/Berg Lake Trail Reservations:
Discover Camping 1-800-689-9025,
www.discovercamping.ca

BC Parks: (250) 489-8540, www.bcparks.ca

126

Home to the highest peak in the Canadian Rockies, Mount Robson Provincial Park protects 224,866 hectares of some of the most breathtaking scenery in a landscape dominated by breathtaking scenery. The massive 3,954 metre (12,972 foot) Mount Robson is the cornerstone of this park, but the park also protects the headwaters of the mighty Fraser River. It is part of the Rocky Mountains World Heritage Site, and was the second provincial park designated in BC in 1913.

The Texqakallt First Nation lived near the headwater of the Fraser, and are the first known inhabitants of the area. They called Mount Robson ÔYuh-hai-has-kun' or 'The Mountain of the Spiral Road', because of the mountain's striated face. The first Europeans arrived in the area in 1820, coming through the Yellowhead Pass. (The pass itself, as well as Tete Juane Cache is believed to be named after the European's native guide, Bostonnais, who had unusually light hair.)

The most famous trip through this area was in 1862, when a group of 115 men and two women made their way through the Yellowhead Pass to reach the Cariboo Goldfields, a story of tragedy, triumph, danger and death that has been the subject of many books, including Bill Gallaher's The Journey.

While the area saw some fur traders and miners before the turn of the century, the first recreationalists came to the area in 1907, to attempt to climb Mount Robson. It took them too long to travel from Edmonton, mostly by horse, and they had to turn back. They tried again the next year, but it wasn't until summer 1909 that they finally succeeded in making it onto the mountain. They turned back at what they thought was the summit, but wasn't. In 1912, the Berg Lake Trail was built, and the same year, Conrad Cain was the first person to actually summit Mount Robson. This trail was an important element in having the area declared a park.

In 1911, the Grand Trunk Pacific Railway was built through Yellowhead Pass and down the Fraser River Valley. Lucerine, on the eastern shores of Yellowhead Lake, was an important terminal for the railway for a little over a decade, until 1924, when the terminal was moved to Jasper, and the place became a ghost town overnight. Shortly after the Grand Trunk Railway was built, the Canadian Northern Railway was built through the Yellowhead Pass as well. However in 1915, with steel for the war effort in short supply, the Canadian Northern line was torn up. In 1918 the two railways were amalgamated into Canadian National Railway, and the second line was never rebuilt. In 1922, intrepid automobilers made their way along the old railway all the way to Victoria, BC. This route became known as the Tote Road, and was the basis for the Yellowhead Highway, which was completed in 1970.

Travelling through the park by train or along the highway remains a popular way to see the park. For people looking for a much more intimate encounter, you need to explore one of its many trails. The Berg Lake Trail is the best-known trail in the park, and one of the most popular trails in the Rockies. The park is also an exhilarating winter destination. None of the trails are groomed for skiing, but they are often well-travelled. Alternatively, guides offer helicopter trips into the backcountry.

CAMPING

To truly appreciate this area, you need to spend a few days exploring, or maybe just relaxing. There are three frontcountry or vehicle accessible campgrounds in the park as well as many backcountry spots. Reservations are accepted at Robson Meadows Campground, while reservations are also recommended for people looking for a backcountry camping spot along the Berg Lake Trail. Camping is available year round, although the gates are closed in winter and services are only offered from mid May until the end of September.

Berg Lake Area (Map 25/E2)
There is a backcountry fee that must be paid if you are planning on overnighting along the Berg Lake Trail. Also note that you can (and probably should) reserve some of the campsites by calling ahead. There are seven campgrounds along the route, with anywhere from five to 26 sites. The seven sites are: Kinney Lake, Whitehorn, Emperor Falls, Marmot Lake, Berg Lake, Rearguard and Robson Pass.

Lucerne Campground (Map 26/F6)
Located at the western end of Yellowhead Lake, there are two separate areas set in a well-treed area. There are 36 vehicle accessible sites at the main site, as well as two walk-in sites. This site is more rustic than the other two vehicle accessible campsites with no running water or flush toilets. A boat launch is found 1.9 km to the east.

Robson Meadows Campground (Map 25/D3)
Set next to the Fraser River, nearby to the Visitor Centre, store and restaurant, this is the largest campground in Mount Robson. There are 125 large, treed sites here, 32 of which are reservable, as well as a playground and sani-dump. Interpretive programs and guided hikes are offered in the summer.

Robson River Campground (Map 25/D3)
This small, well-treed site is found on the shores of the Robson River. It is located a short walk from the Visitor Centre, as well as the Berg Lake Trail. There are 19 drive-in campsites available on a first-come, first-served basis only. Showers are available.

FISHING

The furthest upstream that salmon can spawn on the Fraser is Rearguard Falls, which is located just west of the park boundaries. The park itself holds the usual Rocky Mountain species: bull trout, whitefish, and rainbow trout. You will also find kokanee in Moose Lake. Watch for closures and restrictions.

Berg Lake and Kinney Lake (Map 25/E2)
These two lakes are among the prettiest lakes in the province, which is good, because you're going to be staring at them for a long time if you try fishing here. While the lakes do contain rainbow trout, the water's high glacial till content makes finding them difficult.

Fraser River [Upper Reaches] (Maps 25/A4-26/E7)
The portion of the Fraser River in Mount Robson Provincial Park offers good fishing for rainbow trout, bull trout and whitefish. The best areas are near creek mouths that flow into the Fraser. Another area that provides decent results is the pool formed near Overlander Falls. Watch for special restrictions.

Ghita Creek (Map 26/D6)
Ghita Creek flows along the valley between Ghita Mountain and Sleeper Mountain in Mount Robson Provincial Park. The creek is accessible from Highway 16 and provides fair fishing for rainbow trout, bull trout and whitefish.

Grant Brook (Map 26/D5)
Grant Brook crosses under Highway 16 just west of Yellowhead Lake in Mount Robson Provincial Park. The stream provides fishing opportunities for rainbow trout, bull trout and whitefish. The further you hike away from the highway, the better the fishing usually gets.

Moose Lake (Maps 25/G4–26/B5)
Moose Lake is a big lake just south of Highway 16. The lake has rainbow, lake and bull trout, as well as kokanee, whitefish and burbot. There is a boat launch at the eastern end of the lake.

Moose River (Map 26/A1-C5)
The Moose River is a remote river flowing from the Continental Divide to the Fraser River just east of Moose Lake. Access to the upper reaches is limited to hikers with good navigational skills. Fishing in the river is fair to good in sections for generally small rainbow trout and whitefish, although the bull trout in the river can reach up to 2 kg (4.5 lbs) in size. Streamer pattern flies or lures work best for the larger bull trout.

Robson River (Map 25/D3)
This dynamic river flows from the glacial fed Berg Lake south into the Fraser River. The river is quite scenic as the mighty Mount Robson dominates the landscape. Fishing in the river is generally fair in places for small rainbow trout, bull trout and whitefish.

Whitney Lake (Map 26/E6)
This small, remote lake can be reached by trail from the south side of Highway 16. Fishing in the lake is fair to good at times for small, stocked rainbow trout.

Yellowhead Lake (Map 26/F6)
Yellowhead Lake is found off Highway 16 near the eastern entrance to the park. Anglers will find small rainbow trout, whitefish and burbot, as well as the odd lake trout that can reach 5 kg (11 lbs). There is a campground and boat launch at the west end of the lake.

PADDLING

While there are a number of rivers in the park, few are accessible by road. In fact the only paddling that does not lie adjacent to Highway 16 is the section of the Robson River from the Berg Lake trailhead. Hardcore whitewater kayakers are not going to find a lot of water here to keep them interested except for running Overlander Falls, but canoeists and intermediate paddlers will find some interesting places to explore.

Fraser River East of Moose Lake (Maps 26/E6-B5)

Stretching from the Rocky Mountains to the Pacific Ocean, the mighty Fraser River begins its journey west in Mount Robson Provincial Park. The most easterly put-in along the Fraser River in Mount Robson Park is located just west of Lake Yellowhead, where Highway 16 crosses the river. There is a nearby picnic area where you can park your vehicle. Downstream from the first put-in, where Highway 16 crosses the Fraser River again, there is another access to the river. This area doubles as a take-out for the first put-in. Most people take out at Moose Lake. This particular stretch of river is rated as Grade II water and allows for one of the most scenic water routes in the province. It is more of a scenic paddle than an exhilarating white water run and can be run by intermediate Kayakers and canoeists.

Fraser River West of Moose Lake (Maps 25/G4-B4)

West from Moose Lake, there are several access points available along the Fraser River. Highway 16 parallels the river from Tete Jaune Cache to Moose Lake and provides good access to the river. You can literally pick and choose the length of your run. This portion of the Fraser River flows past the largest peak in the Canadian Rockies, Mount Robson, and offers plenty of impressive white water. Along this stretch of the Fraser River, you can experience everything from Grade II to Grade V type runs, depending on the water level and which sections you choose to run. Before dipping your paddle, be sure to scout the run that you choose, to ensure it is within your capability. The one advantage of planning a paddling excursion along this part of the Fraser is that there is a wide range of difficulty offered to appease paddlers' needs. In fall, paddlers will be amazed to see spawning salmon that have travelled almost 2,000 km from the Pacific Ocean to the final inland barrier at Rearguard Falls.

Moose Lake & Marsh (Maps 25/G4–26/B5)

While not an extremely common activity, it is possible to canoe Moose Lake, which is found just south of Highway 16. More common is to canoe in Moose Marsh, where you will see plenty of wildlife. In fact, the marsh is one of the best places to see wildlife such as moose and deer and birds in the park.

Robson River (Map 25/D3)

This wild, beautiful river is not for the inexperienced. The Berg Lake trailhead is the take-out location, while it is about a 4 km (2.5 mi) hike along the trail to the put-in at the bridge over the river at the outflow of Kinney Lake. The trail traverses along an old access road allowing for fairly easy travel with a canoe. The Grade IV river can swell to Grade V during high water. Although the run is short, at about 4 km (2.5 mi), it will test even the best with a series of Class III-IV rapids along with three significant Class VI drops.

Yellowhead Lake (Map 26/F6)

This long, narrow lake lies alongside the northern side of Highway 16. While not known as a canoeing lake (it can get windy), it is an interesting way to see the scenery. This is a great place to see wildlife, too.

TRAILS

When people think of Mount Robson trails, they think the Berg Lake Trail. It's hard not to, as the well kept trail is one of the most popular multi-day hikes in BC. But the Berg Lake Trail isn't the end all, be all of trails in this park. In fact, there are a surprising number of trails in the park, ranging from easy nature trails to difficult slogs that climb steeply up ridges along almost non-existent trails. We have also included a few trails just outside the park for area visitors.

Berg Lake Trail (Map 25/D3-E1)

The Berg Lake Trail is a world-renowned trail system that provides access to the beautiful backcountry of Mount Robson Park. The trailhead can be found at the end of the Kinney Lake Road, which is located near the park visitor centre off the north side of Highway 16. There is a parking area available at the end of the road. From the trailhead, the trail begins by following the Kinney Lake Trail along the Robson River. From Kinney Lake, the Berg Lake Trail continues along the Robson River with Mount Robson dominating the

landscape. The route travels through the scenic Valley of a Thousand Falls to the beautiful Berg Lake. Along the trail, there are a number of campsites to base camp from as well as several side routes to explore. Overall, the Berg Lake Trail is a moderate journey that traverses over 21 km (13 mi) one-way. Anyone planning to attempt this trip should have adequate backcountry experience.

Fraser River Nature Trail (Map 25/D3)

This easy 2 km (1.2 mi) hike can be accessed from Robson Meadows Campground south off Highway 16. The loop trail meanders through the lush forest along the Fraser River providing several opportunities to view the magnificent river.

Hargraves Lake Route (Map 25/F1)

The Hargraves Lake Route ascends from the Marmot Lake Campsite next to Berg Lake, towards the massive glacier hovering above Margraves Lake. This moderate route is just over 2 km (0.6 mi) each way. From the lake, the Mumm Basin Route veers east to Robson Pass.

Kinney Lake Trail (Map 25/D3)

The Kinney Lake Trail begins from the Berg Lake Trail parking area. En route, trail traverses along the Robson River and past Knowlton Falls. At Kinney Lake, you are rewarded with a spectacular view of Canada's tallest mountain, Mount Robson. The return trip for this moderate trek is about 9 km (5.6 mi). This is also the trail to Berg Lake and hikers can wander past the lake to extend the trip.

Labrador Tea Trail (Map 26/E6)

You can find this easy 2.5 km (1.6 mi) trail at the Lucerne Campground on Yellowhead Lake. From the campground, the trail loops around the beach area.

Moose River Route (Maps 26/C3-32/G7)

This difficult backcountry route travels through the heart of Mount Robson Park. The route stretches from Highway 16, east of Moose Lake, all the way to Jasper National Park, deep in the Rocky Mountains. From Highway 16, the route follows along the lush forested shoreline of Moose River eventually breaking into the alpine near Moose Pass on the border of Jasper Park. Depending on how far you wish to travel, this trek could take several days. All travellers should have good maps, compass and the skills to use them. Since the trail can be challenging to follow at times, only experienced and well-equipped hikers should attempt this route.

Mount Fitzwilliam Trail (Map 26/F6)

The trailhead to the Mount Fitzwilliam Trail is located across from the Yellowhead boat launch area on the south side of Highway 16. This scenic mountain route ascends quickly into the backcountry of Mount Fitzwilliam. About half way along the trip, you will find a cluster of backcountry campsites available for overnight use. As you approach the alpine, fantastic views of the Rockies and the Robson Valley can be enjoyed. There are also backcountry campsites available in the alpine areas. In total, the trail to the alpine and back is a 22 km (13.7 mi) journey and regarded as moderate in difficulty.

Mumm Basin Route (Map 25/E1)

The Mumm Basin Route can be picked up from the Margraves Route or the Toboggan Falls Route. This steep route traverses east from Margraves Lake to the Robson Pass. At the pass, the route meanders down to the Robson Pass Campsite, west of Adolph's Lake. This route is approximately 5 km (3.1 mi) in length and is regarded as moderate to travel.

Overlander Falls Trail (Map 25/E3)

Just east of the park visitor centre near Kinney Lake Road, look for the parking area for this trail off the south side of Highway 16. It is a short hike down to the viewpoint where you will find a great view of Overlander Falls. From the falls, you can continue along the trail in a loop that travels about 5 km (3.1 mi) before returning to the parking area. This easy trail also connects with the Lookout Trail.

Portal Lake Trail (Map 26/G5)

Portal Lake is a small lake found near the eastern boundary of Mount Robson Park off the north side of Highway 16. This easy 2 km (1.2 mi) trail circles the small lake providing a first hand view of the lake and its ecosystems.

Robson River Trail (Map 25/D3)

This easy 1 km (0.6 mi) trail travels along the Robson River gravel flats. The trailhead can be found from the Robson River Campground area west of the park visitor centre.

Snowbird Pass Route (Map 25/F1)

From the Berg Lake Campsite, this difficult route is 22 km (13.7 mi) in length. The trail is marked by rock cairns as it skirts past the base of the magnificent Robson Glacier and eventually reaches Coleman Glacier. Needless to say, the scenery in this part of the park is truly wild and exhilarating. This trail is closed in May and June due to caribou calving.

Toboggan Falls Route (Map 25/E1)

This moderate 6 km (3.7 mi) route travels from the east side of Berg Lake to the Toboggan Creek Falls. From the falls, you can explore further into the alpine basin and look for a small cave that is located to the north.

Viewpoint Field Walk (Map 25/D3)

The Viewpoint Field Walk is the perfect way to stretch those travel weary legs. From the visitor centre, you can follow this easy 1 km (0.3 mi) hike around the field area.

Yellowhead Lake Trail (Map 26/F6)

From the information booth at Lucerne Campground, this is a 2.5 km (1.6 mi) interpretive trail. The route makes an easy loop through the forest canopy and back to the beach area at Yellowhead Lake.

Yellowhead Mountain Trail (Map 26/F6)

You can find the access road to this trailhead just east of the Lucerne Campground off the north side of Highway 16. From the trailhead, this moderate route ascends steeply towards Yellowhead Mountain. At the 2 km (1.2 mi) mark, you will find a fantastic viewpoint, providing sights of the surrounding mountains, the Robson Valley and the highway below. From the viewpoint, strong hikers may wish to explore the alpine area around Yellowhead Mountain. It is an 800 m (2,625 ft) grunt over 8 km (5 mi) one-way to the alpine.

Outside Mount Robson Park

There are also a few nearby trails worth checking out.

Little Lost Lake Trail (Map 25/C4)

Off the north side of Highway 16, the trailhead to this route can be found almost opposite the parking area for the Rearguard Falls Trail. The Little Lost Lake Trail is a fairly easy hike that is about 3 km (1.9 mi) in length. The trail ascends to the shore of the small lake. To extend your hike, there is a loop trail around the lake as well as a side trail to a scenic waterfall. The steep branch trail is less than 2 km long.

Lookout Trail (Map 25/D3)

Beginning from the park visitor centre near Kinney Lake Road, you can hike this easy to moderate route up to a scenic lookout over the valley. The trail is 4 km (2.5 mi) in length and cuts through the forest cover eventually breaking out to a magnificent view of the Rocky Mountains.

Rearguard Falls Trail (Map 25/C4)

The Rearguard Falls Trail is located off the south side of Highway 16, just east of the junction between Highway 16 and Highway 5. The short, easy trail leads to a fantastic viewing area along the Fraser River. The Rearguard Falls are quite a sight on their own, although if you happen to visit the falls during late August/early September you will be able to view Chinook salmon leaping at the falls. The Chinook travel over 1,200 km (745 mi) from the Pacific Ocean to this point along the Fraser River. This is truly an unbelievable feat of nature.

Terry Fox Trail (Map 25/D5)

This moderate 12 km (7.5 mi) trail ascends Mount Terry Fox eventually reaching the scenic alpine area below the peak. Look for the access road off the east side of Highway 5, south of Tete June Cache. The trail and park were established in 1982 as a natural monument to the Canadian hero, Terry Fox.

WILDLIFE VIEWING

Mount Robson is a great place to see wildlife, from large ungulates and predators to smaller mammals and birds. Moose, bear and deer are often seen along the highway, while in June, there is a bird blitz, where birders gather in an annual inventory of the park's birds. There are 182 species of birds (along with 42 species of mammals, four amphibians and one reptilian).

One of the best places to see wildlife is **Moose Marsh.** Found next to Moose Lake, moose, deer and elk are common visitors, while small mammals and birds can also be seen. Other good wildlife watching areas include: **Yellowhead Lake**, **Snowbird Pass** and **Kinney Lake**.

In August, Chinook Salmon, which have fought their way upstream from the headwaters of the Fraser 1200 km (750 miles) downstream finally reach their journey's end at Overlander Falls. Incredibly, after months without eating, a very few salmon still have the dogged determination to fight their way up and over Rearguard Falls just downstream to reach this final, impassible obstacle. The best place to watch the returning Chinook is at Rearguard Falls Provincial Park, just a few kilometres west of the park boundary near Tete Juane Cache.

WINTER RECREATION

Mount Robson is a popular destination for winter recreation, although there are no track-set trails. On a clear blue-sky day in the heart of winter, skiing at the base of Mount Robson is one of the most scenic activities imaginable.

The most popular trail, even in winter, is the Berg Lake Trail. Because the trail is at least a day in and a day out, most people who ski the trail also bring along winter camping gear. All the campgrounds along the trail are available for winter camping.

In addition to the Berg Lake Trail, popular backcountry ski trips include the Moose River Trail, Mount Fitzwilliam and the Mumm Basin Route. The difficulty of these routes should not be underestimated and should be left to experienced winter travelers. Avalanches are only one of the dangers to be encountered along the park's remote, infrequently travelled routes.

For something a little different, Robson Helimagic (www.robsonhelimagic. com) offers heli-skiing adventures in Mount Robson Provincial Park.

WillmoreWildernessAdventures

ACTIVITIES

- (i) Park information centre
- ★ Point of interest
- Warden office
- Boat launch
- Mountaineering
- Viewpoint
- Paddling
- Hiking
- Biking
- Cross-country skiing
- Ski area
- Campground
- Picnic area
- Horseback riding
- Fishing
- Swimming
- Cabin/Hut/Lodge
- ▲ Backcountry campsite

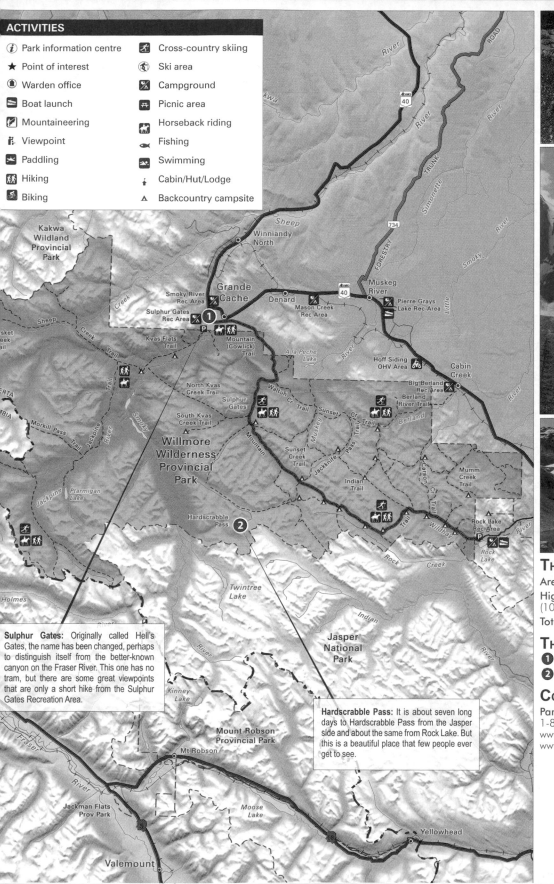

Kakwa
Wildland
Provincial
Park

Sheep

Winniandy
North

Grande
Cache

Smoky River
Rec Area

Sulphur Gates
Rec Area

Denard

Mason Creek
Rec Area

Muskeg
River

Pierre Grays
Lake Rec Area

Kvas Flats
Trail

Mountain
(Cowlick)
Trail

A la Peche
Lake

Hoff Siding
OHV Area

Cabin
Creek

North Kvas
Creek Trail

Sulphur
Gates

Waltoh Cr. Trail

Sunset

Cr
Trail

Berland

Big Berland
Rec Area

Berland
River Trail

South Kvas
Creek Trail

Willmore
Wilderness
Provincial
Park

Muskeg

Mountain

Sunset
Creek
Trail

Jackknife

Pass Trail

Carson Cr

Trail

Mumm
Creek
Trail

Morkill Pass Trail

Jackpine

Jackpine
River

Ptarmigan
Lake

Indian
Trail

Hardscrabble
Pass

②

Rock Lake
Rec Area

Wildhay

Rock Lake

Holmes

River

Rock

Creek

Twintree
Lake

Indian

Jasper
National
Park

Sulphur Gates: Originally called Hell's Gates, the name has been changed, perhaps to distinguish itself from the better-known canyon on the Fraser River. This one has no tram, but there are some great viewpoints that are only a short hike from the Sulphur Gates Recreation Area.

Kinney
Lake

Fraser

River

Mount Robson
Provincial Park

Mt Robson

Hardscrabble Pass: It is about seven long days to Hardscrabble Pass from the Jasper side and about the same from Rock Lake. But this is a beautiful place that few people ever get to see.

Jackman Flats
Prov Park

Moose
Lake

Yellowhead

Valemount

THINGS TO KNOW
Area: 460,000 hectares
Highest Peak: Mount Chown 3,331 metres (10,930 feet)
Total Vehicle Accessible Campsites: 0

THINGS TO SEE
① Sulphur Gates
② Hardscrabble Pass

CONTACT INFORMATION
Parks and Protected Areas:
1-866-427-3582,
www.albertaparks.ca ,
www.willmorewilderness.com

There is a rumour that some Jasper Wardens, when asked by people where they can find solitude and true wilderness, are directing people north to Willmore. Although not as large as Jasper, Willmore Wilderness contains scenery that is different, but every bit as spectacular. It offers an almost perfect blend of soaring peaks, high alpine passes and raging rivers. And, as an added bonus for wilderness seekers, there is no road access into the 4,600 sq km (1,840 sq mile) park. If you want to get anywhere in Willmore, you have got to walk. Or ride a horse. Or bike.

There are three main staging areas for trips into Willmore—Rock Lake, Big Berland and Sulphur Gates Recreation Areas, of which Rock Lake is the largest. Outside of these vehicle access locations, camping is limited to random backcountry sites. But with over 750 km (458 miles) of multi-use trails, some of which connect to the Jasper, there are plenty of places to explore.

The trails range from well-developed valley walks to overgrown routes that lead nowhere. There are also many peaks that can be scrambled by the strong hiker along ridges that are easily followed. As you make your way north, the Rockies are not quite as rocky or angular. Some may find the mountains less impressive (and indeed, there only six mountains over 3,000 metres/10,000 feet in the park), but they are much easier to scramble onto, with ridges that stretch on, sometimes for days.

Yes, it should be a backpacker's paradise but currently, the majority of usage on these trails comes from hunters or day-trippers, most of who are on horse. Willmore is open to fishing, but while some streams can be productive most are often too fast or cold to offer good fish habitat. Still, because few people fish these waters, there are rumours of some monster bull trout in the most remote stretches of water.

The park was set aside in 1959, although it didn't get its current name until 1965, when it was named after the former Minister of Land and Forest. However, the area has a long history. Just outside of the park is one of the world's most extensive dinosaur track finds and inside the park you will find ammonites, corals, fossil fish and even dinosaur tracks. (Remember, removing fossils is illegal.) These are most evident along the rocky ridges in the park.

The area was extensively used by local first nations who travelled into the area to hunt; there were also a number of trade routes over the mountain passes. The Rocky Mountain Cree lived in the area around Willmore and Jasper. When Jasper Park was created, the federal government forced the Cree living there to move; they chose to head into what is now the Willmore area. Even by that time, the area was a haven for outfitters and trappers and there are still a number of active trap-lines (complete with private cabins) inside the park. These trappers and outfitters developed a large trail system in the park, many of which have been lost since the area has been declared a park.

The area is at the centre of a long battle between conservationists and industry. The park boundaries have actually been reduced to exclude areas rich in resources. These areas are also prime wildlife areas and conservationists are worried about the impact on these creature's habitats.

CAMPING

There are no vehicle accessible campsites in the park. There are, however, campgrounds located just outside the park at each of the three main staging areas.

Big Berland Recreation Area (Map 39/A6) 🏕️🚶🐎🐟
This 18 unit site is located off Highway 40. Fortunately, it is far enough away that campers won't hear any noise from the highway. Unfortunately, the site is just about directly below a railway bridge over the Berland River. The site is also popular with anglers. Note that horses are not allowed in this site itself; there is a corral 4 km (2.4 miles) further down the road.

Rock Lake Recreation Area (Map 34/C4)
🏕️🚤🚶🎿🐎⛷️✈️〰️🐟
This is the biggest of the three campgrounds, with 93 campsites. The lake is a popular destination in and of itself and there is a boat launch and swimming area.

Sulphur Gates Recreation Area (Map 37/F4) 🏕️🚶🎿🐎🚣🚻
This small, six unit site is located just north of Grande Cache of Highway 40. The site is functional, but not particularly well designed for destination campers. There is a short trail overlooking the dramatic Sulphur Gates, but the area is mostly just a staging area for trips into Willmore.

BACKCOUNTRY CAMPING

Backcountry camping is random and campsites are easy to find. Most are primitive, but some have tables. The majority of these sites have been developed by guide outfitters and are starting to show signs of too much attention. However, with a major grassroots effort being put into promoting and protecting the area, these sites are being cleaned up. To help preserve this unique area, please practice low impact camping while in the backcountry.

A unique feature of the park is the fact that open fires are permitted at times of low forest fire risk. There are also numerous cabins through the area. Most are trappers cabins and off-limits to tourists. However, there are a few historical cabins that can be used by travellers.

FISHING

The fast, cold nature of many of the streams in Willmore limits the number of good holding areas for trout and grayling. This, combined with the limited access, results in few people willing to trek far enough to find the big fish that are rumoured to roam these waters. Listed below are the bigger tributaries, but do not rule out the many smaller streams that also offer small trout and grayling. Note there are catch and release restrictions on bull trout.

Berland River (Map 33, 38, 39)
A major tributary of the Athabasca River, the Berland itself has dozens of excellent tributaries. Anglers will find grayling and rainbow trout to 1 kg (2 lb), bull trout to 7 kg (14 lbs) as well as rocky mountain whitefish to 2 kg (4 lbs). Access to the upper reaches of the river is gained about 75 km (46 miles) north of Hinton on Highway 40, while a number of minor (and a couple major) backroads provide access to the lower parts of the river. The Big Berland Recreation Area is a popular spot for folks looking to access the trails leading along the upper stretch of this fine river.

Jackpine River (Map 31/F3–37/B7)
Warning! There is no easy way to get to the Jackpine River. It is a long hike in, along some very rough trails, either from Sulphur Gates, or an even longer hike/horseback in from across the BC border. You should also keep in mind that bull trout are catch and release only. For the persistent, there are some very credible rumours of bull trout up to 10 kg (22 lbs) being pulled out of this remote, pristine river.

Little Berland River (Map 34/A2–39/A3)
The Little Berland is a good rainbow trout stream and a pretty good grayling stream, with some bull trout and rocky mountain whitefish to boot. Easily accessed along Highway 40, about 10 km (6 miles) further south than the Berland River.

Muddywater River (Map 36/E7–37/C6)
By foot, the Muddywater is a good half-day hike (15.7 km/9.6 miles) from the nearest road. This has kept angling pressure on this Willmore stream light. But, if people knew about the 4.5 kg (10 lb) bull trout that are to be found here, it might be a better-known river. Then again, as bull trout are catch and release only, chances are the fish will be safe for a few more years.

Sheep Creek (Map 36/B4–37/G2)
If you want to catch fish, conventional wisdom dictates that your best bet is to hike farther upstream than anybody else. Which is true most everywhere but for some reason, the Sheep offers good fishing, even within sight of Highway 40. The fish here are not huge but they are plentiful and seem to like getting caught. The creek contains bull trout to 1 kg (2 lb) as well as rainbow trout, rocky mountain whitefish and grayling, all to about 0.5 kg (1 lb).

Smoky River (Map 32, 37, 38)
The Smoky is one of the big rivers in the region. While its headwaters are inside Jasper Park, the Smoky quickly crosses into—and drains most of—Willmore. It also drains most of west-central Alberta, until it flows into the Peace River, well outside the scope of our maps. Access to the upper reaches of the Smoky means a hike or horseback ride into the vehicle-free Willmore. While few are willing to go to the trouble, it can be a rewarding trip. The river contains pike to 5 kg (10 lbs) in lower reaches only, as well as bull trout to 5 kg (10 lbs), rocky mountain whitefish to 1.5 kg (3 lbs) and grayling and rainbow to 0.5 kg (1 lb).

Sulphur River (Map 33/B2–37/F4)
Although the Sulphur is a long river, most people do not fish much farther than ten or so kilometres upstream of its confluence with the Smoky. That is because the Sulphur is a Willmore River and, although outside the park, the

river is easily accessed from Grande Cache, to fish farther upstream involves a great deal of effort, either hiking or horse packing farther in. Needless to say the bull trout and rocky mountain whitefish in the lower reaches see a fair bit of fishing pressure, while the upper reaches see little action.

Wildhay River (Map 33/E2–35/B1)
The upper reaches of the Wildhay are easily accessible. Highway 40 crosses the Wildhay River 35 km (21 miles) north of Hinton and the Rock Lake Road follows the river for much of the way between the lake and the trunk road. Above Rock Lake, into Willmore, there is good trail access. Farther downstream, however, is more challenging to reach, along long, lonely and sometimes difficult backroads. There is some good fishing for rainbow and bull trout, rocky mountain whitefish and grayling, especially along the Rock Lake to the Forestry Trunk Road section. The Wildhay is catch and release only.

PADDLING
While some people have been known to haul boats upstream, most people don't paddle in Willmore. This is most likely due to the fact that the park has no roads.

TRAILS
With more than 750 km (458 miles) of hiking trails, some of which connect to the Jasper Trails, Willmore should be a major destination for hikers, bikers and horseback riders. However, it is not. Part of the trouble is access. There are no bridged river crossings, so expect to get your feet (legs, thighs…) wet. Care should be exercised at all river crossings. Another problem is the majority of trails that exist are heavily travelled by horses and can be muddy and unpleasant to hike or bike. Still, if you appreciate rugged beauty and solitude, it is worth the effort.

In addition, many of the trails follow old logging or exploration roads, as well as hunting trails that do not lead to scenic viewpoints. The true beauty of this park is found by getting off the main trails and up onto the many ridges. Old game trails, scree slopes or some sort of access usually leads to ridges that stretch on for miles and miles. A new group, the Willmore Wilderness Preservation and Historical Foundation, has been working to clear trail in the park. All the trail distances given in this section are one-way. But it should be noted that while a trail might only be 10 km (6 miles) long, you might have to hike for 30 or 40 kilometres (18 to 24 miles) along another trail to access it.

Adams Creek Trail (Map 38/F7–D6)
A 15 km (9.1 mile) section of trail between the Berland and Muskeg Rivers, the trail sees a lot of day hikers from Big Berland Area.

Adams Lookout Trail (Map 38/F7)
Leaving the Berland Trail at km 14.1 (mile 8.6), this trail climbs another 4.4 km (2.7 miles), gaining 765 metres (2,486 feet). The last couple of kilometres are along an open alpine ridge with great views.

Berland River Trail (Map 33/E2–39/A6)
It is a 32.8 km (20 mile) return trip from the trailhead outside of Willmore to the junction with the Adams Creek Trail. This is one of the main access points into Willmore that is used mostly by horseback riders, as there are several crossings of the cold, fast Berland River. Only the first 5.5 km (3.4 miles) of the trail is open to ATVs. Beyond Adams Creek, you can spend days, if not weeks, exploring the area.

Carson Creek Trail (Map 33/G2)
Although once heavily used, the 8 km long Carson Creek Trail has fallen out of favour. It begins 12 km from the Rock Lake Staging Area along Mountain Trail before climbing steadily up and over Minny Ridge Pass.

Casket Creek Trail (Map 36/C5)
A 10 km (6.1 mile) segment of trail in the far west reaches of the park. The trail passes a small lake at the BC/Alberta divide before continuing south along the divide. This rarely travelled trail is often used as an extension to the Sheep Creek Trail.

Collie Creek Trail (Map 34/D2)
This 30 km (18.3 mile) trail follows Collie Creek across the easternmost corner of Willmore. The trail hooks up with Evans Trail, Mumm Creek Trail and thousands of kilometres of other trails in Willmore, Jasper and even across the border into BC.

Eagles Nest Pass Trail (Map 33/F3)
From the 16.8 km (10.2 mile) mark of the Mountain Trail (see below), this trail continues on for another 17 km (10.3 miles), over the pass and to the old Mile 58 rangers cabin. The trail leads through some impressive alpine scenery and should take hikers at least three days to make it to the pass and back. The more adventurous might want to follow the old Rock Creek Trail back through Jasper, creating a 5 or so day loop.

Eaton Falls Trail (Map 37/E4)
One of the few destinations for day hiking from the Sulphur Gates Staging Area, this trail follows the Sheep Creek Trail for about 2 km (1.2 miles), and then veers right and up to Eaton Falls. The scenic falls are located a little over half a kilometre farther up the trail.

Famm/Trench Creek Trail (Map 36/G4–E2)
Linking the South Kakwa Trail with the Sheep Creek Trail, it is a long way from the nearest trailhead to the start of this trail. In fact, it is about 10 km from where the trail leaves the South Kakwa to the Willmore/Kakwa boundary and about double that to the nearest trailhead on the Willmore side of things.

Glacier Pass Trail (Map 33/B2–F5)
This 16 km (9.8 mile) trail links Willmore and Jasper National Park. Hikers use this trail (along with the West Sulphur Trail) as the Willmore section of a circumnavigation of the Ancient Wall. This area is one of the most spectacular areas in Willmore.

Indian Trail (Map 33/D1–F3)
A main artery for hunters, the 33 km (20.1 mile) Indian Trail is also popular with hikers, horseback riders and mountain bikers. The trail is in good condition and provides access to some of the most scenic areas of the park.

Jackknife Pass Trail (Map 33/C2)
This 9.5 km (5.8 mile) trail connects the North Berland River and Sulphur River via the Jackknife Pass. Although the trail is in good condition, it does not see much use.

Kvass Creek Trail (Map 37/C6–F7)
A difficult crossing of the Smoky River (at Clark's Crossing) means that this 14 km (8.6 mile) connector trail is rarely used. It links the popular Sheep Creek and Mountain Trail systems.

Monaghan Creek Trail (Map 33/A2)
A difficult 12 km (7.3 mile) slog from the Mountain Trail up and over the Monaghan Creek Pass, hooking up with the West Sulphur Trail. Although the trail cuts off a few kilometres, most people prefer to take the slightly longer but infinitely easier, West Sulphur Trail.

Morkill Pass Trail (Map 36/F7)
This old trail has recently been partially cleared and a new campsite has been established near Mount Forget. The area is stunning and, before the trail was cleared, rarely visited, making this, even more than the other trails and routes in Willmore, the perfect destination for those who like to go places few have ever been before.

Mountain Trail (Map 32–34, 37, 38)
At 95 km (58 miles), Mountain Trail is the longest trail in Willmore, running from Rock Lake to Grande Cache. It also provides access to more than a dozen other trails, including the Thoreau Creek Trail, Eagles Nest Pass Trail and the Indian Trail. The first part of this trail is also sometimes called the Wildhay River Trail, as it follows the Wildhay Valley. During high water, fording the Wildhay River at km 4.3 can be difficult and dangerous. The Mountain Trail then branches south along Eagle's Nest Creek to Rock Creek. Eventually the trail links up with the Sulphur River (and a few more river crossings) before venturing north to Cowlick Creek and the final stretch of trail leading to Grande Cache.

Mount Mawdsley Trail (Map 37/F5)
You will need a canoe to get across the Smoky River to the trailhead for this trip, which deters most visitors. The trailhead is across the Smoky River from the Sulphur Gates Staging Area. Because it is so infrequently traveled, the trail can be indistinct and the occasional cross trail can get you moving in the wrong direction. For the truly hardcore, this 22 km (12 hour; 14 mile) return trip is well worth the initial effort. A topographic map is a very good idea on this trip.

Mumm Creek Trail (Map 34/C3–B1)

The Mumm Creek Trail starts where Mumm Creek crosses the Rock Lake Road and heads northwest into Willmore. You will eventually meet Little Berland River, where the trail ventures northeast and follows the Little Berland to a junction with the Evans Trail on the boundary of Willmore. This is a moderate 30 km (18.3 miles) one-way trail. You can either return the way you came, hook up with the Willmore network of trails, head out via Evans Creek or return via the Collie Creek Trail.

Muskeg River Trail (Map 38/B7–C5)

The Muskeg River Trail provides access into the Willmore from the A La Peche Lake area, which is not as easy to get to as the other main access points into Willmore. You will have to cross First Nations lands to get to the trailhead. Although they do not mind you crossing, it is only common courtesy to ask first before heading out. The trail follows the Muskeg River for 32 km (19.5 miles), into the high country of Snow Creek and Rocky Pass.

North Berland Trail (Map 33/D1–38/D7)

This 10 km (6.1 mile) trail connects the Sunset Creek Trail with a bunch of other trails, including the Indian and Jackknife Pass Trails. The trail sees moderate usage.

Pope Thoreau Trail (Map 33/F2)

Linking the South Berland and Wildhay Rivers, this 14.5 km (9 mile) trail follows Thoreau Creek northwest to the Thoreau Creek Pass, then down along Pope Creek.

Ptarmigan Lake Trail (Map 31/G2)

Cleared in 2003, this old trapper's trail leads to Ptarmigan Lake. There are also some other historical trails in the area that may or may not be followed. The lake itself is set in a fairly thick forest, but the view down the lake towards the Draco Peak area is spectacular.

Rocky Pass Trail (Map 37/G7–33/B1)

The high alpine of Rocky Pass is certainly one of the scenic highlights of Willmore. This 10 km (6.1 mile) section of trail takes travellers up and over the pass and connects the Sulphur with the West Muskeg River.

Seep Creek Trail (Map 34/A3)

The Seep Creek trail is a short, heavily used trail near the Rock Lake Trailhead at the start of the Mountain Trail. The trail is only about 4 km (2.4 miles) long but it accesses some prime wildlife country. In the fall the trail sees a lot of traffic from hunters.

Sheep Creek Trail (Map 36/B4–37/E4)

A 65 km (39.7 mile) trail accessing the northwest reaches of Willmore. It is 15.7 km (9.6 miles) to the Muddywater River (Clarke's) Crossing, which is a good place for mountain bikers and hikers to turn around, especially early in the year, when this crossing is dangerously high. During wet weather, this trail is a nightmare for hikers and bikers, as the clay/dirt base of the first part of the trail can get extremely muddy. Also, because the hunting is better in the eastern area of the park, this trail gets little use past Clarke's Crossing. If you can manage the crossing, there are hundreds of kilometres of trails through Willmore, into British Columbia and north into the Kakwa Wildland.

South Kvass Trail (Map 32/E1–37/F7)

The South Kvass Trail is a seldom used, often hard to find 8 km (4.9 mile) trail accessing the north end of Hardscrabble Creek.

Sunset Creek Trail (Map 38/D7)

A difficult 16 km (9.8 mile) trail along Sunset Creek connects the West Muskeg River with the Berland River. The trail sees little use since it is tough to follow and cuts through an area flooded by beaver dams.

Walton Creek Trail (Map 38/B7)

The Walton Creek Trail is a 12 km (7.3 mile) linking trail between the Mountain Trail and the Muskeg River Trail.

West Sulphur Trail (Map 32/G3–33/B2)

The West Sulphur Trail extends 9 km (5.5 miles) from the Mountain Trail and into the high alpine of Azure Pass in Jasper National Park. This trail is often used by Jasper hikers circumnavigating the Ancient Wall and is arguably one of the most scenic trails in Willmore.

WINTER RECREATION

There are no developed recreation activities in Willmore in the winter and few people enter the area. However, there is nothing to stop enterprising and self-reliant travellers from making an extended trip into Willmore on skis or snowshoes. Usually the only people in the area in winter are trappers.

YohoAdventures

Takakkaw Falls: Found east of Field along the Yoho Valley Road, this is one of Canada's highest waterfalls at 254 metres (833 feet). The name means "magnificent" in Cree and this is indeed a good description of the area. July is the best time to see the falls.

ACTIVITIES

- ℹ️ Park information centre
- ★ Point of interest
- Warden office
- Boat launch
- Mountaineering
- Viewpoint
- Paddling
- Hiking
- Biking
- Cross-country skiing
- Ski area
- Campground
- Picnic area
- Horseback riding
- Fishing
- Swimming
- Cabin/Hut/Lodge
- Backcountry campsite

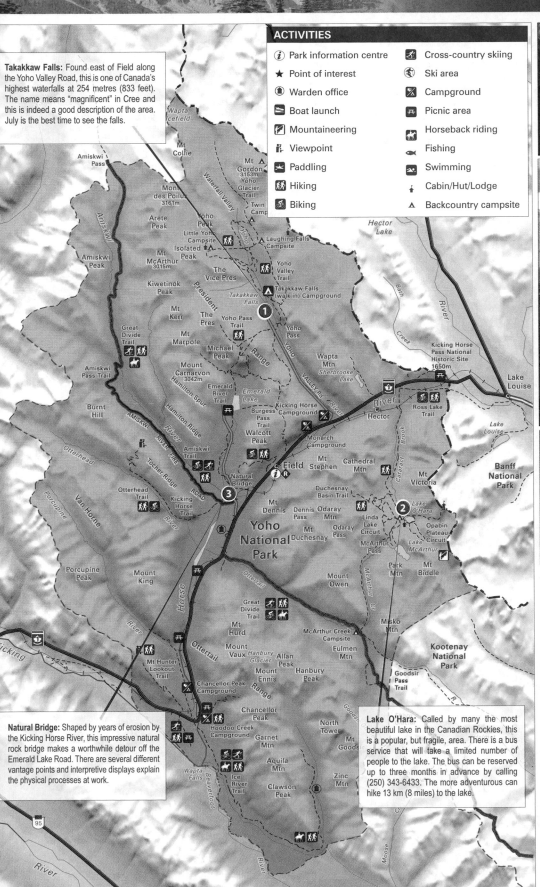

Natural Bridge: Shaped by years of erosion by the Kicking Horse River, this impressive natural rock bridge makes a worthwhile detour off the Emerald Lake Road. There are several different vantage points and interpretive displays explain the physical processes at work.

Lake O'Hara: Called by many the most beautiful lake in the Canadian Rockies, this is a popular, but fragile, area. There is a bus service that will take a limited number of people to the lake. The bus can be reserved up to three months in advance by calling (250) 343-6433. The more adventurous can hike 13 km (8 miles) to the lake.

THINGS TO KNOW

Area: 131,000 hectares
Highest Point: Mount Goodsir 3,562 metres (11,683 feet)
Total Vehicle Accessible Campsites: 259

THINGS TO SEE

1. Takakkaw Falls
2. Lake O'Hara
3. Natural Bridge

CONTACT INFORMATION

Parks Canada: yoho.info@pc.gc.ca, www.pc.gc.ca/yoho
Lake O'Hara Reservations: (250) 343-6433
Yoho Visitor Centre: (250) 343-6783
Emergency: 911
Avalanche Information: 1-800-667-1105, www.avalanche.ca

YohoAdventures

The word Yoho comes from the Cree language. Perhaps it's most appropriate translation is "wow." Okay, that might not be linguistically accurate, but it is apt. Unless you speak Cree, chances are you will be saying "wow" a lot as you explore this land of glaciated peak, thundering waterfalls, colourful alpine meadows and sparkling mountain streams.

At 1,310 sq km (507 sq miles) in area, Yoho is one of the smaller National Parks in the Rockies–only Mount Revelstoke is smaller–but it makes up for it's lack of size in sheer spectacle, with 28 peaks over 3,000 m (9,900 ft) high.

The park was established in 1886 years after James Hector, who was a member of the famed Palliser Expedition, first explored the area in 1858. The area became so well known for the fact that the route for the Canadian Pacific Railway was changed from Yellowhead Pass to the Kicking Horse Pass.

In 1883 William Van Horne, an American who was managing construction on the CP Railway, spoke to the Superintendent of Mines William Pearce about establishing a National Parks system. Pearce came west in 1884 and explored the area. It was from his suggestion that the Banff Hot Springs Reserve was created in 1885 and a year later the area that would become known as Yoho was also set aside. That same year the first train made its way across the continent. One of the most problematic sections of the railway was the Big Hill, east of the settlement of Field. In an effort to prevent wrecks, manned safety switches were built. If a train was out of control, the switch operator diverted the trail onto a runway track. This system remained in place until 1909, when the Spiral Tunnels were built.

In 1909 paleontologist Charles Walcott discovered a fossil bed that has come to be known as the Burgess Shale. The wonderfully preserved fossils in such numbers and varieties were unlike anything he'd ever seen before. In seven years, Walcott collected more than 65,000 specimens, many of which were unknown.

These days, the Burgess Shale is regarded as the finest site for Cambrian-age fossils. The shale was declared a UNESCO World Heritage Site in 1981 and because of its unique and sensitive paleontological nature access to the site is by guided hike only. Collecting of fossils and other objects or artifacts is prohibited. Contact the Yoho Visitor Centre for information on Burgess Shale guided hikes.

The tiny town of Field (population 300) is located in Yoho National Park. It was built to service the CP Railway and survives now as a tourist destination. There is a lodge, a number of bed and breakfasts, restaurants and gift stores in town.

Like all the Rocky Mountain National Parks, this park is governed by a strict set of rules to protect the natural environment. While these may sometimes seem restrictive and arbitrary, they are there for a reason. Parks Canada must try and balance the extremely heavy pressure put on it by humans with the need to conserve and protect the environment.

All groups entering the park are required to pay a fee (on top of any accommodation or camping fees) and are given a parks guide outlining the basic rules. Some of the most important rules include: it is unlawful to touch, feed, entice, disturb or otherwise harass any wild animal; it is illegal to remove any natural object, be it rock, flower, or historic artifact; and obey all closures. Also, permits and reservations are needed for most everything. We suggest you contact the visitor centres before heading out on your adventure.

CAMPING

Unlike other National Parks in the area, Yoho does not have any reservable campsites. That means that all campsites, whether they are walk-in or vehicle accessible, are available on a first-come, first-serve basis. These vehicle accessible campgrounds can open as early as mid-May and are open throughout the summer travel season:

Chancellor Peak Campground (Map 6/B3)
Located near the west boundary of the park beside the Kicking Horse River the campground has 62 sites. It is a rustic, but scenic campground with pit toilets and pump water along with a kitchen shelter. Be sure to visit the nearby Wapta Falls and hoodoos.

Hoodoo Creek Campground (Map 6/C4)
This site is found near the impressive hoodoos and the western entrance to the park. It has 30 sites, playground, kitchen shelters and a sani-dump and is open from early June to early September.

Kicking Horse Campground (Map 11/D7)
Kicking Horse Campground is located just east of Field, alongside the Kicking Horse River and the Yoho Valley Road. It is the biggest campground in Yoho with 88 sites. It features showers, an interpretive program and adventure playground as well as a sani-dump. It is open from mid May until early October.

Monarch Campground (Map 11/D7)
Not far from the Kicking Horse Campground, the Monarch Campground has 44 sites, including eight walk-in, tenting-only sites. It is the first campground to open (usually in early May) and is open until early September). There is a kitchen shelter, showers and sani-dump at the campground.

Takakkaw Falls Campground (Map 11/D6)
There are 35 walk-in tenting sites at this campground located at the end of Yoho Valley Road. Open from mid June until the end of September, the campground is located below the impressive falls. Picnic tables, kitchen shelter and toilets are provided.

BACKCOUNTRY CAMPING

There are six designated backcountry campsites providing bear storage areas, pit toilets and usually up to ten tent pads. No fires are allowed. Random camping in the **Amiskwi, Otterhead** and **Ice River Valleys** as well as the alpine, but be sure to check with the park wardens for certain restrictions. In order to camp in the backcountry, you require a wilderness pass, which can be picked up at the Parks Canada Visitor Centre in Field.

McArthur Creek Backcountry Campsite (Map 6/E3)
Located just below Goodsir Pass on the Ottertail Fire Road, there are ten sites at this backcountry campground. Hikers, bikers and horseback riders all share the trail.

Lake O'Hara Backcountry Campsite (Map 6/F1)
Only a lucky few will be able to spend the night at this beautiful 30 unit site with a kitchen shelter, firewood and chemical toilets. 25 sites can be reserved up to three months in advance. Five sites are set aside and can be reserved the day-before by calling the Lake O'Hara Reservations office at (250) 343-6433. It is open from June 19 to September 30 and can be used for a fee. It is about a 13 km (8 mile) hike in or a shuttle bus service can be reserved.

Laughing Falls Backcountry Campsite (Map 11/D6)
The easiest of all the backcountry campsites to get to, this eight unit tenting site is located along the Yoho River, near Laughing Falls. The falls tumble 30 metres (98 feet) and provide a soothing background noise for tired campers.

Little Yoho Backcountry Campsite (Map 11/C6)
Tucked up behind the President Mountain Range, the Little Yoho Valley is accessed off Iceline or Little Yoho Valley Trail. The ten unit campsite is found below the Kiwetinok Pass nearby to the Stanley Mitchell Hut (see below).

Twin Falls Backcountry Campsite (Map 11/C6)
Located near the headwaters of the Yoho River off the Yoho Valley Trail, the twin falls are quite the site as they fall in tandem off the high limestone cliffs. There are eight backcountry campsites and even a chalet here.

Yoho Lake Backcountry Campsite (Map 11/D7)
Tucked a short distance from the nearest road, Yoho Lake makes a nice overnight destination for area hikers. There are eight campsites here and a series of trails leading further afield.

BACKCOUNTRY HUTS & LODGES

The Alpine Club of Canada maintains several huts in the Yoho backcountry and bordering Banff National Park. Call (403) 678-3200 or visit www.alpineclubofcanada.ca for more information on location and cost. There is also a hostel near Takakkaw Falls as well as a couple lodges to base camp from.

Amiskwi Lodge (Map 11/A4)
Just outside the west boundary of the park, this two-storey lodge rests above Amiskwi Pass. It provides room for up to 16 self-guided people. Contact (403) 678-1800 or visit www.amiskwi.com for more information.

Elizabeth Parker Hut (Map 6/E1)
Found west of Lake O'Hara, this is a beautiful location and a great ski touring destination that sleeps 24. Allow up to 5 hours to reach it.

Lake O'Hara Lodge (Map 6/F1)
For those looking for more luxurious accommodation while exploring the Yoho backcountry, the Lake O'Hara Lodge provides rooms and meals. Reservations are highly recommended. Call (250) 343-6418 for more information.

Scott Duncan Hut (Map 11/E6)
Set below Mount Daily on the Wapta Icefield, this hut sleeps 12. Visitors require glacier travel experience and should allow about 7 hours to reach the hut from the Balfour Hut in Banff.

Stanley Mitchell Hut (Map 11/C6)
Known for its great views and even better skiing, the Little Yoho Valley is a popular destination during summer and winter. The hut sleeps 22 in winter and requires a long day to reach it.

Twin Falls Chalet (Map 11/D6)
In the Yoho Valley, this historic backcountry cabin offers rustic rooms and meals from July to early September. The beautiful log cabin does not have electicity or running water.

Fishing

Despite its smaller size, Yoho National Park provides a surprising number of fishing locations. It is not too hard to find a stretch of water to call you own and soak in the dramatic scenery and hopefully catch a fish or two. The high elevation of the area allows for good fishing throughout the summer months.

National Parks water bodies are governed under their own regulations and you will need a special license to fish. Check with Parks Canada for more information. Regulations can be downloaded from www.parkscanada.gc.ca.

Amiskwi River (Map 11/A5–6/C1)
Accessed by an old road (now open to hiking and biking) and a trail (hiking only), the further you are willing to travel, the less fishing pressure the better pools receive. This river is best fished late in the season after the muddy waters have subsided. Small brook trout and bull trout (average 15–25 cm/8–10 inches) are common but the occasional bull trout will reach 2 kg (4 lbs). Try bait or flies.

Beaverfoot River (Map 6/C5)
The Beaverfoot is a generally lethargic river that winds its way northwest and into the Kicking Horse River. The river holds fair numbers of bull trout, cutthroat and rainbow. Try using a lure, bait or fly. The river forms part of the southwest border of Yoho National Park and has good road access, although the better pools will require some bushwhacking to reach.

Emerald Lake (Map 11/C7)
Found at the end of the paved Emerald Lake Road, this is a very popular tourist destination. There is some fair fishing for rainbow, brook and bull trout (average 25-35 cm/10–14 inches) using a fly, lure or bait. Cast near shore where the fish tend to congregate to avoid the silty, glacier-fed deeper waters.

Emerald River (Map 6/C1–11/C7)
Small brook trout and rainbow to 30 cm (12 inches) can be readily caught with bait or flies. The occasional bull trout is also found in the river, which is best accessed along the Emerald River Trail.

Hidden Lake (Map 11/D6)
Accessed after a short hike from the Yoho Valley Road, this lake has modest numbers of rainbow and brook trout taken on a fly or by spincasting. Camping is available at the lake. No permit is required to fish this lake.

Ice River (Map 6/D5)
This small river is located in the southern portion of Yoho National Park. It contains fair numbers of cutthroat, bull trout and whitefish that are easily caught on a fly or by spincasting. Most of the river will require bushwhacking to reach.

Kicking Horse River (Map 6/A3–11/E7)
This fast flowing river skirts the Trans-Canada Highway (Highway 1) as it winds around the dramatic Rocky Mountains from Yoho National Park to Golden. Due to silty waters, the river offers fair to poor fishing for small brook trout that average 20–30 cm (8–10 inches). However, the odd bull trout to 60 cm (24 inches) can be caught. The section in Yoho requires a national park permit and fishing license to fish it.

Lake Dushesnay (Map 11/C6)
From the Takakkaw Falls Campsite a trail leads to the lake where good fishing for brook trout to 1 kg (2 lbs) exists.

Lake O'Hara (Map 6/F1)
Forming the hub of the park, this gorgeous lake is accessed by trail or private bus. The lake holds fair numbers of small cutthroat in the 20–25 cm (8–10 inch) range caught with a fly or lure. Fishing from shore is your best bet as the fish stay close to shore due to the silty, glacier-fed water. There is a lodge and camping facilities at the lake.

Linda Lake (Map 6/E1)
This clear water lake produces numerous cutthroat in the 20–30 cm (8–12 inch) range. Shore fishing is a possibility with spincasting and fly-fishing proving effective. The lake is accessed by trail off the Lake O'Hara Fire Road.

Marpole Lake (Map 11/C5)
From the Takakkaw Falls Campsite, a 9 km (5.5 mile) return hike brings you to this sub-alpine lake. It contains good numbers of small cutthroat and brook trout. A shelter and camping is available near the lake.

Nara Lakes (Map 6/E1)
Found on the Cataract Brook Trail past Wapta Lake, you will need about an hour to walk to the lakes. Fishing is often good for small rainbow and brook trout.

Otterhead River (Map 6/B2-10/G7)
This small river is found off a fire access road to the west of the Trans-Canada Highway. The river has a fair number of small bull trout, whitefish and brook trout that average 15–25 cm (6–10 inches). Anglers use flies or bait.

Ottertail River (Map 6/C2–F3)
Found across the highway from the Otterhead River, the Ottertail also offers a fair number of small brook trout, bull trout and whitefish to 30 cm (12 inches). Fishing is better in the lower reaches, which can be reached along the fire road.

Ross Lake (Map 11/F7)
Accessed by a short 1.5 km (0.9 mile) hike off Highway 1A, there are a fair number of small rainbow and brook trout (average 20-30 cm) in the lake.

Try fly-fishing or spincasting.

Sherbrooke Lake (Map 11/E7)
A 3 km trail leads from the Wapta Lake Lodge to the lake. There are fair numbers of rainbow and lake trout to 1 kg (2 lbs) that average 20–35 cm (8–14 inches), but the silty, glacier-fed water makes fishing tough. The use of bait or a streamer fly is recommended.

Wapta Lake (Map 11/E7)
Found next to the Trans Canada Highway, you can catch the odd rainbow or brook trout to 1 kg (2.5 lbs) here. A few lucky anglers are rewarded with a large lake trout on occasion.

Yoho Lake (Map 11/D6)
Named after the park, it is surprising to see how tiny this lake really is. It also requires a fairly difficult 4.5 km (2.7 mile) along a fairly steep trail to reach it. Anglers will find generally small rainbow, cutthroat and brook trout.

Paddling

Paddling is not one of the main focuses of the park, but there are a couple beautiful, but definitely different places to dip a paddle.

Emerald Lake (Map 11/C7)
Located in the heart of Yoho National Park, Emerald Lake lives up to its name. Soaring peaks surround this turquoise-coloured lake, and on a clear blue summer day, it is an amazing place to paddle.

Yoho River Paddling Route (Map 11/D7)
The Yoho is not a river to be taken lightly. At low water levels it is rated a Grade IV+, with some features up to a Class V. At high water levels it is even tougher. But, for expert kayakers, this is one of those epic runs that you will talk about for the rest of your life. Give yourself up to four hours to run the 7.8 km (4.8 mile) section from the Takakkaw Falls Campground to the take-out, which is 3.8 km (2.3 miles) above the bridge on the Takakkaw Falls Road. Advance scouting is essential.

TRAILS

There are over 400 km (240 miles) of hiking trails in the park ranging from easy valley walks to rugged treks into the alpine. The hiking season on the lower elevation hikes begins in May and ends in early October. Hikes into the sub-alpine are not accessible until mid-June at the earliest and can be used until mid-September. Mountaineering opportunities are endless but mountain biking is limited to designated fire roads and certain portions of a few trails. During winter, backcountry skiers and snowshoers can access most of the trails. As with all national parks, Grizzly bears are a concern.

The most popular destination is the Lake O'Hara area. There are 34 listed trails in the Lake O'Hara area, from easy hikes along trails like the Alpine Meadow or Mary Lake Trails, to steep routes that should only be attempted by experienced backcountry travellers. The lodge and campground are usually booked well in advance. If you want to visit, booking ahead of time (up to three months in advance) is recommended.

Abbot Pass Route (Map 6/F1)
From the Lake O'Hara Lodge, this 6.6 km (4.1 mile) route heads up to Abbot Pass and the Abbot Pass Hut in Banff. This is a difficult route, mostly used by mountain climbers, that heads up a steep scree slope. The trail begins along the Lake Oesa Trail, before climbing steeply up the slopes of Mount Huber. There are some sections that are prone to falling rock (both from above and from the scree slipping out from beneath your feet) and caution needs to be exercised.

All Soul's Route (Map 6/F1)
From the Lake O'Hara Lodge, this difficult 2.9 km (1.8 mile) trail climbs 440 m (1,450 ft) to a prominent lookout near Schäffer Lake. There are steep sections with loose rocks and care must be taken as you make your way up.

Alpine Circuit (Map 6/F1)
This difficult, 11.8 km (7.2 mile) 4.5 hour trail is one of the more popular routes, but also one of the most difficult in the Lake O'Hara area. The trail is reached by passing the Lake O'Hara Warden Cabin and walking 150 m (488 ft) along the lakeshore to the outlet bridge. From here, it quickly ascends up Wiwaxy Gap to run along some exposed and narrow ledges overlooking Lake O'Hara and the surrounding mountains. The trail then descends to join up with the Opabin Plateau Trail and then the All Soul's Alpine Route.

Amiskwi River Fire Road (Map 6/C1–11/A7)
This gravel road proceeds 24 km (14.6 mile) one-way to the Amiskwi III Campsite gaining 520 m (3,172 ft) to 1,675 m (5,495 ft) in elevation. Given the distance, it is more common to bike up the road, which usually takes up to 5 hours as you pass by remnants of logging and an old mill site. From the campsite, the Amiskwi Pass Trail climbs 305 m (991 ft) past the Amiskwi Falls to the remote pass at 1,980 m (6,435 ft) in elevation. It is possible to descend from Amiskwi Pass into the Blaeberry River Valley on a flagged trail, which begins on the east slope of the valley. This trail leads past the Greens Lodge (for use of the lodge call 250-343-6397) before reaching Branch 27 off the Blaeberry Forest Road. Mountain biking is not allowed north of the Amiskwi III Campground. In the winter, backcountry skiers use the trail.

Big Larches Trail (Map 6/F1)
This trail is only 2.1 km (1.3 miles) long, gaining 160 m (525 ft) in elevation from the Lake O'Hara Lodge to Schäffer Lake. The trail is slightly more difficult than the Alpine Meadows Trail (which also leads to Schäffer Lake), but offers better views.

Burgess Highland Trail (Map 11/D7)
Beginning at the Emerald Lake parking area, the route initially starts along the Emerald Lake Nature Trail before beginning a steady climb to Yoho Pass at 1,840 m (5,980 ft). To reach the pass involves a 7 km (4.3 mile) 3 hour hike gaining 530 m (1,723 ft) in elevation. From the Yoho Pass, a trail heads south some 6.5 km (4 miles) 2–3 hours to Burgess Pass at 2,200 m (7,150 ft). Then, the trail heads downhill to Emerald Lake and the start. In total, the hike is 21 km (12.8 miles) and is an excellent choice if you want a day hike around the alpine with great views of the Emerald Lake Valley.

Cataract Brook Trail (Map 11/F7–6/F1)
The preferred walking route into the Lake O'Hara area, this trail is 13 km (7.9 mile) long and takes about 3 to 4 hours. The trail climbs 410 m (1,333 ft) from the O'Hara parking lot off the Trans Canada Highway to the Hector Gorge. Along the way it crosses several creeks and swampy meadows before reaching the Lake O'Hara Campground.

Centennial Trail (Map 11/D7)
From the Kicking Horse Campground, this short 2.5 km (1.5 mile) hike begins at the bridge on Yoho Valley Road. There is little elevation gain and the trail offers views of old mine portals on the cliffs above. Mountain goats also grace the cliffs.

Duchesnay Basin Trail (Map 6/E1)
This 3.2 km (1.9 mile) trail begins at the west end of Linda Lake and climbs 230 m (784 ft). En route you pass by the Cathedral Lakes, beneath Odaray Mountain and through a wet meadow to hook up with the Cathedral Basin Alpine Route.

East Opabin Trail (Map 6/E1)
This 3 km (1.8 mile) trail takes hikers up to the Opabin Plateau. It follows the shores of Lake O'Hara before climbing through a forest to the plateau. This section of the trail is considered by many to be a bit dull, but it is the easiest route up onto the very scenic plateau, gaining 280 m (920 ft) to Opabin Lake. You can return via a number of routes, including the West Opabin Trail, or take the Yukness Ledge Route to Lake Oesa.

Emerald Basin (Map 11/C7)
From the Emerald Lake parking lot, the trail brings you along the western shores of the lake. At about 1.6 km (1 mile), you will reach a junction at the north end of the lake. Take the left branch of the trail, which brings you to a short, steep hike to a natural amphitheatre of hanging glaciers and avalanche chutes. Overall, the hike is 8.6 km (5.2 miles) 3–4 hours return gaining 275 m (894 ft) in elevation.

Emerald Lake Circuit Trail (Map 11/C7)
This easy, relatively flat walking trail follows the shoreline of Emerald Lake for 4.8 km (3 miles) 1.5–2 hours. It is a very scenic route with lots of vegetation and a great view of Mount Burgess and the lodge area. In the winter, cross-country skiers use the trail.

Emerald River Trail (Map 6/C1–11/C7)
The best way to hike this trail is to use a two-car shuttle system, one parked at Emerald Lake and one at the Amiskwi Picnic Area. The 7.5 km (4.6 mile) 2–3 hours hike starts at the lake and cuts through the dense forest next to the Emerald River as it drops 140 m (455 ft) to the access road 200 m (650 ft) east of the picnic area.

Emerald Triangle (Map 11/C7)
This is a 19.7 km (12.2 mile) route that strings together the Yoho Pass Trail, the Wapta Highline Trail and the Burgess Pass Trail into a nice day-hike from the campground at Yoho Lake. You will gain 880 m (2,887 ft) so it should be considered challenging.

Field to Burgess Pass (Map 6/D1–11/D7)
This trail climbs steeply up to Burgess Pass from the townsite of Field. You will climb 930 m (3050 ft) in 6.5 km (4 miles). It's a difficult, dry trail that leads to a spectacular area. There are easier trails to Burgess Pass, which start higher. A friendlier route would be to get dropped off at Takkakaw Falls or Emerald Lake and hike down to Field via Burgess Pass, spending the night at Yoho Lake.

Great Divide/Ross Lake Trail (Map 11/F7)
Want to sample a piece of one of the most challenging long distance trails in the country? This part of the route starts about 3 km (1.8 miles) west of the Great Divide between BC and Alberta and is an easy, level jaunt to the divide itself. It follows the old road from the Lake O'Hara parking lot through Kicking Horse Pass and is open to mountain bikes. Beyond Ross Lake, a small lake highlighted by a towering cliff face, the trail continues into Banff National Park, a distance of 10.5 km (6.4 miles).

Hamilton Falls & Lake Trail (Map 11/C7)
This easy 1.5 km (0.9 mile) return walk starts from the Emerald Lake parking area and leads to a spectacular falls eroding into a bedrock fault. The hike requires a 50 m (163 ft) elevation gain. For the more adventurous, try the 11 km (6.7 mile) 4 hour hike past the falls to Hamilton Lake. This hike involves a climb of 850 m (2,763 ft) along a steep, forested trail. It is best tried after mid-July due to snow accumulations on the trail and ice on the lake at 2,149 m (6,984 ft) in elevation.

Hoodoos Trail (Map 6/C4)
From the southwest end of the park, a 3 km (1.8 mile) 1.5-hour hike climbs a steep trail along Hoodoo Creek to several viewpoints of the Hoodoos. These Hoodoos are the most spectacular in all the national parks.

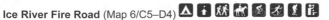

Ice River Fire Road (Map 6/C5–D4)
From the gate at the Hoodoo Trail parking lot, an old fire road leads along the eastern side of the Beaverfoot River to the Lower Ice River Warden Cabin. It is a gentle 19 km (11.6 mile) 4– 5 hour one-way trek through a forested valley that is shared with mountain bikers as well as cross-country skiers and snowshoers in winter. Beyond the warden cabin, the trail crosses the Ice River, leading up the east side of the valley to the Upper Ice River Warden Cabin about 6.5 km (4 miles) 2–3 hours further along. This section is best left to hikers and experienced backcountry skiers since most of the 375 m (1,219 ft) elevation gain occurs after crossing the river.

Iceline Trail (Map 11/C6)
From the Whiskey Jack Hostel on Yoho Valley Road, follow the Yoho Pass Trail as it switchbacks through a large avalanche path to a sub-alpine forest. After passing the Hidden Lakes Trail heading off to the left, you will come to the Iceline Trail, which leads to the right. Hikers can either descend into the Little Yoho Valley for a 22 km (13.4 mile) return circuit or connect to the Lake Celeste Trail for an 18 km (11 mile) circuit. Either way, you can expect to gain about 695 m (2,280 ft) along a very scenic route.

Kicking Horse Trail (Map 6/B2)
From the Natural Bridge it is possible to access the Otterhead River along the Kicking Horse River. This easy 4.5 km (2.7 mile) trail follows the Kicking Horse River, leaving the Amiskwi Trail 1.8 km (1.1 miles) from the trailhead. If you add in the Tally Ho Trail (below), it is a 13 km (7.9 miles) return trip from the Visitor Centre in Field. The trail is open to mountain bikers and is a popular ski route in winter.

Lake McArthur Trail (Map 6/F2)
Accessed from the warden cabin on the Lake O'Hara Road, Lake McArthur is a favourite destination for artists and photographers. It is a beautiful lake surrounded by alpine meadows and a hanging glacier. It is a 7 km (4.3 mile) return climb that takes four hours to complete while climbing 310 m (1,008 ft) in elevation. Since the lake often remains frozen until mid-July, this trip is best taken during the late summer.

Lake O'Hara Fire Road (Map 11/F1–6/F1)
This 11 km (6.6 mile) road climbs 400 m (1312 ft) as it makes its way to Lake O'Hara. The hike isn't that interesting, along the road to Lake O'Hara Lodge (which is also used by the Lake O'Hara bus), but takes visitors to what many people claim is the nicest lake in the entire Rockies. It is the most direct route, but most hikers favour the Cataract Brook Trail.

Lake O'Hara Shoreline Trail (Map 6/F1)
This easy 2.8 km (1.7 mile) trail starts at the O'Hara Warden Cabin and is considered by many to be the nicest trail in the area. It is also a busy trail that makes its way along this superbly beautiful lake.

Lake Oesa Trail (Map 6/F1)
A popular 3.6 km (2.2 mile) 1.5 hour one-way hike, starts at the north end of Lake O'Hara. Follow the lake shoreline about 0.8 km (0.5 miles) to a noticeable fork. Take the left branch and you will begin a steady climb gaining 250 m (813 ft) to the beautiful turquoise-coloured lake at 2,275 m (7,465 ft). From the northern shores of Lake Oesa, you can scramble uphill to Abbott Pass and the Great Divide. The tough, steep climb leads to the windswept pass that is home to a cabin used by mountaineers (for reservations, phone the Alpine Club of Canada at 403-678-3200).

Linda Lake/Cathedral Lake Trail (Map 6/E1)
This trail begins 2.9 km (1.8 miles) south of the Lake O'Hara Campground off of the fire road. The trail crosses the Morning Glory Creek bridge before reaching Linda Lake for a total distance of 1.8 km (1.1 miles) one-way gaining 85 m (280 ft). The tree-lined lake is set below some spectacular peaks of the Great Divide. The trail continues along the north shore of the lake before ascending through a sub-alpine forest and open meadows to Cathedral Lake. This 1 km (0.6 mile) one-way extension gains 225 m (731 ft) and is little more than a scramble up a rocky slope. Allow 3-4 hours to access Cathedral Lake from Lake O'Hara.

Little Yoho Valley Trail (Map 11/C6)
The trailhead to the Little Yoho Valley is found at Laughing Falls on the Yoho Valley Trail, about 4.3 km (2.6 miles) from the Takakkaw Falls parking lot. The trail climbs steadily up the north side of the Little Yoho River to an inviting alpine meadow, which contains the Stanley Mitchell Cabin and the Little

Yoho Campground. The total distance is 10 km (6.1 miles) 4 hours one-way from Takakkaw Falls, with an elevation gain of 520 m (1,690 ft). Backcountry skiers use the trail in winter. Once at the camp, it is possible to take the 2.5 km (1.5 mile) 1.5 hour one-way hike to Kiwetinok Pass, at 2,450 m (7,963 ft) in elevation. This very steep, hard to follow trail brings you to a rocky windswept pass with a small lake.

McArthur Creek Trail (Map 6/E1)
From the Lake O'Hara Warden Cabin, this trail ascends McArthur Pass at 2,200 m (7,150 ft) gaining 165 m (536 ft). Enjoy the view before you begin a steady, 750 m (2,438 ft) descent along McArthur Creek to Ottertail River. This hike is 12.5 m (7.6 miles) 4–5 hours one-way.

Mount Hunter Lookout Trail (Map 6/B3)
From the Trans-Canada Highway at the Wapta Falls turnoff, this trail climbs steadily upwards to the old fire lookout at 1,530 m (4,973 ft). The elevation gain is 400 m (1,300 ft) over the 7 km (4.3 mile) 3.5 hour return trip. You can continue on to the Upper Lookout at 1,965 m (6,386 ft), which is another 6 km (3.7 miles) return. Both lookouts provide excellent views of the Kicking Horse and Beaverfoot Valleys and are used by backcountry skiers in the winter.

Odaray Prospect Trail (Map 6/E1)
Beginning at the Lake O'Hara Warden Cabin, this trail first brings you to Alpine Meadows before heading off to the right at the Alpine Club cabin. From there, climb to one of the best vistas in the Lake O'Hara area where you get a great view of Upper Morning Glory Lake and the Great Divide. The trail is 2.5 km (1.5 miles) 1.5 hours one-way gaining 250 m (813 ft) to the Prospect, at 2,285 m (7,426 ft). From the Prospect, it is possible to access McArthur Pass, Odaray Plateau and Odaray Grandview Prospect. Please limit use of the meadows as this is a fragile wildlife area.

Opabin Pass Route (Map 6/F1)
This high mountain pass route offers access to Opabin Glacier, located between Mount Biddle and Mount Hungabee. The route is partially covered in moraine (the loose, twisty rock and gravel left behind by glaciers). To get to the top of the pass, you will need to travel on the glacier, which shouldn't be attempted without proper equipment.

Opabin Plateau Trail (Map 6/F1)
From the Lake O'Hara Lodge, follow the southwest lakeshore for a few hundred metres. From here, a trail climbs the west side of the plateau to Opabin Lake, gaining 250 m (813 ft) along the way. The trail then loops downhill along the east side of the plateau making it a 6.5 km (4 mile) 4 hour return trip. This is one of the most scenic hikes in the Lake O'Hara area with snow-capped mountain ridges surrounding the alpine valley.

Otterhead Trail (Map 6/B1)
This 9.8 km trail follows the Otterhead River for most of its length, before climbing steeply up to an old fire lookout on Tocher Ridge. You will gain 1,130 m (3,700 ft). The views from the ridge are expansive, but not as immediate as elsewhere in the park, as the ridge is slightly removed from the rest of the peaks. You can bike much of the way, which will cut down on access time.

Ottertail Fire Road (Map 6/C2–G4)
From the Trans-Canada Highway, this old fire road gradually ascends the Ottertail River Valley ending at the McArthur Creek Warden Cabin. The route is about 15 km (9.2 miles) one-way with an elevation gain of 300 m (975 ft) and can be hiked or biked in the summer or skied in the winter. From the end of the road, the trail runs south, crossing the Ottertail River and reaching a fork in the trail about one kilometre later. The left fork leads to Ottertail Falls and peters out (strong route finders can continue on to Ottertail Pass). The right branch leads to Goodsir Pass and other destinations within Kootenay National Park. At McArthur Creek, the view of the Goodsir Towers dominates the scene.

Paget Lookout Trail (Map 11/E7)
This trail gains 520 m (1,706 ft) as it makes its way to the site of an old fire lookout. The trail is 7 km (4.2 miles) return.

Point Lace Falls and Angel's Staircase (Map 11/D6)
This easy 4.4 km (2.6 mile) return trail starts at the Takakkaw Falls Campground. The trail leads slightly upward as it makes its way to these falls.

Sherbrooke Lake Trail (Map 11/E7)

This is a 6.2 km (3.9 mile) trail that starts at the Wapta Lake picnic shelter behind the West Louise Lodge. The intermediate trail climbs steadily for 2 km (1.2 miles), levelling off before reaching the lake at kilometre 3.1 (mile 1.9). The lake sits in a narrow valley surrounded by steep avalanche slopes that may be a concern to skiers in winter. You will gain 165 m (541 ft) in total.

Tally-Ho Trail (Map 6/C1)

This trail is a designated mountain biking route that is used by skiers in the winter. It extends 3 km (1.8 miles) one-way connecting the Trans Canada Highway with Emerald Lake Road and a variety of trails in the area. The trail makes for an easy ride with an elevation gain of 35 m (114 ft).

Walk-in-the-Past Trail (Map 11/E7)

Not really a hike but rather a point of interest. It begins from the Kicking Horse Campground and crosses the Yoho Valley Road to the remains of an old narrow gauge locomotive that was used to build the Spiral Tunnels.

Wapta Falls Trails (Map 6/B4)

From the end of the Falls Access Road, a 2 km (1.2 mile) gravel road, it is a 5 km (3 mile) return forested walk along the flat, easy trail to the spectacular 30 m (90 foot) high falls on the Kicking Horse River. The best view is from below the falls.

Wapta Highline Trail (Map 11/D7)

The Wapta Highline Trail is a long, scenic route through Burgess Pass. Depending on your plans, you can stitch together a number of trails to create a long day or multi-day hike. The trail itself starts at Yoho Lake, which you can get to from Emerald Lake (scenic) or Takkakaw Falls (shorter). The Wapta Highline itself is 6.3 km (3.9 miles) long, with an elevation gain of 425 m (1,400 ft). The trail passes the Burgess Shale (no visits without a guide) and through the spectacular pass. If you started from Emerald Lake, you may wish to return via the Burgess Pass Trail, or continue on to the townsite of Field.

West Opabin Trail (Map 6/F1)

While this trail is a steeper climb to the Opabin Plateau than the Big Larches Trail, it is also more scenic. The trail passes by Mary Lake and then climbs up to Opabin Lake. There is a side trail to Opabin Prospect found at the 1.8 km (1 mile) mark. You can hook up with the All Soul's Route to Schäffer Lake, or return to Lake O'Hara via a number of alternate routes, including the East Opabin Trail.

Whaleback Trail (Map 11/C6)

Linking the Yoho Valley Trail and the Iceline Trail is a moderate 20 km (12.2 mile) trail known as the Whaleback Trail. As the name implies, it climbs up and down a scenic ridge above the Yoho River. Most travellers start the circuit from the Takakkaw Falls Campsite and return on the Iceline Trail, which drops down to the Whiskey Jack Hostel. It is a short jaunt up the road to get back to the start.

Wiwaxy Gap/Huber Ledges Route (Map 6/F1)

From the Lake O'Hara Lodge, this route climbs steeply up to the Wiwaxy Gap. This is easily the steepest trail in the area, climbing 500 m (1,650 ft) in 2.4 km (1.5 miles). The route is not as dangerous as the nearby Abbot Pass Route (see above), but has some exposed sections that some might find too much. This is a pretty area and is home to a large population of mountain goats. While it is possible to climb down the same way you came up, it is much more interesting to descend via Lake Oesa, which will add 5.3 km (3.4 miles) to your trip.

Yoho Lake & Pass Trail (Map 11/D7)

This trail is found on the west side of the Whiskey Jack Hostel parking lot at the end of the Yoho Valley Road. The trail leads steadily uphill through an avalanche chute before reaching a sub-alpine forest. At about 1 km (0.6 miles), a side branch leads to the Hidden Lakes. After passing the Iceline Trail junction, the trail levels off as you reach Yoho Lake. Continue along the southern lakeshore and through an alpine meadow to Yoho Pass where you will find a trail junction, the left branch being the Burgess Highline Trail and the right branch being the Yoho Pass Trail. The hike to Yoho Lake is 3.5 km (2.1 miles) 1.5 hours one-way whereas the hike to Yoho Pass is 4.5 km (2.7 miles) 2.5 hours one-way. The elevation gain is 310 m (1,008 ft) to the pass. Beyond Yoho Pass, you have the opportunity to descend to Emerald Lake via the Yoho Pass Trail or to the town of Field via the Burgess Highline Trail.

Yoho Valley Trail (Map 11/D6)

Beginning at the Takakkaw Falls Campsite off Yoho Valley Road, this trail leads along Yoho River to Twin Falls. The 3 hour hike is 8 km (4.9 miles) one-way gaining 300 m (975 ft) in elevation. The trail passes a number of smaller waterfalls before eventually reaching the spectacular Twin Falls, where you will find a chalet at 1,800 m (5,850 ft) in elevation. The trail is the most popular one in the Yoho Valley area as it is fairly flat and easy throughout most of its length. For the more adventurous, you can make a circuit back to Takakkaw Falls along the Whaleback Trail, which is a total of 20 km (12.2 miles) in distance.

Yukness Ledges Route (Map 6/F1)

This easy (though sometimes treacherous) route links Lake Oesa and the Opabin Plateau. There is only about 60 m of elevation gain along the 2.4 km (1.5 mile) route. The danger comes from the ledges, which are fairly precipitous and can be downright deadly on a wet day. There is an unmarked, hard to find, side trail to Sleeping Poet Pool. Closer to Obapin Lake, an unmarked route heads up to the Yukness Column.

WINTER RECREATION

Yoho is a great place for cross-country and backcountry skiers alike. The trails are ungroomed, but the easy and moderate trails are usually quickly tracked, making them easy to follow. Some trails cross avalanche paths and anyone skiing a moderate or difficult trail should have backcountry skiing experience. Yoho is also home to a number of classic winter ski traverses (like the Bow-Yoho Traverse and the Wapta Traverse), but these are best left to experienced mountaineers. Many of the trails that are hiked in summer can be skied in winter, so we only listed the trails that are unique to winter travel below.

Amiskwi Trail to Amiskwi Pass (Map 6/C1–11/A5)

The long, difficult trail starts at the Natural Bridge and follows part of an old First Nations trade route, which traversed Amiskwi Pass. After crossing the bridge over the Amiskwi River, turn north along the Amiskwi Trail for a daunting 35.5 km (21.7 miles). A large burnt area at Fire Creek provides views in an otherwise heavily forested valley. However, the open slopes of Amiskwi Pass offer terrific views of the Mummery Icefield in the Blaeberry Valley. Backcountry camping is permitted in the Amiskwi Valley if you obtain a wilderness pass. The trip is 75.8 km (46.2 miles) return.

Chancellor Peak Road (Map 6/B3)

From the Trans-Canada Highway, the summer access road to Chancellor Peak Campground parallels the Kicking Horse River and offers easy skiing and great views of the Ottertail and Beaverfoot ranges. The trail is 4 km (2.4 miles) return and is an excellent place to see a variety of animal tracks.

Emerald Lake Connector Trail (Map 6/D1–11/C7)

Start at the Field Visitor Centre and follow the trail along the Kicking Horse River then cross the Trans-Canada Highway and ski up the Tally Ho Trail to the junction for the Natural Bridge or Emerald Lake. The right hand fork continues on to the Emerald Lake Road and then parallels the road through rolling terrain that provides skiers with opportunities to work on technique. After crossing the bottom of an avalanche slope, the trail drops down to follow the Emerald River, with many lovely views and brings you directly to Emerald Lake. You can stop for rest or refreshments, or continue on a variety of trails at the lake, including the popular circuit trail around the lake. This is a 22 km (13.4 mile) return, intermediate route.

Great Divide Trail (Map 11/F7)

From the Lake O'Hara parking lot, just east of Wapta Lake, ski along the road to the picnic shelter and interpretive display. This is an easy 11 km (6.7 mile) return trip. For other options, continue east along the road to Lake Louise in Banff National Park (7.5 km/4.6 miles one-way), or take a side trip to Ross Lake.

Ice River Trail (Map 6/C3–D5)

From Hoodoo Creek Campground follow the road south for 1 km (0.6 miles) to the gate at the beginning of the Ice River Trail. The trail is a former fire road, which ascends gradually over slightly rolling terrain, with some moderately steep hills, to the Lower Ice River Warden Cabin. It is 37 km (22.3 miles) return through a beautiful valley.

Yoho Adventures

Kicking Horse Trail (Map 6/B2)
From the Natural Bridge it is possible to access the Otterhead River along the Kicking Horse River. Ski 2.4 km (1.5 miles) along the road down a gradual hill, past the Emerald River to the Amiskwi River Bridge. Cross the bridge and continue left along the fire road for 4.1 km (2.5 miles) to the Otterhead River. If you add in the Tally Ho Trail (below), it is a 13 km (7.9 miles) return trip from the Visitor Centre in Field.

Lake O'Hara Fire Road (Map 11/F7–6/F1)
From the Lake O'Hara parking lot, just east of Wapta Lake, the trail climbs moderately to the shores of Lake O'Hara. The trail crosses several avalanche paths and is 23.4 km (14.3 miles) return to the lake. At the 10 km (6 mile) mark strong skiers can take the trail to Linda Lake. It is 2 km (1.2 miles) one-way to the lake or 5 km (3 miles) one-way to Duchesnay Basin. Once at Lake O'Hara, there are many great routes to sample. The day-use only cabin, Le Relais, is open on weekends, while lunch is available at the lodge from February to April.

Little Yoho Valley (Map 11/C6)
From the trailhead on the Yoho Valley Road, ski 13 km (7.9 miles) to Takakkaw Falls (see Yoho Valley Road) and continue up the Yoho Valley to Laughing Falls. This last stretch is a gradual climb except for a steep section on Hollingsworth Hill. It is possible to continue on the summer trail from Laughing Falls into the Little Yoho Valley. After a series of switchbacks, the climb moderates to an easy grade until the ACC's Stanley Mitchell Hut. The trail is 44.4 km (27 miles) return.

Lake O'Hara Area (Map 6/F1)
From the Lake O'Hara parking lot, winter enthusiasts can explore the Great Divide Trail, the Ross Lake Circuit or follow the fire road up to the popular lake. The fire road climbs moderately to the shores of Lake O'Hara. The trail crosses several avalanche paths and is 23.4 km (14.3 miles) return to the lake. At the 10 km (6 mile) mark strong skiers can take the trail to Linda Lake. It is 2 km (1.2 miles) one-way to the lake or 5 km (3 miles) one-way to Duchesnay Basin. Once at Lake O'Hara, there are many great routes to sample.

Monarch Trail (Map 6/D1–11/D7)
This easy 12 km (7.3 mile) trail begins from Yoho Brothers parking lot, across the road from the Field Visitor Centre and extends to Monarch Campground on the Yoho Valley Road. From the parking lot, it drops down to follow along the north bank of the Kicking Horse River for 1 km (0.6 miles). Cross the Trans-Canada Highway and follow the trail along the base of Mount Field, across two small avalanche paths and on to Monarch Campground. Here you can see the old portals from Kicking Horse Mine in Mount Field and from Monarch Mine across the valley in Mount Stephen.

Ottertail Trail (Map 6/C2–F3)
From the Trans-Canada Highway, 7.8 km (4.8 miles) west of Field, the fire road climbs moderately for the first few kilometres then becomes more gradual for the remainder of the trip. At McArthur Creek, the view of the Goodsir Towers dominates the scene. The moderate trip is 28 km (17 miles) return, but skiers can travel an additional 6 km (3.7 miles) to the base of Mount Goodsir.

Ross Lake Circuit (Map 11/F7)
From the Lake O'Hara parking lot, follow Highway 1A until you reach the Ross Lake trailhead sign on your right. The trail climbs gradually for 1.3 km (.8 miles) to this small lake bounded by a great rock wall. Turn west at the lake and continue for 3.2 km (2 miles) to the Lake O'Hara Fire Road. Turn north (right) at the fire road to return to the parking lot. There are some narrow and fast sections on this circuit, which is 9.5 km (5.8 miles) total.

Sherbrooke Lake (Map 11/E7)
From the parking lot behind West Louise Lodge on Wapta Lake, the intermediate trail climbs steadily for 2 km (1.2 miles), leveling off before reaching the lake at kilometre 3.1 (mile 1.9). The lake sits in a narrow valley surrounded by steep avalanche slopes. If you continue to the back of the lake, a further 1.4 km (0.9 miles), you will be in avalanche terrain. The return trip is an exciting run, best accomplished on fresh snow. This route is 6.2 km (3.8 miles) return.

Tally Ho Trail (Map 6/C1)
From the Visitor Centre, this easy trail follows the Kicking Horse River downstream for 0.5 km (0.3 miles) then crosses the Trans-Canada Highway to join the Tally Ho Trail. This trail, originally a carriage road, was built at the turn of the century so visitors could travel to the Natural Bridge and Emerald Lake. The trail climbs gradually for about 1.5 km (0.9 miles) through an avalanche area before descending to a junction. The left trail descends to the Natural Bridge, where it links to the Kicking Horse Trail. The trail on the right is the Emerald Lake Connector trail. The return trip is 7 km (4.3 miles).

Wapta Falls Trail (Map 6/C4)
This easy trail is 8.2 km (5 miles) return and starts from the Trans-Canada Highway in the park's west end. The first 1.6 km starts on the summer access road before joining the hiking trail. There are a few rolling hills but the effort is rewarded with a spectacular view of frozen Wapta Falls. The trail continues to a lower viewpoint down river from the falls. Mist makes this lower section too icy to ski.

WILDLIFE VIEWING

The mountain park is home to a variety of large ungulates and predators, like moose, bighorn sheep, mountain goat, cougars, wolves and bears. While bears are a fairly common sight, the other predators are much shyer and rarely seen. Many of these animals can be seen alongside the highway and the sheep and goats are a common site on the bluffs above the Yoho Valley Road.

Index

The index location references consist of a **page number** and a letter, number combination. In the example found below the city *Duncan* is found on page *11/E6*.

The grid lines found in the example below are used for illustrative purposes only, the blue grid lines found on the maps refer to UTM coordinates.

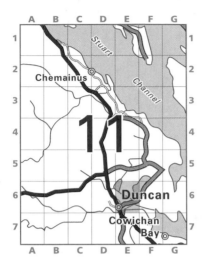

IMPORTANT NUMBERS

General

Alberta Camping Association..........................(403) 453-8570
Alberta Conservation Association 1-877-969-9091
Alberta Trailnet Society.....................www.albertatrailnet.com
Alberta Off-Hwy Vehicle Association ....www.aohva.com
Alberta Snowmobile Fed ....www.altasnowmobile.ab.ca
.... (780) 427-2695
Government of Alberta.. gov.ab.ca
.... Outside of Edmonton (Alberta only): 310-0000
....Outside of Alberta: (780) 427-2711
Report a Poacher 1-800-642-3800
Report a Forest Fire 310-FIRE
Road Reports .... www.ama.ab.ca
.... 1-800-642-3810
Edmonton .... (780) 471-6056
Red Deer .... (403) 342-6611
Tourism Alberta ....www.travelalberta.com
.... 1-800-252-3782
Canadian Avalanche Centre.............. www.avalanche.ca/cac
Updates ....www.backroadmapbooks.com
Weather Conditions ....www.weatheroffice.ec.gc.ca

Parks

Heritage Canada (National Parks)........ www.parkscanada.ca
.... 1-800-651-7959
Parks and Protected Areas...................www.albertaparks.ca
.... 1-866-427-3582
Campground Reservations..............reserve.albertaparks.ca.
East Central Parks Office ....(403) 340-7691
West Central Parks Office ....(780) 960-8170
Parks Canada .... www.pc.gc.ca
Elk Island National Park ....(780) 922-5790
Jasper National Park ....(780) 852-6176

Sustainable Resource Development

Fishing Information .... http://www.srd.gov.ab.ca/fw/fishing/
SRD Information ....(403) 944-0313
Fish & Wildlife Services ....(403) 427-3574

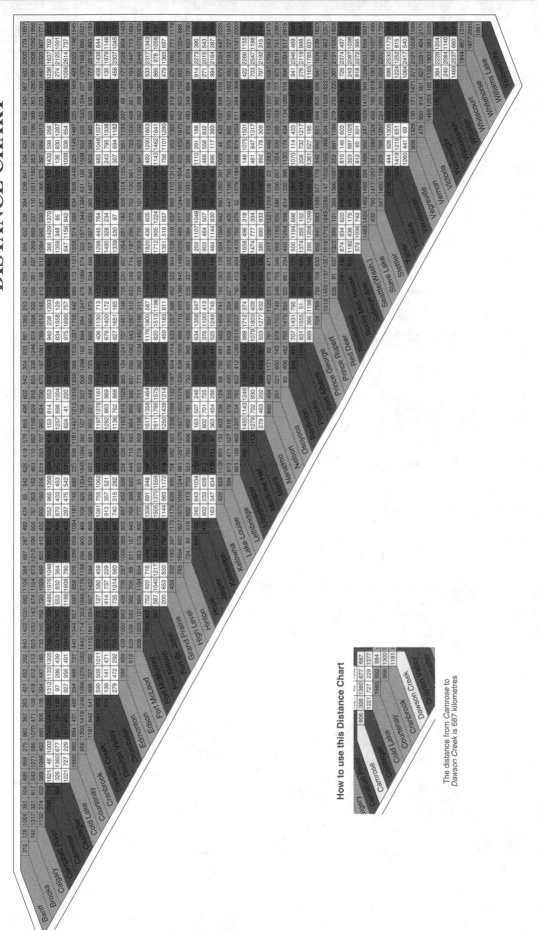

BRITISH COLUMBIA/ALBERTA DISTANCE CHART

How to use this Distance Chart

The distance from *Camrose* to *Dawson Creek* is 687 kilometres

SPEED CONVERSION CHART

Km/hr
MPH

1 Kilometre = 0.621 Mile   1 Mile = 1.6 Kilometres

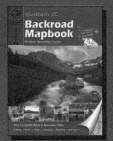
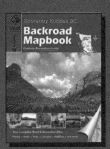
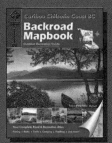
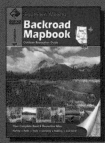
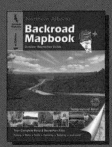
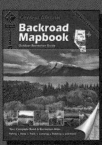
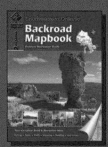
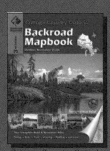
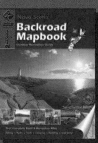